Essential Elements for Effectiveness

A Step by Step Guide
to Personal and Professional Success

Second Edition

Juan R. Abascal, Ph.D.

Laurel Brucato, Ph.D.

Patricia Stephenson, Ph.D.

Dominic Brucato, Ph.D.

PEARSON

Custom
Publishing

Cover art by Wayne Hopkins.

Printed in the United States of America

10 9 8 7 6 5

ISBN 0-536-72910-7

BA 996768

SS

Please visit our web site at *www.pearsoncustom.com*

PEARSON
Custom
Publishing

PEARSON CUSTOM PUBLISHING
75 Arlington Street, Suite 300, Boston, MA 02116
A Pearson Education Company

About the Authors

Juan R. Abascal, Ph.D., a graduate of Rutgers, the State university, and Kent State University, is a clinical psychologist and Associate Vice Provost for Academic Programs at Miami-Dade Community College. Dr. Abascal has conducted numerous personal effectiveness and stress mastery seminars and workshops with people from all walks of life, from the lay person to the professional health care provider. In conjunction with two of the other authors, he co-founded MindWorks, Int., Inc., a stress management center and comprehensive private practice of clinical psychology. He is committed to the principle that any individual willing to follow a step-by-step process can become effective and happy with life, and learn to thrive from stress.

Laurel Brucato, Ph.D., a graduate of the University of Illinois and Kent State University, is a clinical psychologist in private practice at MindWorks, Int., Inc., the stress management center she co-founded in 1988. Dr. Brucato has conducted numerous stress mastery seminars and workshops on developing assertive skills. She has trained health professionals in the use of state-of-the-art relaxation technologies in psychotherapeutic practice. In her clinical practice Dr. Brucato specializes in the treatment of anxiety and phobic disorders, OCD, depression, sexual dysfunctions, eating disorders and marital problems. She has also taught at Miami-Dade Community College as an adjunct professor. Dr. Brucato has dedicated the thrust of her clinical work to helping individuals learn to become more effective in their lives and to master stress.

Patricia Stephenson, Ph.D., a graduate of the University of Florida and Florida State University, is a professor of psychology at Miami-Dade Community College, Kendall Campus. Dr. Stephenson has been a counselor, director, and Associate Dean prior to returning to her first love—teaching. She received a national award for contributions to staff and organizational development, and has served as a consultant to faculty groups writing curriculum. As a health care professional, she is also an avid promoter of wellness lifestyles. Dr. Stephenson has presented numerous workshops for students, faculty, and health care practitioners on stress management, wellness, assertiveness and self-development. She is devoted to the teaching/learning process and helping individuals grow into their personal and professional promise.

Dominic Brucato, Ph.D., a graduate of the University of Notre Dame and Kent State University, is a clinical psychologist and psychology professor at Miami-Dade Community College–North Campus. Along with his wife, Dr. Laurel Brucato, and Dr. Abascal, he co-founded MindWorks, Int., Inc., the state-of-the-art stress management center in Miami, Florida. Dr. Brucato divides his time between teaching and his clinical practice. He specializes in teaching courses aimed at helping students increase their effectiveness and coping skills. A dynamic speaker, Dr. Brucato has conducted numerous stress mastery and effectiveness workshops for people from all walks of life. He has also trained health professionals in the use of cutting-edge relaxation technologies. Dr. Brucato has dedicated himself to helping students and individuals achieve their full potential.

Contents

Preface

TO THE INSTRUCTOR

In the fall semester of 1998 a new course was introduced at Miami-Dade Community College, PPE 1005, the Psychology of Personal Effectiveness. This was a unique course at the college in that it was developed from information obtained from groups including college and university faculty, graduates of Miami-Dade Community College, and potential employers in our community. They were asked to help identify the knowledge and skills that graduates need to be successful in the workplace and in upper-level university settings. A mountain of interview and survey responses was collected, summarized, analyzed, and examined which served as the basis for the competencies for this course. Many faculty and staff members at the college worked on the Educational Review Project which resulted, among other changes, in this course as a new offering to our students.

PPE 1005 can perhaps be best described as an applied psychology course. It differs from traditional university courses in that its focus is not solely on educating students about theory and research, but rather on educating students in how to make use of this theory and research in their daily lives. As such, the goal of the course is not to have students who know a lot *about* effectiveness, but students who have learned *how* to be effective. This book was specifically developed to address the unique objectives of this course. While it certainly addresses psychological theories and research, this is presented as the underpinning of the applied aspects rather than the central focus. In this manner, it also differs from most college textbooks as it does not present an exhaustive list of theoretical perspectives. The National Science Foundation has described the current trend in the teaching of the sciences as being "a mile wide and an inch deep." The argument typically espoused by proponents of this approach is that we must pass on all the knowledge in a field. However, although we may be covering all the material, evidence suggests that even if students learn it all, they are quickly forgetting it because they are not using it. In contrast, this book is organized around a limited number of principles which are continually addressed and approached from various perspectives. We believe that when application is the goal, knowing a lot about a little is far more effective than knowing a little about a lot. Therefore, this book addresses a narrower number of critical topics in much greater depth.

We have consciously attempted to make this book conversational in nature rather than didactic. Our goal is to address the student directly through its pages, to literally encourage the reader to engage in a dialogue with the book. When appropriate we have incorporated material presented in our effectiveness seminars. We have also sought to frequently include humor and amusing anecdotes to help engage the reader, particulary given that the ability to find the humor in life is one of the characteristics of effective functioning. You will find that in the Introduction for students we have included the competencies for this course as created by the College Wide Social Science Discipline Committee.

We encourage you to require your students to actively involve themselves with the exercises, techniques and suggestions included in this book, and not just to read the book and regurgitate the information on tests, as with so many other texts. The value of this book is in the doing, not just in reading and/or memorizing facts. To that end we invite you, the instructor, to do the same so as to heighten your ability to teach this material and truly model effectiveness for your students. We have found that assigning students to keep a journal provides an excellent foundation for processing the lessons and techniques presented in the forthcoming chapters.

Acknowledgments

The authors would like to thank the members of the college-wide committee charged with developing this psychology course for the new General Education Curriculum as part of the Educational Review Process. These faculty members spent countless hours contributing their professional expertise in the planning of the Psychology of Personal Effectiveness course. In addition to three of the authors, other committee members were Frances Aronovitz, Neil Burns, Raul de la Cruz, Ron Fisher, Manny Garcia, Jan Mese, Ron Seveik, and Lois Willoughby. An additional thank you to Mary Ann Miller, who served as the liaison with the College District Office of Education.

Introduction

TO THE STUDENT

Hey you! Yes, you. We *are* talking to you. At least that's what we would really like to establish with you—a dialogue. Now you might ask yourself: "What do you mean . . . a dialogue? To dialogue takes two people; all I have is me and this book!" But that's not true. You have your classmates, your professor, your friends, your family, *and* this book. We sincerely hope that you take the principles and ideas contained within its pages and discuss them. Talk about them. Consider their validity. And most importantly, try them out in your own life.

You see, the material you encounter in this book will best serve you if you use it. We recognize that using it will likely require some changes on your part. And we all know that changing is not always easy. Dialogue about that too. With others for support, explore ways in which what you are learning can have an impact in your life. Expect it to happen, and you might be pleasantly surprised.

So, let's begin. To make the most out of this book, we suggest you take a moment to think about what motivated you to pick it up. Why are you reading it? Even if your initial response is that it was required for the course, think . . . is there something else you want to get, other than a good grade, from reading this book? If you were able to change something as a result of your experience with this book, what would that be? What would be different about you? How would you look, feel, and act differently? Take a moment now to think about these questions.

There is a story about a group of scientists who were walking along the countryside when they saw a field of fruit-bearing trees. A local inhabitant told them that the fruit was called "Mango" by the natives of this land. This kind of fruit was unknown to them and they wanted to learn all they could about it. Half of the scientists went into one side of the field and began measuring the mangoes' weight and their size. They noted the color and the shape and recorded their findings. These scientists now *knew about* mangoes. The other half of the scientists went into the field, each took down a mango from the tree and tasted it. These scientists *knew* mangoes.

Did you do what we suggested in the first paragraph? Did you take a moment to think about what you wanted to get from using this book? If you did, you are like the scientists who ate the mangoes. Continue tasting what we have to offer and we can promise you will notice a significant positive difference in your life. But if you didn't, your tendency might be to read this book much like the scientists who measured and weighed the mangoes. With that approach, this book may provide you with some interesting facts and general knowledge, but it is doubtful that it will create any significant changes in your life. The material discussed in this book will work for you only if you use it; only if you *do* it. Merely knowing about it is not enough. So if you have not considered the questions posed earlier, we invite you to go back and think about what you want to get, how you want to be different, and notice the results *after* you've tasted the mangoes. This way, you will not just know a lot *about* effectiveness when you are done. Instead, you will know how to *be* effective.

THE HISTORY OF THE COURSE

This is a unique course at the college as it was developed from information obtained from groups including college and university faculty, graduates of Miami-Dade Community College, and potential employers in our community. They were asked to help identify the knowledge and skills that graduates need to be successful in life. A mountain of interview and survey responses was collected, summarized, analyzed, and examined and served as the basis for the competencies for this course. Many faculty and staff members at the college worked on the Educational Review Project which resulted, among other changes, in this course as a new offering to our students.

This book was specifically developed to address the unique objectives of this course. We have consciously attempted to make it conversational in nature, to address you, the student, through its pages. We have done this because we painfully remember how unexciting it was when we were students and we had to cope with textbooks that merely presented dry information. As such, this textbook is unconventional. It seeks to talk to you. We hope that although it is different, you find it useful. At times, we have attempted to bring some humor into our writing. We certainly laughed and had fun while writing it. It is our sincere wish that you laugh, too, when you are reading it. Following are the competencies that were recently revised for this course by the College Wide Social Science Discipline Committee and which are addressed in this book.

COURSE COMPETENCIES FOR THE PSYCHOLOGY OF PERSONAL EFFECTIVENESS:

1. **The student will explore theoretical perspectives regarding personal effectiveness by:**
   a. describing an overview of the major theoretical approaches to personality and human behavior.
   b. analyzing the theory of self-concept and the factors involved in its development, relating this to personal behavior.
   c. distinguishing the causes and characteristics of high and low self-esteem and the relationship of these to behavior.

    d. discovering the holistic nature of humankind including the cognitive, emotional, social, spiritual, and physical influences on behavior.

2. **The student will learn to manage stress by:**

    a. demonstrating knowledge of stress, its sources, and the physical, psychological and behavioral outcomes.

    b. applying effective stress management theory.

    c. demonstrating effective self-management in the use of resources such as time, money, and personal assets.

3. **The student will understand the theories of healthy and successful relationships by:**

    a. describing how these theories apply to family, friends, social groups, work teams, and culturally diverse groups.

    b. practicing effective verbal and nonverbal communication.

    c. applying effective listening skills.

    d. applying theories related to assertive behavior.

    e. practicing conflict resolution skills and analyzing the process.

4 **The student will understand the changing nature of the world of work by:**

    a. exploring future occupational and academic trends.

    b. using knowledge and skills of personal and interpersonal effectiveness to achieve career related goals.

    c. valuing diversity in the workplace.

5. **The student will understand the role of personal responsibility in workplace success by:**

    a. describing the characteristics of effective employees and their responses to performance assessment and varying leadership styles.

    b. demonstrating understanding of the necessity for policies and procedures in the workplace.

    c. demonstrating knowledge of job satisfaction, including intrinsic and extrinsic work motivations.

    d. describing factors which interfere with effective job performance such as alcohol and drug use; sexual harassment; racial, gender, and age discrimination; and violations of ethical and moral standards.

JOURNALING YOUR EXPERIENCE

In order to support you in becoming personally effective, we strongly suggest and invite you to journal your experiences. While daily journal writing is certainly commendable, two entries per week, for at least the first half of the semester, will suffice. The act of writing down your experiences and reflecting on them is an exquisite vehicle for remaining conscious and aware of all their different aspects. This, in turn, allows you to remember the many choices you, in reality, have when confronting any situation.

THE MECHANICS OF READING THIS BOOK

This book is divided into three main sections. The first section deals with topics involving personal effectiveness, how you can become more effective in your daily life. The second section involves becoming more effective in your interpersonal relationships, at home, at school and at work. The last section is geared towards promoting effectiveness in your career and in your workplace.

We suggest that you will benefit if you follow a set of specific steps as you read this book. First, make sure to study the Table of Contents to get an overview of the terrain you will be covering. Spending a little time wondering about the different concepts and ideas you will encounter will prepare you to make use of them. Surveying material before you read it has been found to be an effective means of really learning it. An appropriate analogy is that of a computer. Imagine you save new data to the hard drive without using directories or subdirectories. After a short time, although the information is stored in your computer, you can no longer find it! There is so much disorganized data that it's hard to find what you are looking for. Our memory works in much the same way. When you survey data to be learned, it is as if you are creating a directory in which the data will be organized to facilitate retrieval of the information. For the same reason, it is important that prior to each section, you contemplate the brief outline for that section.

Something else we know about learning is how important it is to review what you have just learned. This is because revisiting the information is a powerful way to ensure that the neural pathway to requisite data is active and open. To use another analogy, think of your memory as a dense forest where your thoughts reside. Each time you review the information it is as if you are going through the path with a machete and cutting away the vegetation. The more often you review the information the more you assure that the path through the forest remains clear. For this reason, we suggest that after reading the chapter, you spend time reviewing the chapter by studying the key terms and answering the end of chapter questions.

In a similar vein, many educators recommend a study method known by the acronym of the "**SQ3R**". If you use this technique for studying this book or any other texbook or course, you can find that will greatly enhance your understanding and retention of course material. The SQ3R method consists of the following:

- **Survey:** For all the reasons stated above, survey the Table of Contents and before reading each chapter, look it over to get an overview of what information will be covered in that particular section.

- **Question:** Before reading each chapter in full, briefly skim it and ask yourself questions about the material.

- **Read:** Carefully read the chapter and find answers to the questions that you previously created while skimming the chapter.

- **Recite:** Paraphrase what you have learned. Putting material into your own words greatly enhances your ability to understand and retain information. One helpful hint for doing this is to explain the material to yourself as if you were attempting to explain it to a friend or younger sibling.

❖ **Review:** After each chapter, go over the material carefully including answering the end of chapter questions and making sure you know the definitions to all key terms.

REMEMBER, DON'T JUST READ THE BOOK. TASTE IT!

One of our favorite sayings from the Sufi masters is: "We eat at all tables that serve good food." We invite you to eat at our table and sample the different dishes we have to offer. Resist the temptation to decide you don't like any particular one until you try it. Taste them first and notice the results. Others before you have discovered that learning and using the strategies of effectiveness has made a powerful impact on their ability to succeed and thrive in both their work and personal life. We suggest you give yourself a chance to do the same.

Are you willing to take this on? Take a moment to decide. If you are, and you willingly do the things that we suggest, we can guarantee that you will notice a significant positive difference in your life as you learn and apply the strategies of personal effectiveness. Have fun as you read this book and partake of this course. May your journey be adventurous and fruitful.

SECTION ONE

Personal Effectiveness

Recognize That Reality Is All in Your Head

Know That the Buck Starts and Stops with You

Love Who You Are

Develop Mastery Over Stress—Part I

Develop Mastery Over Stress—Part II

Create a Vision

Manage Yourself in Time

1

Recognize That Reality Is All in Your Head

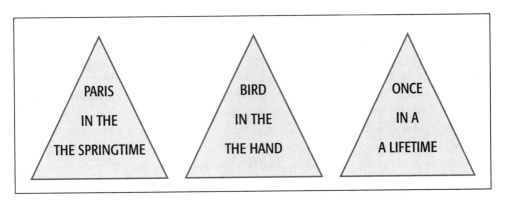

What do you think you just read within the three triangles above? Are you sure? Why don't you go back and read them again just to make sure and come back to this point.* Are you still seeing "Paris in the springtime", "Bird in the hand", and "Once in a lifetime"? After all, you certainly know how to read five little words. If you are so sure, would you be willing to bet your car on this? What about betting your next year's entire income? When we present this to our students in class, some of them are not willing to bet anything because they figure that something is up if the professor is setting the stakes so high and willing to wager at the same level. A small minority are not willing to bet because they recognize that it does not say what the majority of their classmates think it says. But the overwhelming majority are willing to bet the farm. Because after all, they can certainly trust what they see! They certainly *can* read three simple five word sentences. What about you? Did you see the double "the" and the double "a"? At what point did you see it? When you first read it, or when we invited you to reread it, or even after that? You know why ? Because we really don't see what is there; **we see what we think is there**. And, believe it or not, this doesn't happen just with spiffy, little, five word, optical illusions like we presented above, this happens in every area of your life. Every time you face a situation, what you perceive is at least as much dependent upon your perspective as it is upon the external reality.

An important distinction is drawn within the field of psychology between what is termed "sensation", and what we call "perception". **Sensation** involves the physical process of receiving stimuli which connect with our sensory organs and receptors, and then translating that into electrochemical impulses or signals within our nervous system and brain. **Perception** occurs when our brain interprets these signals and ascribes meaning to them. Both mechanisms are essential for us to make sense out of our environment. But recognize that in this process each individual brings his or her unique interpretations to these environmental stimuli.

In a classic experiment psychologists Bruner and Postman (1949) cleverly demonstrated the fact that what we see does not always correspond to what is really there. These researchers created a normal deck of playing cards, except that some of the suit symbols were color reversed. For example, the nine of diamonds had black colored diamonds instead of red. These special cards were shuffled into an ordinary deck, and then were displayed one at a time to subjects who were asked to identify them as fast as possible. At first the cards were shown very briefly, too fast for accurate identification. Then the display time was gradually increased until all the cards could be identified. The interesting thing is that while all the cards were eventually identified with great confidence on behalf of the participants, none of the subjects noticed that there was anything peculiar about any of the cards! Subjects identified the red six of spades as either a six of spades or a six of hearts, but were not aware that anything was amiss. When the display times were lengthened even more, subjects hesitated and got confused, making comments such as, "this is a six of spades but there's something wrong", but still had difficulty determining what was out of the ordinary. Subjects were eventually able to identify the cards as being the wrong color only when display times were greatly lengthened. This result illustrated in spades (pun intended) that we see what we expect to see, and not necessarily what is there to see.

THE CONCEPT OF FRAMES

Therefore, how you view any event or situation in your life is greatly influenced by your expectations, your beliefs, your pre-conceived notions. This has been called by many names. Thomas Kuhn referred to it as a **paradigm** in his landmark book, *The Structure of Scientific Revolutions*. Others have called it a **perspective** or a **mind map**. We prefer to call it a **frame**. Have you ever purchased an unframed print or painting which you later got framed? Can you remember when you first saw your picture with its new frame? Didn't it look clearer somehow, more in focus? It was finished now. Can you recall the sense of satisfaction you experienced when you hung it on the wall and stood back? Each and every one of us is adept at developing **frames of reference** or paradigms to enable us to organize and understand our world, our perceptions, our experiences. Every situation in which you engage, you eventually put a frame of reference around it in order to understand it, to make sense out of it. Most of the time this happens instantly and you are not even aware of it. When you are "confused" about something it takes longer to sort the experience into a frame of reference. Indeed, that is one definition of confusion, the inability to make sense of something or *place it within a frame.* It is likely that we humans are hardwired, genetically programmed, to create frames of reference to organize our experiences. Without this inherent ability to construct frames the world would be a very perplexing and unpredictable place.

Experiences are made up of multiple perceptions, sensations and bits of data which we need to categorize. For instance, imagine this situation. Night is approaching as the sun has recently set. You hear a knocking at your door. You wonder who it could be because you are not expecting any visitors. You walk over and peek out of the window at the top of the door. You see two figures who are wearing masks and dark clothing. Your immediate reaction is confusion, even fear, and you are unsure how to respond. Who are these guys and what do they want? Should you open the door? Why are they wearing masks? You wonder if you are in danger and should call the police. Rather than take any chances and open the door you yell out, "Who's there?" Your question is answered by the macabre duo as they answer, "Is the party here?" You suddenly remember that it is Halloween weekend and your neighbors are having a costume party. Once you have sorted this odd experience into a familiar frame of reference (i.e. it's Halloween and some partygoers have come to the wrong house), you now know what you are dealing with and how to respond appropriately.

Thus you are genetically predisposed to develop frames of reference which are shaped by your learning history, what you learned from your parents, your peers, in school, in church, from the media and our culture. Some frames of reference remain in flux, but most become fixed. In fact, the more a frame of reference is utilized, and the more successful it is in helping you to derive meaning from your experiences, the more entrenched it becomes. You tend to forget that it is only a paradigm, a frame. The degree to which you are able to recognize that you are operating within a frame, and shift that frame when appropriate, enhances your flexibility of thought and ability to solve problems. So how well can you do this? Try this problem now. **Connect the nine dots using only four straight lines and not lifting your pen off the paper.** By the way, use a pencil for we guarantee you will need to erase!

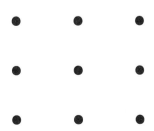

Figure 1.1 The Nine Dot Problem

Were you able to solve the problem? If you are like most people you will find that it takes you five lines to be able to connect all the dots without lifting your pencil or bending the lines. Is this problem impossible to solve? Only if you stay within the parameters and limitations of your current frame. We suggest you try going outside the box. When you look at the nine dots, what do you see? If you had to give those dots a name, other than "nine dots", what would you call it? Most people would call it a square or a box. Change that frame. As long as you hold onto the paradigm that this is a square and act accordingly, you will be unable to solve the problem. Go ahead and try it again, this time allowing yourself to go beyond the square. Were you successful? If not, here's another hint. Can you see it as a sort of an arrow? Adopting this frame of reference might help. If all else fails, look at the next page for the solution.

Obviously, to solve this problem you had to go beyond the nine dots, beyond the originally preconceived square which you likely perceived. Your paradigm that this was a square led you to use the corner dots as the edges, which effectively inhibited you from solving this problem. Is this just another clever riddle? Or does it show us that we are predetermined to see things in a particular or familiar way, and what we see dictates how we interact with that reality (in this case how we attempt to solve the problem).

OBJECTIVISM VS. CONSTRUCTIVISM

So what does this say about the nature of reality? To answer this, let's talk a bit about two competing models. One can consider the question, "what is reality?" from two different models. These models have been termed **Objectivism** and **Constructivism**, and hold inherently different assumptions, or paradigms. Objectivism assumes that there is a separate reality independent from the observer of that reality. Meaning, when you look at a chair what you see exists out there in the world, independent of you. The chair would be the same whether or not you are looking at it. Based on this assumption proponents of this model suggest that the task of science is to discover reality. This, after all, makes sense if you believe that reality is separate from you. As a consequence of this an Objectivist values truth, that which is out there to be discovered.

Constructivists, on the other hand, hold that there is no separate reality. The chair that exists when you look at it is different somehow than the chair that exists when you are not gazing at it. Now we know that you may be saying to yourself, "What? What do you mean the chair is different?" For now we ask you to allow for the possibility that such an interactive reality may exist. If we are somehow involved in the reality that we experience, then it makes sense that proponents of this model are not seeking to discover reality, but to invent it. Now, if the task is to invent reality, then it is no wonder that constructivists value usefulness, not just truth. It is not that constructivists devalue truth, but rather that they view truth as relative, constantly changing, depending on the frame of reference of the observer. For example, consider the fact that eyewitness accounts of strangers who viewed a crime scene or a car accident typically vary considerably. Why is this? Is it that all eyewitness accounts are a pack of lies? No, rather each witness' account is greatly influenced by his or her expectations, biases, memory ability, perceptual acuity, etc. Numerous research studies have demonstrated that reports of eyewitnesses are often distorted and unreliable. In one classic study (Loftus and Palmer, 1974), subjects shown a movie of a car crash perceived the speed of the cars quite differently depending on the way they were later questioned (which subtly affected their expectations) about what they saw and remembered. There have also been many people recently released from prison when DNA evidence proved that the eyewitness and victim testimony that led to their convictions was simply not true, even though those testifying were *certain* of their perceptions. This phenomenon is known as **memory distortion**. Considering this, we encourage you to bear in mind the strong possibility that your "memories" are not nearly as accurate as you assume, and may contain numerous inaccuracies and/or omissions.

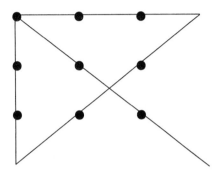

Figure 1.2 The Nine Dot Solution

But what about the aforementioned chair? Surely that doesn't change, whether or not you are looking at it. Now, look at a chair or any other object in your environment. What color is it? Is that color a property of the chair? Perhaps surprisingly to you, the answer is no. That chair has no color. The chair is merely reflecting a multitude of wavelengths of light which, when received by the cone receptors in your eyes, followed by a series of convergences where the signal is transmitted through a complex network of neurons, gets interpreted by your brain as the particular color. You see, the color literally does not exist unless you are there to look at it. By the way, this is the same concept reflected in the oft quoted riddle, *"if a tree falls in the forest and no one is there to hear it, does the sound still exist?"* Again the answer is no. For sound to exist it requires the tree to fall AND your ear to hear it. Without your ear there are only sound waves.

You remember Sir Isaac Newton. He's the guy you read about in science class who was sitting underneath an apple tree, saw an apple fall in front of him (although we prefer to think the apple fell on his head), and discovered gravity. Newton was a scientist/physicist who is a great example of the Objectivist scientific view. He proposed a very mechanical and clockwork frame of the universe which greatly advanced physics, astronomy, and other sciences. Newton's laws helped predict a wide range of phenomena that were previously poorly understood. However, this predictability value decreased sharply when we began considering the subatomic level.

Then along came the guy who has frequently been described as looking like he stuck his finger in a light socket. You know, of course, we are referring to Albert Einstein.

Einstein can be seen as an example of the Constructivist model. He postulated the theory of relativity, the concept that time and space exist only in relation to each other. While a detailed exploration of the theory of relativity is clearly beyond the scope of this book and perhaps beyond the scope of our brain (at least the authors'), perhaps a simple explanation would help. Einstein proposed that time and space are not independent but are relative to each other and the speed of light. That is, the experience of time changes as we approach the speed of light. So that, theoretically, if you were to travel in a spaceship nearing the speed of light for what you experienced as one year, when you returned to Earth, many more years would have passed here. Your body would have aged one year, but your friends and relatives would likely be dead by then. This concept revolutionized physics and as a consequence is influencing every other scientific discipline. Einstein's theories are more useful because they have greater predictive value, particularly when addressing the subatomic level. They don't deny Newtonian physics, they just expand it.

PARADIGM SHIFTS AND THE HISTORY OF SCIENCE

If reality is interrelated, then it makes perfect sense that as Thomas Kuhn observed in his book, all major scientific discoveries are preceded by a **paradigm shift**, a change in the overriding theoretical framework that governs a scientific discipline. Kuhn described in great detail how almost every significant breakthrough in the field of scientific endeavor is first a break with tradition, a break with old ways of thinking, a change of old paradigms. For example, in the second century A.D. the great Egyptian astronomer Ptolemy held that the earth was the center of the universe. This belief came to be known as the *geocentric* theory where all objects in the sky revolved around a stationary Earth. This made perfect sense because it certainly appeared that the sun revolved around the earth every 24 hours, rising in the east and setting in the west. So if seeing was believing, this paradigm made all the sense in the world. The Ptolemaic view dominated from ancient times until the early 1500's when a rebel named Copernicus dared to posit that the earth revolved around the sun. This idea came to be known as the *heliocentric*, or sun-centered theory. Unfortunately, his view was considered to be heresy, since it contradicted the biblical view that we are the center of the universe. It wasn't until the mid 1600's when Galileo took up the fight, that, after considerable struggle, this new view prevailed. This new frame on things made possible a host of other discoveries and advances.

Similarly, medicine was revolutionized by germ theory which made a host of previously confusing phenomena understandable. For example, prior to postulating that small organisms invisible to the eye could enter our bodies and be responsible for illness and even death, doctors were baffled as to why following a battle, patients with relatively minor wounds would often die, while patients with more serious wounds would survive. What would occur was that patients would be "triaged". That is, surgeons and nurses would prioritize patients into those they could do nothing for and would let die, those who could wait before help had to be tendered, and those who needed immediate attention. Surgeons would then operate on the latter, proceeding in order until those least injured were helped. The problem was that they would use the same instruments from one patient to the next without recognizing the need to sterilize these instruments. No wonder the ones who came last were more likely to die! But without considering the possibility of germs, there was no reason for these surgeons to think that it was their behavior that was leading to infection, and often the deaths of their patients. By the way, germ theory was postulated prior to us developing the tools to see these germs. Indeed, the reason we developed the tools, such as microscopes, is because we believed in the possibility of extremely small, unseen creatures.

In the *Structure of Scientific Revolutions* Kuhn observes that the history of scientific advancement in all disciplines is a result of paradigm shifts. Science, which Kuhn refers to as "normal science", proceeds by building a foundation of research and data based upon proving and expanding existing theoretical paradigms. But invariably anomalous results begin to turn up, findings which cannot be understood or accounted for by the overriding paradigm. Often these anomalies are ignored or discounted. Scientists who reveal or publicize these seemingly bizarre results are dismissed, and often even discredited within their profession. New theories or paradigms which attempt to explain the anomalies by expanding or changing the existing paradigm are often treated as heresy. Inherent in this is a struggle between the old guard of a discipline (who believe they have the truth), and the mavericks who dare to challenge the accepted paradigm. It is no wonder that successful challenges to existing paradigms often come from outside the discipline, developed by individuals with a fresh perspective or different viewpoint. Eventually, the mass of anomalies builds to the point where the discipline must become open to a new paradigm in order to stay viable. Thus a scientific revolution occurs when the paradigm shifts. This may occur suddenly, but typically, given the resistance of the old guard, this is a more gradual process. Two or more paradigms may co-exist for a while with separate adherents, but eventually the paradigm with greater predictive value will win out.

A good example of a gradual paradigm shift exists within the field of psychology. Early in the 1900's Sigmund Freud posited his theory of psychosexual development. Initially this appeared to explain the development of mental disorders and it provided a framework for the treatment of emotional difficulties. It was the first global theory of how personality was formed and it described both normal and abnormal behavior. This new paradigm stimulated the development of a new treatment modality, that of talk therapy, and it provided avenues for new research. But then holes began to appear in the theory. Psychoanalytic theory was a cumbersome model for explaining many emotional problems and psychoanalysis, as a treatment, often failed. Psychoanalytic theory had great explanatory value, but little if any, predictive value. Competing models were developed.

Learning theory explained behavior in terms of conditioning and reinforcement (i.e. rewards and punishment). These theorists were called Behaviorists since they believed that behavior was not a result of repressed psychosexual impulses, as Freud believed, but was driven by the consequences that followed the behavior. At around the same time, humanistic thought came into prominence. The humanists held man to be not quite as dark as Freud postulated, driven by sexual and aggressive impulses. Instead, they professed that humans are driven to continually improve themselves, to move towards self-actualization.

Freud's theories were a natural outgrowth of the population he studied, namely, his patients who were primarily neurotic females living in a highly repressive, Victorian society, and himself (and we are here to tell you that despite his brilliance, Freud has his problems too). Behavior theories stemmed primarily from laboratory research such as the pioneering work of Ivan Pavlov on Classical Conditioning, and B.F. Skinner on Operant conditioning. Humanistic theories evolved from studying the best society had to offer as evidenced by Carl Rogers' research with college students, and Abraham Maslow's work with highly successful, self-actualized individuals. (In fact, Maslow initially studied gorillas, but they were the most dominant gorillas in the pack). With such varying experiences influencing their observations, no wonder such different paradigms emerged. For many years, perhaps even up until the present, these different frames coexisted which led to continual debate about what was truth in psychology. Now, a great majority of psychologists would agree that human behavior is best explained and predicted via the Cognitive-Behavioral model, which we see as a combination of the Humanistic and Behavioristic schools of thought. Freud's original paradigm, while not completely discarded, has been greatly expanded and refined. So, to quote Kuhn:

> "Examining the record of past research from the vantage of contemporary historiography, the historian of science may be tempted to exclaim that when paradigms change, the world changes with them. Led by a new paradigm, scientists adopt new instruments and look in new places. Even more important, during revolutions scientists see new and different things when looking with familiar instruments in places they have looked before. It is rather as if the professional community had been suddenly transported to another planet where familiar objects are seen in a different light and are joined by unfamiliar ones as well. Of course, nothing of quite that sort does occur: there is no geographical transplantation; outside the laboratory everyday affairs usually continue as before. Nevertheless, paradigm changes do cause scientists to see the world of their research-engagement differently. In so far as their only recourse to that world is through what they see and do, we may want to say that after a revolution scientists are responding to a different world."

PARADIGM SHIFTS IN EVERYDAY LIFE

"The important thing is not to stop questioning."
Albert Einstein

OK. So when we put new frames on what we see, we begin to perceive something quite different. It is as if our reality changes. We are able to find solutions and explanations to previously baffling and unpredictable phenomena. So why don't we just do it? Because old paradigms, old frames tend to resist being changed. Remember we said they tend to become entrenched? They focus our perceptions but also limit them. We tend to only look at the picture within the frame. That is why as Kuhn observed, prior to every major scientific paradigm shift, there was incredible resistance to it. Galileo was imprisoned and forced to recant his ideas. Can you imagine what people first thought when a colleague told them about hypothesized "germs", those invisible organisms? There is an "old guard" that will fight against changes and attempt to hold on to the familiar.

Lest you think this happens only with "major scientific paradigm shifts", let us assure you that this phenomenon of resistance occurs whenever we seek to change most of our own personal frames. There is an "old guard" within us that wants to hang on to the old. And what compounds the problem is that most of what we perceive supports our original frame. This is called **selective perception**, the tendency to perceive that which we expect to be there. You see, when we frame something, we tend to see only that which lies within the frame. Phenomena outside of it, tend to be ignored or labeled anomalies. More often than not, we need to see things differently in order to discover the truth that it is so. Or as we often tell our students, if not the truth, then a whole new pack of lies to be considered until a new, more useful pack comes along. For example, as Mark Twain in his witty and clever manner noted, *"When I was sixteen, I was flabbergasted by how ignorant my father was. By the time I was twenty-one, I was amazed at how much the old man had learned in five years."*

While in the process of writing this chapter one of the authors had a personal experience which typified the process of developing an everyday paradigm, using selective perception to reinforce it, and then undergoing a paradigm shift. This occurred as a result of watching the popular horror movie *The Sixth Sense*. For those of you who have not seen this movie we suggest you skip the next paragraph, rent the movie and watch it twice. Why twice? You will understand after you have seen it once, and most people desire to see it twice. After watching this movie you will understand how it is relevant to the concepts presented in this chapter. For those of you who have already seen it you will no doubt relate to what the author experienced.

> "At the end of the movie when I realized that the Bruce Willis character was dead, I was astonished. How could he be dead? I distinctly remembered that he had conversations with the boy's mother and with his wife. How could this be the case if he were a ghost? I was immensely curious to find out how I could have been so thoroughly tricked. So when the movie was available on video, I rented it and watched it carefully a second time. Due to a very clever screenplay and a combination of optical and auditory illusions, I, and most other viewers were led to adopt the belief (the paradigm) that Bruce Willis' character, the psychologist, had survived the gunshot. Upon the second viewing I discovered that in the scene with the child's mother, not a word of dialogue was spoken between her and the psychologist. But that is not how I perceived it, nor how I remembered it. Why? The scene was composed to make you assume that they had been talking. Due to selective perception and selective memory I remembered this scene as though they had actually conversed. The restaurant scene was also cleverly set up to make you assume that his wife was talking to him, when rather she was just talking to herself. But due to selective perception, I saw what I expected to see, that she was talking to him. Despite all my supposed sophistication and the fact that I too am a psychologist, all of this combined to fool me. I remembered events as I thought they had occurred, distorted by the lens of my expectations and beliefs. When I discovered that the character was really dead, of course I experienced a paradigm shift, motivating me to reassess my original perceptions."

So what does all this have to do with effectiveness? As Einstein observed, *"the significant problems we face today can not be solved at the same level of thinking we were at when we created them."* In order to solve them you are required to experience a paradigm shift, or a **reframe**. As we will discuss in Chapter 8, we have been taught to look out there for the source of our problems or difficulties. In *The Seven Habits of Highly Effective People,* Steven Covey emphasizes that effective people are adept at questioning their frame and recognizing that *"**the way** we see the problem is the problem"*. Thus what we are after here is helping you build your skills at changing the way you think.

REFRAMING

There is an oft repeated story of a Chinese farmer that goes something like this . . .

> A farmer and his only son were busily plowing their fields when their horse broke free from its harness and ran off into the nearby hills. When their fellow villagers heard of their plight they began to commiserate, "Oh, what terrible luck! How unfortunate! What will you do?" To which the farmer responded, "Good luck, bad luck . . . who knows?" Several days later the farmer's horse returned with two other horses in tow. His fellow villagers were astonished as they exclaimed "What wonderful luck! You lose your only horse and end up with three!" To which the farmer responded," Good luck, bad luck . . . who knows?" Several days later the farmer's son was attempting to break one of the horses so as to put it into service on his land. The son was thrown from the horse and broke his arm. All the villagers were united in their opinion that this was indeed bad luck. The farmer as usual responded, "Good luck, bad luck . . . who knows?" The very next week the Imperial Army marched through their village conscripting all the able-bodied young men into the service. The farmer's son was spared due to his broken arm. The villagers were once again impressed with this man's extraordinary good luck and told him so. And he replied, "Good luck, bad luck. . . . who knows."

This story illustrates what we call reframing. Because the farmer was able to see things differently (i.e. think about them differently than his fellow villagers) he was able to respond differently, and experience an emotional calmness and equanimity that evaded those around him. As with most things, this is easier said than done. However, be assured it is definitely easier on you to learn to do it than to not do it. We promise you that if you commit to practicing the strategies outlined in this book so that they truly become part of who you are, you will be amazed at the change in your life. Reframing is like trying on different pairs of glasses and paying close attention to your responses. We've all heard of "looking at the world through rose colored glasses" as a way to describe chronically optimistic people. And all of us have heard of people who act as if they have blinders on, because of their refusal to see things that are readily apparent to everyone else around them. What we would like to offer you are some different pairs of glasses to try on and experiment with their effects.

Entering the Funhouse

> An older gentleman approached his doctor with a problem. "Every morning at eight a.m. I have a regular bowel movement", he complained. His doctor was somewhat perplexed and responded, "That doesn't seem to be a problem to me. Most of my patients would be thrilled to have a regular bowel movement at eight a.m." The patient replied, "The problem is that I don't wake up and get out of bed until nine a.m.!"

Humor is the most familiar way in which reframing is used. We are led to believe a situation is one way and then suddenly we see it differently through an amusing lens. This contrast leads to the experience of laughter. Whenever you can bring humor to your perceptions your emotions can shift and your effectiveness is potentially increased. There is even research documenting that laughter is conducive to creative thinking for problem solving, as well as for changing frames of reference in general. In one study (Isen, 1991) psychologists found that subjects who watched a highly amusing video were much better at solving a complex puzzle where the solution required creative thinking about combining or using familiar objects in unusual ways. Subjects who only watched a neutral video were more prone to lapse into **functional fixedness**, wherein they got locked into thinking about using objects only in the most conventional or familiar ways, therefore they had far more difficulty solving the puzzle. The researchers concluded that laughter was instrumental in promoting flexibility of thought; that it literally seems to help people to think more expansively and associate more easily, making connections that might otherwise go unnoticed. This strongly implies that one way to help someone think through a problem is to tell them a joke.

Consider the American amusement park phenomenon—the Funhouse. We enter, frequently in the dark, and are beset by all manner of stimulation. The ground is unsteady, strange noises and blasts of air occur seemingly at random intervals, scary images jump in and out of our visual field, and bizarre mirrors distort our reflection. We are alternately scared, startled, laughing, and emerge having had a pretty good time. Sounds a lot like life. Often our most interesting and funny tales are our descriptions of harrowing or embarrassing moments from our past, told from the safety of the present moment. As we step outside of the experience and see ourselves in it, we see it differently and we can therefore feel differently. You need strategies for modifying your feelings and emotions so that you can choose an effective response. Here are some ideas to help you create your own personal Funhouse.

Life as a Sitcom

This is a simple strategy for changing your point of view. Imagine that your life is being videotaped and consider what this difficult moment might look like to your viewers. One of the authors discovered this strategy accidentally while moving a very heavy sofa with several friends.

> The sofa was so awkward and heavy that everyone had to stop periodically to rest and readjust their grip. While we were doing this, I was intermittently warning all my friends to be careful not to set this large object on their feet. At that very moment I proceeded to lower the sofa onto my own foot! (And I realized that, indeed, it really was a very heavy sofa!) Just as my mouth was opening to ask for help, I mentally shifted to an outsiders view of my situation and started laughing hysterically. I had become Jerry Lewis or one of the Three Stooges, and I simply could not stop laughing long enough to speak. Luckily, my friends, also laughing now, realized I was pointing at my foot and removed the couch.

While we still recommend being careful with heavy objects, this incident demonstrates the power of shifting your point of view. The pain and upset would have been far more intense had our colleague not been caught up in the hilarity of the moment.

Life as a Novel

Frequently, when going through a prolonged difficulty we tend to put ourselves down and negate our effectiveness by seeing ourselves as failures, now and forever. It is as if we have forgotten that *things have not come to stay but have come to pass.* Try considering your current difficulties as one chapter in a long autobiography. This gives you a different perspective and reminds you to *take a longer view of your life's possibilities.* Think about the life stories of great men and women. Almost invariably they are stories of failures that were converted into learning experiences which then led to success. For example, were you aware that Abraham Lincoln lost eight elections, failed in business, went bankrupt and suffered a nervous breakdown before he was elected president? There was a guy who didn't let failure get in the way of his success. His numerous failures built his character and made for a fascinating life story. Let your imagination roam into a successful future and look back at this time. What are you learning? In what way will it lead to your success?

Special Effects

The two reframing strategies we discussed above are essentially about viewing your life literally from an outside or observer perspective. The second strategy includes playing with this perspective over time. This grouping of strategies is built upon a simple realization. Consider the fact that every special effect you have ever seen in the movies was first imagined by someone. This means that your imagination is capable of duplicating anything you have ever seen and fully capable of changing your experience in any given moment. For example, a very popular method of disrupting anxiety over public speaking is to imagine that your audience is nude. (There are a minority of people who find this particular image really scary.) It is important to remember that we are in the Funhouse to play and experiment. The next time you are bothered by a thought about the past or about the future, play with some of the following special effects:

- Change the voices in a memory to sound like Donald Duck and his nephews.
- Imagine that someone who is being particularly critical of you is suddenly seized with an attack of belching or flatulence.
- Add circus music to the soundtrack.
- Go beyond observing yourself. Watch yourself watching yourself.
- Imagine that an individual who always manages to intimidate or anger you is wearing a clown hat, or mismatched clothes with dirty smudges, or is sitting on the toilet, or is half-nude, etc. The idea here is to create an image that is so ludicrous that it evokes your amusement rather than your anxiety or your anger.
- Pretend. Pretend. Pretend. Be childlike.

Case Study in Reframing—Using Special Effects

Julie was happily engaged to her boyfriend, and he had given her no concrete reasons to be jealous or to doubt his fidelity. Nonetheless, she found herself feeling quite jealous of an attractive, younger girl who lived in the same apartment building as her fiance. Often she and her fiance would run into this girl in the building or at the pool, and she would feel angry when her boyfriend chatted with her, although these conversations were not flirtatious and not of the sort that should have aroused her suspicions. When she confronted her fiance with her feelings and asked him not to speak to this girl, he was annoyed and advised her to work on her feelings of jealously. Since his actions were totally innocent and just friendly, he felt it was unfair for him to have to totally ignore this girl just to make Julie comfortable. When Julie considered the situation, by putting herself in her fiance's shoes (a technique discussed in more detail in Chapter 8), she decided there was merit to his point of view and suggestion that she work on her jealously. To facilitate this end she used reframing strategies to counteract the anxiety she felt when she saw the girl. Since the most common place she ran into this girl was in the elevator in her fiance's building, she used that as the setting for her visualization. Julie imagined that she and her boyfriend ran into the girl on the elevator. Once the doors shut the girl was immediately beset with an uncontrollable fit of gas, resulting in both audible flatulence and burping. Imagining this ridiculous scene made her double over with hilarity, and also resulted in Julie feeling sorry for the poor girl and her embarrassment. Julie was amazed that when she next saw the girl in question, all feelings of anxiety and jealousy were replaced by amusement and recollections of her silly, yet very useful, fantasy.

THE MAP IS NOT THE TERRITORY

"Reality is an illusion, albeit a very persistent one."
Albert Einstein

So we invite you to always view your perceptions as just that, your perceptions, nothing more, nothing less. Your perceptions are like maps you use to get around in your world. Remember that a map is not the territory (Bandler and Grinder, 1975). It is just one representation of a territory. And some maps are more useful than others, depending on the circumstances. If you want to drive from Atlanta to Washington, D.C., you will need a good road map. A topographical map of the southeastern United States will be useless. On the other hand, if you want to fly your own plane from Atlanta to Washington D.C., a good road map will not help you, but a topographical map which helps you identify landmarks, will come in very handy. The same is true of your perceptions. Given that we each have a unique set of blinders which color our perceptions, it is useful to don a set of blinders which will be most useful in a given situation. Be open to the possibility that the solution is found in a reframe. To give you some practice with shifting your perceptual frame of reference, try the following exercises.

Figure 1.3 Is the Book Looking Towards You . . . or Away from You?

Figure 1.4 Two Faces . . . or One?

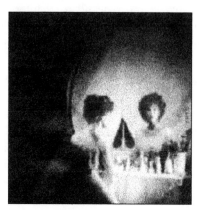

Figure 1.5 Woman in Vanity . . . or Skull?
Hint: Move the book a bit farther away
from you to see the skull or the woman
looking at the mirror.

Figure 1.6 Man Playing Horn . . .
or Woman Sillhouette?

Figure 1.8 A Rabbit . . . or A Duck?
Hint: The duck is looking to the left,
the rabbit is looking to the right.

Figure 1.7 A Vase . . . or Two Faces?

Figure 1.9 A Face of a Native
American . . . or an Eskimo?

Figure 1.10 Old Woman . . .
or Young Girl?
Hint: The old woman's nose is the
young girl's nose and chin.

The previous optical illusions represent what psychologists refer to as **ambiguous figures**. These illusions clearly illustrate the importance of the meaning (i.e. perceptions) we attribute to any given sensations. In summary, the context of the stimuli along with our learning histories and expectations all combine to influence how we perceive and interpret our world. In the real world, we are faced with ambiguous stimuli and sensations all the time. But the recognition that *your perceptions are not reality, but just your perceptions,* can facilitate the development of flexibility of thought, improved problem solving, and ultimately your effectiveness as a human being.

SELF EXERCISE

1. Is there a situation where you are habitually stuck because you are totally unwilling to part with your point of view about it? We guarantee that if you think hard enough you will find that the answer to this question (for everyone) is typically yes. Can you think of a particular instance? Pick one of the reframing techniques and practice shifting your perspective on your issue. If you at a loss for how to proceed, then experiment with reframing a past mistake or failure as a valuable learning experience. Think about how your life might have improved or been enriched today, either directly or indirectly, as a result of this experience. You may have to dig deep to adopt this perspective, or to see connections between past mistakes and current successes, but if you persist you will be rewarded.

KEY TERMS

Sensation	Objectivism	Memory Distortion
Perception	Constructivism	Reframing
Paradigm	Paradigm Shift	Ambiguous Figures
Frame of Reference	Selective Perception	Functional Fixedness

CHAPTER 1 QUESTIONS

True or False (T or F)

1. _____ We always see exactly what is there.

2. _____ Sensation and perception are the same thing.

3. _____ All frames of reference are constantly in flux.

4. _____ Our perceptions are greatly influenced by our expectations, beliefs, and pre-conceived notions.

5. _____ Effective individuals are flexible in their thinking.

6. _____ Eyewitness accounts of accidents or crimes are always accurate.

7. _____ Traditional thinking is what stimulates scientific development.

8. _____ Paradigm shifts typically happen very easily.

9. _____ Humor tends to decrease our flexibility of thought.

10. _____ Reframing is one method for creating paradigm shifts within yourself.

Short-Answer Questions

1. Humans are adept at developing _____ to help us organize and understand our world.

2. _____ believe that reality exists independent from you.

3. _____ believe that there is no separate reality.

4. Newtonian physics is an excellent example of the _____ scientific view.

5. _____ causes us to perceive what we expect to be there.

6. Einstein's theory of relativity is an excellent example of the _____ scientific view.

7. Major scientific discoveries are typically preceded by a _____.

8. _____ is a way of creating a paradigm shift on a small level in your personal life.

9. Getting locked into viewing things in only conventional or familiar ways is termed _____ _____.

Essay Questions

1. Differentiate between the Objectivist and Constructivist models.

2. What is a paradigm shift and how is this phenomenon important?

3. Why are paradigms (in science and in everyday life) so resistant to change?

4. Why is the 9 Dot Problem so hard to solve for many people?

5. Describe the process of reframing and how it could prove useful in your life.

6. Describe several strategies for creating reframes.

2

Know That the Buck Starts and Stops with You

Have you ever wondered, at some time in your life, "why am I the way that I am?" One of the authors recalls a question frequently asked of him at the start of his graduate career while in training to become a psychologist:

> 'What made you choose to become a psychologist?', people would ask me. My traditional retort was, 'because I'm screwed up and I want to figure myself out'. I guess that I was searching for the *truth* about myself. Along the way I discovered that I was not as screwed up as I feared I was, the "I'm OK, You're OK" school of thought as proposed in the book with the same title by Thomas Harris. And later I concluded that maybe I was a bit screwed up, but that wasn't so bad, the "I'm not OK, You're not OK, and that's OK" school of thought proposed by Sheldon Kopp, in his book *If You Meet the Buddha on the Road, Kill Him!* But most importantly I realized that there was no one truth, since the truth was dependent upon *the frame of reference*, or school of thought that I adopted. Early in my career, while enveloped in the Freudian mystique, I blamed my parents for my troubles and felt that I was the victim of an, at times, traumatic childhood. When studying Behavioral theories I concluded that I was the product of an unusual reinforcement and conditioning history. But the Humanists and the Cognitive-Behaviorists helped me realize I had some choices in the matter of who I was, and who I would ultimately become. I realized I was who I was, not because of what had happened to me, but because of the choices I had made in response to what had happened in my life.

DETERMINISM VS. FREE WILL

The history of science reveals that the various scientific disciplines developed, in part, in order to determine the causes of events. Meticulous observations and measurements led scientists to the conclusion that everything which occurs in nature has a cause. Theories of causation were postulated and then tested by scientific experimentation. This belief in cause and effect relationships has been termed **Determinism**.

As psychology matured as a science, social scientists, in turn, began to posit that human behavior may also be the product of causal relationships, and therefore determined. That is, if nature encompasses all of humanity, then human behavior must also be the result of various determining factors. Determinists espouse the view that all human actions are caused by something, even if we are oblivious to these causative factors. Strict determinists go so far as to imply that free choice does not exist, that all our actions and decisions are the product of outside determining variables over which we have no control. At the other end of the spectrum we find the **Free Will** camp. According to this point of view humans can and do typically ignore so-called determining factors (such as genetics or environmental influences) and freely choose how and when to act. Psychological theories of personality and behavior can be placed on a continuum between determinism, the belief that who we are is largely governed by outside forces, and free will, which obviously assumes that who we are is a result of the choices we make.

There are three main deterministic theories. The first of these are the biologically based theories which postulate that we are almost exclusively a product of our genetic heritage. Proponents of these theories claim that all of our behavior, both normal and abnormal, can be traced back to particular configurations of our genetic makeup. Support for these theories comes from the obvious fact that abilities, talents, and certain emotional and physical disorders clearly run in families. For example, it is evident that singing ability is passed down from generation to generation. Just look at the late, great reggae artist, Bob Marley, and his son Ziggy Marley, or Julio Iglesias and his son, Enrique Iglesias, or Nat King Cole and his daughter Natalie Cole, or Judy Garland and her daughter Liza Minnelli. Or consider athletics where sons often follow in their father's footsteps like quarterback Peyton Manning and his quarterback father Archie Manning, or baseball superstar Ken Griffey, Jr. and his father Ken Griffey, Sr. As another example, let's take the rather severe emotional disorder known as **schizophrenia**. Individuals suffering from this malady have difficulty differentiating traditional reality from their own internal fantasies or fears. Schizophrenic individuals are prone to "**psychotic episodes**" where they lose contact with reality, and suffer from **hallucinations** (seeing or hearing things that aren't really there), and/or **delusional thinking** (believing in ideas that are not reality based, like those involving fears of persecution). Research clearly shows a

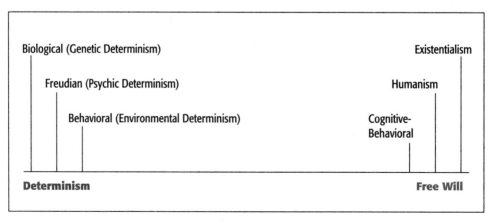

Figure 2.1

strong genetic component to this disorder (Mirsky & Quinn, 1988). The **concordance rate** (the probability that two individuals display the same trait or characteristic) of schizophrenia is much higher for identical twins (who have the same genetic makeup) than for fraternal twins (whose genetic makeup is the same as any sibling), or siblings in general. All of these, however, were much higher than for non related individuals raised in the same environment (Gottesmann, 1991; Cannon et. al, 1998). So theories of genetic determinism espouse a view of reality that "my grandparents did it to me. I am who I am because of my genes (and we don't mean the kind you wear on your body)."

A second set of deterministic theories are those of psychic determinism which postulate that you are who you are because of how you were raised. The most famous of these is Freud's **Psychoanalytic Theory**. Proponents of this theory believe that your personality is determined by your early experiences, and that by the time you reach six years old, it is pretty well set. So such things as the tenor of your toilet training or your mother's style of feeding you have a profound influence on your later development. This theory says "my parents did it to me. I am who I am because of the way they brought me up."

The third set of deterministic theories, known as **Behaviorism**, postulates that we are a product of our conditioning and learning histories, and of our current reinforcement schedules. There is a wealth of data that the aforementioned factors greatly influence the behavior of both animals and humans. In order to insure that psychology was accepted as a "science", Behavioral theorists argued that the only unit worthy of study was overt, observable behavior. According to theorists such as B.F. Skinner, and Ivan Pavlov, it is our overall environment that shapes our personality and behavior. Thus, you became a good student because you were rewarded for academic achievement. Or you learned how to be fearful because you copied the behavior of significant others who modeled being afraid. These theories say, "my environment (teachers, parents, bosses, coaches, siblings, peers, etc.) did it to me. I am who I am because of the pressures they exerted and the rewards they provided."

But are these theories based on reality? Is this really all there is to human behavior? Are we just essentially victims of our genes, our upbringing, and our environment? The proponents of the Free Will theories would argue that these deterministic paradigms only tell a part of the story. They are accurate maps of a portion of the territory, but fail to include a key component of the human existence. The fact is, we believe that while you are certainly influenced by all of these factors, human beings are ultimately free to choose. Perhaps the earliest of these theories is based on the European philosophy of **Existentialism**, as popularized by John Paul Sarte and Albert Camus. These philosophical theories, when translated into psychological thought, basically posited that although, undoubtedly, life throws waves at you that are outside of your control, how you ride those waves is up to you. You could choose to be drowned by the rising waters, or you could learn to tread water, or you could master surfing.

Here in America this view was developed further by the **Humanists**, such as Abraham Maslow and Carl Rogers. They too hypothesized that our personalities and our behavior were not so much a product of our conditioning and our conditions, but of the choices we made in response to those. They were much more optimistic than the existentialists by promoting a belief that if anything occurred naturally, it was human beings striving towards self-actualization, towards becoming all that we can be. These humanistic theories developed partly in reaction to the strictly deterministic Freudian view which dominated psychology and psychotherapy practice at the time.

Cognitive-Behaviorists, such as Albert Ellis, Aaron Beck, and Martin Seligman pointed out that, when studying humans, we should not focus solely on the study of overt behavior, as the strict Behaviorists would have it, but must take into account "covert behavior", our thoughts, the internal self talk that preceded the behaviors. The strict Behaviorist model is an S-R (stimulus-response) model. Simply stated, this cause and effect model holds that all behavior is controlled by the stimulus which precedes it. For example, you walk into your house and your spouse or parent screams at you (the stimulus) for being late, and as a consequence of this you get angry and yell back (the response). This model was based on research with animals, which appear to be more stimulus bound. But for humans a more descriptive model is that of S-O-R (stimulus-organism-response). A stimulus impinges upon you, but before you respond, you have a thought about that stimulus, you imbue it with meaning. It is *that thought* that leads to your particular response. To go back to our earlier example, after you've been screamed at, if your first thought is, "how dare you?" or "that jerk, she/he is always picking on me", you are likely to respond in kind. However, if your first thought is "he/she must have been really worried about me", you are much more likely to respond with an apology. You see, it was not the screaming that led to your response, but what you said to yourself about the screaming. It is here, between the stimulus and the response that choice resides. To quote, Stephen Covey, *"Between stimulus and response humans have the greatest freedom, the freedom to choose that response."* The difficulty lies in the fact that our thoughts tend to be automatic and rather telegraphic, and we are generally not aware of them. But more on this later in this chapter.

Human history is replete with examples of individuals who, when faced with extraordinarily difficult situations, stimuli which would overwhelm most of us, exercised this freedom to choose their responses. Take, for example, the story of Ruben "Hurricane" Carter, as described in his book *The Sixteenth Round*, and popularized in the 1999 movie "The Hurricane". Carter, a successful boxer, was falsely imprisoned for nineteen years for a triple murder he did not commit. He refused to allow prison to rule his life. He opted to wear pajamas rather than prison garb. He chose to sleep by day and be awake all night to avoid the normal prison routine. This was not just an act of blind opposition; rather, he used his time to educate and transform himself. He read extensively and spent years working on the manuscript that later became his autobiographical work. His book inspired others to work on his behalf, eventually leading to his release. His goal while in prison, besides, of course, to get released, was not to be bound by the routines and prescriptions of prison life, but to make his own world within the prison walls. Those of you who have seen the movie "Life is Beautiful", which won the 1998 Academy Award for best foreign film, will recognize it as a perfect example of our freedom to choose our actions even when faced with intolerable circumstances. Those of you who haven't seen it, we strongly recommend that you *choose* to do so. Lest you think that this is just a romanticized version of a possible response to the tragedy which was the Holocaust, we recommend reading Victor Frankl's autobiographical account of his time in a concentration camp, as described in his book *Man's Search for Meaning*.

If we take an objective look at the body of knowledge and data amassed in psychology over the last hundred years, the inescapable conclusion is that human behavior can best be understood as lying somewhere in the middle of the free will vs. determinism continuum. There is conclusive research evidence that certain emotional disorders (such as schizophrenia and bipolar disorder) have a strong genetic component, in the same way that inherited predispositions towards diabetes or heart disease run in some families. Likewise, we cannot ignore the overwhelming evidence that we are strongly affected by environmental factors ranging from our past experiences and our learning histories, including what we have learned through operant and classical conditioning as well as observational learning. Could it be that our belief in free will is just a fantasy? Do we harbor an illusion of free choice because at any given moment we are bombarded with so many determining variables that we are unable to perceive them or sort them out? Most psychologists have come to the conclusion that human behavior is affected by a combination of determining forces along with each individual's inherent ability to choose, to set and pursue goals, and to decide to change the path set by determining factors. Not all humans rise to this challenge, however, but the capability to do so exists nonetheless. This mixed viewpoint has come to be known as *soft determinism*. The psychological theory which fits best in the middle of this continuum is the cognitive-behavioral school of thought.

PROACTIVITY

This freedom of choice, referred to in the current literature as **"proactivity"**, is undoubtedly the most important paradigm guiding the behavior of effective individuals. We have found that a good way to begin to understand the nature of proactivity is to consider your first responses to the word *responsibility*. What first comes to mind when you hear this word? If you are like most of our students and workshop participants you think of things such as paying your bills, doing your homework, picking up the kids, cleaning the house, cooking dinner, washing your clothes or your car, etc. These are things you feel you should be doing. The image that frequently comes to mind is that of a large ball and chain attached to your ankle, which drags you down and limits your freedom. But, proactivity involves placing a different frame around the concept of responsibility, as aptly described by Steven Covey in his seminal book, *The Seven Habits of Highly Effective People:*

> "While the word *proactivity* is now fairly common in management literature, it is a word you won't find in most dictionaries. It is more than merely taking initiative. It means that as human beings, we are responsible for our own lives. Our behavior is a function of our decisions, not our conditions. We can subordinate feelings to values. We have the initiative and the responsibility to make things happen. Look at the work *responsibility—* 'response-ability'—the ability to choose your response. Highly proactive people recognize that responsibility. They do not blame circumstances, conditions, or conditioning for their behavior. Their behavior is a product of their own conscious choice, based on values, rather than a product of their conditions based on feelings."

Locus of Control

The concept of proactivity has also been previously referred to, by psychologist Julian Rotter, as an internal locus of control. **Locus of control** is on a continuum ranging from external to internal. Individuals with an **external locus of control** see themselves as victims, buffeted and abused by external events over which they have no control. Individuals with an **internal locus of control** believe that they are responsible for the ultimate outcomes in their life. They do not wait for fate to lead them in directions, rather they endeavor to take active control over their own life. For Covey, an internal locus of control is "proactivity", while an external locus of control is "reactivity". Reactive persons are at the mercy of forces beyond their control. Have you ever heard someone say, "It's raining outside, how can I be happy?", or "It's Monday so I don't have any energy". For these people their mood or their energy level are determined by the weather or the day of the week. Proactive people, while certainly influenced by their environment, recognize that they are response-able to choose their responses to these conditions. If you are curious to see where you fall on the continuum of locus of control, we suggest you take the time to fill out the following inventory.

TABLE 2.1 Student Locus of Control Inventory

Check Yes if you agree with a statement; check No if you do not agree.

YES	NO	
____	____	1. If I can do the work, I can get a good grade in any course no matter how good or bad the instructor may be.
____	____	2. If the teacher isn't a good speaker or doesn't keep me interested, I probably won't do well in the class.
____	____	3. I believe that I have the power to control what happens to me.
____	____	4. I believe that I have very little control over what happens to me.
____	____	5. When I make a mistake, it's usually my fault.
____	____	6. When I make a mistake, it's usually because someone didn't make clear to me what I was supposed to do.
____	____	7. My grades are the result of how much studying I do.
____	____	8. My grades don't seem to be affected by the amount of studying that I do.
____	____	9. I can adapt easily to a change of plans or events.
____	____	10. Adapting to change has always been difficult for me. I like things to be as predictable and orderly as possible.
____	____	11. When I fail a test, it's either because I didn't study or I didn't understand the material.
____	____	12. When I fail a test, it's either because the test was unfair or the instructor didn't cover the material sufficiently.
____	____	13. I usually don't need anyone to push me or make me study.
____	____	14. I can't seem to make myself study.
____	____	15. I am a self-motivated person.
____	____	16. I need someone to motivate me.

If you checked "yes" to mostly odd-numbered statements, then you tend towards having an internal locus of control. We congratulate you! The rest of this chapter will help you refine and polish skills to make you an even more proactive individual. On the other hand, if you found yourself endorsing more even-numbered statements, then we suggest you consider the possibility that your locus of control is more external. If effectiveness is your goal, then we strongly recommend that you take the ideas and strategies presented in the rest of this chapter and incorporate them into your behavior. Remember, it is not enough to know about mangoes, you must be willing to taste them.

Students with an internal locus of control recognize the connection between the effort they put forth and the grades they receive. These students tend to be self-motivated and optimistic. They believe in themselves and that they can do whatever they set out to accomplish. They welcome challenges and are not afraid of change. If a student with an internal locus of control fails a test, he/she does not blame the teacher nor the test questions. He/she takes responsibility for the failure, and attempts to determine what action is needed to avoid this in the future. When these students make mistakes, they endeavor to figure out what they did wrong or what they did not understand. These students don't believe that their grades are a function of luck or fate. When things go wrong, they look to see what they can do to put things right.

Students who have an external locus of control cannot see a connection between the effort they put forth in a course and the grades they receive. If they do poorly on a test or in a course, they may focus their blame on the teacher, believing the tests were too hard or the grading standards too stiff. These students tend to be pessimists who need someone to motivate them and give them a push to succeed. They believe that many of the things they want in life are out of reach or that other people are holding them back. They may be afraid of change and prefer to follow familiar routines. When they make mistakes, they blame others for being unfair or for not giving them the right information. They see themselves as victims in the drama that is their lives. When something goes wrong, they may feel there is nothing they can do about it. They forget that the way they see the problem is the problem.

Three Ways to Increase Proactivity

Perhaps we have convinced you that being proactive is a skill you want to spend some time cultivating. You might be asking, "OK, but how do I go about doing that?" We have found that a useful method for increasing proactivity involves focusing on three key areas: (1) your thoughts; (2) your language; and (3) your actions. We believe that all things are created three times. First, when you think about it; second, by how you speak about it, and lastly by when you take some action to make it happen. You will find that we deal with this last aspect of the process in more depth in Chapter 6. Creating the reality of becoming a proactive individual involves a sustained focus on all three areas.

Focusing on Your Thoughts

Reactive individuals tend to be worriers. If a worrier were conscious of the direction of his or her thoughts, he or she would discover that the focus is mostly on the bad things that could possibly happen. We are not suggesting that you should not plan for the possibility of negative eventualities, but to spend most of your time doing this is clearly counterproductive. This is particularly the case if you consider that *fully 80% of what we worry about never happens!* Yet the effects on our emotional and physical health, as well as our productivity, are similar to what might have occurred if the feared event had actually happened. This topic will be dealt with in more detail in Chapters 4 and 5. Are you a worrier? Proactive people make a conscious effort to give more time for considering what might go right and how to make it go right. In other words, they are more likely to be considered optimists.

Focusing on Your Language

Have you ever heard yourself saying things like, "he made me angry", or "I couldn't make it to class, I was just too tired to get up on time"? If you have said things like this, and who among us has not, realize that you are speaking reactively. You were giving your freedom to choose away and giving someone else control of your emotions, in the first example, or letting circumstances (i.e. apparent fatigue) determine what you could or could not do, in the second example. Proactive individuals realize that they are ultimately in control of their feelings and emotions, and speak in a way that creates and reinforces this reality. So instead of, "he made me so mad", they might say, "I am angry about what so and so did". We hope the difference between these two is clear. When you say, "I am angry about what he did", *you* are in control of your response. Please don't think that this is merely semantics. Our language is one of civilized man's prominent ways of defining reality. How we speak has a profound impact on how we view the world.

Focusing on Your Actions

Increasing proactivity in this area simply requires adopting two habits: (1) making promises and keeping them; and (2) setting small goals and working to achieve them. Proactive individuals are keenly aware of the power of their word. Unfortunately, the authors have noticed that many people fail to grasp or heed this important concept. So people say things like, "I'll call you", after running into someone they haven't seen in a while, when, even at the time, they know they are highly unlikely to follow through. Or many students promise themselves that they will study for that test in plenty of time, only to, at best, end up cramming desperately at the last minute. Such behavior has the unfortunate consequence, not just that others stop believing in what you say, but more importantly, that you stop believing in yourself. We recognize that it might not be possible to keep your promises 100% of the time. But at least don't sleaze out. Be willing to acknowledge the lapse and seek ways of amending it.

Most people can't wait to be successful so they can do just what they feel like doing. It is this thought, however, that can interfere with ever achieving success in the first place. The bottom line is that *effective people do the things that ineffective people don't feel like doing.* They don't feel like doing those things either, necessarily, but they want to do them out of the strength of their purpose. We strongly believe that there is a big difference between wanting and feeling. Feeling is merely a momentary desire (i.e. "I don't feel like getting out of bed"), wanting encompasses not just the present but the future consequences of the present behavior. A proactive individual acknowledges his present feeling (i.e. "I feel tired"), but decides to want to get out of bed because he wants the results of this action, like doing well in class, or keeping his promise. Now at this point you might be thinking, "this is all well and good but it is easier said than done". You are absolutely right. As is often remarked, "Talk is cheap". But to quote an old mentor of ours, Norman Brenner, *"to be effective you must be willing to do what is necessary"*. Perhaps even more proactively stated, "you want to be willing to do what is necessary". So what about you? What do you choose?

DEALING WITH IRRATIONAL SELF-TALK

To make the process of becoming proactive a doable enterprise we thought it would be helpful for you to learn some specific strategies for modifying the way you think and the way you talk in a more proactive direction. A powerful way humans undermine their effectiveness is by doing what Albert Ellis (1975) called **catastrophizing**, when you give yourself messages that a situation is too awful or overwhelming to bear or that the worst is about to happen. These messages, also termed **self-talk** by Ellis or **automatic thoughts** by Aaron Beck (1970) refer to the running commentary that goes on in your head during the course of the day. Most of it is mundane and benign, but problems will arise when your perceptions are influenced by automatic thoughts reflecting irrational beliefs. Many studies have documented the link between irrational beliefs and anxiety (Bonner & Rich, 1991). These typically fall into two general categories: (1) beliefs that the world, someone, or something should be different; and (2) beliefs that your perceptions reflect reality rather than your subjective impressions of reality. Many times these irrational beliefs operate on a subconscious level, yet guide your emotional reactions nonetheless.

Self-talk tends to be circular in nature. Figure 2.2 illustrates this cycle. It begins with events in the environment, events that have no valence until you are there to interpret them or ascribe meaning to them. Next, we have your sensory impressions of the event (i.e. your perceptions and sensory input). This is followed by your cognitions and interpretations of your perception of events (i.e. your self-talk about the event). This may include irrational ideas or self statements. The next step is the reaction of your emotional and physical system, not so much to the events themselves, but to your interpretations

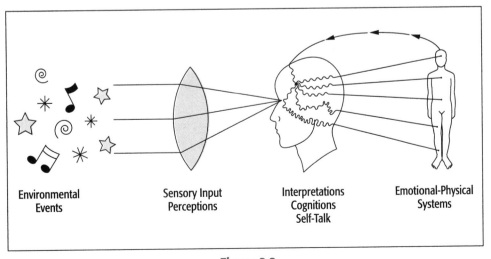

| Environmental Events | Sensory Input Perceptions | Interpretations Cognitions Self-Talk | Emotional-Physical Systems |

Figure 2.2

(self-talk) about the events. These physical/emotional reactions then feed back into your self-talk. For example, if you are feeling disappointed or depressed because of how you have interpreted an event, this sadness will then further influence your self-talk, predisposing you to further negative cognitions. And the cycle goes on. Negative thoughts create unhappiness, and depression stimulates further pessimistic thinking.

At the root of all irrational thinking is the assumption that things are done to you, rather than recognizing that events happen in the world. Going back to the S-O-R model presented earlier: you experience those events (**S**); engage in self-talk about those events (**O**); and then experience an emotion (**R**) resulting from your self-talk. **S** does not cause **R**, rather it is **O** that causes **R**. If your self-talk is irrational and unrealistic, you will create negative emotions. The two common forms of irrational self-talk are: (1) statements that catastrophize; and (2) statements that revolve around absolutes. Catastrophic thinking involves expecting the worst and/or giving nightmarish interpretations of your experience (i.e. being a worrier). Thus, a momentary chest pain becomes a heart attack, your boss' bad mood means you are going to get fired, if you do poorly on a test you assume that you will fail the course. The emotions that follow such expectations are very unpleasant, but you are responding to your own description of the world. Irrational self statements involving absolutes typically include words such as "should, must, ought, always and never". Here you assume that if things are not a certain way, or if you do not conform to some standard, it is disastrous. Any deviation from that particular value or standard must be bad.

Cognitive Restructuring

A potent strategy for refuting irrational beliefs and changing your self-talk involves the use of **cognitive restructuring techniques**. The first step in this process is to attempt to identify the irrational belief that is underlying your reaction. Once you have uncovered this belief you may immediately notice the absurdity of it. Common irrational beliefs include:

1. Everyone needs to like you. It is awful if someone dislikes you.
2. You must be competent and perfect in all that you undertake.
3. Mistakes are sure proof that you are a failure.
4. You should never hurt anyone or refuse a request/favor.
5. It is horrible if things don't turn out the way you want.
6. You are helpless and have no control over your feelings or experiences.
7. You will be rejected if you don't go to great lengths to please others.
8. There is a perfect love and a perfect relationship.
9. You shouldn't have to feel pain. Life should always be fair.
10. Your worth as a human being depends on how much you achieve and produce.

The next step is to examine and challenge the irrational belief with your rational mind. Notice how so many of the irrational beliefs above revolve around a "should", or a "must", or the idea that it is catastrophic if something doesn't turn out in a particular way. Challenging irrationalities can be facilitated by asking yourself the following questions:

1. Is there any reason to think that this belief is true?
2. Is there evidence that this belief might not be true?
3. If I reject this belief, what is the worst that could happen to me?
4. If I reject this belief, what good things might happen as a result?

The third step is to substitute a new, rational belief in place of the old, irrational idea. Initially this may seem artificial, a bit phony. But replacing the negative thoughts that led to painful emotional responses with more positive and rational alternatives is a good start, even if you don't completely believe it at first. In time you will start to believe your rational thoughts, particularly after you experience improvements in your situation reflecting the change in you. The changes in your thinking patterns will become natural and comfortable after a while. With practice, it will get easier and easier to reframe reality, and to view things from a more positive viewpoint. Cognitive restructuring does not imply that you should repress your thoughts. It is a process of acknowledging those thoughts and feelings that are reactive in nature, then examining/challenging them, and finally replacing them with more rational thoughts when appropriate. For example, the rational statements below can be substituted for each of the irrational thoughts above. These are not the only options. We invite you to create your own rational alternatives if the choices below do not fit for you. Notice that these rational statements utilize elements of reframing. Oftentimes, the process of thinking rationally involves the process of reframing, of learning to view a situation from a different, more rational, perspective.

1. It is impossible to be well liked by everyone. No one achieves that. It certainly isn't the end of the world if _____ (insert the name of the person or persons in question) doesn't like me. And, who knows, next month the situation could be totally different.

2. It is impossible to be good at everything. Besides, if I did succeed at being extremely competent in everything I did, many people would no doubt resent me.

3. Everyone makes mistakes. Mistakes can be learning experiences that lead to eventual success. "Failure" is just another word, not an enduring part of my character.

4. _____ will surely survive if I don't do things his/her way.

5. It is unfortunate if things don't turn out the way I would like, but it is hardly the end of the world and I can handle it. By this time next year I will no doubt be completely indifferent to this whole situation.

6. I *always* have a choice over how I respond to situations.

7. If I don't go out of my way to please someone there is a chance I might get rejected, but it certainly is not guaranteed. And, if I need to go to great lengths to please someone in order for that person to like me, then that individual is not someone that I care to have as a friend. I want to be liked and appreciated for who I am, not for what I can do for someone.

8. There are no perfect relationships. I will focus on making this a healthy, honest, enjoyable relationship and learn to accept the inevitable disappointments and imperfections.

9. Life isn't always fair. Feeling pain is part of being human. If I had never experienced sadness or despair I would not know what it means to be happy and content.

10. My worth as a human being is much more dependant on my capacity to be fully alive, feeling everything it means to be human, the good with the bad. My worth depends more on how I am in relation to the people who are important to me.

David Goodman, in his book *Emotional Well-Being through Rational Behavior Training*, offers six rules or guidelines for rational thinking. You may find these rules to be quite useful for guiding you to think rationally and challenge your irrational beliefs.

1. **It does not do anything to me.**
   That is, the situation does not make you anxious or afraid. The things you say to yourself are what produce the negative emotions you may feel at any given moment. In the same vein, no one can make you feel anything. How you feel is always your choice. Other people may provide provocation, but ultimately, you always choose how you feel in response.

2. **Everything is exactly the way it should be.**
   The conditions for things or people to be otherwise do not exist. To say things should be different is tantamount to believing in magic. Things are the way they are because of a long series of causal events. To say things should be different is to throw out causality.

3. **All humans are fallible creatures.**
   This is an inescapable truth. If you have not set reasonable quotas of failure for yourself and others, you increase the prospects for your disappointment and unhappiness.

4. **It takes two to have a conflict.**
   Before pointing your finger in blame, consider the 30% rule. Any party to a conflict is contributing at least 30% of the fuel to keep an argument going.

5. **The original cause is lost in antiquity.**
   It is a waste of your time to try to discover who did what first. It is often impossible to find the original cause of chronic painful emotions, as such dilemmas are usually extremely complicated, and often the product of multiple interactions. The best strategy is to make decisions to change your behavior now.

6. **We feel the way we think.**
   To again quote Covey, *"The way you see the problem is the problem"*. And what you say to yourself determines your feelings.

Correlation ≠ Causation

Irrational thinking takes other forms as well. In our attempts to make sense of our world we often make a common error in thinking by assuming that if things occur together or are associated in some way, that one must therefore cause the other. In statistical terms, when two variables tend to be reliably associated with one another, this is called a **correlation**. The greater the degree of association, the higher the correlation. When a correlation is present, it could be that one variable does cause or influence the other (such as in the relationship between height and weight), but this is not necessarily the case. It may be that some other factor or variable is actually influencing or causing the correlation. For example, let's take the common characterization of the bespectacled intellectual (i.e. the high IQ kid with the thick glasses). There is a reason for this stereotype. A correlation does exist between myopia (nearsightedness) and intelligence, as individuals with higher IQ's are more likely to be nearsighted. But what does this mean? Is it that being myopic somehow magically makes you smart? Or does having a high IQ somehow harm your vision (maybe from reading too many books!)? We are sure you would agree that both of these positions are totally absurd. Rather, this correlation is the byproduct of other genetic variables which are beyond the scope of this book to discuss.

Some of the studies and research cited throughout this text are correlational in nature. We advise you to be very wary of inferring any causation from the results of correlational research. Disclaimers of this nature will pop up periodically in reference to these correlational studies. It is only through controlled experimentation that we can get valid information about causation.

When combating irrational thinking, remember that just because two things occur together, that alone does not offer proof that one has caused the other. A prime example of the folly of inferring causation from correlation was found in the field of psychology. For decades it was widely thought that childhood schizophrenia was caused by the "schizophrenogenic mother", a parent who was cold, aloof and gave a child inconsistent and confusing messages. Although a correlation does exist between parenting styles and the incidence of schizophrenia, we now know that this disorder is primarily a function of a genetic, biochemical disturbance in the brain, and is not caused by cold parents. It is actually more likely that the so-called schizophrenogenic parenting style could have been in reaction to, rather than the cause of raising an emotionally troubled child.

It is also relevant at this point to alert you to be aware of the very human tendency to perceive a correlation or relationship between things that really does not exist. We call this an illusory or **spurious correlation**. If we believe there is a relationship between variables, we will likely (and unconsciously) use selective perception to detect and recall only those circumstances which confirm our belief. This is one way stereotypes and racial prejudices get ingrained. All of us fall prey to perceiving spurious correlations and using selective perception to reinforce these mistaken notions. Being aware of this tendency can help you combat this form of irrational thinking. Remind yourself that incidents that superficially appear to confirm your beliefs could just be nothing other than random coincidences.

OPTIMISM

As we have already alluded to, effective individuals are optimists. We recommend that you consciously choose to adopt optimistic perceptions. Why? Because that particular map of the world will be the most useful for helping you be achieve your goals. Effective individuals develop the habit of perceiving and interpreting potential problems in ways that give their life meaning and a sense of control. That is, they look for reasons to be happy and satisfied with life, imperfect as it is. They have become adept at turning lemons into lemonade and finding the proverbial silver lining in the cloud. Optimists are not necessarily unrealistic, or unwilling to accept or face negative circumstances, rather they choose to focus on what is right, rather than bemoaning all that is wrong. It is a matter of focus. They look for evidence that life is good and that they are doing all right. When misfortune strikes, as it does in everyone's life at some point, optimists recover more quickly because they find lessons in adversity that continue to give their life meaning. Optimists simply refuse to let go of their positive expectations. Just as irrational or negative self-statements can create depression, anxiety, or other negative emotions, positive or optimistic self-statements can create and reinforce effectiveness and happiness.

Research indicates that your level of optimism vs. pessimism has been found to be a powerful determining factor in your physical and emotional health. Indeed, a review of the research on happiness has consistently identified four traits manifested by happy people: (1) optimism; (2) good self esteem; (3) an internal locus of control; and (4) extroversion (Myers and Dreiner, 1995). Given that these were correlational studies, it is unclear whether these four personality dimensions lead to happiness or the reverse. But in any event, it is surely safe to conclude that these characteristics help to maintain happiness. Pessimism has been associated with high stress levels, depression, psychosomatic problems, higher levels of physical illness and premature death (Miley, 1999). Likewise, where a person falls on the optimism-pessimism continuum is related to health in the future and how quickly that individual will recover from serious illness (Scheier & Carver, 1993). You might also be surprised to learn that optimism is actually a better predictor of college academic success than standard measures such as SAT scores or high school GPA's! That was exactly what researchers at the University of Pennsylvania found when they measured the optimism levels of 500 incoming college freshman and then compared that to their later college grades. A strikingly similar result was obtained at the University of Kansas when freshman were administered measures of their level of "hope" (a major factor in optimism). Again, hope was a better predictor of freshman grades than the usual standard measures. These researchers concluded that the students' emotional attitudes were the critical factor in academic success.

We encourage you to test your own level of optimism by completing the following survey. There are no right or wrong answers to the questions. It is important to take the test prior to reading the interpretation of scores, in order to assure that your answers will not be biased. Read the description of each situation and vividly imagine it happening to you. It is likely that you have not experienced some or even most of these situations, but that does not matter. If neither response seems to fit for you, go ahead anyhow and answer either A or B, choosing the cause likelier to apply to you. You may not like some of the responses offered, but don't choose what you think you should say or what would sound right to other people, choose the response that would be most likely for you. Don't leave any blank, make the best choice.

TABLE 2.2 Optimism Questionnaire

1. You get a flower from a secret admirer.
   A. I am a popular person.   1
   B. I am attractive to him/her.   0

2. You run for a community office position and you win.
   A. I devote a lot of time and energy to campaigning.   0
   B. I work very hard at everything I do.   1

3. You miss an important engagement.
   A. Sometimes my memory fails me.   0
   B. I sometimes forget to check my appointment book.   1

4. You fail an important examination.
   A. I wasn't as smart as the other people taking the exam.   0
   B. I didn't prepare for it well.   1

5. You prepared a special meal for a friend and he/she barely touched the food.
   A. I made the meal in a rush.   1
   B. I wasn't a good cook.   0

6. You lose a sporting event for which you have been training for a long time.
   A. I'm not good at that sport.   1
   B. I am not very athletic.   0

7. You ask a person out on a date and he/she says no.
   A. I was a wreck that day.   0
   B. I got tongue-tied when I asked him/her on the date.   1

8. Your boss gives you too little time in which to finish a project, but you
   get it done anyway.
   A. I am an efficient person.   1
   B. I am good at my job.   0

9. You save a person from choking to death.
   A. I know a technique to stop someone from choking.   0
   B. I know what to do in crisis situations.   1

10. Your employer comes to you for advice.
    A. I am an expert in the area about which I was asked.   0
    B. I am good at giving useful advice.   1

11. A friend thanks you for helping him/her get through a bad time.
    A. I care about people.   1
    B. I enjoy helping him/her through tough times.   0

TABLE 2.2 Optimism Questionnaire *(continued)*

12. Your doctor tells you that you are in good physical shape.
    A. I make sure I exercise frequently.   0
    B. I am very health conscious.   1

13. You win a prestigious award.
    A. I was the best employee.   1
    B. I solved an important problem.   0

14. They won't honor your credit card at a store.
    A. I sometimes overestimate how much money I have.   0
    B. I sometimes forget to pay my credit-card bill.   1

15. Your stocks are at an all-time low.
    A. I didn't know much about the business climate at the time.   0
    B. I made a poor choice of stocks.   1

16. Your romantic partner wants to cool things off for a while.
    A. I don't spend enough time with him or her.   1
    B. I'm too self-centered.   0

Scoring

If your score is 14 to 16, you are very optimistic.

If your score is 12 to 13, you are moderately optimistic.

A score of 8 to 11 is average. You vacillate between optimism and pessimism.

If you score is 6 to 7, you are moderately pessimistic.

If your score is 6 or below, you are very pessimistic.

There is a whole school of metaphysical thought that presumes that you create your own reality with your thoughts. If this is indeed true, then by adopting an optimistic world view you are maximizing your chances for success, happiness and getting what you want. What have you got to lose by trying? Some of you may answer, "If I expect a positive outcome and it does not happen, then I will be disappointed". You would be a subscriber to the *"don't expect anything and you will never be disappointed"* philosophy of life. But if you are really honest with yourself, you will admit that even if you truly expect nothing, there's still a small part of you that hopes, and if what you hope for fails to materialize, you still end up disappointed. The problem with expecting nothing is that you might not do what is necessary to get what you want in life. There is an old saying, *"If you want your ship to come in, you must go to the dock"*. The problem with being a pessimist is that you might not bother to go to the dock. Optimists go to the dock and find ways to enjoy their time there whether their ship comes in or not.

When to Be Optimistic

In what situations is it most effective and useful to be optimistic? Martin Seligman, Ph.D., in his book *Learned Optimism*, advises that first you need to ask yourself what it is that you want to accomplish. If you are in an achievement situation (i.e. sports competition, going for a promotion at work, etc.) you may increase your chances for success if you are optimistic. If you are concerned about your feelings (i.e. trying to avoid depression or anxiety), adopting an optimistic framework will help considerably. If you are concerned about your physical health, by all means use optimism. By the way, optimism is one of the major emotional factors affecting how long cancer patients live and whether they survive. And if you want to be in a leadership role, or to influence or inspire others, you will be far more likely to succeed with an optimistic approach. On the other hand, there are situations where you would be well advised to avoid optimism. If your goal is to plan for a risky and/or uncertain future, it is not wise to rely solely on optimism. This is not to say you should mire yourself in pessimism, but rather you need to make a realistic assessment of the risk of negative contingencies and plan accordingly. Similarly, If your goal is to give support or advice to others with a grim future, do not use optimism initially. It is wiser to begin by being empathic to their situation. However, once you have established rapport it may be helpful to introduce some optimistic reframes.

How to Become an Optimist

Dr Seligman offers a variety of suggestions for channeling your thinking in an optimistic direction. Many of the cognitive techniques for doing this are similar and/or identical to the cognitive restructuring methods for defusing irrational thinking. This is not surprising because in many instances pessimism is just one form of irrational thinking. Optimism is not about being unjustifiably positive about the world, but rather about learning to challenge negative thinking. Learning to think optimistically involves learning to dispute pessimistic thoughts. Dr. Seligman recommends the following four strategies for defusing negativity.

Look for Evidence

The most convincing way of combating a negative belief is to show that it does not fit the facts, that it is clearly incorrect. Since pessimism is usually either an overreaction or dead wrong, the facts will typically be on the side of a more optimistic viewpoint. This does not mean that we are recommending that you naively repeat positive affirmations to yourself in the hope they will somehow change your life. Most educated people are too scientifically minded or skeptical to blindly believe a positive affirmation without some confirmation that it could be true. *Just repeating positive thoughts to yourself is not a guarantee of success or happiness. Rather, it is how you deal with your negative thoughts that determines whether optimism or pessimism will rule.* In general, negative beliefs that accompany or follow adversity are almost always untrue. For example, let's say you fail an important exam. Common negative thoughts include assuming you are stupid, or that you can't cut it in college, or that you are destined to flunk out so why try at all. This is another example of catastrophizing, of picking the worst possible alternative from all the possibilities. One of the most effective techniques is to look for evidence pointing to the distortions in your disastrous explanation of events or catastrophic expectations of what will occur. Evidence to the contrary might include the fact that you got a B on a test last week, that failing one test does not necessarily mean that you will fail every test or flunk out in general. Our professors in graduate school continually reminded us to *never generalize from one piece of data*. You could also remind yourself that even smart people can have a bad day and do poorly at times.

Generate Other Alternatives

Most things that happen in life have multiple causes rather than just one cause. Most things that will happen in your life are a product of interactions among many factors. It is useful to keep this truism in mind. Pessimists make a habit of latching onto one cause and one cause only, and typically it is the worst of all the possible causes. They usually pick the cause that it is the most *permanent*, *pervasive* and *personal*. Challenging this typically has reality on its side. To effectively challenge your negative thoughts look for all the possible alternatives. What else could have caused the situation? What else could happen as a result? Focus on what is *changeable*, what is *specific* and what is *non-personal*. Returning to our failed exam example, you could focus on the fact that you didn't study hard enough (a condition that is changeable), that the exam was unusually hard (a specific instance that may not repeat in the future), and that the rest of the students also fared poorly (a nonpersonal explanation for your poor grade). You may have to work hard to generate alternatives, and you may not be thoroughly convinced they are accurate. But the process of searching for alternatives trains you to think differently, and oftentimes you will come up with an alternative that makes a lot more sense than your worst case scenario. But you have to look for the alternatives to get to that place. Latching onto the worst possible alternative and stopping there is a sure fire recipe for undermining your effectiveness.

Realistically Assess the Implications

What do you do if the facts are not on your side, if your negative belief turns out to be true? In that case you need to use a technique called decatastrophizing. Ask yourself what the implications are if your belief is true. Generate a variety of alternatives. Challenge the most negative alternatives by asking yourself just how likely those implications really are. For example, let's say that you haven't just failed an exam, but that you are actually in danger of flunking out of college altogether. What does this mean? Is it a catastrophe which guarantees that you will never get a good job, that you will be a failure in life? Of course not. Having a college degree certainly helps, but with the right attitude and willingness to do what is necessary, anyone can succeed, even without a college degree. This is not to say that flunking out is a good thing, but it is also *not the end of the world*. Other people have gone on to success without making it through college. Even flunking out of college once does not preclude coming back at a later time and being successful. And, in addition, you need to remind yourself that flunking out is not a foregone conclusion. You have some choice in the matter depending on how seriously you take your studies from this point forward.

Evaluate Usefulness

Occasionally there are situations where the consequences of holding a belief are potentially more problematic than the belief itself, true or not. You need to evaluate whether the belief is potentially dangerous. For example, if you truly believe you are stupid, even if you are not a rocket scientist, the damage to your self-esteem could be heavy. There are other instances when the best strategy is to distract yourself from a belief rather than taking time to challenge it. This is the case when negative thoughts interfere with your performance. Engaging in negative thinking or the evaluation of such is not useful in a situation where you need to perform now. Distracting yourself and focusing on the task at hand is the most useful response.

Other Tips for Becoming Optimistic

When faced with adversity optimists typically follow the steps outlined below:

- **Face the problem squarely.** Pessimists tend to avoid dealing with problems because of their negative expectations.

- **Develop a plan.** Optimists create specific plans to deal with situations.

- **Accept the reality of the situation.** Contrary to popular belief, optimists are realists. It is just that they expect (and thus are more likely to get) positive results or the eventual resolution of the situation. It is this hopeful belief that allows optimists to persevere.

- **Learn to grow from adversity.** Optimists make the best of a bad situation and are cognizant of the personal growth they can experience as a result. Pessimists cannot see the value in adversity and typically quit trying because they only expect negative results.

SELF EXERCISES:

1. The next time you find yourself feeling anxious or depressed, look deeper into yourself, and determine whether there are any irrational thoughts fueling your feelings. Look at the list of irrational thoughts and check whether any of your unconscious cognitions are a close match. If so, follow the three step Cognitive Restructuring technique to counteract those irrational messages.

2. Identify that area of your life about which you are most pessimistic. Experiment with the four techniques presented above and notice how you are able to shift your perceptions or expectations in a more optimistic direction.

KEY TERMS

Determinism	Locus of Control	Psychotic Episode
Free Will	Internal Locus of Control	Delusional Thinking
Psychoanalytic Theory	External Locus of Control	Hallucinations
Behaviorism	Self-Talk	Concordance Rates
Existentialism	Cognitive Restructuring	Optimism
Humanism	Catastrophizing	Pessimism
Cognitive-Behaviorism	Correlation	Spurious Correlation
Proactivity	Schizophrenia	

CHAPTER 2 QUESTIONS

Short-Answer Questions

1. The _____ theory of personality claims that you are who you are because of your upbringing.
2. The _____ theory of personality claims that you are who you are because of your learning history.
3. The existentialists epitomize the concept of _____.
4. Effective individuals are typically _____.
5. Students who take responsibility for their performance on a test have an _____ locus of control.
6. Students who blame the teacher if they do poorly in a course have an _____ locus of control.
7. Individuals who are not proactive (i.e., reactive) tend to have an _____ locus of control.

8 The two common forms of irrational self-talk are statements that
_____ and statements that involve _____.

9. _____% of what we worry about never happens.

10. Proactive individuals typically have an _____ outlook.

11. A reliable relationship between variables is termed a _____.

Essay Questions

1. What is the main difference between Determinism and Free Will?

2. Which theory of human behavior is the most deterministic and why?

3. What drives mankind according to the Humanistic theorists?

4. Differentiate the Cognitive-Behaviorists from the strict Behaviorists.

5. What are the characteristics of a proactive student?

6. What are the three areas that you need to focus on in order to increase your proactivity?

7. Describe the three steps of cognitive restructuring.

8. Explain whether causation can be inferred from correlation.

9. How does optimism differ from repeating positive affirmations to yourself?

10. Explain how pessimism is incompatible with proactivity.

11. Name and explain the four strategies for promoting an optimistic outlook.

3

Love Who You Are

How is self-esteem relevant to effectiveness? The simple answer to this question is that effective individuals have learned to value themselves, to have what psychologists refer to as "high self-esteem". But what does that mean?

THE CONCEPT OF SELF-ESTEEM

Self-esteem refers to the relationship you have with yourself, the degree to which you regard yourself in a positive or negative light. It is a measure of how much you value yourself and feel useful and necessary in the world. To understand self-esteem it might help to view it within the larger framework of the **self-concept**. Your self-concept is your paradigm about yourself and is reflected in how you might describe yourself, while your self-esteem refers to how you judge and evaluate yourself based on this paradigm. This is influenced by what Carl Rogers (1959) described as the discrepancy between your **ideal self** (the person you feel you should be) and your real self (the person you actually are).

While there is certainly a global measure of self-esteem, that is, the degree to which you like yourself in general, the fact is that self-esteem also fluctuates depending on how you regard yourself in specific areas. For example, you might have high self esteem and confidence in yourself as an athlete, but low self esteem as a scholar. Studies have identified several key areas which help determine self esteem including physical appearance, scholastic ability, work performance, popularity and social skills, and athletic ability (Fleming & Courtney, 1984). The importance that you place on each of these areas will determine the weight it carries in influencing your global sense of self-esteem. For example, if you overemphasize the importance of physical appearance and you believe that you are unattractive, your self-esteem will be in the dumpster.

Why is having high self-esteem, or positive self-regard, so important to your effectiveness? Because when you have faith in yourself, it enhances your ability to do your best, which in turn improves your performance and further reinforces your good feelings about yourself. As aptly described by Brehm (1998), "when your self esteem is strong, mountains become molehills. A positive self-regard attracts others; when you are happier with yourself, you are happier with life and a pleasure to be with. A healthy self-esteem is essential to clear communication. When you value yourself, you value your thoughts and feelings and can express them more clearly to others. A positive self-esteem allows you to give more of yourself and enjoy other people. Best of all, a positive self-regard gives you freedom, the freedom to try new things, to make the most of opportunities, to be the best you can be, and get the most out of life."

On the other hand, low self esteem is a circular, self-defeating process where your negative feelings about yourself result in negative attitudes in general. These negative attitudes then become a driving force in your negative behaviors. Such negative behaviors then promote negative feelings, and so on. Thus the person with low self-esteem becomes a psychological prisoner of his or her own poor self-image. The Neo-Freudian theorist Alfred Adler described individuals with chronically low self-esteem as having an **"inferiority complex"**. Figure 3.1 illustrates both the positive cycle described above by Brehm and the contrasting negative vicious cycle.

Lastly, having high self-esteem greatly facilitates your ability to cope with stress. When you have positive self-regard it is much easier to be an optimist, to view life's difficulties as opportunities for growth and self discovery rather than as problems.

A word of caution here: Don't make the mistake of confusing high self-esteem with being conceited or self-centered. Some people are afraid to hold themselves in high regard because they fear it will make them seem stuck-up. Keep in mind, people who are conceited or stuck up are braggarts. If you truly have high self-esteem you will not need to broadcast it. There is an old saying which sums this up perfectly, *"when you have arrived, you don't need to shout"*. People with high self esteem don't need to boast about themselves or their achievements. Those who feel the need to brag typically are trying to compensate for insecurity or low self esteem.

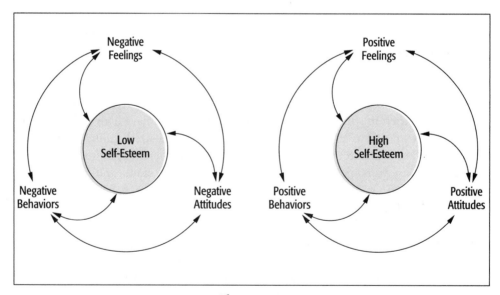

Figure 3.1

The Question of Self-Worth

So self-esteem is based on your appraisal of your **self-worth**. But, what is your self-worth based on? When we ask this of students in our classes, they typically respond with answers such as their achievements, caring for others, physical appearance, intellectual attributes, financial success, and even the extent of their material possessions (i.e., whether they drive a "hot car" or have fashionable clothes). They are often startled by our suggestion that your *self-worth is based on nothing*. It is a given. It is your birthright. Ideally, your self-esteem should be based on a recognition of your inherent sense of worth as a human being independent of your achievements and attributes. You are worthy because you are a unique individual with your own special potentials. Too often we define our self-worth based on our performance or accomplishments. While your achievements are an integral part of who you are and will undoubtedly contribute to your self-esteem, you will be doing yourself a great disservice if you define your worth solely on the basis of this dimension. You are worthy because you are human. It helps to believe that you are basically good, kind, caring, and worthy of being loved despite your faults or temporary failings. This is, of course, only a frame, but a very useful one, one that will lead to high self-esteem and greatly enhance your effectiveness as a human being. To quote the well known author and motivational speaker Tony Robbins, "*I used to have to achieve to feel happy, now I happily achieve*".

If you are curious about your level of self-esteem, we invite you to complete the questionnaire that follows. Be honest with yourself. Answer the questions to reflect how you really feel about yourself.

SELF-ESTEEM SELF-ASSESSMENT

Answer the following questions by assigning each one the appropriate number from the following scale:

1 = strongly agree   2 = agree   3 = disagree   4 = strongly disagree

Self-Esteem Scale

_____ 1. I feel that I am a person of worth, at least on an equal basis with others.

_____ 2. I feel that I have a number of good qualities.

_____ 3. All in all, I am inclined to feel I am a failure.

_____ 4. I am able to do things as well as most other people.

_____ 5. I feel I do not have much to be proud of.

_____ 6. I take a positive attitude toward myself.

_____ 7. On the whole, I am satisfied with myself.

_____ 8. I wish I could have more respect for myself.

_____ 9. I certainly feel useless at times.

_____ 10. At times I think I am no good at all.

_____ TOTAL SCORE (**Read directions below before adding**)

Scoring: **On questions 3, 5, 8, 9, and 10 convert your numbered answers as follows: Change 1 to 4; change 4 to 1; change 2 to 3; change 3 to 2. Now total your responses. The lower your score the higher your self-esteem.**

   10–15   High Self-Esteem
   16–20   Good Self-Esteem
   21–30   Moderately Low Self-Esteem
   31–40   Very Poor Self-Esteem

So how did you do? Where do you lie on the continuum of negative to positive self-esteem? Now that you have an added measure of your level of perceived self worth, lets look at the characteristics of individuals with high vs. low self-esteem.

The Pathological Critic

How is it that we sabotage our self-esteem? Each of us has an inner voice which evaluates and judges our actions and ourselves. The nature of this inner voice reflects the quality of your relationship with yourself. Psychologist Eugene Sagan coined the term **"pathological critic"** to describe what he saw as a negative inner voice that attacks and judges you. Although it is true that for most people their inner voice tends to be critical, this is clearly not necessary nor particularly effective. Perhaps a more appropriate metaphor would be that of a misguided critic or coach. The intention behind this inner coach's behavior and communications is always positive, i.e. it is always trying to help you do or not do that which it believes is best for you. However, the way that it goes about this frequently accomplishes just the opposite of what it is trying to do. Our goal is not to help you get rid of this coach altogether, but to train it in using methods which are more aligned with assisting you to improve your self-esteem, to value yourself more positively.

To illustrate this point, we ask that you entertain the notion that change or growth in the human being occurs in a similar fashion as that of the task of toilet training a child. Initially, the child does not even recognize that she is not to relieve herself in her clothes. After some training, she knows what is expected, but cannot translate this into appropriate anticipatory behaviors. Thus she can only report to us once she has already messed her clothes. Later on she can recognize it as it is happening, and thus can change her behavior midstream (pun intended). After a while she can anticipate the need to defecate or urinate and can go and do it in the toilet. Now, we know that toilet training occurs quickest and most effectively if we acknowledge and reinforce (reward) the child every step of the way, for indeed this is clearly a process of step by step learning. If we want to make toilet training difficult and lengthy, then we need to criticize and demean the child for the mistakes she makes. The same holds true for how we deal with ourselves. If we criticize and demean ourselves, we get stuck repeating the same behavior or mistakes over and over again, and as an added bonus we lower our self-esteem. But if we approach ourselves as we would someone we respect, admire and love, then we find we feel better about ourselves and can notice changes in ways which promote our growth.

TABLE 3.1 Characteristics of People with High and Low Self-Esteem

High Self-Esteem	Low Self-Esteem
• Believe that they are worthwhile and valuable.	• Believe that their worth is based on their accomplishments or the opinions of others.
• Sees demanding goals as a challenge.	• Is highly critical of self and others.
• Recognizes the strengths and achievements of self and others.	• More likely to be prejudiced.
• Acknowledges their personal power without being manipulative.	• Doubt their personal power.
• Takes responsibility for their own actions without blaming or making excuses.	• Likely to be hero worshipers.
• Able to take risks. Is not afraid of failure.	• Resistant to change.
• Do not view failure or rejection as a reflection upon their self-worth.	• Fearful of taking risks that may lead to failure.
• Accepts compliments.	• View failure or rejection as evidence of their lack of self-worth.
• Accepts and values constructive criticism.	• Discounts praise from others.
• Generous with their praise for others.	• Show an inability to accept constructive criticism.
• Is able to give themselves positive self messages.	• Give self negative internal messages.
• Do not feel the need to continually prove themselves.	• Tend to be highly competitive.
• Is able to communicate their needs and wants effectively.	• Feel a need to win to prove themselves.
• Is able to develop satisfying interpersonal relationships.	• May resort to workaholism to prove their worth.
• Recognizes the value of all experiences.	• Have difficulty communicating their needs.
• Is capable of working well as a team member.	• Are likely to remain in unsatisfying relationships.
• Have trust in themselves.	• Tend to value appearances over substance.
• Seeks balance in their life.	• Inability to make decisions and take action without clearly defined rules.
• See the value in continued personal growth and self exploration.	• Doubt themselves.
• Surround themselves with people who validate them.	• Lack balance in their lives.
• Are seldom controlled by guilt.	• Are threatened by personal growth experiences.
• Are optimistic about themselves, others and the world.	• Often attract people who denigrate them.
• Value the power of their word.	• Are guilt ridden.
• Are proactive.	• Are pessimistic about themselves, others and the world.
• Accept all of their feelings as natural, human and a part of life.	• Typically don't live up to their word.
• Are good losers.	• Are reactive.
• Are not afraid to be different or take an unpopular stand.	• Consider negative emotions as further proof of their lack of worth.
	• Are poor losers.
	• Resort to fadism to be included in the "in crowd".

THE ROOTS OF SELF-ESTEEM

Self-esteem has its roots, not in genetics, but in learning. Children are not born with high or low self-esteem; they learn it as a result of their life experiences. Many people and events in your life combine to shape your self-esteem from the moment of your birth. Infants can sense whether people respond to them with acceptance and love, contempt, or indifference, which helps lay the early groundwork for self-esteem (Pelham & Swann, 1989). Your self-esteem is influenced by your parents, siblings, relatives, school-teachers, peers, bosses, co-workers, etc. Although many of these individuals may no longer be involved in your life, what you learned from them may still wield a dramatic impact on your self-perceptions. The foundation for self-esteem appears to be laid very early in life, and it is believed that some children have poor self-esteem even prior to starting school.

Parental Influences

For most of us, our parents are the most significant influence in shaping our self-esteem, particularly early in life. In most cases, they were our major source of love, security and need fulfillment. If you were fortunate enough to have been raised by parents who cherished you and treated you as a valued human being, worthy of love, you will probably enjoy positive self-esteem in your later life. However, if your parents were too preoccupied with their own troubles, or with work, to give you the attention and love you deserved, the development of high self-esteem, while not impossible, would certainly be more difficult.

Many theorists have speculated on how parental behavior influences the self-esteem of children. Carl Rogers observed that children develop positive self-esteem when parents show them **unconditional positive regard**, which refers to their acceptance of them as having intrinsic merit regardless of their behavior at the moment. Unconditional positive regard involves a consistent expression of love and esteem for the child as a person. When parents show children **conditional positive regard**, that is, they judge the child's value and deliver their love based on the acceptability of the child's behavior, children develop **conditions of worth**, meaning that they only think they are worthwhile or lovable if they behave in certain ways or meet certain standards. Karen Horney (1956) suggested that parents often unknowingly diminish their children's self esteem by being erratic, domineering, overprotective, demanding, critical, overindulgent, partial to other siblings, or indifferent. Harry Stack Sullivan (1953) noted that when children are treated badly they can develop what he described as **the malevolent attitude**—the belief that one is surrounded by enemies. As a result of this attitude the child comes to view him or herself as someone who is detestable and will always be treated poorly, and moreover, who does not deserve to be treated well.

Returning to our coach metaphor, it is safe to say that for most of you, your original coaches did the best they could and most likely had your best intentions in mind, however, their coaching styles may not have always been healthy. If your coach over utilized criticism, that took a toll on your self-esteem. Perhaps even more crucial, many of your coaches may have failed to differentiate between you and your behavior when correcting or disciplining you. Have you ever heard, "You are a bad boy", or "You are so lazy", or "How stupid could you possibly be"? These statements are directed at the self and teach you to evaluate yourself negatively. Had your coaches been able to differentiate between you and your behavior, they may have made comments like, "I don't like it when you act that way", or "That behavior is unacceptable", or "I get angry when you do. . . ." In addition, your level of self-esteem is also a byproduct of how you saw your coaches treat themselves, that is, what they modeled for you. If your coach was overly self-critical you may have learned to adopt this particular style. The bottom line is that how you treat yourself, or more specifically, how you coach yourself, typically resembles how you were coached.

Parenting Styles

At this point you may be wondering what kind of parenting is likely to maximize the opportunities for the healthy development of self esteem in the child. To answer this we first need to consider what have been termed parenting styles. Diana Baumrind (1991) identified three basic parenting styles that impact on child development: (1) **authoritarian parenting**; (2) **authoritative parenting**; and (3) laissez-faire (permissive) parenting. Other theorists (Maccoby and Martin, 1983) further differentiated permissive parenting into two subgroups: (1) **permissive-indifferent** and (2) **permissive-indulgent**. Authoritarian parents have a restrictive, punitive style of parenting focusing on following rules and assuming that the child is incompetent. Permissive-indifferent parents are uninvolved in their child's life. They are not particularly harsh or punitive, but basically treat the child as if he/she is not particularly important. Permissive-indulgent parents are very involved in the child's life and often very loving, but they fail to set limits or provide meaningful controls over the child's behavior. They may be very indulgent without requiring the child to earn any of the rewards, thus the child may end up quite spoiled. Authoritative parents are warm and nurturing while at the same time setting meaningful limits and controls for the child. These parents are very involved in the lives of their children.

It may seem rather obvious to you that the authoritative parenting style should be the most effective for fostering self-esteem in the child. You are correct if you have made this assumption, and it useful to know that research backs this up, as well. The classic research of Coopersmith (1967, 1975) demonstrated this by studying the self-esteem patterns of fifth and sixth grade boys. The boys with high self-esteem typically came from homes where their parents were strict, but not harsh. Their parents were affectionate, accepting, very involved in their son's activities, and used consistent, reasonable discipline for enforcing clear cut limits. Boys with low self-esteem came from families where the parents were in some ways more permissive, but were quite harsh when discipline was enforced. These parents were far less involved in their son's lives, often oblivious to misbehavior until it reached a critical point where the parents might overreact. The parents of the high self-esteem boys were more demanding of their sons in terms of achievement and meeting standards, but their involvement in their son's lives communicated a deep caring and value for the child. Coopersmith also found that once self-esteem was established it remained relatively consistent across the school years.

But is this always the case? You may be interested to know that other researchers have found that some children develop high self-esteem even though they were raised in very dysfunctional environments. For example, Emmy Werner (cited in Hamburg, 1994) conducted a longitudinal study of 700 children from dysfunctional homes, where parenting styles were far from ideal. Some of the children in this study had healthy self-esteem despite inadequate parental influences. These resilient children all appeared to have four characteristics in common: (1) they took an active approach to problem solving, believing they could find solutions; (2) they found positive ways of framing their experiences, even the bad ones; (3) they were adept at getting positive attention from others; and (4) they were optimists. How did this happen? We are not certain from the research, but somehow these children had learned to be more proactive, perhaps on their own, or perhaps out of their proclivity to attract positive people into their lives (i.e. teachers, coaches, etc.) to serve as mentors.

Other Important Influences

Obviously, parents are not the only agents who influence self-esteem. Teachers can often have a deep impact on the development of a child's self-esteem, particularly in the early years. A highly critical teacher can certainly inflict damage on a child's self image, especially if it involves being ridiculed in front of the class. On the other hand, a good teacher, one who encourages and praises a child's progress, can help repair the faltering self-esteem of a child who is very unsure of her abilities. Certainly peer influences are paramount as well. The agony of being rejected by peers, ostracized on the playground in elementary school, left out of the cliques in middle school, not being invited to parties, or picked for sports teams in P. E. class, can each take a heavy toll.

But the development of our self-esteem is not only dependent upon what we have learned from others or how we were treated by others. It is also a byproduct of what we learn from experiencing life independently. Failure experiences can certainly undermine self-image, whether this occurs in childhood or in adulthood. Given that our level of self-esteem represents an ongoing process, events in adulthood can either enhance or detract from our perceived level of self-worth. So if you enjoy success at work and/or in your relationships, you will likely experience enhanced self-esteem. If you are losing jobs or failing to gain advancement at work, or you are suffering disappointments in love, you may experience diminished self-esteem

HOW TO BOOST YOUR SELF-ESTEEM

If your self-esteem is a measure of how you evaluate yourself, then let's return for a moment to two previously mentioned concepts which are central to your level of self-esteem, that of your real self and your ideal self. Your real self, your evaluation of yourself regarding various characteristics and attributes is, for most people, regularly compared to your ideal self, the desired state of being which you seek to achieve. Many people hold their ideal self to be something they *should* be and then feel disappointed with themselves when they fail to reach this goal. What many people forget is that the ideal self is just that, an IDEAL. It serves as a guiding light in your continual process of growth rather than a grade you need to achieve. The person with high self-esteem realizes that their real self is in an everlasting process of change, moving towards their ideal self but never reaching it. This is what Carl Rogers described as "The Process of Becoming".

The first step in learning to improve your self-esteem is to realize that your current level of self-esteem is, ultimately, your choice. This is, of course, not to say that the myriad of past and present influences on your level of self-esteem, both positive and negative, did not influence how you feel about yourself. These experiences *influenced* your self-image, but they do not determine it. You can choose to work towards developing a satisfying level of self-esteem. The task of enhancing and then maintaining high self-esteem is a life long process of personal growth in which we all proceed slowly, step by step. This is made challenging by the fact that the world is often a far less than ideal place to live. Disappointments occur, things change, events will not always go your way. You will inevitably make mistakes, and you will not succeed at everything you attempt. Your self-esteem can be a casualty in this process unless you have learned how to nurture yourself. What follows are strategies and guidelines for building a nurturing relationship with yourself that will allow you to truly appreciate who you are, in bad times as well as good times.

Uncovering Irrational Beliefs

To begin, we suggest you examine your paradigm regarding the qualities you believe a person worthy of high self esteem must possess. Could some of your beliefs be based on unrealistic expectations or irrational thoughts? As described in the last chapter, it is important that you take a look at the irrational thoughts which may be influencing the frame by which you evaluate yourself. Albert Ellis and others have described the way irrational beliefs affect the way we feel about ourselves. Irrational beliefs which impact on self-esteem typically take the form of what we should and should not do and be. These *shoulds* are generated by parental, cultural, and peer expectations, as well as by your need to feel loved, to belong, and to feel safe and good about yourself. What gives these shoulds their power is your belief that they represent the truth. This is the *tyranny of the shoulds:* the absolute nature of beliefs, this unbending sense of right and wrong. If you don't live up to your shoulds, you then judge yourself to be a bad, unworthy person and your self-esteem goes out the window.

The following is a list of some of the most common irrational beliefs people hold about themselves. Look through this list carefully. If a statement fits you, even occasionally, place an X in the space next to it. This exercise will help you identify your irrational beliefs and give you insight about thoughts which stand in the way of your self-esteem.

COMMON PATHOLOGICAL SHOULDS QUESTIONNAIRE

1. _____ I should be the epitome of generosity and unselfishness.
2. _____ I should be the perfect lover, friend, parent, teacher, student, spouse, and so on.
3. _____ I should be able to endure any hardship with equanimity.
4. _____ I should be able to find a quick solution to every problem.
5. _____ I should never feel hurt. I should always feel happy and serene.
6. _____ I should be completely competent.
7. _____ I should know, understand, and foresee everything.
8. _____ I should never feel certain emotions such as anger or jealousy.
9. _____ I should love my children equally.

10. ____ I should never make mistakes.

11. ____ My emotions should be constant—once I feel love, I should always feel the same.

12. ____ I should be totally self-reliant.

13. ____ I should never be tired or sick.

14. ____ I should never be afraid.

15. ____ I should always be busy; to relax is to waste my time and my life.

16. ____ I should have achievements that bring me status, wealth, or power.

17. ____ I should always put others first; it is better that I feel pain than cause anyone else to feel pain.

18. ____ I should be unfailingly kind.

19. ____ I should never feel sexually attracted to _____.

20. ____ I should care for everyone who cares for me.

21. ____ I should make enough money so that my family can afford _____.

22. ____ I should be able to protect my children from all pain.

23. ____ I should not take time just for my own pleasure.

24. ____ I should be more like other people.

Overcoming the Tyranny of the Shoulds

How many of the above items did you endorse? Even if only a few, recognize that the pathological critic feeds and thrives on these shoulds. What image comes to mind when you hear statements such as, "You should be successful", "You should always be considerate of others", or " You should never get angry"? For most people the image that comes up is that of a parent or authority figure pointing their finger and scolding them, telling them what they should or should not do, or think, or feel. To increase your self esteem, we encourage you to *stop shoulding on yourself.* You have the right to question any and all of these shoulds. When you recognize that your behavior is being guided by a should, ask yourself, "Should according to whom?" Are these your choices, or are you merely parroting some often heard messages that you have gotten from others? If the latter is so, realize that you are being reactive, literally giving away your power to that internalized authority figure. You would be proactive if you can say with certainty that these are values that you truly want for yourself, and you decide to set them as the standards by which you live. The irrational beliefs which undermine your self-esteem, the *tyranny of the shoulds,* are a subset of the irrational beliefs discussed in Chapter 2. Remember that many of us were taught unrealistic beliefs such as those above. That is why we have such terrible feelings when someone does not like us or when we fail. In spite of their commonness, though, these beliefs are irrational. They are based on the premise that our self-worth is solely determined by the approval of others and by continual striving for perfection. We urge you to challenge the frames by which you are judging yourself using the techniques of cognitive restructuring we discussed in the previous chapter.

According to Ellis and Harper, the negative self-statements used by the pathological critic, which are generated by these irrational beliefs, must be replaced by positive self-statements. Following the four step framework for challenging irrational beliefs presented earlier in Chapter 2, question your shoulds. You will find that by replacing these with more rational self statements, your self-esteem will steadily climb. For example:

It is definitely nice to have people like and approve of me, but even without that, I can still accept and love myself.

Doing things well is satisfying, but it is human to err.

It is healthy for me to relax at times. It is important to recharge my batteries.

Not all problems lend themselves to quick solutions.

It is part of the human experience to occasionally feel emotions such as anger, sadness, jealousy and hurt.

One of the most salient differences between individuals with high self-esteem vs. individuals with low self-esteem is in the nature and content of their self-talk. People with high self esteem do not continually barrage themselves with negative messages or observations about themselves. This does not mean that they are unaware of their faults or that they discount constructive criticism, but rather that they tend to give positive, self-affirming messages to themselves. For example, a person with high self-esteem who is preparing to give a speech and is nervous about the upcoming performance would help prepare himself by recalling other successful public speaking experiences, and by reassuring himself that he knows his material. A person with low self-esteem in the exact same situation would likely remember only uncomfortable public speaking experiences, and tell himself that he was going to do poorly, or make a fool of himself, etc.

Research has shown that people with low self-esteem can successfully change irrational negative beliefs about themselves. Individuals with low self-esteem tend to attribute their failures to internal causes (weaknesses and shortcomings), reflecting doubts about their self-worth. However, when these individuals succeed they tend to attribute their success to external sources such as luck. Brockner and Guare (1983) hypothesized that by inducing people with low self-esteem to ascribe their failures to possible external causes (factors beyond their control), and their successes to internal causes (ability and effort), self-esteem could be modified. In addition, they theorized that people with low self-esteem could be encouraged to try harder, thereby maximizing their chances for success, which could further elevate their self-esteem.

In their study, college students were divided into two groups based on low and high self esteem. All students were then given an insolvable task so that each student experienced failure. Following this initial failure experience each student was given a task that was solvable. Prior to the second task, some subjects in both groups were told that their previous failure stemmed from external causes (e.g. the task could not be solved). Other subjects in both groups were led to believe that their previous failure was due mostly to internal causes. And the remaining subjects in both groups were given no information regarding possible causes of the initial failure. The results indicated that students with low self-esteem were able to accept that failure may be due to external causes. But more importantly, the students with low self-esteem who were led to believe that the initial failure was not their fault, performed the best of any group on the second task! So a positive cycle had been set in motion. Now, this does not imply that it is wise to teach people with low self-esteem to always attribute all failures to external causes, that certainly would not be proactive. But the process of challenging irrational, perfectionistic beliefs can assist individuals with low self-esteem to evaluate themselves more realistically and fairly.

Eliminating Cognitive Distortions

Irrational beliefs are also fueled by **cognitive distortions**, which refers to the tendency to look for verification to support your existing opinion of yourself. In other words, via selective attention we tend to pay attention to that which supports what we already believe about ourselves. Epstein (1992) points out that individuals with low self-esteem are prone to look for evidence of where they fall short, rather than appreciating their achievements. If your self-esteem is low and you are focusing only on where you come up short, return to the guidelines for facilitating optimism covered in Chapter 2. Using the method of looking for alternative evidence, challenge your cognitive distortions. If you look for contrary evidence, it is quite likely that you will find it.

Alternative Ways of Framing Mistakes

> "I have not failed 10,000 times, I have successfully found
> 10,000 ways that will not work."
> —Thomas Edison

Most people think of a mistake as something they did wrong. But this is simply not the case. A more appropriate definition is that a mistake is any behavior which you do or fail to do which later, as you reflect about it, you wish you had not done or had done differently. The key word here is LATER. At the time you behaved or did not behave in a particular fashion, you did the best that you possibly could. All decisions are made on the basis of insufficient information, for none of us has the power to foretell the future. "Mistake" is a label which you apply later on, when you wish you had done something else based on 20/20 hindsight. The issue here is awareness. At the time you did or did not do something, you were functioning with a certain degree of awareness. By the time you labeled something a mistake, you had more information and were more aware of the consequences. Within that awareness you always behave in a way that you believe will best meet your needs. If you want not to "repeat the same mistakes", we suggest you focus on expanding your awareness, that is, gathering more data before acting, or learning to anticipate the consequences of actions, rather than just resolving to never make the same mistake again. Unless you expand your awareness, it is almost guaranteed that you will repeat the same mistakes. In addition, the more you berate yourself for having made them, the greater the probability that you will make them again.

Thus a mistake becomes a mistake only after some time has passed. The length of time is not important. What is important is that at the time you did it, you did the best you could. It makes no sense to criticize yourself about it. Thinking about mistakes in this fashion allows you to see them in a different light or to reframe them. To further this new perspective consider that a strong case can be made that mistakes serve as invaluable teachers. They provide you with information about what works and what does not work. When you were a toddler learning how to walk, you needed to fall in order to learn your balance. Had you been afraid of making mistakes, you would still be crawling! This is true for everything in your life. Mistakes are an absolutely necessary part of the learning process. Rather than fearing them you need to welcome them. It might help to think that the more mistakes you make, the more you are learning. Ultimately, there is no such thing as mistakes, only feedback. If you set perfectionistic standards for yourself, you rob yourself of the ability to accept yourself as a fallible but worthwhile human being.

Another way to view mistakes is to think of them as warnings. If you get a poor grade on a test, that could be a warning that you need to study more or change your study habits. It is only when you think that you need to be perfect that mistakes become an indictment rather than a warning.

Yet another way to throw a different frame around mistakes is by realizing that if you are going to behave in a spontaneous fashion, you will most certainly make some mistakes. Without the willingness to make mistakes, you can only act in totally predetermined ways in familiar situations. How boring! You would also kill your self-expression, since to say what you feel or what you think does not always have predictable results, i.e. you risk making a mistake. If you don't allow yourself to say the wrong thing, then you are never free enough to say the right thing.

In his book *Building Self-Esteem,* Glenn Schiraldi recommends utilizing a particular technique for maintaining your self-esteem in the face of mistakes. This technique is called *"Nevertheless",* which helps you to acknowledge your mistakes while simultaneously affirming your basic self-worth. People with low self-esteem typically are likely to engage in "because . . . therefore" thinking, reflected in such statements as, *"because of _____, therefore I am no good".* You can replace this with *"even though _____, nevertheless".* So for example, instead of saying, *"because I did poorly on this test, therefore I am stupid",* you could say, *"even though I did poorly on this test, nevertheless I am capable of doing much better if I study harder".*

We hope by now you may be beginning to see mistakes in a different light, perhaps as friends rather than enemies. Some people believe that all mistakes are to be avoided, that intelligent, competent people somehow don't make them. That is nonsense. A much wiser position is to allow for a quota for mistakes, for without them you would not be human.

KEY ATTITUDES FOR MAINTAINING SELF-ESTEEM

We feel this chapter would not be complete without sharing with you a framework that the authors found particularly meaningful. While not a well researched paradigm, case studies support the efficacy of this viewpoint. At a workshop years ago, Heidi Schlieffer, a noted author, trainer, and marriage and family counselor told the story of her mother, a Holocaust survivor. She described how, in order for her mother and her fellow prisoners in the concentration camp to maintain their self-esteem, they developed a set of five daily practices. These are:

Hello

Have you ever had the opportunity to watch a two year old child when he first walks into a room? Most two year old children walk with their mouth agape and their eyes wide open in awe, taking in all the novel sights and sounds. They look at strangers with curiosity and wonder, perhaps even reaching out to touch the stranger's nose or hair, or fingering some glittery jewelry. Because most two year olds are not yet self conscious and socialized not to touch or stare, they are free to explore and express their joy of discovery. The prisoners in Heidi's mother's barracks would remind each other to walk and carry themselves as a two year old, searching for the new and exciting opportunities offered them in their sparse environment. They would look out the window at the sunlight as it cast shadows on the various structures in the compound, to remind them to enjoy the beauty of a sunny day. They would welcome a cloudy day for the changes it would bring, the different feel and smell of the air. They would remember to greet each other genuinely and take the time to support one another and appreciate that support. Can you imagine yourself assuming this attitude of hello in your particular environment? We suggest you try it and notice the results.

Bravo!

In an environment devoid of most human pleasures and privileges, the prisoners found that focusing on their little achievements and victories greatly increased their will to live. They would make any occasion a cause for celebration, for congratulating each other and themselves. A multitude of research supports the effectiveness of reinforcement as a tool for heightening self esteem, as well as for motivating behavior. We invite you to be on the lookout for things you can applaud about your behavior, your accomplishments, and yourself in general. Realize that often it is an accomplishment just to get up in the morning and tend to your responsibilities. Give others and yourself frequent bravos throughout the day.

Expect Miracles, but Do Your Part

There is a story about a town that was surrounded by three rivers. Forecasters predicted that a terrible storm was approaching and cautioned that the torrential rains would cause the rivers to overflow and engulf the town. To aid in the evacuation, the authorities dispatched buses to carry all the residents in need of transportation to safety. One particularly devoutly religious man rejected this help, asserting that he knew that God would save him. As the storm began its relentless downpour, authorities sent all-terrain vehicles to rescue him and the other remaining inhabitants. While most left, some, including this man, refused to go. But the waters continued rising as the rains would not let up. Boats were then dispatched to save the remaining hold outs. All but our man chose to leave. He was certain that he would be saved. Unfortunately, the waters overcame him and he drowned. He was really angry as he waited for his audience with God in the afterlife. When his turn came he angrily demanded of God, "How could you leave me to die?" To which God replied, "What do you mean? Who do you think sent the buses, the jeeps, and the boats?" Expect miracles, but do your part. Always have positive expectations of success, but remember to do what is necessary to make your expectations a reality.

Laugh and Dance a Little Everyday

The prisoners discovered that taking some time everyday to literally sing and dance helped raise their spirits and maintain their good feelings about themselves. While you might choose to make this a daily activity, what we recommend is that you practice seeking joy in your daily experiences. It is important that you play and have fun for this is essential for maintaining good feelings about yourself.

Love Your Inner Child

Speaking metaphorically, of course, we all carry within ourselves a child, the child we used to be. Our perceptions of how others treated us as children are later reflected in how we treat this child within, also referred to as the "**inner child**". If you are critical with yourself, or at best try to be logical and rational with the inner child all the time, it will inevitably fail to have the desired effect since, like most children, your inner child does not respond to logic and rationality. Have you ever tried convincing a four or five year old that there is no monster in the closet? What works to reassure an insecure child are communications indicating that she is safe, protected, loved and that, she will certainly survive. Part of maintaining your self-esteem is having this compassionate relationship with your inner child.

> One of the authors recalls a time, as a young graduate student, when he arrived late at a workshop with a renowned speaker that greatly interested him. The presentation had already begun, so he walked cautiously into the room filled with hundreds of participants. He noticed way up in the front a lone vacant seat. As he considered making his way to that seat, he heard a voice inside saying, "you can't walk up there. You'll be embarrassed. Everyone will see that you are late!" He recognized this as the voice of his inner child, the school boy afraid to make waves in the classroom. He proceeded to imagine taking this boy by the hand as he walked down the long aisle towards the front of the lecture hall. By the time he had to cross in front of the speaker to reach the vacant seat, he was carrying the child in his arms. He made his way to seat and sat happily with the "child" on his lap.

SELF EXERCISES

1. While this exercise may not seem logical, following through with it will prove to be invaluable in terms of building your self-esteem. What we want you to do is to experientially give yourself permission to make mistakes. The most effective way of achieving this is for you to go out and deliberately make a mistake. We want you to think of a relatively harmless, innocuous mistake you can make, preferably one that is humorous, and to plan it out and set a date to do it. It could be something as silly and mundane as wearing two different color sucks or putting your make-up on wrong. But be creative and let your child play. By the way, did you catch our mistake above?

2. **Looking at yourself through the eyes of someone who loves you:** Think of someone who you believe really loves you and values you for who you are. Imagine that person standing in front of you as vividly as you can. Look at them looking at you with that expression which lets you know how much they appreciate you. Now imagine in your mind's eye that you can look at yourself through their eyes. Seeing, perhaps for the first time, what someone who loves you sees as they look at you. Watching and listening closely to your own gestures, words, looks, as perceived by someone who loves you. Can you recognize qualities and attributes which were perhaps viewed as faults by your own eyes? Allow yourself to perceive what it is about you that this person cherishes. Now describe yourself to yourself as you know this person would, highlighting your endearing qualities and traits, using the positive adjectives you know this person would use.

KEY TERMS

Self-Esteem	Conditions of Worth
Ideal Self	Malevolent Attitude
Real Self	Authoritarian Parenting
Self-Worth	Authoritative Parenting
Self-Concept	Permissive-Indulgent Parenting
Pathological Critic	Permissive-Indifferent Parenting
Inferiority Complex	Cognitive Distortions
Unconditional Positive Regard	Inner Child
Conditional Positive Regard	

CHAPTER 3 QUESTIONS

True or False (T or F)

1. _____ Unfortunately, once your self-esteem is set, it cannot be changed.

2. _____ Low self-esteem creates a negative vicious cycle.

3. _____ People with high self-esteem are always conceited.

4. _____ People with high self-esteem are afraid to take risks.

5. _____ People with low self-esteem are prone to resort to fadism in order to be accepted and included.

6. _____ High self-esteem leads to proactivity and vice versa.

7. _____ People with low self-esteem give themselves negative internal messages.

8. _____ People with high self-esteem cannot accept constructive criticism.

9. _____ People with low self-esteem are often very competitive.

10. _____ Self-esteem is genetic.

11. _____ Children can develop high self-esteem even if raised in very dysfunctional environments.

12. _____ Self-esteem can be influenced by irrational beliefs.

13. _____ You should ignore your inner child so that it will finally grow up.

14. _____ One of the biggest differences between people with high vs. low self-esteem is in how they talk to themselves.

Short-Answer Questions

1. Your self-esteem is influenced by the discrepancy between your _____ and your _____.

2. The negative inner voice that attacks and judges you has been termed the _____.

3. Carl Rogers observed that children develop positive self-esteem when parents show them _____. When parents treat children with _____, the children develop _____, whereby they think they are only lovable if they meet certain standards.

4. Harry Stack Sullivan noted that when children are treated badly, they can develop the _____, where they believe they are surrounded by enemies.

5. Research and observations indicate that the _____ parenting style has the healthiest impact on the self-esteem of children.

6. You can challenge your *shoulds* using _____ techniques.

7. Looking for evidence to support your existing view of yourself can result in _____.

Essay Questions

1. How does self-esteem differ from self-concept?

2. What should self-worth be based upon?

3. Describe the characteristics of the parenting style that is most conducive to fostering positive self-esteem in the child.

4. How does the *tyranny of the shoulds* impact upon self-esteem?

5. What do the authors suggest you do to avoid repeating the same mistakes over and over?

6. Why is it that mistakes are not bad?

7. Summarize the key attitudes for maintaining self-esteem according to Heidi Schleiffer.

4

Develop Mastery over Stress

Part I: Understanding Stress

Effective individuals have learned how to become *masters* over stress. This chapter and the next will prepare you to master the stress in your life by first giving you a thorough understanding of how stress affects you, and then teaching you a variety of strategies and techniques for modifying your thinking and your physiology in ways that will allow you to develop resistance to and mastery over stress.

STRESS MASTERY VS. STRESS MANAGEMENT

You may notice that we refer to the concept of **Stress Mastery** in this chapter rather than using the more common name: Stress Management. This is not just a semantic difference. We really see a difference between the ability to achieve mastery over stress versus the ability to merely manage your stress. See, the key is not just *surviving* stress, but *thriving* from stress. Stress management is suggestive of one more "thing" to do. As if you didn't have enough things to do already! Stress mastery is more a part of the fabric of your life. It is not *work;* it is a *craft*. It is a way of taking the raw material of the stresses of life and creating a reality in which you can live. With the passage of time, your craft improves. It does not take time away from your schedule. It actually adds time to your life. Often people see stress management as having to do specific exercises in order to lower stress. But stress mastery is really about cultivating wisdom. It is not mechanical or rote. It is about becoming increasingly aware of your situations and, perhaps even more so, of your reaction to these situations. The truth is, life is not always a calm sea of tranquility. Life throws waves at you, and these waves do not appear to be of your choosing. You do have a choice, though, on how you ride these waves. Do you choose to surf them gracefully, making use of the opportunities presented, or do you choose to go under, feeling as if you can't breathe and might drown at any moment. Stress mastery is organic. It changes and it is flexible, while always remaining consistent with certain core skills and habits. Stress mastery is planting a garden that is enriched year after year. Stress management is opening another can of beans.

Stress Management	vs.	Stress Mastery
One more "thing" to do		Part of the fabric of your life
Work		Craft
Takes time		Adds time
Do exercises		Cultivate wisdom
Mechanical		Increase awareness
		Organic

A Three-Week Commitment

The core skills and strategies presented in this chapter and the next form the foundation on which stress mastery is based. They are absolutely necessary if you are to be able to cope gracefully with the demands placed on you by life. To acquire them will require an initial investment of time and focus. We ask that for the next three weeks, you dedicate yourself to Stress Mastery Training. There are only two requirements to do this. The first is that you commit 15 minutes a day to practice so that you may learn to be able to quiet your body. The second is that you commit to remember you are in training as you go about your daily routines. These are your three weeks of Stress Mastery Training! Make thinking about and applying what you read a priority during this time. We promise that you will ultimately gain time as a result of the increased energy and improved concentration you will experience. As you learn to master your stress, other priorities in your life will become clearer. You might find that you are not only climbing the ladder of success, but that you know for sure that the ladder is against the right wall. As a result, the quality of your time would improve.

In order to support you in achieving these outcomes, we strongly suggest and invite you to include your experiences with Stress Mastery Training in your journal. The act of writing down your experiences and reflecting on them is an exquisite vehicle for remaining conscious and aware of all their different aspects. This, in turn, allows you to remember the many choices you, in reality have when confronting any situation.

THE DEFINITION OF STRESS

What is stress? When we ask students, employees, employers, and workshop participants this question, they typically respond that it is tension, nervousness, headaches, having deadlines to meet, etc. Basically what we hear is a list outlining the effects of stress, or specific causes of stress. The official definition of stress is that **stress is anything that requires an adaptive response on the part of the organism.** But, what does that mean?

It means that anything that requires you to respond, to make a change or an adjustment is stressful. So, when people say they want to get rid of stress, the reality is that this is impossible. That is not to say that you cannot reduce the amount of change or responsibilities you have in your life. Indeed, this is at times recommended as a way of minimizing your stress level. But we want you to understand that, even if you went and hid out on a mountaintop in order to escape the rat race, you would probably eventually get bored and boredom itself is stressful. See, the fact is, **stress is an inescapable part of modern life.**

That is not necessarily as bad as it may sound. One of the best-known experts on stress, a Canadian scientist by the name of Hans Selye, was quoted as saying that *"stress is the spice of life."* Just as spice can make your food tasteful and come alive, stress can give your life meaning and excitement. This depends, of course, on the amount and type of spice you use. We all know that the wrong spice, or too much spice can make you sick to your stomach (with a possible visit to the porcelain throne). Selye (1956) differentiates between these two types of stress, referring to **positive stress as "Eustress" and negative stress as "Distress."** So stress is not all bad. In fact, in one study adult volunteers who were placed in a completely stress free environment (a sightless, soundless, weightless, motionless liquid heated to body temperature) soon began to manifest disturbances of mood, thought and action. Most asked to be quickly released. We all need an optimal level of change and stress in our life to keep things interesting. And that level varies from person to person.

Given the pejorative connotations given to stress, it is easy to forget that an appropriate level of stress in your life is often helpful. Stress can help motivate you to perform and meet the challenges you will face. The physiological and psychological aspects of the arousal produced by stress can be useful, and unless you are routinely overloaded and aroused, stress may not necessarily harm you (Kobasa, 1982). It may surprise you to find out that you need an optimal level of stress and arousal in order to perform at your best. This fact was established many years ago by pioneering psychologists Yerkes and Dodson (1908) who demonstrated that performance on a given task improves as physiological arousal increases until some optimal point, after which performance declines as arousal continues to climb. This optimal level of arousal varies with the type of task. The more complex the task for an individual, the less arousal can be tolerated before performance suffers. In layman's terms, when you are totally cool, calm and collected in a performance situation, you may not have the required motivation or edge necessary to perform at your best. If, on the other hand, you are panic-stricken or a nervous wreck, your high arousal will interfere with your performance. **Many tasks are best performed with moderate levels of arousal.** This relationship is known as the Yerkes-Dodson Law. This is useful to remember next time you have to speak before a class, or group, or are in any type of performance situation. There is a misconception that you should be "cool as a cucumber". This is not necessarily true, for you will actually perform better if you are moderately aroused (i.e., stressed). What does this have to do with stress mastery? If you are under aroused you will experience the stress of boredom. If over aroused you will experience anxiety. If you can find your optimal level, where you are stimulated and performing at your best, you can experience satisfaction and master stress.

STRESS AND ILLNESS

Do you believe that stress can make you sick? If you are like most people, you would answer with a resounding, "YES!" When we ask people this question in our workshops and classes all of them believe that stress can affect their emotional well being, and the majority realize that it can lead to physical illness. Unless you have been living off planet for the last few years, you have had some exposure to the fact that stress can and does have deleterious effects. However, had we asked this question just twenty-five or thirty years ago to people in general, or even to a group of health professionals, the majority would probably have denied the relationship between stress and our health. Then we were just emerging from the era of infectious diseases where we believed that illnesses were caused by exposure to germs and bacteria, and that the way to keep healthy was to create vaccines and medicines to combat these external agents. At that time, to have considered the notion that stress could lead to illness would have been *avant garde* thinking.

Then, Thomas Holmes, M.D., a professor at the University of Washington School of Medicine, began doing research on the effect of changes (i.e., stress) on our physical and emotional well being. Together with Richard Rahe, Dr. Holmes developed a questionnaire measuring life changes and set out to study whether there was a relationship between the number, seriousness, and pervasiveness of changes, and our frequency of illness (Holmes & Rahe, 1967). Using army personnel, because they were a captive audience and their progress could be followed easily, they demonstrated that the questionnaire could help them predict with remarkable accuracy those soldiers who would get ill within the next two years and those who would remain healthy. We suggest that you complete and score the Holmes-Rahe Life Readjustment Scale to determine your own level of stress as measured by this inventory.

LIFE READJUSTMENT SCALE Part A

Instructions: Think back on each possible life event listed below, and decide if it happened to you within the last year. If the event did happen, check the box next to it.

	Check here if event happened to you.	Mean Value (Use for scoring later)
1. A lot more or a lot less trouble with your boss.	_____	_____
2. A major change in sleeping habits (sleeping a lot more or less, or change of sleep habits)	_____	_____
3. A major change in eating habits (a lot more or a lot less food intake, or very different meal hours or surroundings)	_____	_____
4. A revision of personal habits (dress, manners, associations, etc.).	_____	_____
5. Major change in your social activities (clubs, dancing, movies, visiting, etc.).	_____	_____
6. A major change in your usual type and/or amount of recreation.	_____	_____

7. A major change in church activities (a lot more or less than usual).   _____   _____

8. A major change in number of family get-togethers.   _____   _____

9. A major change in financial state (for better or for worse).   _____   _____

10. In-law troubles   _____   _____

11. A major change in the number of arguments with your spouse.   _____   _____

12. Sexual difficulties.   _____   _____

LIFE READJUSTMENT SCALE Part B

Instructions: In the space provided, indicate the number of times that each applicable event happened to you within the last two years.

	Number of times	×	Mean Value	Your Score
13. Major personal injury or illness.	____		____	____
14. Death of close family member (not spouse).	____		____	____
15. Death of a spouse.	____		____	____
16. Death of a close friend.	____		____	____
17. Gaining a new family member (through birth, adoption, oldster moving in, etc.).	____		____	____
18. Major change in the health or behavior of a family member.	____		____	____
19. Change in residence.	____		____	____
20. Detention in jail or other institution.	____		____	____
21. Minor violations of the law (traffic tickets, jaywalking, disturbing the peace, etc.).	____		____	____
22. Major business readjustment (merger, reorganization, bankruptcy, etc.).	____		____	____
23. Marriage.	____		____	____
24. Divorce.	____		____	____
25. Marital separation from spouse.	____		____	____
26. Outstanding personal achievement.	____		____	____
27. Son or daughter leaving home (marriage, attending college, etc.).	____		____	____
28. Retirement from work.	____		____	____
29. Major change in working hours or conditions.	____		____	____
30. Major change in responsibilities at work (promotion, demotion, lateral transfer).	____		____	____
31. Being fired from work.	____		____	____

32. Major change in living conditions (building a new home, remodeling, deterioration of home or neighborhood). ____ ____ ____

33. Wife beginning or ceasing work outside the home. ____ ____ ____

34. Taking on a mortgage greater than $25,000 (purchasing a home, business, etc.). ____ ____ ____

35. Taking on a mortgage or loan of less than 25,000 (making a large purchase). ____ ____ ____

36. Foreclosure on a mortgage or loan. ____ ____ ____

37. Vacation. ____ ____ ____

38. Changing to a new school. ____ ____ ____

39. Changing to a different line of work. ____ ____ ____

40. Beginning or ceasing formal schooling. ____ ____ ____

41. Marital reconciliation with mate. ____ ____ ____

42. Pregnancy. ____ ____ ____

YOUR TOTAL SCORE ____ ____ ____

Scoring

The "Mean values" for each life event are listed below. Write in the mean values for those events that happened to you. For items in Part B, multiply the mean value by the number of times an event happened, and enter the result in "Your Score." Add up the mean values in Part A and scores in Part B to get your total score.

Life Event	Mean Value	Life Event	Mean Value
1	23	22	39
2	16	23	50
3	15	24	73
4	24	25	65
5	19	26	28
6	18	27	29
7	19	28	45
8	15	29	20
9	38	30	29
10	29	31	47
11	35	32	25
12	39	33	26
13	53	34	31
14	63	35	17
15	100	36	30
16	37	37	13
17	39	38	20
18	44	39	36
19	20	40	26
20	63	41	45
21	11	42	40

Interpreting Your Results

The more change you have, the more likely you are to get sick. Of those people with a score of over 300 for the past year, almost 80% get sick in the near future; with a score of 200 to 299, about 50% get sick in the near future, and with a score of 150–199, only about 30% get sick. A score of less than 150 indicates that you have a low chance of getting ill. So, the higher your score, the harder you should work to stay well. Stress can be cumulative. Events from two years ago many still be affecting you now. If you think this applies to you, repeat this test for the events of the preceding year and compare your scores.

But this questionnaire has a major flaw. Do you know what that is? It fails to take into account individual differences in our abilities to cope with the changes and demands of our lives. Since that time a number of other inventories have been designed attempting to measure a variety of factors associated with stress. One that we have found particularly useful is a computerized *Brief Stress Inventory* which pinpoints your particular sources of stress and the current effects these are having in your life. In addition, it identifies your present resources for dealing with stress along with specific suggestions for enhancing your ability to cope.

NEGATIVE EFFECTS OF STRESS

So what are the negative effects of stress? What can happen when stress overloads your coping resources; when your skills are inadequate to deal with the demands placed on you by circumstances? **Stress negatively affects your physical, psychological, and occupational functioning** in a variety of ways.

Physical Consequences

The relationship between stress and your health is not simple nor straightforward. Stress will not automatically cause you to become physically ill. The impact of stress on your health is mediated by a variety of personality variables, as well as your genetic makeup and environment. But physically, it is clear that when you are under prolonged stress your immune system can be weakened, creating vulnerability to illness and bodily system breakdown. Recent research has revealed that chronic high levels of stress hormones, known as **glucocorticoids**, cause white blood cells to migrate to the bone marrow and hide out, making them less available for combating disease. This appears to be one specific mechanism by which chronic stress weakens immune functioning, leading to an increased susceptibility to diseases, including cancer. Furthermore, as illustrated by the list below, stress can create a wide assortment of psychosomatic problems in which the weakest link in your system of organs, muscles and glands is affected. For some individuals the heart is affected, for others the stomach or the pancreas, thus some develop heart disease, others ulcers or diabetes.

- Eighty percent of all visits to doctors offices are for stress related disorders.
- At least 50% of all deaths in the U.S. are caused by cardiovascular diseases such as heart disease and stroke, in which stress plays a significant contributing role.

❈ Most heart attacks occur around 9:00 a.m. on Monday mornings.

❈ Severe stress is one of the most potent risk factors for stroke—even more so than hypertension—even 50 years after the initial trauma. A study of over 500 World War II veterans found that the rate of stroke was 8 times higher for those who were POWS.

❈ Hypertension (high blood pressure), a stress related disorder, afflicts at least 30 million people in the U.S. with some estimates going as high as 80 million.

❈ Cholesterol levels in the bloodstream rise during periods of stress.

❈ One of the top gastro-intestinal specialists in the U.S. reports that 90% of all people with chronic diarrhea (irritable bowel syndrome or colitis) have no organic basis for their condition.

❈ Ulcers, spastic colon and similar gastro-intestinal disorders are the direct result of elevated acidity brought on by the stress hormone cortisol.

❈ There are 50–100 million headache sufferers in the U.S. Headache is the number one complaint seen by physicians in this country and 80% of all headaches are tension headaches. Migraines compose 18% of headaches but even these (despite the genetic predisposition) are often triggered by stress and tension.

❈ A 1991 study showed that people ranking high on a test of perceived stress were more likely to develop colds when intentionally infected with a virus. A repeat of this study in 1998 revealed that chronic stress increased the odds of catching the cold as much as 3 to 5 times.

❈ Fifty million Americans suffer from chronic pain and lower back pain accounts for 50% of this total. Negative emotions and stress can aggravate pain and cause acute pain to develop into chronic pain. The stress hormone ACTH can impede endorphin production (**endorphins** are our bodies' natural painkillers) leading to increased pain and discomfort.

❈ Recent research indicates that stress even plays a significant role in the development of osteoporosis in women due to increased levels of stress hormones.

❈ Dentists report that a high percentage of patients show signs of nocturnal bruxing (teeth grinding at night).

❈ Stress is also implicated in rheumatoid arthritis. The hormone prolactin, released by the pituitary gland in response to stress, triggers joint swelling.

* Studies reveal that during college exam week students possess lower levels of salivary immunoglobulin, a defense against respiratory infections. Studies also report that students' acne worsens when they are under stress.

Psychological Consequences

It is not surprising that stress is also a key factor in the development of emotional difficulties and behavioral problems. Can you remember a time when you felt there were too many demands placed on you? What was that like for you? Did it affect your ability to relax and enjoy life? Stress clearly influences our psychological well-being in a host of different ways as elucidated below:

* Stress is a major factor in the development of anxiety, phobias, panic attacks, depression, PTSD (post traumatic stress disorder), obsessions, compulsions and all major psychiatric disorders. In 1996 it was estimated that 1.5 billion individuals worldwide were suffering from some form of psychiatric disorder including 115 million dependent on alcohol and/or illegal drugs and 400 million suffering from anxiety disorders.

* According to the World Health Organization, depression, clearly a stress-related condition, is the number one cause of disability worldwide.

* It has been demonstrated that stress alters serotonin pathways. Imbalances in serotonin levels have been linked to depression and in some cases aggression.

* There are over 30 million Americans suffering from insomnia. Sales of sedatives are second only to aspirin.

* An estimated 24 million Americans are using drugs to cope with stress. The three best selling drugs in the U.S. are Tagamet (for ulcers), Inderal (for hypertension) and the tranquilizer Xanax (for anxiety).

* Alcoholism is the third major cause of death in the U.S.. An estimated 10 million Americans are alcoholic. Relief of stress and anxiety is one of the primary motives for the use and abuse of alcohol. Repeated use for that purpose is viewed as an important factor in the development of habituation and addiction.

* Fifty-five percent of all marriages end in divorce. Experts report that stress is a major contributing factor to relationship conflicts and the rising incidence of divorce. Frustration tolerance decreases, thus individuals are more likely to mis-attribute the source of their stress and blame their spouse.

Consequences in the Workplace

At times of stress, how well can you concentrate on the task at hand? Do you find thoughts, preoccupations, and fears interfering with your ability to function? The ability to concentrate is significantly affected by stress. It is no wonder that an inability to cope with life stressors leads to lowered productivity and an increased frequency of mistakes on the job. In addition, you are more likely to miss work due to both emotional and physical illness. As the following list demonstrates, this leads to major financial losses for business, industry and employees.

* People are more accident prone during periods of stress. U.S. businesses claim that most industrial accidents are stress related, accounting for 2 million disabling injuries per year, more than 15,000 deaths, and 3 billion dollars annually in lost productivity.

* At least ten billion dollars a year is lost to industry due to absenteeism from physical or psychological problems. It is estimated that individuals suffering from chronic pain miss over 700 million work days per year, with a cost of 60 billion dollars per year. A 1995 estimate by the American Heart Association indicated that cardiovascular diseases alone cost the economy $20.2 billion in lost production for that year.

* Data suggests that 80–90% of all business dismissals are somehow linked to tension and subsequent mental and physical problems.

* Stress is eroding the bottom line for business. The combination of decreased productivity, absenteeism and spiraling medical costs may be costing the economy as much as $150 billion annually according to some surveys.

* At least 25% of the people in the U.S. suffer from stress overload at work. According to a 1995 Gallup Poll 37% of American workers reported daily job stress, while 75% reported significant stress at least once weekly. A study by the National Center for Health Statistics revealed that more than half of 40,000 workers surveyed reported experiencing moderate to severe job stress in the previous two weeks. A 1998 Gallup poll strongly suggested that stress continues to mount for American workers as fully 80% reported being significantly stressed at work. This poll also revealed that women feel more "stressed out" than men and, interestingly, that stress increases as income levels rise.

* Insurance companies have recently been plagued by a nationwide epidemic of sick, disabled and wealthy professionals, especially doctors, but also accountants, architects, insurance agents and lawyers filing claims for disability due to stress related disorders.

THE PHYSIOLOGY OF STRESS

There is more than sufficient data demonstrating that stress can lead to physical, emotional and behavioral maladjustments. But how does this happen? How is it that changes in our lives lead to ill health? The answer lies in a physiological mechanism known as the "**Fight or Flight response**". The fight or flight response is a survival mechanism present in humans and most animals which prepares us to deal with physical danger. Imagine our ancestors, cavemen and cavewomen, exploring their terrain, perhaps even enjoying the wonders of their prehistoric environment, when suddenly out of the corner of their eyes they spot a saber-toothed tiger, licking his lips in anticipation of a tasty human morsel. The fight or flight reaction would kick in preparing their bodies to either fight or flee from the tiger. It would do this through a series of instantaneous physiological and psychological changes which prepare us to take immediate physical action in the face of danger. These changes and their resulting physical signs are outlined in the following Tables.

In short, fight or flight shows a picture of autonomic hyperactivity. If we return to the example with the cave dwellers, the caveperson's body and mind would be on "red alert" in order to deal with the impending danger. This activation would not go on for long, however. If the tiger had his way and caveperson ended up serving as a meal, he/she would definitely be relaxed as the deceased tend to show no autonomic activity. If, on the other hand, our friend was lucky enough to escape and tell the story to his/her cronies back in the cave, his/her physiology would return to a state of **homeostasis** or balance. After a slight period of recovery, caveperson would be no worse for the wear. Visually, this may be represented as follows:

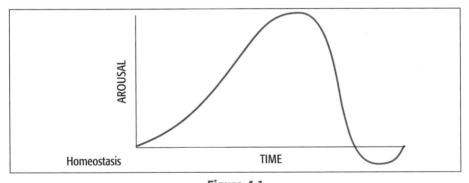

Figure 4.1

It also appears that men and women often respond differently to stress. Women's blood pressure goes up less than men's in reaction to stress, but women tend to react to a wider range of stressors than men. Women feel stress more often because they take a more holistic view of everyday life.

TABLE 4.1 Signs of Fight or Flight

Racing Thoughts	Attention Span Narrows
Rapid Pulse	Pounding Heart
Gritting of teeth	Muscular Tension
Can't sit still	Jaw clenching
Tremors	Stomach tightens
Rapid, shallow breathing	Perspiration increases
Serious, concerned expression	Field of vision narrows
Numbness	Cold, clammy hands
Impulsive behavior	Gripping emotions
Inability to concentrate	Dry mouth

TABLE 4.2 Anatomy of "Fight or Flight" Response

❁ The breathing rate becomes more intense and rapid, increasing the oxygen supply in the blood.

❁ Breathing becomes more shallow, switching from diaphragmatic to thoracic respiration, again shifting the oxygen/carbon dioxide balance.

❁ Muscles tense in preparation for strenuous action.

❁ Heart rate speeds up insuring sufficient blood supply to needed areas, especially to the brain for optimized control over conscious functions as well as to major muscles to prepare the individual for action.

❁ Peripheral blood vessels constrict again to send the bulk of the blood supply and the oxygen it carries to needed areas. Blood clotting mechanisms are also activated to protect against injury. This prevents excess bleeding should the caveperson be cut in the struggle.

❁ The increased heart rate and constriction of peripheral blood vessels cause blood pressure to soar.

❁ Digestion ceases, so blood may be diverted to muscles and brain.

❁ Stored sugar and fats pour into the blood stream to provide fuel for quick energy.

❁ The adrenal gland is activated releasing adrenalin into the system, along with the hormones epinephrine and norepinephrine.

❁ Triggered by the pituitary gland, the endocrine system steps up hormone production.

❁ All senses are heightened. Pupils dilate making vision more sensitive. Hearing becomes more acute.

❁ Electrical resistivity (perspiration/galvanic action) and skin temperature change.

❁ Perspiration increases and saliva decreases.

❁ The urethra and anal sphincter muscles (controlling bowel and bladder function) initially loosen, in order to evacuate waste if necessary, but then constrict to prevent waste elimination when running or fighting. So when people say, "I was so scared that I peed in my pants," there is a physiological mechanism underlying this humiliating phenomenon.

The Downside of the Fight or Flight Reaction

This mechanism is clearly an adaptive response to the presence of physical danger. The problem is that the response is triggered not only by actual physical danger, but by perceived danger. The tigers that chase modern man and woman are not of flesh and blood. They are things like deadlines, unpaid bills, confrontations with others, rush hour traffic, demands from children, spouses, bosses. All these and many more trigger the fight or flight response in the person of today. But it gets worse, for not only are the tigers the actual events, but also those events remembered and anticipated by us. So not only does the act of asking the boss for a raise lead to increased autonomic activity, but also our anticipation of our meeting, along with the recollection of the event, particularly if we didn't obtain the desired results. The predicament lies in the fact that the fight or flight reaction prepares us to either fight or run away and neither of these responses is particularly useful nor adaptive for dealing with most of the stresses we face in our modern world. To further aggravate the situation, caveperson's stresses had a distinct beginning and a definite ending, whereas the tigers we face today seem to be much more ongoing. No sooner have we begun to recover from fight-flight activation when another event, real or imaginary, triggers the response. Thus, we never really have the chance to fully recover and return to homeostatic balance before we are faced with the onslaught of new or old stressors recurring in our environment. This can be expressed visually as follows:

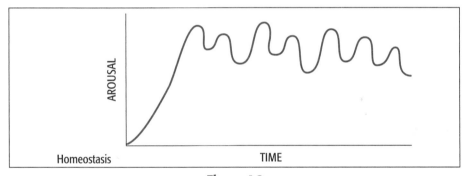

Figure 4.2

Day after day we are faced with a continuous barrage of stressors. We get some relief at night when we sleep, but even in our sleep we might dream about our stressors, again triggering the fight-flight response, and the next day we awaken with our physiology just a bit above homeostasis, to begin the whole cycle over again. After years of this pattern we forget what relaxation really feels like, as we habituate to a state of autonomic arousal. This state feels relaxed in comparison to full blown fight-flight activation, but in reality it is higher than true homeostasis, which we need to maintain health. This is illustrated in the graph on the next page.

Thus a person under chronic stress is like a car with its idle set too high. Imagine for a moment a car whose engine is idling just a little too fast. What would happen to it? For one thing, it would use more gas, just as we tend to spend more energy for diminishing returns when we are under stress. In addition, the engine will wear out

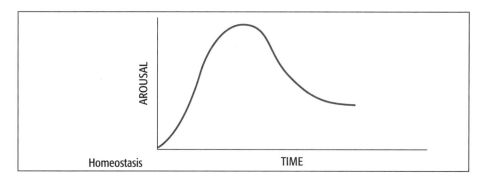

Figure 4.3

prematurely as it similarly appears to happen to our bodies. The stress researcher Hans Selye, mentioned earlier, described this phenomenon as a three stage process which he named the **General Adaptation Syndrome** (or **GAS** for short). The first stage of GAS, called the **Alarm Reaction**, is basically the fight or flight response. If the stressor continues, as is typical of modern day tigers, we enter into the **Stage of Resistance** where our bodies habituate to the specific stressors. Overt signs of the fight or flight reaction disappear or go underground, but subtle signs persist (our neural and glandular systems remain hyperactive) leaving us overstimulated and vigilant. The last phase, known as the **Stage of Exhaustion**, occurs when stressors are prolonged despite our best attempts at coping. Just as we have to rest, so must our glandular system rest in order to regain balance. Without rest it wears down and eventually out, resistance deteriorates, and stress related symptoms resurface. Clearly, if there is no relief, even death is possible (Selye, 1982). See Figure 4.4.

Stress Sensitization

To make matters even worse, before the Stage of Exhaustion overtakes us, recent research indicates that we can become sensitized, or acutely sensitive, to stress. That is, we may respond to stress as we do an allergy. Once that happens, even the slightest stress can trigger a torrent of chemical reactions in both our brain and body that besiege us from within, making stress the psychological equivalent of ragweed. Even though at some level we realize that what we are facing is a normal, everyday stressor, our brain is signaling our body to overreact. We may not think we are getting worked up over running late for an appointment, but our brain is responding as though it were a life or death situation. Years of research has demonstrated that people become sensitized to stress and this sensitization actually alters physical patterns in the brain. We may produce too many excitatory chemicals or too few calming ones; either way we are responding inappropriately.

The fact that stress itself lowers our ability to cope with further stress led to yet another distressing finding. Sensitization to stress may occur before we are old enough to prevent it ourselves. New studies suggest that animals ranging from rodents to monkeys to humans may experience still undetermined developmental periods during which exposure to extreme stress is more damaging than in later years. For example, we have known that losing a parent when you are young is much harder to handle than if your

STRESS
THE GENERAL ADAPTATION SYNDROME

In the short term it's vital, but over time it turns destructive. New research shows how chronic stress breaks down the body and makes way for disease.

1. IMMEDIATE

In response to a perceived threat, the body channels resources for strength and speed.

Brain: Stress protectively dulls the body's sense of pain. Thinking and memory improve.

Eyes: Pupils dilate for better vision.

Lungs: Take in more oxygen.

Liver: Sugar stored as glycogen is converted to glucose for energy.

Heart: The bloodstream brings extra oxygen and glucose – fuel for power. Heart rate and blood pressure rise.

Adrenal Glands: The medulla secretes fight-or-flight hormone Epinephrine (adreneline).

Spleen: Extra red blood cells flow out, allowing the blood to carry more oxygen to the muscles.

Intestines: Digestion halts, allowing the body to dedicate energy to the muscles.

Hair: Body hairs become erect. Puffed-up hair makes animals look bigger and more dangerous.

Muscles: Tense to prepare to fight or flee.

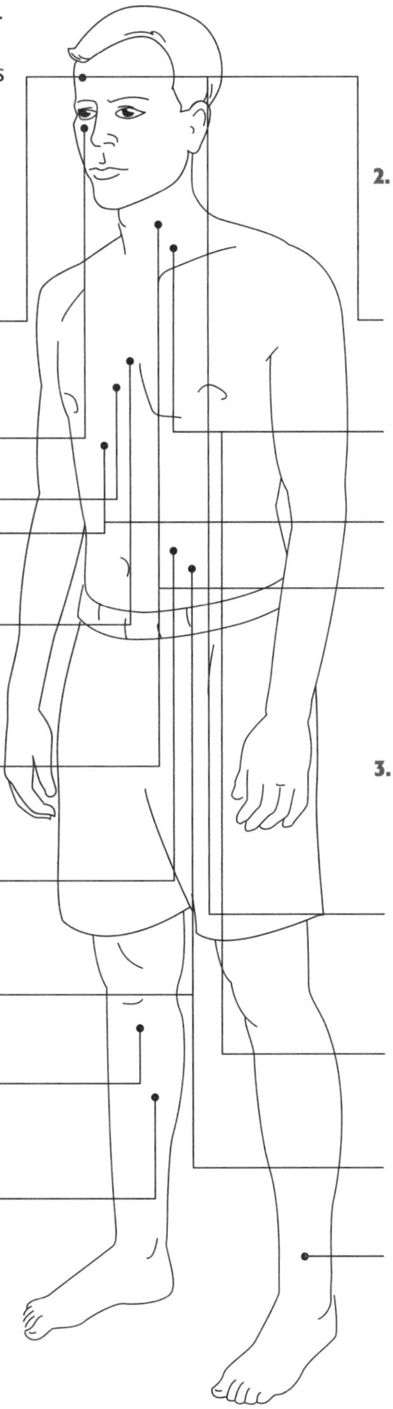

2. DELAYED

A few minutes after the fight-or-flight response, the body makes changes to stabilize and replenish itself.

Brain: The hippocampus, a center of memory/learning, gets activated to process the stress.

Immune System: Infection fighting is diminished, perhaps increasing available energy.

Liver: Fat-stored energy is converted into usable fuel.

Adrenal Glands: The cortex secretes cortisol, which regulates metabolism and immunity. Over time, though, this can be toxic.

3. CHRONIC

If activated too often, the response may harm the immune system, heart, and brain.

Brain: Cortisol becomes toxic to the brain cells, potentially damaging cognitive ability. Fatigue, anger and depression increase.

Immune System: Repeated suppression of disease-fighting cells ultimately weakens infection resistence.

Intestines: Decreases in blood flow leave mucous lining vulnerable to ulcers.

Circulatory System: Elevated blood pressure and heart rate damage elasticity of blood vessels.

Figure 4.4

parent dies when you are an adult. What we now believe is that a stress of that magnitude occurring in childhood may rewire your brain's circuitry, throwing the system off kilter, leaving you less able to handle normal, everyday stress. So clearly, stress does not just grab us for a time and then release us. It changes us by altering our bodies and our brains.

WHAT IS POSSIBLE?

But enough of this doom and gloom scenario! Are we totally at the mercy of our past and current stressors? Is there nothing we can do? Research and an overwhelming amount of anecdotal evidence supports the idea that, just as we have the potential to slowly destroy ourselves, our mind/body system can also create miraculous beneficial results. What is possible can sometimes border on the unbelievable.

For example, you may have heard the story of Norman Cousins, who wrote about his remarkable recovery from a supposedly incurable and very painful connective tissue disease that leads to spinal deterioration and paralysis, in his best selling book *Anatomy of an Illness*. Mr. Cousins refused to buy into the gloomy predictions of his physicians (who gave him a 1 in 500 chance of recovery), so he designed a regimen of self healing based largely on using humor as a stress reducer. As part of his regimen he spent several hours daily watching movies of the Three Stooges and the Marx Brothers. Initially he reported that ten minutes of belly laughter had a powerful anesthetic effect, allowing him to sleep at least two hours without analgesic medication (painkillers). Laughter also reduced his inflammation, probably by stimulating the release of endorphins. Ultimately, much to the surprise of his physicians, he went into a complete remission.

The Power of Belief

Or what about the amazing story reported by Ernest Rossi in his book *The Psychobiology of Mind-Body Healing*. Dr. Rossi recounted the story of Mr. Wright, as told by his personal physician, Dr. Phillip West, over 30 years ago. Mr. Wright suffered from advanced malignancy of the lymph nodes known as lymphosarcoma. His condition was terminal and he had deteriorated to the point where his physician thought death was imminent. He had tumors the size of oranges in his neck, groin, chest, and abdomen. His spleen and liver were grossly enlarged. Copious amounts of fluid were drawn from his chest on a daily basis. He was bedridden and having severe difficulty breathing. All standard cancer treatments of that time, including radiation, had proved useless. Although his doctors had given up hope for his recovery, Mr. Wright maintained an optimistic attitude, for since the onset of his illness he held fast to a belief that a miracle drug would come along to save the day. This expectation was fulfilled when newspapers reported that a newly developed drug, "Krebiozen", showed significant promise in the treatment of cancer. This hope was further heightened when he learned that the hospital where he was staying would be included in a research project studying the effectiveness of this new drug. Even though he did not fit the criteria for inclusion in the study (because of the advanced nature of his condition), he begged his doctors to include him in the treatment protocol. Against their better judgement his doctors included him in the study, fully expecting he would die within the week, thus freeing up a supply of

Krebiozen for another patient. His response to the drug was nothing short of miraculous! Within several days he went from death's door to walking around the ward, joking with nurses. His tumors were half of their original size. After ten days of Krebiozen treatment, he was discharged from the hospital with his cancer in complete remission. In the meantime, early results of the study indicated that this miracle drug appeared to be ineffective in the treatment of cancer. Unfortunately, Mr. Wright became aware of these initial reports of the lack of effectiveness of the drug, and within a short period of time he completely relapsed.

Clearly, it wasn't the Krebiozen that was responsible for his improvement, but the power of his belief. In order to test this out, his doctors decided to see if they could recreate the previous results. They deliberately lied to him and told him not to believe the discouraging results he had read in the newspapers. They further informed him that Krebiozen was highly effective, and that his relapse occurred because his last doses had deteriorated on the shelf. They further added that he would be receiving double strength dosages from a fresh shipment of the drug which should restore him to health. They then, with great fanfare, proceeded to inject him with saline solution, nothing but a placebo. What do you think happened? Again he made a remarkable recovery, even quicker than the first time. He was discharged from the hospital and remained in complete remission for two months, until reports appeared in the press that Krebiozen had proven to be totally worthless in the treatment of cancer. Mr. Wright quickly relapsed and was readmitted to the hospital, dying two days later.

What can be learned from this? You could conclude that the lesson here is that Mr. Wright should have stopped reading the newspaper! But obviously what is evident, and rather amazing, is that it was the power of Mr. Wright's belief that affected his physiology. Doctors would dismiss this as a dramatic example of the **Placebo Effect**. We often hear our colleagues in the health profession refer to similar, if less dramatic, results with their own cases as "just a placebo." To us, the fact that **IT'S JUST A PLACEBO!** opens up a whole new range of possibilities. Rather than an area to be dismissed, we consider this to be a phenomenon to explore fully. The consensus in the field is that 30% of the effectiveness of any treatment, including drugs, can be accounted for by placebo effects. One highly respected researcher in the area of stress reduction and mind/body connection, Herbert Benson, believes the placebo effect is responsible for 80% of the success of all treatments!

THE MIND-BODY CONNECTION

So clearly, just as we have the capacity to do ourselves tremendous harm through our reactions to stress, so too do we have the ability to create dramatic positive outcomes in our lives. The first step is acknowledging this possibility. Our mind and body are not as separate as was once thought. In fact, they are profoundly interconnected and interdependent. As a result of this shift from the old paradigm where mind and body were thought to operate separately, a whole new branch of psychology, called psychoneuroimmunology or PNI, has developed over the last fifteen years. PNI is the study of the relationship between stress, our immune system and health outcomes in order to uncover the workings of the mind-body connection, and discover how to use these mechanisms to fight illness, ranging from AIDS to the common cold.

One facet of PNI research is focused on proving the mind-body connection by establishing a direct physiological link between the body's immune system and the brain. This is based on a new theory (Maier and Watkins, 1998) which hypothesizes that the immune system functions as a messenger which signals the brain of injury or impending illness by releasing cytokine proteins which travel to the nervous system and the brain. In response, the brain then releases its own cytokines to prompt the nervous system to discharge a cascade of responses, such as fever and fatigue, which assist the body's healing mechanisms by lowering activity level and thus conserving energy. These researchers question whether the depressive response in humans may have developed as a survival mechanism for saving energy during times of illness.

PNI researcher Margaret Kemeny, Ph.D. and her colleagues at UCLA are exploring a new theory which challenges and expands upon Selye's well accepted G.A.S. model of the stress response. Kemeny and her associates propose that there are actually two potential stress reactions: (1) the classic fight/flight reaction Selye describes; and (2) a withdrawal response where people cut back to conserve energy (by for example, getting depressed rather than anxious). Kemeny's team is also studying the cognitive aspects of these two reactions. They have found that people respond differently to the same stressful events depending on the meaning given to the stressor. That is, the interpretation given to the stressor helps determine whether a person withdraws or becomes agitated. Our bodies respond not so much to our environment, but to our interpretation of our environment. By now this should be starting to sound familiar to you. This aspect will be dealt with in much greater detail in the next Chapter which focuses on how to cope with stress.

A related theory about alternative stress reactions (Taylor, 2000) posits that women will often respond with "tend and befriend" behaviors rather than fight/flight reactions. That is, when under stress females will often initiate nurturing behaviors to protect their children and their loved ones, as well as themselves.

Your Immune System Can Learn!

Experiments with animals have demonstrated that the immune system is capable of learning by association (i.e. classical conditioning). In one study, rats were given sweetened water (the equivalent of rat Coca-Cola) which contained a drug which suppressed immune functioning, and, not surprisingly, they began to get sick at an abnormally high rate. After a hiatus when no sweetened water was available, it was reintroduced but without the drug. Guess what? The rats started getting ill again, as the flavor of the water created a conditioned response that once again inhibited their immune functioning even though the immunosuppressant drug was absent. In another rodent experiment, mice were bred to be genetically vulnerable to an autoimmune disease (where an overactive immune system literally attacks the body's own tissues). They were then fed a flavored solution which included an immunosuppressant drug, and, as a result, it delayed the onset of the disease because their immune systems were suppressed. The researchers then continued giving the mice the flavored solution minus the drug, and the mice continued to resist the disease. Once again the immune system had learned to inhibit itself by association to a taste. In yet another mouse study, mice were repeatedly exposed to the smell of camphor while simultaneously receiving an injection which enhanced "natural killer" (NK) cells. NK cells are a type of white blood cell which is vitally important to immune functioning as they kill germs. Later on, when these mice were exposed to the smell of camphor without the injection, their NK activity increased once again.

More Research Evidence for the Mind-Body Connection

On the human level, researchers have demonstrated that NK cells decreased in medical students preparing for exams, but those students who were calmer and had slower heart rates exhibited less immune suppression. Similarly, another study showed that unhappily married women had lower numbers of certain immune cells than happily married women. Individuals caring for relatives with Alzheimer's disease, which is a very stressful task, have also been shown to have higher than average cortisol levels and lower levels of antibody response to influenza vaccines. In a 1991 English study, the stress levels of 420 subjects were evaluated immediately following an administration of nose drops containing a cold virus. These subjects were then quarantined for nine days, and those reporting the highest levels of stress were more likely to catch the cold. In a similar study in the late 1990's at the University of Pittsburgh, 276 heathy adults were given cold virus nose drops. Those under the most stress manifested the most severe cold symptoms, but mainly when their stress levels were affected by serious problems such as troubled marriages or unemployment. In another study, 100 subjects were monitored for one year and were required to keep a diary of life events and their emotional reactions. Periodically they were examined for bacteria in throat cultures and antibodies to viruses in their blood. The results showed that stressful events were four times more likely to proceed rather than follow incidents of illness.

With regard to healing from injuries, one study found that a biopsy wounds healed more slowly in women who were under high levels of emotional stress. In another experiment, students' wounds healed slower if inflicted just before an examination rather than just before vacation. Slow healing has also been reported in people caring for relatives with Alzheimer's disease.

Social stress appears to be even more damaging than physical stress for animals as well as humans. Our poor friends the rodents were once again tortured in this next study where one group of mice were put into a cage with highly aggressive mice. Another group were kept in tiny cages without food or water for long periods of time. Then both groups were exposed to a bacterial toxin. The mice who were socially stressed were twice as likely to die as the mice who were just physically stressed.

For humans, isolation often inhibits immune functioning. Some studies have reported lower NK cell activity in separated and divorced men compared to married men. Medical students who are lonely have been found to have lower NK activity than non-lonely med students. In a year long study of people caring for spouses with Alzheimer's, decreases in immune functioning were greatest in those who had the weakest social networks and the least outside help. In general, good social support is strongly correlated with stronger immune functioning in the elderly, even after factoring out variables such as emotional health, health habits, stress levels, etc. In the University of Pittsburgh study mentioned above, social support was correlated with resistance to the cold virus, that is, those with the weakest social networks were four times more susceptible to the cold than those with the strongest ties.

There have even been a few studies of the effects of traumatic stress on our immune functioning. According to one report, four months after Hurricane Andrew, Miami residents in the most heavily damaged neighborhoods demonstrated reduced activity in four out of five immune indicators. Similar results were found in a study after the Los Angeles earthquake. Weakened immune functioning has been reported among women who are victims of physical abuse. Another article suggested that men with a history of PTSD (Post Traumatic Stress Disorder), even though recovered, showed weakened immune functioning which may indicate a long lasting suppression of their immune systems.

The studies cited above were reviewed in the Harvard Mental Health Letter which summarized these findings and concluded that . . .

> *"Animal experiments suggest that the nervous system responds differently to acute and chronic stress. The acute stress reaction is often a healthy response to a challenge. But chronic stress may cause the feedback controls to fail, turning the emergency response into a condition that persists when it no longer has any use. Stress hormones and sympathetic activity remain at high levels, suppressing immune function and possibly promoting illness. The immune systems of people who are under chronic stress may also respond abnormally to acute stress."*

The Healing Power of the Mind

What really matters is whether our minds can influence our immune system to prevent or lower the risk of illness or injury, and also promote healing. At this point you may have several questions such as, "How can I cope better with stress?", or, "How can I get the mind-body connection to work for me?" We now know enough of the necessary steps to harness this power. What remains is to learn and then practice these steps. If you follow the techniques and suggestions outlined in the next chapter and in Chapter 6 (the section on using visualization techniques to promote healing), we promise you will reap significant benefits. But let us caution you that knowing the steps is not enough, it is only in the doing that solutions are found.

SELF EXERCISE

1. Be aware of the relationship between stress and the fight or flight response in your own life. Next time you are feeling anxious or shaky, note what is triggering this reaction. Is it actual danger or more likely just perceived danger? Conversely, the next time you are faced with a stressor, pay attention to how your body reacts. Awareness of increased arousal or fight/flight activation is the first step in learning to calm yourself, which is the subject of the next chapter.

2. Reflect back on your own life. Can you recall a time when you were under a lot of stress and then may have gotten quite ill shortly afterwards? On the other hand, can you recall a time when you were feeling content or when your stress level was low, and you successfully avoided getting ill even when close friends or relatives were succumbing to illness and you were exposed to, say a bad cold or flu bug that was going around?

KEY TERMS

Stress Mastery	Fight/Flight Response
Stress	Homeostasis
Eustress	Stress Sensitization
Distress	General Adaptation Syndrome (GAS)
Glucocorticoids	Placebo Effect
Endorphins	Psychoneuroimmunology

CHAPTER 4 QUESTIONS

True or False (T or F)

1. _____ A commitment to mastering stress will add time to your schedule.

2. _____ It is definitely possible to escape all the stressors in your life.

3. _____ We all need an optimal level of eustress in our lives to keep things interesting.

4. _____ There is no clearcut relationship between stress and emotional and physical health.

5. _____ The more changes in your life, the less likely you are to get sick.

6. _____ The fight or flight response can be triggered not just by actual physical danger, but by any perceived danger or stressor.

7. _____ The fight or flight response is a natural mechanism which prepares us to either fight or flee.

8. _____ Death is possible if there is no relief from the Stage of Exhaustion of the General Adaptation Syndrome.

9. _____ Despite popular myths, the mind and the body function separately.

10. _____ The mind/body connection is capable of facilitating healing.

11. _____ Psychoneuroimmunology is the study of the relationship between neurosis and neurological damage.

12. _____ Divorced men are less likely to get sick than married men.

Short-Answer Questions

1. _____ is anything that requires an adaptive response on the part of the organism.
2. Many tasks are best performed with _____ levels of arousal.
3. Stress negatively affects your _____, _____, and _____ functioning in a variety of ways.
4. _____% of all visits to doctors offices are for stress-related disorders.
5. The _____ response is a survival mechanism present in humans and most animals that prepares us to deal with physical danger.
6. When _____ sets in, it is possible to respond to stress as you would to an allergen.
7. When people report feeling better after being given a sugar pill and told it is a painkiller, this is an example of the _____ _____.

Essay Questions

1. Distinguish between eustress and distress.
2. Explain the Yerkes-Dodson Law and its implications in performance situations.
3. Describe the physiological changes that occur during the fight or flight response.
4. Discuss the General Adaptation Syndrome (GAS).
5. What is stress sensitization?
6. What conclusions can be drawn from research in psychoneuroimmunology?

5

Develop Mastery over Stress

Part II: The Art of Coping Gracefully

THE MAGIC IN BREATHING

The path towards stress mastery is a life long process. If you choose to incorporate the concepts and techniques presented in this chapter into the daily fabric of your life, your capacity to cope with and thrive from stress will flourish. Clearly, to deal with stress effectively, you must pay attention to both your body and your mind. A dramatic example of this is a study which showed that meditators tended to age slower than non-meditators. During meditation one focuses on quieting both the body and the mind through the act of fixing on a single thought, image, or visualization.

Truth be told, the distinction between body and mind is really an artificial one. We now know that body and mind are really one, an intricately interrelated system where thoughts give rise to our physical reactions and, in turn, our physical reactions trigger our various thoughts. But for the purpose of training, of learning how to begin traveling on the path towards stress mastery, it is useful to talk about addressing your body first. It is very difficult to change the way you think if your body is simultaneously sending messages of danger. Addressing the body is best accomplished by learning **active relaxation**.

Most people confuse inactivity with relaxation. You might say, "I do relax. I go home and sit down in front of the TV, watch my favorite programs, and let the stress of the day melt away." But the fact is that when subjects' level of stress, as indicated by physiological arousal, is measured while watching TV, negligible, if any decrease is evident. You see, **passive relaxation** such as this is not nearly as effective in reducing stress. What is needed is relaxation aimed at reducing the fight/flight response and thereby restoring balance or homeostasis. Active relaxation involves becoming aware of your body and your physiological reactions so that you may consciously reduce your level of arousal.

Diaphragmatic Breathing

Any journey which you undertake begins with a first step. The key to any practice of active relaxation is to relearn proper breathing patterns. Breathing slowly, deeply, and regularly is the easiest and most accessible relaxation technique (Loehr & Migdow, 1986). Most of the time you are no doubt oblivious to your breathing patterns. Let's first begin by discovering where you are now. Sit with your back supported, your feet flat on the floor and your eyes closed. Put one hand on your chest, and the other on your diaphragm, the muscle right above your stomach, as you focus on your breathing. Notice the pattern and rhythm of your breath as you breathe in and out. Then, take a few deep breaths, noticing as you breathe in and out which hand moves more. Does the hand on your chest move up and down, with the shoulders rising and falling, as you breathe? Or is it the hand on your abdomen that does most of the movement? Take a few moments to do that now.

So what happened? Which hand moved more as you breathed deeply? We notice in our classes and workshops that for the majority of students and participants, it is the hand on the chest that evidences more movement. If you have ever seen a baby breathing while he/she is at rest or asleep, you may have noticed that it is the stomach that moves up and down, while the baby's chest remains relatively still and quiet. This is called **diaphragmatic breathing** and it is a natural antidote to stress. Diaphragmatic breathing involves deep, slow, rhythmic breaths.

Pay attention to what happens to your breathing the next time you feel stressed. You may notice that your breathing became quicker, more shallow and irregular. Some people even hold their breath or begin to hyperventilate when under significant stress. What happens to many adults is that after years of frequently activating the fight/flight response, the fast, shallow, upper chest breathing characteristic of this physiological reaction becomes a habit. This breathing is ineffectual, disrupting the proper balance of carbon dioxide and oxygen in your blood stream and thereby creating a continual, if not full blown, over-activation response. There is an optimal balance of oxygen and carbon dioxide that needs to be maintained in your bloodstream for you to remain calm. Rapid, shallow breathing causes over-oxygenation of the bloodstream. The side effects of too much oxygen include muscle tension, dizziness, and feelings of anxiety. That is why hyperventilation is so counterproductive. The more quickly you breathe, the worse you feel.

Practicing Diaphragmatic Breathing

Retraining yourself is, in most cases, a rather simple procedure. What is required is just about five minutes a day of conscious focusing on your breathing. You can do this by practicing the following technique, once a day, for three weeks. (Three weeks are generally required to bring tone to the diaphragm muscle.) We have discovered that a few minutes prior to going to sleep is a good time to practice for many people. Others prefer to take five minutes when they return home from either work or school. It is important for you to discover which time is best for you.

Find a quiet place where you are unlikely to be disturbed. Recline and put one hand on your diaphragm and one hand on your chest. Focus on allowing the hand on your diaphragm to rise as you breathe in, as if your stomach were a balloon filling with air. Then watch it go back down as you breathe out and the balloon deflates. Notice the rhythm of the rising and falling of your abdomen as you inhale and exhale. Focus on the particular feelings and sensations you experience in your diaphragm as the breath comes all the way into your lungs and then completely empties from your lungs. Do this for about five minutes, gently focusing your attention on your breath.

If you find yourself having difficulty initially lifting your abdomen as you breathe, try imagining that you are putting on a tight pair of jeans, when they come out fresh from the drier. You would let all the air out of your lungs first, as if you wanted to touch your spine with your bellybutton, then slowly inflate the balloon as you let the air come all the way into your lungs.

Yet another technique that has proven successful for many people is to use a heavy book placed on top of your stomach as you practice your breathing exercises. You could watch the rising and falling of the book as you breathe in and out. This method has the added advantage of providing a weight against which the diaphragm is rising and falling, thereby conditioning the muscle much quicker. Most people find that with just a little attention and practice they can return to that slow, diaphragmatic breathing they knew as a child.

We cannot stress enough how important this first step is. Without shifting your breath to a calm, relaxed, diaphragmatic pattern, it will be very difficult to start your journey on the path towards stress mastery. The type of breathing you employ is the key to unlocking the magic. We know it sounds simple, but it is nonetheless true.

Take as an example research done with people suffering from panic attacks, a disorder in which intense anxiety (often accompanied by hyperventilation) is experienced at various times, often causing the individual to withdraw and increasingly restrict their activities in the hope of preventing the attacks. In the extreme, these individuals develop a condition known as "agoraphobia" where they become house bound as a way of coping with the fear of the attacks reoccurring. Developing appropriate diaphragmatic breathing patterns has been identified as essential in learning to overcome the panic.

Other research has shown that the speed of your breathing affects your perception of time. When you breathe faster, a typical byproduct of shallow breathing, time seems to speed up. You are more likely to perceive a shortage of time, creating a sense of time pressure. This, in turn, increases your level of stress. As you slow down your breathing, time also appears as if it is slowing down, resulting in a much more calm and relaxed attitude.

Focusing on your breathing helps keep you in the present moment. Your worries, anxieties and stress occur when you focus on either the past, (i.e. mistakes you have made or things you wish would have happened differently), or you focus on the future, (i.e. worrying about what is going to happen and how you will be able to survive). But the past has already happened, there is little you can do to alter that except change your attitude or perception about what happened. And the future is yet to come. You can only affect it by working in the present, the here and now. Breathing helps you exist in the now in a way which increases your effectiveness.

Most spiritual traditions recognize the importance of the breath. It is often considered our direct link to God or a Higher Power. The word "inspiration" has a double meaning, being used both to describe breathing as well as being infused with spirit and motivation. Alterations in breathing can create dramatic effects on our consciousness.

Holotropic breathing, an alteration in breathing in which controlled hyperventilation is employed, for example, has been shown to create dramatic shifts in consciousness in the practitioners, akin, if somewhat less intense, than those experienced when using hallucinogens. So breathing is clearly a powerful tool. One that can create numerous changes in our body and in our experience of ourselves and our world.

Once you can breathe comfortably using your diaphragm as you think consciously about it, it becomes important to be able to generalize that response to your daily life. One easy way to do this is to set up a number of reminders in your everyday environment. For example, do you know those sticky colored dots that are often used in offices to color code charts? You could take a few of these (3–5) and place them in different places around your home and work environment. We suggest that you resist the temptation to place these dots on the foreheads of people who are a source of stress to you. However, feel free to use your imagination. Each time you see a dot, stop for a second, take one or two breaths using your diaphragm, and then go on with your activity. This will allow you, with minimal effort, to remind yourself to breathe this way at different times during the day. In just a short time you will be pleasantly surprised, as you focus on your breathing, to discover that you are automatically breathing deep, diaphragmatic breaths.

Another way to insure that you generalize the correct breathing response to a variety of situations is by using a higher order classical conditioning principle. This principle states that when a new behavior is paired, and thus eventually associated, with a behavior which is frequently emitted, the new behavior becomes conditioned. Now to translate from psychologeeze, this means that you will learn how to breathe correctly faster and better if you do it at the same time that you are doing things which you do frequently, like answering the phone, going to the bathroom, or stopping at red lights.

Another obvious way, and indeed, the first building block, is to remember to breathe from your abdomen whenever you feel yourself becoming stressed. This will help interrupt the automatic cognitive and behavioral strategies you may be using now, which merely lead to an escalation of the stress response. Remembering to breathe in these situations allows you a pause which opens up the possibility of thinking or behaving differently, thereby using stress rather than being used by it.

We should caution you, however, that it is not wise to use only situations when you are feeling stressed as reminders to practice your breathing. You will clearly find it more difficult initially to successfully focus on appropriate breathing at these times. Until you have learned and feel comfortable with abdominal breathing, you need to practice in situations which are less demanding and in which the Fight/Flight response is not fully activated.

You need only do the most basic breathing awareness exercises to achieve a much more relaxed state of body and mind. As long as your breathing is becoming slower, quieter, and deeper you are moving in the right direction. Quite frankly, the hardest part is remembering to remember to be aware of your breathing and then to practice. But the fact remains that wherever you are you still have to breathe, so you might as well practice doing it properly in a manner that will help keep you calm yet alert.

Cultivating Awareness

By now you have become more aware of your breathing. You can notice just how you are breathing. Are you using your diaphragm or your thorax? Are you breathing deeply and slowly, with a comfortable rhythm? Or is your breath fast and chaotic? In any situation, if you notice you are engaged in unhealthy, stress producing breathing, this aware-ness allows you the opportunity to shift the pattern to a more appropriate one.

Can you do this? If you can't, we strongly urge you to continue your practice. With-out the ability to breathe appropriately, it will be difficult for you to master stress. If you can, we congratulate you! You have taken the first, and most essential step towards stress mastery. It is important that you now remember to do this throughout your day, in a vari-ety of settings. That you think about it at work, and at home. That you notice your breath-ing as you are going to sleep, and shortly after you wake up. It is important that you remember to notice your breathing. The more you do this, the more you are cultivating awareness. You are replacing your automatic behavior with conscious behavior.

THE VALUE OF SELF-AWARENESS

You see, all human beings have the ability to be aware, not just of our breathing, but of a multitude of things that make up who we are. Let us demonstrate what we mean. Imag-ine, in your mind's eye, that a part of you can float out of your body, floating up to a par-ticular corner of the room, so that you can see yourself, from that perspective, sitting there reading this book. What would it be like to do this, what would it feel like? How would you describe the particular sensations the you who is sitting there is experiencing right now? Focus in on a particular part of your body and become aware of your experience there. Perhaps you can be aware of pressure, or temperature. Or perhaps some other sen-sation. It's not important what the specific sensation is, just your ability to notice it. How about your overall mood? How would you characterize that? What can you say about your thoughts? Are you thinking about what you are reading right now, and yet perhaps at the same time wondering what's the point of all this? As you answer these questions, make sure you get back into your body. We certainly wouldn't want you to remain float-ing around the room somewhere while you continued reading this chapter.

The Witnessing Stance

By doing what you just did, answering the questions we just asked, you have demon-strated your ability for **self awareness**. All human beings share the ability to be aware of ourselves. The fact that we can do this, that we can stand apart from our feelings and our thoughts suggests that we can have some control over them. Ram Dass, formerly known as Richard Alpert, a Harvard psychologist who studied extensively in India and is renowned for integrating both Eastern and Western techniques, describes our ability to stand apart from ourselves, to view ourselves from the outside, as assuming the **wit-nessing stance**. Whenever you are involved in the many experiences that make up your life, you have the choice to be a witness to your own life. This shift in perspective pro-vides you with the possibility that you can change the particular situation. The fact is (as we addressed in Chapter 2), that you cannot always change situations (i.e. external stres-sors or events) you are faced with, but you can always change your reaction towards the stressor. Assuming the witnessing stance allows you to do this. Remember that, as we mentioned earlier, what inappropriately triggers your fight/flight response and therefore your stress, is not actual physical danger. Not many of you have guns pointed at your head, at least not on a daily basis. What triggers your stress response is your perception of danger. And whether you perceive something as dangerous or not depends on the meaning you give the particular situation. Fortunately or unfortunately, human beings are the kind of beings that give meaning to everything. And what we say, especially to ourselves, about a situation or event determines our attitude towards it. Assuming an observer perspective allows you to get a glimpse of the meaning you are ascribing and therefore provides you an opportunity to change your attitude.

Psychologists also have other labels to describe the processes involved in becoming self aware. The term **metacognition** refers to becoming aware of your thought processes, and **metamood** to becoming aware of your emotions. The process of assuming the witnessing stance allows you to step back from your experience, to go "meta", where you hover somewhere above the main flow, aware of what is happening rather than being immersed and therefore lost in it, which facilitates getting a better perspective. This refers to the difference between being furious and having the thought, "I'm feeling anger". But this subtle shift in mental activity is the first step in gaining some control. Becoming aware of your underlying thoughts and emotions is essential to developing emotional self control. Certainly, there is a big gap between being aware of a feeling and being able to change it, but the two often go hand in hand. That is, if you recognize that you are in a rotten mood, typically you will want to get out of it. Self awareness appears to have a greater impact on intense negative feelings. The recognition of what it is you are feeling gives you that slight bit of distance that sets in motion an awareness of alternatives, such as the option to attempt to let go of the feeling.

Attitude Is Everything!

Research has revealed that the attitude you have at the beginning of a task determines the outcome of that task more than any other single factor. For example, if you believe you will be able to succeed at a particular undertaking (i.e. if you are optimistic) and you approach the endeavor with a sense of excitement and joyful expectation, your chances of achieving success are much higher than if you face the task with dread and apprehension. Self-fulfilling prophecies can be positive or negative, depending on your expectations. So your attitude is more important than any other possible factor, both external and internal. This is clearly true when it comes to stress and whether we thrive from it or are buried by it.

Remember Thomas Holmes and his research showing that there was a relationship between the number, severity, and pervasiveness of life changes and our physical and emotional health? We mentioned that the major flaw of this series of studies was a failure to take into account individual differences in abilities to cope with the changes and demands. This research only focused on the effects of external events or stressors. A psychologist by the name of Suzanne Kobasa decided to focus her research interests on individual differences in coping skills. What makes some people capable of handling enormous amounts of change and demands without suffering the devastating physical and emotional consequences predicted by the Holmes research? Kobasa studied individuals whose lives seemed so filled with stressors that, according to Holmes, they should have been growing massive tumors on the sides of their heads. Yet, these folks were successful in their endeavors and seemed to be suffering no apparent negative consequences from their demanding life style.

STRESS HARDINESS ATTITUDES

Kobasa discovered three attitudes which these people all shared and which appeared to make them resistant to the negative effects of stress. She called these three attitudes, **the Stress Hardiness Attitudes** because individuals who possess them appear to be "stress hardy", i.e. capable of dealing effectively with stressors. These three attitudes are **control**, **commitment**, and **challenge**. These attitudes are also referred to as the **three Cs of stress hardiness** (Kobasa, 1979).

Control

Let's take a look at the first, the attitude of **control.** Stress hardy individuals believe that they are in control of their lives, rather than stressors having control over them. They recognize that they have resources and options that allow them to influence events in their lives. Although stress hardy individuals recognize that they may not always have direct control over the actual onset or occurrence of an event, they certainly have control over their own response to the stressor. And this is not only true of humans, but also true of such higher life forms as rats. For example, let's say you placed two rats in cages capable of delivering an electroshock to their unsuspecting paws. (Psychologists do, indeed, do this and other perhaps less kindly things to these animals. That is why our standing as a profession is rather low in the rat community!) Using what is known in experimental psychology as a "yoked research design", both rats are then shocked simultaneously at various intervals. One rat has a lever available in its cage which if pressed will discontinue the shock. The second rat has no such escape opportunity. When the first rat presses the lever, it stops the shock for both rats. This assures both rats are exposed to the same level and intensity of the shock, but only the first rat has control over discontinuing the stressful event. Can you guess what happens? The first rat, the one with control, is minimally, if at all affected by the series of shocks. The second "helpless" rat, on the other hand, suffers negatively, developing multiple psychosomatic symptoms such as ulcers.

These differences in stress response are maintained even when the escape lever is removed and replaced merely by a light which precedes the shock. In this design, the first rat had no means of escape, but was warned that a shock was imminent. Although the rat could do no more than dance around the cage, the effects of the stressor were somehow reduced, perhaps because the rat knew it was going to be dancing around and was therefore more prepared to do so. Thus, our sense of control is also affected by the extent to which we can anticipate and prepare for the onset of stressors and change. Involvement in exercise is a perfect example of this. We know that physical exercise is stressful. Yet it is stress over which we have control because we typically can choose when to begin and when to end our exercise routine. Stress researchers conclude that it is this sense of control which is at least partially responsible for the beneficial effects of repeated exercise.

So, stress hardy individuals refuse to see themselves as victims, buffeted and abused by external occurrences over which they have no control. Persons exhibiting this attitude see themselves as active players in their own lives. They possess what was discussed in Chapter 2 as an **internal locus of control**, for such individuals believe that they are responsible for the ultimate outcomes in their life. They do not wait for fate to lead them in directions, rather they endeavor to take active control over their own life. This is the same attitude described by Stephen Covey as **proactivity**.

Commitment

The second attitude characteristic of stress hardy individuals that was identified by Kobasa involves **commitment**. It is not merely the persistence in following through with a goal, it is an attitude which expresses a real *"joie de vivre"*, a zest for life. Commitment involves believing that what you do is of value and importance. Individuals exhibiting this attitude seem to possess an almost romantic relationship to their own life and the pursuits which they choose. When they wake up in the morning they don't start their day with, "Oh God, I wonder what could go wrong today? What horrible ambush can life have planned for me?" Instead they wake up expectant of the possible surprises and wonderful experiences that the day has in store for them. They have an optimistic outlook. Stressors are viewed as potentially interesting and meaningful. Commitment is the opposite of alienation and is characterized by involvement.

It is not surprising that research has linked how one answers two simple questions with the likelihood of developing heart disease. The two questions are: Are you happy? And do you like your job? If you answer yes to both of these, your chances of developing heart disease are much lower. Clearly the reverse is true when the answer is no. We are not implying here that overall life/job dissatisfaction causes heart disease, obviously there are many other factors operating in the development of cardiovascular problems. But your attitude towards your life is one important contributing factor. What is your attitude when you first open your eyes in the morning? We suggest you begin with an **attitude of gratitude**. One that says, "thank-you. I'm glad I'm alive. I wonder what adventures and experiences this day has for me." You see, happiness is not a condition, but a decision. You can choose to focus on all that can make you miserable. If you do, you will get results fitting this attitude. Or you can choose to count your blessings, to be thankful for all you have, and all you still have coming. To quote the great comedienne Gilda Radner shortly before her untimely death, *"Happiness is not about getting what you want, but about appreciating what you have."*

Challenge

The third and final attitude discovered by Kobasa to be typical of stress hardy individuals is that of **challenge**. This attitude can perhaps be best explained by considering the concept of crisis. The Chinese write this word using two characters as illustrated below:

dangerous   opportunity

The first character is the symbol for dangerous, the second is the symbol for opportunity. Think about that, what a wonderful way to describe a crisis. Not a catastrophe, or a problem, but a dangerous opportunity. Individuals exhibiting the attitude of challenge focus not so much on the danger aspect of the crisis, but on the opportunities available as a result. Every crisis, no matter what, has inherent opportunities. Those who cope well look for these opportunities and capitalize on them. Those who cope poorly get paralyzed by the inherent danger. To quote Don Juan,

> *"The basic difference between a warrior and an ordinary man is that a warrior sees everything as a challenge. While an ordinary man sees everything as either a blessing or a curse."*

Or to quote another colorful literary character, Zorba from *Zorba the Greek* by Nikos Kazantzakis,

> *"Life is trouble, only death is not. To be alive is to undo your belt and go looking for trouble."*

Hardiness and Stress Resistance

Take a moment and fill out the Stress Hardiness Inventory on the following page. Research has documented an association between high hardiness scores and lower rates of physical illness among white collar male executives and women in various occupations (Rhodewalt & Zone, 1989), blue collar workers (Manning, Williams, & Wolfe, 1988), college students (Roth et. al., 1989), and adolescents (Sheppard & Kashani, 1991). Hardiness is also associated with psychological health. Stress hardy individuals report lower anxiety levels, less depression, greater job satisfaction and lower levels of tension at work. In other studies hardy subjects were shown to have stronger physical tolerance for stress. When exposed to a stressor they have a lower increase in diastolic blood pressure (Contrada, 1989) and a smaller increase in heart rate (Lawler & Schmied, 1987).

One interesting study (Allred & Smith, 1989) demonstrated that male college students who scored low on hardiness experienced high levels of tension before the onset of a stressor (i.e. as they waited and anticipated), while those scoring high on hardiness measures displayed higher arousal only during exposure to the stressor. It appeared that the hardy subjects got aroused only when they needed an adrenalin surge to confront the stressor more effectively, while the others spent valuable energy worrying. Hardy individuals do get physiologically aroused but at the right time and to the right level.

Strong resistance to stress is associated with optimism, and clearly the ability to think positively is a defining characteristic of the stress hardy. Stress resistant people are more likely to use problem-focused coping measures, positive thinking, and support-seeking strategies when faced with stress (Cohen & Edwards, 1989; Holt, Fine & Tollefson,1987; Nowack, 1989). Those scoring low on measures of hardiness tend to respond passively to stress, whether with avoidance or maladaptive behaviors. Hardy individuals are much more likely to take care of their health, which helps boost their stress resistance. A strong sense of personal control over one's life is associated with better health habits, such as exercise and good nutrition, lower likelihood of abusing alcohol, drugs or nicotine, or of aggressive acting out when under stress.

STRESS HARDINESS SELF-ASSESSMENT INVENTORY

Use this scale to indicate how much you agree or disagree with the statements below:

0 = Strongly disagree	1 = Mildly disagree
2 = Mildly agree	3 = Strongly agree

_____ A. Trying my best at work and school makes a difference.

_____ B. Trusting to fate is sometimes all I can do in a relationship.

_____ C. I often wake up eager to start on the day's projects.

_____ D. Thinking of myself as a free person leads to great frustration and difficulty.

_____ E. I would be willing to sacrifice financial security in my work if something really challenging came along.

_____ F. It bothers me when I have to deviate from the routine or schedule I've set for myself.

_____ G. An average citizen can have an impact on politics.

_____ H. Without the right breaks, it is hard to be successful in my field.

_____ I. I know why I am doing what I'm doing at work or school.

_____ J. Getting close to people puts me at risk of being obligated to them.

_____ K. Encountering new situations is an important priority in my life.

_____ L. I really don't mind when I have nothing to do.

To get your scores for control, commitment and challenge, write the number of your answer, from 0 to 3, above the letter of each question. Then add and subtract as shown below.

$$\underline{\quad} + \underline{\quad} = \underline{\quad} \qquad \underline{\quad} + \underline{\quad} = \underline{\quad} \qquad \underline{\quad} + \underline{\quad} = \underline{\quad}$$
$$\text{A} \qquad \text{G} \qquad\qquad\qquad \text{C} \qquad \text{I} \qquad\qquad\qquad \text{E} \qquad \text{K}$$

$$\underline{\quad} + \underline{\quad} = \underline{\quad} \qquad \underline{\quad} + \underline{\quad} = \underline{\quad} \qquad \underline{\quad} + \underline{\quad} = \underline{\quad}$$
$$\text{B} \qquad \text{H} \qquad\qquad\qquad \text{D} \qquad \text{J} \qquad\qquad\qquad \text{F} \qquad \text{L}$$

Control _____   Commitment _____   Challenge _____

_____ _____ _____

Control + Commitment + Challenge = Total Hardiness Score

Score	Interpretation
10–18	Hardy personality
0–9	Moderate hardiness
Below 0	Low hardiness

The Three Cs in Action

The authors had an opportunity to witness, firsthand, how stress hardiness attitudes affected the ability of literally thousands of people to cope with a monumental crisis. Being based in Miami, Florida we, along with thousands of other people, experienced Hurricane Andrew, one of the strongest storms ever to ravage the mainland U.S.A. The scale of property destruction and disruption of normal life for months afterward was unprecedented. Just about everyone in the hurricane zone (including the authors) suffered severe damage to their homes, businesses, cars, and personal property. Rebuilding took years and normal routines were totally disrupted for at least six months for most. As psychologists we paid close attention to how individuals coped with the aftermath of the storm and we found that three distinct styles emerged: (1) The Whiners—individuals who spent months bemoaning their plight and all the inconveniences, hassles, and property losses they suffered; (2) The Stiff Upper Lip Crowd—individuals who were very upset but focused on cleaning up, rebuilding, and didn't spend an inordinate amount of time complaining, but internally they focused primarily on how awful it all was; (3) The Adventurers—individuals who did not deny the reality of the damage but who focused on how interesting, how exciting, what an adventure it all was. These people relished rebuilding their homes with insurance money. They delighted in the sense of camaraderie and community that developed between neighbors who found themselves in the same boat, who previously had barely spoken to one another. Needless to say, the latter group experienced far fewer emotional disturbances and physical illnesses than the other two groups. They believed that they could *control* their destiny, even in the face of incredible ruin. They were *committed* to making the rebuilding process as joyful as possible. And they viewed the crisis as a *challenge* and opportunity to recreate their living situation and make new friends. For them, the hurricane became an epic, fascinating story to share with friends rather than merely a tragic event.

Clearly, you should be able to perceive the wisdom in Steven Covey's oft quoted phrase, *"The way you see the problem is the problem."* Ultimately, whether something is stressful or not depends on the way you look at the situation. Remember, it is not the world out there that makes you a victim, it is your perception of the circumstances and events which lead you to be either defeated by stress or to survive and thrive from the challenges and opportunities presented to you. You may not have control over all that happens to you, but you certainly always have control over the meaning you give to the events in your life. There is an old saying, *"When God closes a door, he opens a window".* Remember this as you face apparent hardships in your life. Always look for the windows; we guarantee that they will be there, no matter what the circumstances.

ACQUIRING BODY WISDOM: THE WARRIOR STANCE

If you have been applying what you have learned thus far, your breathing will be becoming slower, deeper, and quieter. Your awareness will be keener as you notice that you can observe and stand apart from your attitudes and emotions. It is from this very place that all systems of personal change and development begin. Now that you have gotten your feet wet, it is time to dive a little deeper and focus your new tools more intently on both body and mind.

This section will focus on acquiring what we call body wisdom. Usually we think of wisdom as having an awful lot to do with the things we say and think. For many it is a measure of how many facts they know or how intelligent they are. Body wisdom, however, is not about how thoughts affect your body but about how your body affects your thoughts. We maintain that the body is intelligent, wise if you will, and that this wisdom can be tapped to improve your health, well-being, and performance.

Midway through graduate school one of the authors made a personal discovery which has guided his work as a therapist, trainer, and student ever since. The story illustrates the central premise of this concept.

> It was the most difficult emotional period I had ever experienced in my life. I was a novice psychotherapist facing the pressures of a new job, a new relationship, physical illness, and the most difficult examinations of my academic life. My symptoms were classic: difficulty eating and sleeping, obsessive thoughts, a lack of energy and feelings of hopelessness. Since I had never experienced anything like this before, I had no clear idea how to get better. The difficulties lingered for months, even after many of the problems had been resolved. It certainly didn't make sense to me that it just kept going on and on. It was as if my emotional life was going downhill and all I could do was watch. I was alternatively frightened, sad, and bewildered by my inability to feel the way I used to feel, joyful and engaged in life. Finally, one afternoon as I sat alone in my office, particularly exasperated, I asked myself the key question. How did I act when I felt better? I was, as they say, sick and tired of being sick and tired. Thinking alone had not really changed anything for me. I knew I used to be different and I began to focus on **acting** that way again. Quite literally I decided to change my posture, the speed of my walk, the tilt of my head, the expression on my face. I walked out of my office **in character**, whistling a happier tune in my head, and asked the first person I saw how **they** were feeling. I played this part the remainder of the day and I noticed that I felt better. I decided to continue playing the role for a while longer and soon forgot that I was playing the role. I simply began to be the way I was with one important difference: I now knew there was a way out of the darkness. I knew I would never be quite that lost again. This was the beginning of a series of physical and mental practices that have served me very well over the years. My body had led me out of the wilderness the way a horse carries an injured rider back to the stable.

Shakespeare once wrote *"If you lack the virtue, act the virtue."* Today we say *"Fake it, til you make it."* What we are suggesting is that there is a stressed stance as well. If you act stressed, holding your body in the manner characteristic of the fight or flight response, you will feel stressed, even if there is no particular reason to be stressed. Luckily, there is an antidote for this and that is to discover what we call the **warrior's stance**.

At first blush the notion of a warrior's stance leading to a more peaceful, less stressed existence may seem like an oxymoron. Why not a monk's stance or a gardener's stance? However, since life, business, and relationships are often presented in terms of struggles, battles, conflicts, and competitions, we might find it useful to examine this metaphor more carefully. Contrary to popular belief, successful warriors are ultimately peaceful individuals whose primary battles are fought internally. They display a relaxed and balanced posture. This enables them to have exceptional reaction times and full freedom of movement. This capacity for relaxed balance also begets a fluidity of response that allows them to pull an opponent who pushes them or push one who pulls. It is a capacity to literally flow around obstacles. Anyone who has gone white water rafting has been given the wise counsel to let the river carry you to a safe place when you have been thrown from the boat. To resist overpowering force is to risk being thrown into the rocks. A warrior knows that it is best to stay relaxed and alert and float feet first so you can be aware of genuine routes of escape.

A warrior cultivates fearlessness. This does not mean recklessness. It simply speaks to the survival value of being able to notice the body's response to a threat and, by the force of the regular practice of a discipline, still maintain the ability to choose a course of action. This grace under fire is often the difference between life and death in survival situations. Fear is a process that necessitates that we step out of the moment and contemplate the past or future. An intense focus in the here and now is the best way to keep fear at bay. The easiest way to maintain this focus is to cultivate the breathing and relaxed posture of the warrior. A warrior does not seek out or create conflict. Their preference is to walk away. But once engaged in battle, they are fully committed to their chosen course of action.

This is truly a critical piece of information for individuals who have attempted to change their lives by changing the content of their thoughts through endless affirmations. In our experience, "nice thoughts" have very little impact on someone's long term well being if their body is wracked with tension and stress related hormones. You must actively change your physiology if you hope to contend successfully with stress. Consider a parallel from the study of communication. The best estimates that we have suggest that only 7% of the meaning of any communication is actually in the words themselves. The remaining 93% of the meaning is communicated by our body language and the tone and tempo of our speech. In a similar vein, if we wish to communicate to ourselves the value of a more relaxed stance, we will need more than words. We need to speak to our bodies in a way that they will understand.

However, in the realm of relationships, the behavior that most of us are in need of cultivating is listening. This is no less true of our relationship with our body. The disorders that are brought on by chronic, excessive muscle tension begin as mere brief episodes of tension. We may grit our teeth in anger and still maintain some residual tension even after the cause of our anger is gone. Over time this can develop into **bruxism**, the grinding and gnashing of the teeth while sleeping. We may tighten our neck and shoulder muscles in response to fear or anxiety and again retain excess tension even after the threat has disappeared. This is how tension headaches begin. Why exactly does this occur?

You might say that in each of the cases above someone failed to listen to his or her body. Now the body's usual response is to continue communicating in its language of rising tension. Ultimately when we are stricken with a stress related illness, the body is now screaming, "Why didn't you listen when I was whispering?" This is the primary aphorism of this chapter: **IF YOU LISTEN TO YOUR BODY WHEN IT WHISPERS, YOU WON'T HAVE TO LISTEN TO IT SCREAM.**

Once again we return to the issue of awareness. To listen to the whispers of tension we must be aware of what it means to be truly relaxed. In point of fact, most people simply do not know what it means to be relaxed. We have seen many clients claim that they are relaxed only to be shown otherwise when they are monitored by biofeedback equipment. As noted earlier, breathing is the starting point of your relaxation practice. But to go deeper into relaxation requires an additional practice and we would like to introduce that to you next.

PROGRESSIVE MUSCLE RELAXATION

In 1929 the book *Progressive Relaxation* by Edmund Jacobson, a Chicago physician, was published. He theorized that physical tension leads to mental tension which further exacerbates physical tension. Therefore, learning to relax your body should promote mental relaxation and lowered stress levels. This technique has been used very effectively to treat a wide variety of stress related disorders (Seaward, 1997). The theory of its use is simple, that is, if you induce a feeling of deep relaxation in your body you simply cannot be feeling stressed. As your body experiences a return to homeostasis, your body's natural inclination towards healing and health is activated and enabled.

While we will present a formal protocol which you can follow to implement Progressive Relaxation, it is most important that you understand the principles and guidelines that will allow you to succeed as long as you commit to regular practice for several weeks. The reward for this short term commitment is that you will be able to reduce the time needed to reach a relaxed state from 25 minutes down to 5 to 7 minutes. Before you begin you may find the following guidelines to be helpful for your practice:

- Prepare a convenient time and place, and practice regularly. Remove distractions.

- Set up a regular practice schedule. Several times weekly is recommended until you have mastered the technique. You can then use it on an as needed basis.

- Be comfortable. Wear loose fitting clothing. Recline on your bed, sofa or in a cozy recliner chair. Some people place a rolled towel under their knees and lower back to maintain a comfortable spinal alignment.

- Avoid falling asleep, unless you are using this procedure to facilitate sleep.

- Don't try too hard. Paradoxically, if you try too hard to relax it will only increase your level of tension.

- Allow yourself to "let go". Sometimes people fear letting go, for it is equated with losing control. The only thing you have to lose here is unhealthy muscle tension. Learning to relax increases your control, but first you have to let go and allow this to happen

- If you find your mind wandering, gently bring your focus back to your breathing and to this technique without scolding yourself or passing judgement.

- Finish your relaxation practice by coming back slowly. At the end of your practice session, slowly bring your attention back to the here and now, gently stretch your muscles, and open closed eyes. If you are lying down, roll over slowly onto your side, pause, and then sit up. When your muscles are deeply relaxed you do not want to contract them suddenly. Coming back slowly allows your relaxed state to linger for hours.

One goal of this procedure is to help you become aware of the difference between feelings of muscle contraction vs. muscle relaxation. Begin by taking a few moments to scan your body for tension and to focus your attention on any physical sensations. The basic method in Progressive Relaxation is to first carefully tense a particular muscle or group of muscles. This is to further develop your *awareness* of that part of your body, specifically when that part is tense. It is important that you contract the muscle only to a low level of tension. Be particularly careful not to over tense any muscle or muscle group where you are prone to experience muscle spasms. Contracting a muscle as hard as you can only leaves you more tense and does not cultivate relaxation. Tense each muscle group for up to 5 to 7 seconds, and then release the muscle and focus your awareness on how the muscles feel as they relax for the next 20 to 30 seconds. Allow yourself to focus on any sensations of warmth and heaviness. As you continue from muscle to muscle, slowly but surely the sensation of warmth and heaviness begins to spread throughout your body. It can help to talk to yourself during this process with self instructions such as the following:

Clench your right hand into a fist. Tighten your fist and study the tension as you do so. Become aware of the tension and discomfort in your hand and forearm as you tense. Now let go of the tension and let your hand go limp. Pay careful attention to the feelings of relaxation spreading in your hand as the tension drains away. Notice the difference between the comfortable sensations of relaxation in your hand now, compared to the uncomfortable feelings of tension. Let go more and more, letting the muscles in your hand and forearm grow more and more deeply and fully relaxed.

The typical sequence of movements would be as follows:

PROGRESSIVE RELAXATION SEQUENCE

1.	Hands and forearms	Clench fists—left then right; bend hands backward at wrist, left then right
2.	Biceps	Flex by bending elbows and bringing hands up to your shoulders
3.	Triceps	Straighten arms and push down against the chair or floor
4.	Forehead	Wrinkle forehead
5.	Eyes	Squeeze tightly shut
6.	Jaw	Press teeth together; then let jaw drop
7.	Tongue	Press into roof of mouth
8.	Lips	Press together
9.	Head and neck	Push head back; bend head forward—touch chin to chest
10.	Shoulders	Shrug and try to touch ears
11.	Chest	Take three deep breaths—hold each several seconds
12.	Back	Arch
13.	Abdomen	Suck stomach in; make stomach hard as if it was going to be hit
14.	Thighs	Tense thigh muscles—stretch legs out
15.	Ankles and calves	Point toes toward face; point toes downward

After you have gotten familiar with this sequence of movements, there are a number of techniques for coordinating your breathing, language, and imagination to creatively deepen and enrich your experience.

- ❀ Experiment with coordinating your breathing with the tensing and relaxing of each muscle group. Inhale and briefly hold your breath as you tense the muscle group. Exhale as you let go. Be aware of the sounds of the breath as you relax as well as the feelings of relaxation. Over time the hissing of the slow release of breath will become associated with relaxation and speed up the process of letting go.

- ❀ Some people prefer to visualize their breath as light that carries warmth and relaxation to their muscles. In this scenario, as you tense a muscle and inhale you are pulling light to the muscle group. As you exhale you expel darkness and tension from the muscles. Gradually you build an image of your body filled with light. If another set of colors feels better to you feel free to experiment. For instance, some people like to use the color blue to symbolize relaxation and red to indicate tension. Once you have reached a relaxed state you can really embrace your relaxation experience by imagining a scene that is pleasant to you. (e.g. lying on a beach or walking in the woods).

- ❀ There is also a time honored method known as **Autogenic Training** in which one literally talks oneself into relaxation. This is done by repeating certain phrases over and over while focusing your attention on a particular muscle group. For instance, if after going through a Progressive Relaxation exercise, you still feel residual tension in a body part, then you would repeat to yourself, "My (name the part, i.e. arm, hands, thighs) feel warm and heavy". Or you could say to yourself, "My (arms) feel loose and relaxed". In fact, this method of systematically repeating relaxing phrases over and over again can be used on its own to induce relaxation. It can, however, be terminally boring, so be certain to tailor your program to your needs and interests. Create a routine that interests you and you will increase the likelihood of following through and mastering this skill.

One main goal of Progressive Relaxation training is to help you achieve **differential** relaxation throughout your day. Accomplishing this means that you are able to contract only those muscles which are necessary to accomplish the task at hand, while keeping all other muscles relaxed (McGuigan, 1984). For example, there is no need to clench your jaw, stiffen your shoulders, or squeeze the steering wheel while driving. But your arm and leg muscles will certainly need to contract in order to operate a car.

THE IMPORTANCE OF STRETCHING YOUR MUSCLES

As noted earlier, an intrinsic part of the fight/flight response is muscle tension. When muscles tighten they also shorten. One way to reverse the fight/flight response is to lengthen your muscles. This is accomplished quite simply by stretching the muscles. Our goal here is not to provide a comprehensive manual on stretching exercises, but we would like to mention some guidelines for stretching intuitively.

Intuitive Stretching

As you cultivate body awareness and relaxation you will notice an urge to stretch your body in various ways. Many people notice that yawning is accompanied by an almost instinctual urge to lean back and extend one's arms. We are very aware of the need to stretch after sitting in a car or at a desk for a prolonged period of time. Anyone who has dogs or cats can watch them stretch when they awaken or when they anticipate they will go for a walk. The point we are making is that while we would suggest it is a good idea to read a manual on stretching or to take a yoga class to learn a specific routine, your body is actually a very good guide to this procedure if you will pay attention to it. After all, someone figured this stuff out without referring to a textbook. Nor has anyone found the family dog curled up in front of the fireplace with an autographed copy of *The Autobiography of a Yogi*. This information is inside of you. These are guidelines for intuitive stretching:

- Set up a comfortable environment for your practice. This might include soft music.

- It is always easier to stretch muscles when they are warm. Thus, some light exercise like walking until you begin to break a sweat is recommended. Another alternative would be to stretch after or while in a hot shower.

- Stretch on a firm padded surface such as an exercise mat.

- Pay attention to what you are doing. It should not hurt when you stretch. Pain is a sure signal that you are doing something with too much intensity or in a direction that your body was not meant to accommodate. Progress in stretching will come rapidly, within weeks, but it is accomplished in small, incremental steps. Stretch and move your body until you feel a solid pull on the muscles and maintain that position as long as you feel comfortable. Return to your original position slowly.

- Move slowly, and do not bounce into any stretch.

- Do not hold your breath while stretching, but keep your breath flowing. Visualize or sense your breath carrying oxygen to the areas being stretched. See and sense them loosening.

- Rest for a short time after each stretch.

- At the end of your stretching period take time to cool down and relax. An excellent time to do a breathing meditation or Progressive Relaxation is following stretching.

- While it is optimal to do a set stretch routine on a daily basis, do not limit your stretching to only one time or place. There are many moments throughout the day, at your desk, stopped in your car, etc, where you can relieve the stress and tension in certain muscle groups with a quick stretch.

❧ The muscles that support the head and neck are also intensely involved in the fight/flight response as primates (including humans) tend to pull their shoulders up to protect their necks, and appear bigger when threatened. Over time chronic tension in these muscles leads to tension headaches. Pay particular attention to these muscles in your stretching routine.

STAYING HEALTHY

Given the mind-body connection, it naturally follows that what is good for your body will be good for your mind and vice versa. Another important aspect of mastering your stress involves adopting a healthy lifestyle. A new branch of psychology called health psychology was developed in the 1970's to study the psychological factors that cause or contribute to illness and to promote behaviors that foster wellness. In particular, there is a focus on **psychosomatic illness**, where a physical disorder is affected (or in some cases even caused) by stress and/or emotional/psychological factors.

An unhealthy lifestyle, characterized by lack of exercise, poor diet, cigarette smoking, and alcohol or drug abuse will definitely increase your stress level, and eventually impact on your health and even your mortality. One study (Powell, Spain, Christenson & Mollenkamp, 1986) found at least half of premature deaths in the U.S. were a direct result of such unhealthy behaviors. A few years earlier the 1979 U.S. Surgeon General's report reached this same conclusion and went on to state that seven of the ten leading causes of death in the U.S. (such as from heart attacks, stroke, etc.) could be significantly reduced by adopting the following six lifestyle modifications:

❧ **improving diet**

❧ **quitting smoking**

❧ **getting regular physical exercise**

❧ **eliminating substance abuse**

❧ **practicing stress management techniques**

❧ **properly following medication regimens (especially for hypertension)**

Breslow (1983) found that when people adopted these healthy lifestyle behaviors, mortality rates declined significantly over a nine year period. In addition, this study showed that older people derived an even greater benefit from adoption of healthy behaviors that younger people, and the effect of lifestyle in general appeared more crucial to the health of males as compared to females.

The Importance of Exercise

By far, one of the simplest and most effective methods of stress management is to engage in regular exercise. Your body immediately reacts to stress by gearing up to respond physically to a stressor. Given that the original evolutionary purpose for the "fight or flight response" was to enable humans to fight or to flee physical danger, it follows that the natural outlet for built up physiological arousal is some type of vigorous physical activity or exertion. Exercise releases pent up muscular tension and allows your body to return to equilibrium.

Throughout most of human history our ancestors got plenty of exercise while taking care of basic living tasks such as searching or hunting for food, walking from one place to another, chopping wood for fires, etc. In current times, the advent of modern conveniences such as the automobile, elevator, supermarket, washing machine, etc, have greatly reduced the need for physical activity in order to accomplish basic tasks. It has gotten to the point where we don't even have to move to change the channel on the TV, thanks to the ever present remote control! Consequently, if you don't make a point of exercising you are probably leading a sedentary lifestyle, unless you are involved in a job or profession involving physical labor or physically exerting activities. But the vast majority of us have sedentary occupations, sitting behind a desk, barely flexing our arm muscles to push papers. The majority of college students train for and hold sedentary jobs after graduation. Leisure activities often involve sedentary pursuits as well. Thus, even though the tempo of modern life and the rate of change is accelerating (further adding to our stress), our activity levels are falling. And this comes at a time when our need for regular exercise to bolster coping resources is increasing.

The Benefits of Exercise

Is there proof that exercise helps us to cope with stress? Research clearly indicates that exercise is an effective stress reducer. Indeed, many studies have found that one of the most reliable differences between individuals with high vs. low levels of stress resistance was exercise and activity level (Brown, 1991; Kobasa, Maddi, & Puccetti, 1982; Roth & Holmes, 1987, just to name a few). In one study, McGilley and Holmes (1989), found that individuals who exercised regularly had lower cardiovascular and subjective responses to psychological stress than individuals who were not physically fit. Studies have also been done linking regular aerobic exercise to reductions in depression (McCann and Holmes, 1984), anxiety (Long, 1984) and improvements in self-esteem (Sonstroem, 1984). Furthermore, it is important to note that the amount and intensity of exercise necessary to produce stress management effects need not be overly extensive.

Research suggests that regular exercise, even of only moderate intensity, literally provides a dress rehearsal for dealing with stress. Why is this the case? Because the way your body responds to exercise is very similar to the way your body reacts to stress. During exercise your heart rate increases, blood pressure rises, respiration quickens, stress hormones are released, and muscles tense to perform the activity. Does this sound familiar? Therefore, engaging in regular exercise gives your body practice in experiencing stress, allowing you to develop more strength and stamina to cope.

It appears that the stress reducing effects of exercise are both short and long term. Many people find a single exercise session to be an excellent way of releasing tension. Proponents of regular exercise, who exercise at least three times weekly, typically report lowered levels of tension overall, even on days when they are less active (Holmes & Roth, 1988). So clearly, exercise has powerful positive effects on both our psychological and physical well being. These are some of the most notable benefits that are possible from engaging in regular exercise:

THE CUMULATIVE BENEFITS OF REGULAR EXERCISE

- **Improved sense of well-being, decreases in depression.**
- **Lowered anxiety and muscular tension.**
- **Greater ability to handle domestic and job-related stress.**
- **Increased endorphin production.**
- **Decreased production of stress hormones such as adrenalin and cortisol.**
- **Improvements in concentration and productivity.**
- **Quicker recovery from acute stress.**
- **Decreased fatigue; more energy and stamina.**
- **Reduction in blood pressure and resting heart rate.**
- **Improved cardiopulmonary functioning. Lower risk of heart disease.**
- **More restful sleep.**
- **Fewer physical complaints in general. Boosts in immune functioning.**
- **Better self-image and more self-confidence.**
- **A more attractive physique.**

The Role of Proper Nutrition

The old adage, *"You are what you eat",* is more true than you might imagine. Why is this? Because how well or how poorly you eat has a direct relationship to your ability to handle stress. Your body needs 40 to 60 nutrients to stay healthy. When you are under stress your need for all nutrients increases, especially the B vitamins (which help you combat stress) and calcium. Calcium is especially important because it counteracts the lactic acid buildup created by muscular tension. If your diet is deficient in milk and leafy vegetables your ability to reduce high levels of lactic acid related to stress would be impaired. This would leave you feeling more fatigued, anxious and irritable when under stress than if your diet was more balanced. You also need to realize that certain foods provide the biochemical building blocks for the neurotransmitters (brain chemicals) that affect mood and behavior, and consequently your ability to handle stress. For example, your body synthesizes the neurotransmitter **serotonin** from the amino acid tryptophan which is found in certain high carbohydrate foods such as bread, potatoes and pasta. Healthy levels of serotonin help you to stay relaxed, sleep well and have less sensitivity to pain. That is why we tend to crave carbohydrate rich foods when we are in a bad mood in order to get a temporary lift. On the other hand, it is well known that an over reliance or heavy consumption of caffeinated beverages can significantly heighten your arousal, and consequently increase your stress level. And it is also important to know that protein rich foods tend to improve concentration and alertness, particularly if you have them for breakfast. Missing breakfast altogether can deprive your brain of essential nutrients needed for effective functioning throughout your day. You can learn to make changes in your diet that will help you to cope with stress and increase your productivity level by heeding the following seven steps to good nutrition:

1. **Eat a Variety of Foods.**
2. **Eat More Whole Foods.**
3. **Avoid Caffeine.**
4. **Avoid Alcohol.**
5. **Take Vitamin and Mineral Supplements.**
6. **Eat Frequent, Calm Meals.**
7. **Maintain a Healthy Weight.**

SELF EXERCISES

1. The next time you are feeling stressed or anxious, or anticipate that this will be the case, take the time to focus on your breathing. It is likely that you will note more rapid, shallow respiration. Take several deep, slow, diaphragmatic breaths to center yourself, and notice the difference this makes. As suggested earlier in this chapter, practice this relaxed breathing pattern at non-stressful times to insure mastery of the technique for when you really need it.

2. If you are feeling tense, or are suffering from a tension headache, neck or shoulder soreness or stiffness, or have back pain, take the time to practice Progressive Relaxation exercises. Relieving the tension in various muscle groups will go a long way towards improving how you feel. Remember, pain can be reduced up to 40% just by relaxation alone! In fact, much of the effectiveness of painkillers comes from the fact that these medications relax you. Better yet, make practice of Progressive Relaxation exercises part of your regular routine and you will find that the frequency and severity of stress related aches and pains will decrease sharply. That is, you can prevent your body from cramping up in the first place.

KEY TERMS

Active Relaxation	**Witnessing Stance**	**Bruxism**
Passive Relaxation	**Stress Hardiness**	**Progressive Relaxation**
Diaphragmatic Breathing	**Warrior's Stance**	**Autogenic Training**
Self-Awareness	**Body Wisdom**	**Differential Relaxation**
Metacognition	**Psychosomatic Illness**	**Serotonin**
Metamood		

CHAPTER 5 QUESTIONS

True or False (T or F)

1. _____ Passive relaxation, such as watching TV, is not nearly as effective for reducing stress as practicing active relaxation techniques.

2. _____ When under stress most people breathe slowly, deeply and rhythmically.

3. _____ Rapid, shallow breathing causes too much oxygen to enter your bloodstream, which increases feelings of anxiety.

4. _____ When you breathe slowly, time seems to speed up.

5. ____ Stress hardy individuals have an internal locus of control.

6. ____ Stress hardy individuals focus on the problems inherent in adversity rather than waste their time attending to opportunities.

7. ____ Stress hardy individuals tend to be pessimistic so that they can be ready to deal with potential problems.

8. ____ Your body will let you know which muscles need to be stretched.

9. ____ Exercise is a potent stress management technique because it can provide a dress rehearsal for dealing with stress.

10. ____ The foods you consume have no bearing on your stress level or your ability to cope with stress.

Short-Answer Questions

1. _____ relaxation techniques are aimed at decreasing fight or flight arousal and restoring balance or homeostasis.

2. _____ breathing is a natural antidote to stress.

3. Adopting the _____ stance makes it easier to be objective about a situation and therefore helps you to choose the most effective response.

4. Stress hardy individuals possess attitudes of _____, _____, and _____.

5. _____ Relaxation Exercises are an effective method for reducing and/or eliminating muscular tension.

6. _____ is the type of breathing that triggers or accompanies panic attacks.

7. Proper _____ and getting plenty of regular _____ are vital not only for staying healthy but for stress management.

8. The neurotransmitter _____, which helps keep us calm, is synthesized from amino acids found in certain carbohydrates.

Essay Questions

1. What is the difference between passive relaxation and active relaxation methods?

2. How does diaphragmatic breathing differ from everyday breathing, anxious breathing, and hyperventilation?

3. What is the benefit of adopting the witnessing stance?

4. Describe the stress hardiness attitudes and how they contribute to stress resilience.

5. How does body wisdom differ from the typical conception of wisdom?

6. How can acting as if you feel better before you actually do feel better promote positive changes?

7. Describe the warrior's stance.

8. What is Progressive Muscle relaxation and how does it work?

9. What is the value in stretching your body, either by following a prescribed routine or following your intuitions?

10. Give some examples of the relationship between your nutrition and your ability to cope with stress.

11. Explain why exercise can be an effective stress reducer.

6

Create a Vision

"Each path is only one of a million paths. Therefore, you must always keep in mind that a path is only a path. If you feel that you must not follow it, you must not follow it under any circumstances. Any path is only a path. There is no affront to yourself or others in dropping it if that is what your heart tells you to do. But your decision to keep on the path or to leave it must be free of fear or ambition. I warn you! Look at every path closely and deliberately. Try it as many times as you think necessary. Then ask yourself, and yourself alone, one question . . . It is this . . . Does this path have a heart? All paths are the same. They lead nowhere. They are paths going through the brush or into the brush. Does this path have a heart is the only question. If it does, then the path is good. If it doesn't, it is of no use. Both paths lead nowhere, but one has a heart and the other doesn't. One makes for a joyful journey; as long as you follow it you will be one with it. The other will make you curse your life. One makes you strong, the other weakens you."

—Carlos Castenada, *The Teachings of Don Juan*

In the 1970's a song with a somewhat obvious but very true lyric was published. Joe Jackson wrote, *"You'll never get what you want til you know what you want."* One of the hallmarks of effective people is that they have a very clear sense of where they are going and how they intend to get there. The "how" of getting to their destination transcends specific techniques and stops along the way, and also includes a deep awareness of their values which guides their choices at each step. It can be said that they are on a mission based on a vision that emanates from their heart. Unless you are one of those rare individuals who seem to have always known what they want, you will need to do what has been done from ancient times. You will need to go on a vision quest.

THE VISION QUEST

"Dream lofty dreams, and as you dream, so shall you become.
Your vision is the promise of what you shall one day be."

—James Allen

A **vision quest** can be thought of as a search for or recognition of an aspect of your destiny. Not only does it include a strong sense of a place that you are moving towards, but also an awareness of allies that will help you along the path of your journey. In archaic times shamans, the spiritual guides and healers of their cultures, would direct individuals to undertake ordeals, oftentimes involving strenuous, food deprived quests after objects or animals. Sometimes these vision quests involved the ingestion of psychedelic substances which can produce an ordeal in their own right.

Dreams were also interpreted to assist the seeker in discovering what they really want. The object of all these techniques was to help an individual transcend the limitations of their everyday perceptions, and thus the limits that may have been placed on their own possibilities. Even today, many people report that it was in moments of extraordinary stress and upheaval, often life threatening, that what they wanted from life became crystal clear and ever after directed their actions.

Now before you close this book out of concern that we are going to recommend that you bungee jump out of a helicopter to determine your heart's desire, relax. There are alternatives available. In fact, the first step is one you've been playing with since childhood. Your vision quest can begin with a *wishing quest*. We all know the stories of three wishes conferred upon some fortunate soul by an enchanted being. We also know that these stories usually end with those so-called fortunate souls making some very bad choices. Subtly, we can be discouraged from the wishing process because we fear that we are not worth it (due to low self esteem), or that we will just screw it up, or that we will be disappointed if our wishes don't come true. Nonetheless, this is where it begins and we recommend that you start by engaging in a process we call **wishstorming**.

Self Exercise: Wishstorming

Wishstorming is basically brainstorming about what you would wish for if you had an unlimited supply of wishes. In fact, you *do* have an unlimited supply of wishes. There are no wish police out there making certain that you don't exceed the wish limit. As in brainstorming, let your imagination run free, but be as *specific* as possible when wishing and write your wishes down on paper. In other words, don't just wish for a car. Wish for a specific make, model, and color. Don't just wish for a relationship. Wish for someone with specific qualities. Wish for as many things as you can imagine, one hundred or more. Do this now and you will have taken the best first step towards freeing your imagination and establishing your mission.

A Consultation with the Grim Reaper

"No one on their death bed wishes they had spent more time at the office."

Anonymous

Wishing is like stretching in that you begin to become more comfortable with your desires. Common sense suggests that you can't go after all your desires simultaneously. And a closer look at your wish list will certainly suggest that some wishes are more of a priority to you than others. One of the ways to begin to narrow and clarify a vision is to make the possibility of your death part of the equation. You can do this in fantasy without risking life and limb. After all, it is true that not one of us is promised any more life beyond this moment.

Leo Buscaglia suggested that you can begin this process by answering the following question: What would you do if you had six days to live? What activities would you seek to do? Where would you like to visit? Who would you like to see? What would you want to say to them? How would your answers change if you had six months to live rather than six days?

Steven Covey suggests a slightly different strategy for using the specter of your own death to clarify your goals and values. He recommends an exercise wherein you attend your own funeral, and listen to several individuals eulogize you. These individuals should come from different areas of your life experience. For example, you might listen to a friend speak about you. Alternatively, you could listen to a family member, a wife or husband, a boss, a professor, or a child of yours even if it is yet to be born. Done properly this exercise will help you discover what things are really important to you. We are rather certain that you will realize that you must take into account the importance of relationships in the pursuit of your goals. Success in the presence of failed relationships can hardly be called success at all.

Ground Hog Day

By now you may be thinking, "I've had enough already of this death stuff". Is there another way to approach the process? We maintain that there is always another way to look at things. Another strategy is what we call Ground Hog Day, named afer the movie of the same name. In this film the main character is faced with the dilemma of living the same day over and over again. Initially this is a frightening situation for him, but soon he realizes that he is virtually immortal. He can do whatever he wants each day with no fear of death. In the beginning he indulges himself in all manner of pleasures. However, in time he becomes bored with a purely hedonistic life and becomes depressed to the point of wanting to commit suicide. He cannot though, because he cannot die. Thus he is forced to look deeper inside himself to find that which he really loves to do. Ultimately, the only thing which brings him satisfaction is to help others, and to master various skills (i.e. piano, sculpture, French Literature) which bring him joy.

Use your imagination and put yourself in a similar scenario. What would you do with eternity? What warms your heart and excites you? What can you do that leads you to become so absorbed in it that you lose track of time? What would be a part of a perfect day for you? The key in this plan is to do what Joseph Campbell, the renowned expert in the study of mythology, recommended to all of his students, *"Follow your bliss."* So often we can let the outside world dominate our choices of what to do. We end up doing what we "ought" to do or "should" do. No one else can tell you what you love to do. It is a most personal and crucial decision because life already has enough difficulties even when you are doing what you love to do. When you are doing something that doesn't really reflect your heart's desire, life can become downright miserable.

Getting Clarity: The Goal of the Goal

By now you should have a list of goals that excite you. But before you can proceed taking action toward the goals, you must take another action first. You must examine the goals themselves. In *Heart of the Mind*, Connie Rae and Steven Andreas recommend a number of steps that will assist you in thinking about your goals in a way that can increase the likelihood of your meeting them. But before we detail these steps, it is worth considering another critical question raised by the Andreases. They suggest that many people choose unrealistic goals, goals that are really impossible to achieve. For example, people might want to live lives free of mistakes or want to be loved by everyone. Their recommendation is to seek out the "goal of the goal" by asking this important question: *"What will this goal get for me?"* This question enables you to dig deeper into what it is that you really want. Many people have the goal of becoming rich and famous. Yet a moments glance at tabloid T.V. or the history of the rich and famous shows that this is not a group of very happy people. The more basic issue is: "What do you hope to get by being rich and famous?" If the goal of the goal is to feel worthwhile or loved then clearly there are other ways to achieve this without pursuing fabulous wealth and fame.

If you are pursuing a specific career, say medicine, because you believe it will secure money and respect, but you really hate studying science, then it would be wise to consider many other options that offer money and respect. You don't have to narrow the doorway to one specific career path. By seeking the goal behind the goal you broaden the number of options available to you for getting what you want. Thus, it is worth examining your goals carefully to make sure you really want them. Oftentimes what we really want is much more basic and involves feelings of safety, security and self-worth. In Chapter 7 we address the process of goal setting again by stressing the value of composing a "personal mission statement" which can assist you in prioritizing your goals. The lessons on goal setting in this chapter can be applied to the development of your mission statement.

SIX STEPS FOR SECURING YOUR GOALS

Assuming now that you know what you really want, we can move onto the steps the Andreases recommend for securing your goal.

STEP 1: *The goal must be stated in positive terms and in a way that you can achieve it yourself, regardless of the behavior of others.*

Rather than saying, "I no longer want to be lonely and overweight", it would be better to say, "I would like to have a healthier lifestyle and spend more time with friends." This way of thinking motivates you instead of reminding you of the aspects of yourself you dislike. It is also critical to set goals that do not depend upon others. For example, if your goal is , "I want my girlfriend to be more affectionate", you have set a goal over which you have only indirect control. This is when it is appropriate to ask, " What is the goal of the goal?" What would getting more affection from her do for you? Would it help you feel confident or more secure? You would probably benefit more from working directly on feelings of self-confidence that would allow you to ask for what you want and move on if it is not forthcoming.

STEP 2:   *Make certain you know how you will know that you have reached your goal.*

There are a couple of things to note here. One is that you don't generally achieve your goals in one step. It will take time, and it is good to have small benchmarks along the way that let you know that what you are doing is working. For instance, you may want an A grade in a course you are taking (perhaps even this course). In that case it makes sense to keep track of your grades on all tests and projects along the way. This is realistic evidence that lets you know if you are on the path to success. Sometimes people rely on evidence that does not give them useful feedback. For example, you are not necessarily an effective parent because your children tell you that you are doing a great job. Nor are you an effective employee on the rise in your career because you feel good at the end of the workday. Perhaps you feel great because you spend your time at work catching up on your sleep! Performance evaluations are a better measuring rod. Therefore, take the time to ask how you would know if you are reaching your goals. Then take the time to feel satisfaction at each step along the way.

STEP 3:   *Describe your goals as specifically as you can.*

This will be particularly important when we discuss the actual processes of moving towards your goals. Where, when, and with whom you want to reach your goals are critical questions that will help you clarify your goals. If one of your goals is to feel more passion and excitement about your life, do you want to feel that all the time, at every moment? Is passion and excitement what you want to feel at a funeral, or while having lunch with your grandmother? Do you want to feel passion and excitement during a proctological exam? As you prepare to reach your goals ask yourself what will be the sights, sounds, and feelings that will accompany reaching your goal. For example, "When I hear my professor assign a large term project, I will feel challenged and confident that I can do what is necessary to get the grade I want."

STEP 4:   *Are your goals compatible with each other?*

Sometimes you may find yourself in situations where you need to choose between two or more different goals or alternatives that are incompatible or contradictory. When you are being pulled in different directions, you are in what is called a "conflict situation". Lewin (1935) identified four basic forms of conflict situations.

> ❖ **The Approach-Approach Conflict.** Here you are forced to choose between two options or goals, both of which are very desirable. For example, you may want to see two movies, both of which are playing at the same time and you have to make a choice. Most people initially vacillate between the two alternatives, but then resolve the dilemma by deciding that one option is slightly better than the other.

- **The Avoidance-Avoidance Conflict.** In this situation you are stuck choosing between two equally undesirable alternatives. These scenarios bring to mind the old adage, *"being between a rock and a hard place".* For example, let's say you get sick with a bacterial infection. You may hate going to the doctor but you are also aware that if you don't you may get sicker. Often, people react to this dilemma by freezing in place, that is, by doing nothing. Sometimes a conflicted person will bail out completely, a response called "leaving the field." This type of conflict is much harder to settle than the approach-approach conflict. Typically it is resolved more slowly and only after considerable fretting and indecision.

- **The Approach-Avoidance Conflict.** This common situation occurs when a goal has both negative and positive aspects, leading to a tendency to both approach and avoid it simultaneously. For example, you might be offered a job you really dislike, but it offers a great salary that would bail you out of your financial problems. Resolving this conflict often involves making a partial approach and attempting to split the difference (i.e. trying to find a happy medium between the positive and negative aspects). Returning to our example, you could decide to take the job for the short run to get ahead financially, while continuing to look for one more to your liking, even with a lower salary.

- **The Double Approach-Avoidance Conflict.** Most of the conflicts we face in life are far more complex than the former three. More typically you will find yourself in situations where the options contain multiple positive and negative aspects. For example, you might be offered your dream job, but it requires relocating out of state, away from your family and friends. As with the Avoidance-Avoidance conflict, individuals tend to vacillate between the two alternatives.

Most of us have more than one goal we want to reach. This step simply asks that you make sure you find a way to reach both goals or once again return to evaluating what you really want. For example, since the women's rights movement many women were faced with the dilemma of balancing career and motherhood. Now, having a career and being a mother are not incompatible goals, but it requires very clear thought about how they are to be balanced or sequenced in order to support reaching both goals.

STEP 5: *Assess what you already have and what you are going to need in order to reach your goals.*

In other words, what are your skills, your assets? If you want to be a stand-up comedian, you may already possess a wonderful sense of humor and a quick mind. You may need a lot of confidence building, public speaking skills and practice, an ability to withstand criticism so as to grow a thick skin and continue to improve, or even some training regarding how to formulate an act. This kind of thinking allows you to direct your energy in the appropriate directions.

STEP 6: *Make a plan.*

A journey of a thousand miles begins with a single step. It is often useful to work backwards from the place where you want to be to the place where you are now in order to determine your very next step. For example, if you've decided upon a career as an attorney, the step just before entering practice is passing the bar exam. The step before that is completing law school. The step prior to that is getting into law school which requires taking and scoring well on the law boards (LSAT). And of course you need to have a bachelors degree before the law boards results are significant. Obviously we can take this process all the way back to toilet training, as most attorneys do not practice in diapers either. However, the point is that there is a next reasonable step to take and you need to take that step. Working backwards from your goal lays out a path for you to follow.

The Role of Rewards in Goal Setting

It is vitally important that the goals you set for yourself be realistic. If you set goals that are clearly impossible to attain, you are setting yourself up for failure and disappointment. On the other hand, if you set your goals too low you will deprive yourself of the satisfaction of achievement and never develop your full potential. Albert Bandura (1982), has also offered rules for appropriate and realistic goal setting which emphasis the role of rewarding yourself. This process of setting goals and then rewarding yourself for progress towards the goal is called **self-regulation**. He recommends the following four steps:

1. Establish short term, specific goals. Or break your goal up into a series of sub-goals or steps. This recommendation echoes the tips above.

2. Reward yourself with something concrete (i.e. a movie, a massage, new clothes, dessert, etc.) when you attain a short term goal.

3. Establish your own standards for success. Don't let your friends, parents, etc. determine what success is for you. Let your own standards be your guide.

4. Make a realistic appraisal of your abilities and adopt goals that draw from your strengths.

VISUALIZATION

As an infant, before you learned to speak, you were able to think, but this rudimentary thinking took the form of images rather than words or phrases, which you had not yet mastered. That is why, for most people, our earliest memories from childhood tend to be fragmented images rather than conversations or events. Indeed, mental imagery is perhaps the most basic way that your mind represents and stores information. And imagery is the primary medium by which your **unconscious mind** operates. Freud, in his psychodynamic theory, developed the concept of the unconscious mind to describe that part of the mind containing aspects of our functioning of which we are totally unaware. Freud believed that the mind is like an iceberg which is mostly hidden underwater. He saw our conscious mind as being the part of the iceberg that is above the waterline. But below the surface is the much larger unconscious region containing thoughts, wishes, feelings and memories of which we are largely unaware, but which influence our feelings and behaviors nevertheless. When asleep, as you detach from your conscious mind and waking verbal thought, your unconscious mind emerges and dream images abound. The imagery of the unconscious mind is not confined to just mental pictures, it can represent impressions from any of your senses (i.e. remembered sounds, feelings, aromas, tastes, etc).

Visualization is a time honored method of deliberately using imagery, visual and otherwise, to alter your feelings, your behavior, and even your physiology. Because of the dominance of imagery in the functioning of your unconscious mind (which has a powerful effect upon your motivation), visualization practice can have a profound effect on your emotions or behavior, over and beyond your conscious efforts to change. Over one hundred years ago, the French pharmacist, Emil Coue, wrote that the power of the imagination exceeds that of the conscious will. That is, you may or may not be able to will the achievement of a specific goal, but repeatedly visualizing attaining that goal greatly increases the probability of success. Mastery of the art and practice of visualization will help propel you down the road to effectiveness.

Steven Covey, in his Seven Habits book, also speaks to the importance of this as he exhorts you to *"begin with the end in mind"*. With this he is talking both about the importance of setting goals *and* being able to visualize the achievement of those goals as necessary prerequisites to effectiveness.

Applications to Sports Performance

In a now classic study (Richardson, 1969) three groups of boys were tested on their ability to make free throws on a basketball court. After the initial assessment they were instructed to spend the next two weeks in one of three ways. One group practiced shooting free throws. Another group did nothing with a basketball for two weeks. The third group was instructed to mentally rehearse shooting the basketball, to visualize themselves shooting and making free throws. All the groups were then retested. The group that did nothing showed no change in their free throw proficiency. The group that actually practiced with the ball improved 24%. The group that only visualized improved 23%! This is only one of many demonstrations of the power of human beings to achieve extraordinary results by controlling the content of their thoughts.

In a comprehensive treatise called *Peak Performance*, Dr. Charles Garfield documents extensive research done with world class athletes in Russia and the United States. He states unequivocally that almost all world class performers are visualizers. In fact, in the realm of the world class athlete, he cites a study done in the then Soviet Union where researchers compared different training regimens among their athletes. Some athletes spent almost 100% of their time in physical training for their event. Others spent between 25%, 50%, and 75% of their time in mental training and rehearsal (i.e. visualization for their event). The results showed that performance results improved as the amount of time devoted to mental practice increased. Dr. Garfield also points out that, "peak performers are highly motivated by a deep and personal sense of mission which is distinctly different from the highly specific and measurable goals each person may set."

In yet another fascinating demonstration of the power of imagery and belief, Talbot (1991) cites a study done at Hebrew University in Israel. In this study several groups of soldiers were sent on a march of 25 miles. Each group of soldiers, however, was given different information as to the actual distance they had marched or had yet to march. When stress hormone levels were measured in each group the levels reflected how far the soldiers thought they had marched, not the actual distance. In other words, their bodies responded to their *imagined* stress, not the reality of the extent of their exertion!

Applications for Healing

Cancer researcher Dr. Carl Simonton, in his book *Getting Well Again*, reports increased longevity in cancer patients who practice relaxation and visualize their diseases remitting. This process literally involves creating vivid mental images of the disease process, a tumor for instance, and then deliberately imagining that the image is changing. For example, you might imagine a tumor as a black octopus with tentacles reaching into various body parts. You then imagine that your chemotherapy or radiation treatment is acting as a weapon, shrinking the octopus, damaging its arms, changing or fading its color to white, and causing it to eventually disappear. While this treatment approach is still controversial, it is becoming a widely used technique in fighting cancer.

In *Nothing is Impossible*, Christopher Reeve's moving account of his life as a quadriplegic as a result of a 1995 fall off of a horse headfirst, he eloquently describes how he employed visualization techniques for healing a very serious, deep decubitus ulcer on his ankle. His doctors had advised him that his foot would need to be amputated if this wound would not heal. For months the ulcer had worsened and resisted standard antibiotic treatment and amputation loomed.

> "I was put on a ten-day course of a powerful antibiotic administered intravenously. As I sat on the porch of our summer home in Massachusetts, gazing for hours on end at the hills surrounding our property, **I kept picturing my ankle as it used to be**. . . . It was far more difficult to sit on the porch with my leg propped up on pillows constantly trying to push doubt and negativity out of my mind. One minute I would think, *'I can do this—I can heal this wound.'* The next minute I would think, *'What are you talking about? You don't have any special powers'.* Then I would try yet again to picture my ankle as it used to be and tell myself that it deserved to be whole. I reminded myself that I had always recovered from all kinds of setbacks. . . . Six months later the wound had closed. Within a year the ankle appeared perfectly normal.
>
> I don't claim to understand precisely why my wound healed and my leg was saved. Certainly the prescribed antibiotic is an aggressive therapy. But even the strongest antibiotics don't always work. I had learned that from other treatments when I was in rehab. Looking back at it now, I believe that I wouldn't have recovered without the drug. But I also believe that I wouldn't have recovered without an ironclad agreement between my mind and my body that I had to keep my leg."

Simonton is far from alone in his faith in the power of belief and visualization. Both Jeanne Achtenberg and Bernie Siegel in their respective texts, *Imagery in Healing*, and *Love, Medicine and Miracles*, cite many examples that indicate that our beliefs affect our physical health for better or worse. When you believe you will survive and thrive, your probability of doing so increases. If you believe your disease is a death sentence, then unfortunately that becomes true with increasing frequency as well. In fact, Achtenberg achieved a 95% rate of accuracy in predicting who would survive their illness and who would die simply by a careful analysis of patients' drawings of themselves, their cancers, their immune systems, and their treatment.

Biofeedback practitioners have found that their patients are able to affect aspects of their physiology with visualization. For example, patients are routinely taught (via the autogenic training technique described in Chapter 5) to deliberately warm their hands and/or feet by imagining that their hands and feet are in tubs of hot water or under a heat lamp. The latter has applications for lowering blood pressure and the former is used for counteracting migraine headaches.

The placebo effect, as discussed in Chapter 4, also stands as powerful proof of the role of belief and how we see things in the creation of our reality. In fact, in the realm of metaphysical and spiritual practice it is understood that the eyes are more than simply receptive organs. The root word of eye actually translates as "fountain". That is, the eyes send energy out and thus are involved in creation itself. Pick up virtually any revered text of wisdom teachings and you will find references and specific instructions for controlling and shaping your thoughts and images to manifest the life you desire. This is best summed up by Michael Talbot in his book *The Holographic Universe.*

> "Paramahansa Yogananda advised people to visualize the future they desired for themselves and charge it with the 'energy of concentration'. As he put it, 'Proper visualization by the exercise of concentration and will power enables us to materialize thoughts, not only as dreams or visions in the mental realm, but also as experiences in the material realm.'
>
> Indeed, such ideas can be found in a wide range of disparate sources. *'We are what we think,'* said the Buddha. *'All that we are arises with our thoughts. With our thoughts we make the world.' 'As a man acts, so does he become. As a man's desire is, so is his destiny,'* states the Hindu pre-Christian Brihadaranyaka Upanishad. *'All things in the world of Nature are not controlled by Fate for the soul has a principle of its own,'* said the fourth-century Greek philosopher Iamblichus. *'Ask and it will be given you . . . If ye have faith, nothing shall be impossible unto you,'* states the Bible. And, *'The destiny of a person is connected with those things he himself creates and does.'* wrote Rabbi Steinsaltz in the kabbalistic *Thirteen Petaled Rose.*"

The Role of Modeling

The principle of **modeling** describes the ability of humans to learn how to do something simply by observing others. This is also referred to in the literature as **observational learning**. It works whether the models are live or on a TV screen. It also apparently works when the models are in your imagination. *And* it also works well when the model is a new, improved, and more successful you. How is it that this occurs? One explanation seems to be based on principles first outlined by Albert Bandura in his Social Cognitive Learning theory. While this theory has many elements, it relies on thoughts, beliefs, and a principle known as modeling to explain why you behave as you do and how you acquire behaviors and skills. The importance of this principle will become clearer as you proceed in learning how to visualize and enhance your ability to attain your goals.

THE PROCESS OF VISUALIZATION

Now that a case has been made for the power of **visualization**, it remains for us to specify how to actually use this capacity in a way that works to your advantage. What follows is a discussion of critical principles in understanding and using this process.

1. Begin by mastering voluntary relaxation skills.

This is an absolutely critical element in the use of visualization. Your body is a reflection of your mental state. If you are tense, anxious, fearful, or lack confidence, this is reflected in your musculature. Thus you may verbalize positive thoughts and even conjure up positive images. But if your body is presenting a competing picture of negativity then you are sending mixed messages to yourself and your results will be mixed at best. When you relax completely prior to your visualization practice, you are creating on a blank sheet of paper. There are no competing images to interfere with the process of your learning. You might also think of this process as familiar to recording music in a studio. Recording studios are deliberately soundproofed so that only the music played in the studio is recorded, not the sound of traffic or conversation in the hallway. Relaxation is the moral equivalent of silence in your body, and allows for a clearer recording of the behaviors, skills, and attitudes you wish to acquire.

The techniques discussed in Chapter 5 will allow you to master the act of relaxation. In addition, we will also end this section with a discussion of basic meditation technique which is another pathway to relaxation and the quieting of competing thoughts.

2. Garbage in, garbage out.

Your consciousness is an equal opportunity employer. It really doesn't care if what you visualize is good or bad for you. It just produces results. In this case, **what you see is what you get.** Consider this analogy. You can think of visualization as being to your mind what food is to your body. Positive images are the equivalent of health food and negative images are like feeding yourself junk food. If you recall, earlier we stated the necessity of stating your goals positively. This is to avoid the pitfall of visualizing and manifesting what you *don't* want. For example, one of the author's discovered this principle in a rather embarrassing fashion . . .

> I was waiting at the first tee of the golf course with my father and some of his friends. The first tee is the one place on a golf course where you are being observed by many people. My concern, my absolute preoccupation, was that I did not want to embarrass myself by hitting a terrible shot in front of my father and all of these people. To that end I began saying to myself, "just don't shank the ball", a particularly bad shot. I kept thinking this over and over again until it was my turn to hit. In short order, I stepped up to the ball and shanked it! I got exactly what I didn't want because I had rehearsed it so thoroughly.

3. Visualization is much more than images.

You don't necessarily see things when you visualize. This is a crucial point because many people are not aware of the visual aspect of their thoughts. If you ask them to visualize something they panic because they believe that they should be seeing a mental television set with crisp, clear images. For those of you that can do this, that is wonderful. For those of you that cannot, there is no need to worry because *all* of your senses are involved in the visualization process. It is sufficient to have a *"sense"* of what it would be like if your imagined future or outcome was occurring. In other words, as long as you "know" what your image would look like if you could see, or hear, or feel it, that is good enough for the purposes of creation. In an ideal scenario the outcome that you imagine should be developed as vividly as possible. You should see, hear, and feel your future in as much detail as possible. For instance, if your goal is to be more assertive in your communications, it would be best not only to hear the words in the appropriate speed and tone of voice, but also to see yourself acting in an assertive fashion. You could also see the people you are speaking to responding appropriately and receptively to your communication. And lastly, you should feel what it would be like to communicate in this way.

Self Exercise: Enhancing Your Visualizations

If you have difficulty with making visual images and would like to learn to enhance your ability, try this simple exercise. Just close your eyes and allow yourself to recall your bedroom, or a pleasant experience, either recent or from childhood, or what you ate at your last meal, in as much detail as possible. Pay special attention to the colors, shapes and lighting, as well as any tastes, smells, textures, temperatures, sounds, physical sensations and feelings you experienced. If you are not a strong visualizer that likely means that you tend to store your memories in another **representational system**. We use representational systems to encode information in our brain. There are five primary representational systems relating to each of the five senses: **auditory** (our hearing represented in sounds, words and language); **visual** (our vision represented in mental pictures); **kinesthetic** (our sense of touch represented by feelings and physical sensations); **gustatory** (taste); and **olfactory** (smells). Each person has a dominant representational system, a sense that they favor for encoding and remembering information. Although the visual system is typically dominant, many individuals prefer another representational system for storing memories. If this is the case for you, remember any experience by tuning into whatever sense is most dominant for you, and then imagine any visual images associated with these other sensory images. So, for example, if you are remembering your bedroom, first recall the sensation of lying in your comfortable bed and feeling the softness and warmth of your comforter or bedspread while listening to your stereo. Now connect that with actually seeing what that comforter or bedspread looks like. What color is it? Does it have a pattern? What color are the walls in your room or the floor? Where is your dresser, or your desk? What can you see when you look out of your window? Basically, you can use memories from one sense to bridge into memories from any other sense. Doing this enables you to make your visualizations more vivid by giving them the depth of multiple sensory representations.

4. Use participant and observer imagery.

This brings us to another subtle but critical distinction in the visualization process, participant and observer imagery. Consider for a moment that all of the movie special effects you have ever witnessed originated first in someone's imagination, therefore, these are available to you as well. Special effects have different effects on you as you watch them. For example, most likely you have experienced simulation rides (such as those at

Disney World or other amusement parks) and their powerful impact on your physiology. You can actually feel as if you are on a roller coaster or an airplane if the ride presents you with the sights and sounds you would experience if you were actually on the plane or coaster. This is what is referred to as participant imagery—you feel as if you are actually participating in the experience. Observer imagery occurs when you see a roller coaster or airplane "out there" or in the distance. The difference in your experience is that you may have feelings about the airplane or coaster, but you don't feel as if you are on it, directly experiencing it. It is the difference between watching a mental image of yourself riding the coaster (a third person experience) vs. imagining yourself actually riding it (a first person experience). Depending upon the results that you want, you need to use these two variations appropriately.

Participant imagery involves actually practicing the result you want in your mind. This is how world class athletes prepare for their events without leaving their rooms. You feel what it is like to be doing what it is you want to be doing. Your muscles are actually experiencing the same electrical impulses that they would during the actual activity. In other words, there really is no difference to your brain between real and imagined. Observer imagery has a different effect. In this context it tends to be more motivating. As you see yourself behaving, looking, and sounding as you would like, you tend to be positively motivated to expend the energy to do what is necessary to achieve the result. Using observer imagery can also be helpful when imagining yourself doing something which is frightening or anxiety provoking for you. Since you are viewing yourself at a distance when using observer imagery, it can give you more emotional distance, and as a result help allay anxiety. You can then shift to participant imagery once you feel comfortable with your observer images.

5. *The recommended sequence for the process of visualization would be as follows:*

    a. Decide on your goal, the actions and attitudes you wish to adopt.

    b. Find a model who can do what you want to do.

    c. Get into a comfortable position.

    d. If possible, make sure that your environment is relatively quiet and free from distractions.

    e. Use a relaxation technique to establish a receptive mental state.

    f. Begin to imagine or sense your model doing the desired goal or behaviors.

    g. Study what the model does, how do they look, sound, move, etc., until you can vividly "sense" them in your imagination.

    h. Substitute yourself for the model. That is, see yourself doing the desired goal and allow yourself to feel motivated.

    i. Step into the image and see, hear, and feel what you would feel if you were doing the desired goal.

    j. Practice this for 15 minutes daily. For faster results practice 2–3 times daily.

6. Let go and be patient.

This part is a little trickier. Visualization is effective. You do it all the time effortlessly. When you begin to deliberately direct it, it is often difficult to maintain that effortless quality. After all, you want something and have been taught that you need to try your hardest to get those things you want. Unfortunately, trying hard can be counterproductive because it is associated with tension which interferes with the visualization process. Also, there is a tendency when embarking on this process to worry whether or not it will work. You may remember other things you wished for and never got. You may find yourself looking for results each day and feeling frustrated that your progress isn't more obvious. All we can say is to continue to practice, relax, and let go. All of the other worry and concern leads to visualizing all of the things you don't want. If you are having difficulty with this, review the lessons from Chapter 2 on maintaining an optimistic perspective. Visualization is similar to gardening. You plant seeds of positive thought through imagery and pluck out the weeds of negative thoughts by refusing to invest your energy in contemplating all the things that can go wrong. When you plant a seed, you don't dig it out of the ground every day to check it's progress. Now we are not suggesting that you never plan for the possibility of things not going your way. Life will definitely surprise you. But, when you are exercising the power of visualization it is important to keep your eye on the prize. Obviously, what is required is a mind able to maintain a focus on the present moment. This is also a skill that can be learned and is the primary benefit of the practice of meditation.

MEDITATION

There is no shortage of reading material regarding the value of meditative practice (Goleman, 1977; Kabat-Zinn, 1990; Ram Dass, 1990). Nor is there any lack of scientific research demonstrating that the practice of meditation indeed works to reduce and relieve pain (Kabat-Zinn, 1990), to lower blood pressure and the advance of atherosclerosis (Benson, 1984; Ornish, 1992) and to facilitate healing in general. Deep relaxation, euphoria, and heightened awareness can also be byproducts of meditative practice (Wallace & Benson, 1972; Kabat-Zinn, 1994; Alexander et al., 1993). People who regularly meditate report less stress, anxiety, depression, and hostility than non-meditators. However, while meditation has these many benefits, they are ultimately not the point of the practice. All meditation methods are like roads leading to Rome. There are lots of ways to get there. In this case Rome is the ability to maintain a focused awareness in the present moment. It is to be in each and every moment without being preoccupied with thoughts of the past or the future. It is to realize that you are much more than you think you are. That realization depends upon recognizing that you are more than your thoughts. Meditative practice is designed to break you out of your habitual patterns of perceiving and thinking about the world and who you are. While practical results abound in terms of improved concentration, relaxation, health, and awareness, it is ultimately a spiritual journey of discovery. *Every* religious tradition has some practice within it which can be considered meditative.

Attitudes for Mindfulness Meditation

Before we embark on a discussion of technique it is important to consider the attitudes that you want to bring to whatever practice you begin. In his book *Full Catastrophe Living*, Jon Kabat-Zinn suggests cultivating the following attitudes as part of the practice of meditation, particularly the practice of mindfulness.

1. Non-Judging

As you begin a meditative practice you can be sure you will immediately discover that you are making judgments about every aspect of your experience: "This is good." "This is bad." "Who cares about that?" These judgments create feelings and often stress. When you notice this kind of thinking arising, remind yourself to suspend judgment and just notice whatever comes up including the tendency to judge.

2. Patience

We discussed patience earlier in this chapter. Suffice it to say that things emerge in their own time. You cannot make a butterfly emerge from its cocoon sooner than necessary without damaging the butterfly. You can generally recognize impatience when you decide that there is something missing in this moment, a kind of judgment. All these practices take time and you make progress by accepting each moment of practice as being just where you need to be for now, simply because it is now.

3. Beginner's Mind

To quote Dr. Kabat-Zinn, *"We tend to take the ordinary for granted and fail to grasp the extraordinariness of the ordinary."* To see things with the wonder of a child seeing things for the first time is to practice **beginner's mind**. So often we don't really see, hear, or feel what is here, but instead react to our memories of similar moments, but not this moment. How many times have you walked in a familiar place and suddenly seen something that you never noticed before and realized it had *always* been there. That is all too typical of our perceptions. We often see those closest to us as we remember them and not as they are now. Experiment with this. Look at someone familiar to you and see them as they are now.

4. Trust

This is a most crucial point. Just as there is no shortage of texts about meditation, there is no shortage of teachers and gurus either, and not all necessarily have your well-being or best interests at the top of their agenda. Ultimately you must learn to trust your own internal guidance and intuition. Everyone makes mistakes along the way. The best teachers will strive to help you develop this trust in *yourself*. You are not here to imitate others and follow their orders and ideas about who you should be. You are here to become more fully yourself.

5. Non-Striving

This is very similar to a recommendation for a "passive attitude" that Dr. Herbert Benson makes in his landmark text *The Relaxation Response*. Most everybody begins meditation because they want something. The promise of meditation is that you will get something, but not if you try too hard. You simply need to do the technique and not worry whether it is working. If you notice that you are unable to let go of a preoccupation with certain thoughts, simply notice this instead of striving to rid yourself of these thoughts, and then return to your technique.

6. Acceptance

Dr. Kabat-Zinn again summarizes this attitude beautifully. Although he does not talk directly about effectiveness per se, the relevance of adopting this attitude to the cultivation of personal effectiveness should be obvious.

> "Acceptance does not mean that you have to like everything or that you have to take a passive attitude toward everything and abandon your principles and values. It does not mean that you are satisfied with things as they are or that you are resigned to tolerating things as they 'have to be'. It does not mean that you should stop trying to break free of your own self-destructive habits or to give up on your desire to change and grow, or that you should tolerate injustice, for instance, or avoid getting involved in changing the world around you because it is the way it is and therefore hopeless. Acceptance as we are speaking of it simply means that you have come around to a willingness to see things as they are. This attitude sets the stage for acting appropriately in your life, no matter what is happening. You are much more likely to know what to do and have the inner conviction to act when you have a clear picture of what is actually happening than when your vision is clouded by your mind's self-serving judgements and desires or its fears and prejudices.

7. Letting Go

If you know how to fall asleep you know how to "let go". If you have ever had insomnia you also know how difficult letting go can sometimes be. You cannot will yourself to fall asleep. Paradoxically, sleep comes when you let go and stop trying to fall asleep. Letting go means that it is important not to try to hold on to any aspect of our experience but simply to notice it and let it go. When we want to hold on to certain thoughts, this can tell us a lot about what may be causing difficulty in our lives. There are things to discover in the practice of meditation that go beyond the power of words to say. No one of us is ultimately any better or worse or less capable of discovering the beauty of their existence. However, you do need to practice something to move you down the road toward Rome. What follows is a discussion of basic techniques to get you started.

The Practice of Meditation

Meditation can be divided into techniques which emphasize focused concentration on a word, phrase, sound, image, physical movement or posture, or on techniques which emphasize the cultivation of mindfulness or awareness in each present moment.

Focused Concentration

To begin the practice it is best to find a quiet place and to sit in a comfortable position with an erect spine. You could do this practice lying down or in a recliner but very often the tendency is to then fall asleep and not cultivate concentration and awareness.

So for that reason we recommend that you do your practice in an upright sitting position. You next need to choose a mental device, i.e. something upon which to focus your concentration. Some people choose to focus on their breath, the sound and feel of the process of the breath moving in and out of their body. Some focus on the word *"in"* as they breath in and *"out"* as they breath out. Other people simply choose a word or phrase to focus on such as *"relax"* or *"peace"*. Still others choose a sound with resonance which is referred to as a **"mantra"**. A common example of a mantra is the sound *"Ommmm"* which is repeated over and over again in the mind. An important point to note here is that there is data that suggests that focal points which have some spiritual significance or deep meaning for the meditator have led to more clinical improvement and more disciplined practice (Benson, 1984).

Once you have chosen your focal point simply sit and bring your attention to it. To use breathing as an example, you would bring your attention to the in and out movement of the breath and, if you like, repeat in your mind the word *"in"* on the inhalation and *"out"* on the exhalation. That is basically it in terms of technique. What you will initially and over time experience may vary considerably. One thing is certain: You will find your mind wandering everywhere and that is fine. When this occurs, notice that you are thinking and label it as thinking. Then return to the in and out of your breathing. Do not try to stop thinking because that is just doing more thinking. Notice your thoughts and let them go. You may want to think of your thoughts as bubbles rising before your eyes. Let them float by and return to noticing your breath. With continued practice and cultivation of the proper attitudes you will begin to notice the differences in your life.

If you were to practice chanting, or **Tai Chi** (a moving meditation) or **Qi Gong** (a focus on the movement of energy) or any other discipline, the challenge and ultimate results tend to be quite similar. All roads lead to increased awareness and that is to be treasured above and beyond any specific path. These paths take you toward awareness by way of concentration. That is, as you gain the ability to concentrate you are able to stay more aware and involved in the moment, and you are less distracted by the meanderings of your thoughts.

Mindfulness

Mindfulness is the cultivation of awareness by practicing awareness. Virtually any activity whether eating, walking, lovemaking, driving, bathing, etc. can become the vehicle for your practice. You can even consider the breathing meditation above as a kind of mindfulness practice. Attention brought to the breath over time generally results in slower, quieter, deeper breathing, i.e. relaxation.

Perhaps mindfully eating is the best place to get a feel for how unaware we are and how practicing mindfulness can increase awareness and lead to very practical results. How many times have you sat down to a meal and ate without truly tasting more than the first bite or two? Do you eat while reading or watching TV? Do you eat when you are not really feeling hungry? No, this is not a chapter on dieting, but a lack of mindfulness of all of the processes involved in eating can certainly lead to gaining weight. Try this mindfulness experiment when you have some quiet, uninterrupted time to enjoy a meal.

Self Exercise: Mindfulness Meditation

Set your plate down and simply look at your food. Attend to the colors, shapes, and textures. Notice the aromas or perhaps steam rising up from the dish. Also at this moment attend to your own body. Is your mouth salivating? What is your tongue doing? Is your stomach growling? Do you find it difficult to be patient while doing this exercise? What are your thoughts like? Does this seem pointless to you? Do you wonder if you are doing this correctly?

As you prepare to take your first bite notice your intention to pick up your utensil. Feel your arm, hand, and fingers move to grasp the fork or spoon. Feel the utensil in your hand. Are you breathing or holding your breath? Feel the additional weight of the food on your fork. Notice your arm rising, your mouth opening. Now taste the food. Notice the actual action of chewing and the change in taste as the food moves around your mouth. Be aware of the impulse to swallow. Keep chewing. Swallow. Feel the food go down your esophagus. Perhaps feel one bite heavier. Set your silverware down with full awareness. Are you breathing? Begin again.

> What did you become aware of in this process?
>
> How satisfying can a single bite of food be?
>
> Do you think you would eat more or less if you ate mindfully?
>
> Did the food really taste good? Did you taste something different from what you expected?
>
> How might your experience change if you were blind or had a head cold?

This same intensity can be brought to observing any process including your own thinking. To bring this discussion full circle, there is incredible value in observing your thoughts because that is how you create the world of your experience. If you remember, earlier in this chapter we said that visualization works whether you want it to or not. Meditative disciplines not only have the capability of giving you the relaxed concentration necessary to making the visualization process work, but they also illuminate that which you have been visualizing all along, but which may have been operating on an unconscious level, out of your awareness. As we said at the very beginning of this text, you create your reality. Meditation allows you to see how you have been doing it. If you take the responsibility and make the commitment to practice, you can reshape your life. If you are creating your reality with your thoughts, words, and images, why not be proactive and deliberately choose to create an effective reality by consciously employing thoughts, words and images that promote your effectiveness.

THE LARGER CONCEPTUAL FRAMEWORK

"Have you ever felt helped by unseen hands?"

"Do you ever feel sorry for the man who has no invisible means of support?"

Bill Moyers' questions to Joseph Campbell

Our discussion thus far of creating a vision, goal setting, and the place of meditative practice has alluded to a spiritual reality which frequently goes unacknowledged in psychology textbooks. And yet when we consider what we are discussing here, the path of our lives' endeavors, how can we not consider questions regarding the ultimate meaning and purpose of life.

To discuss a spiritual perspective in a book about personal effectiveness may impress some as painfully obvious, and others as patently unscientific and unnecessary. After all, we, the authors, are scientists and as such are obligated to attempt to cite evidence to substantiate our point of view. Traditionally, spiritual matters have been outside the realm of the scientific and relegated to the corridors of faith and speculation, or, at worst, merely the superstitions of those with an unsophisticated grasp of probability theory, placebo effects, and psychopathology. Yet the vast majority of people on our planet hold to some kind of belief system which affects their day to day quality of life. These beliefs, unscientific or not, can be sources of great pain, guilt, feelings of inadequacy, hopelessness, confusion, and fear. But they can also be the source of love, compassion, joy, vitality and a peace that surpasses understanding. A complete treatise on this subject is well beyond the scope of this text, but to leave it unaddressed is to abandon our charge of presenting you with a wide buffet of ideas regarding the process of becoming an "effective individual".

But what if you are scientifically minded? Then you are in great company because many of the leading scientific minds of our time and the past century realize that, in fact, the most advanced representations and speculations about the nature of reality do not preclude the possibility of a spiritual reality. Furthermore, they do not suggest a reality which is capricious and unlawful. They simply suggest that our most sophisticated attempts at measurement, in the scientific sense, have led us to the realization that consciousness, the activities of our minds, directly affects the "reality" around us. This is indeed a slippery slope for science because it implies that the results of experiments may vary solely due to the intentions of the researchers. This is a variable that is seldom controlled, and frankly, in most situations, was thought to be something that did not need to be controlled, outside of placebo studies.

While much of modern Western psychology has been based on extrapolations of work with animals to create models for human experience and treatments for problems, there is no shortage of theories regarding the interface between psychology and spirituality. These various models are grouped under the rubric of what has come to be known as **Transpersonal Psychology**. That is, these models speak to the belief that humans are much more than a bag of skin and bones with a very sophisticated computer animating the machinery. Carl Jung's most important work began after he broke with Freud over Freud's unwillingness to see humans as anything more than advanced, complicated animals driven by sex, aggression, and pleasure seeking. Jung took a larger view of humankind and explored the possibilities of spiritual experience with concepts like the **collective unconscious**, a storehouse of experience to which all of us are connected, and **synchronicity** which refers to meaningful coincidences.

Currently, theoreticians like Stanislov Grof, Ken Wilbur, and Jean Houston are actively pursuing ideas like the reality of the soul, reincarnation, and the whole realm of paranormal phenomenon. There is even a division of Transpersonal psychology within the American Psychological Association, and a journal dealing with transpersonal issues.

As we proceed through the remainder of this chapter we will cite references, when appropriate, to current theoretical models which bridge what appears to be the gap between the spiritual and the scientific.

"We do not know what anything is. The summarization of our existence is Mystery, absolute, unqualified confrontation with what we cannot know. And no matter how sophisticated we become by experience, this will always be true of us."

Da Free John

We began this book with a tale of tasting mangoes. Our simple premise being that it is one thing to know about mangoes intellectually and quite another to truly taste a mango, savor the experience, and be fully alive in that moment. After all, when we cut through all of the words and rationalizations about mastery and personal effectiveness, what we are after is a sense that we are really alive and living an existence that is meaningful to us. Some might refer to this as a spiritual quest. This chapter, too, is full of words and ideas and questions, but if you do not taste them, chew on them, and mull them over then you will have missed the point. Words, while they are wonderful tools, always reduce experience. They aren't the experiences themselves. Joseph Campbell once related in a lecture that the best things in life cannot be told because they are beyond thought. The next best things are misunderstood, and the next best are those things about which we talk. Consider the words written here as only fingers pointing at the moon. As the ancient expression goes, *"focus too much on the fingers and you miss the heavenly splendor above"*. If you get caught up in the rightness or wrongness of these words you will fall into the trap of being right that we discuss in Chapter 8, and miss the opportunity to choose happiness. Paraphrasing the words of the mystic Rumi, out there beyond ideas of right doing and wrong doing there is a field. We would like to meet you there. We'll bring the mangoes.

This is about coming to terms with what we believe are fundamental human concerns that we all must confront if we are to truly become masters of living our lives joyfully and effectively. Something that is fundamentally stressful to humans is the experience of having an inadequate map for a territory that they are exploring. Unfortunately or fortunately, depending on your perspective, life lived well will present you with the unexpected and you will be scrambling to find directions and maps to guide you. We would like to humbly offer some landmarks that we hope will help you find your way, or at least help you learn to enjoy being lost. Remember, maps are never the territory that they represent. You do not eat the menu when you go to a restaurant. We hope these maps are useful. Some may even be true!

This discussion is also about how you face the inevitable choices and decisions that you must make throughout the course of your life. If you avoid making these choices, ultimately they will be made for you. If you want to maximize your effectiveness by enhancing your sense of control, you need to again consider the maps on which you base your decisions. You must determine what is important to you, or your life will not be your own and surely your effectiveness will be undermined.

What follows are simply guideposts, ideas worth considering. When you find yourself struggling to get your bearings, attempting to make some sense out of life and your place in it, remember these things.

Life is a mystery.

For one of the authors, who was educated largely in Catholic schools, a very frustrating memory of childhood was being told that the answer to his inquiries about God and life was *"It's a mystery"*. Now, he appreciates the essential truth of that assertion. No matter how many books we read, how much knowledge we acquire, or experiments we conduct, there will always remain that which is elusive, mysterious. Consider building a fire on a moonless night deep in the woods. The larger the fire the more trees we illuminate. However, the amount of darkness that we become aware of expands in direct relationship to the areas of light. Of this you can be sure, nobody knows what's really going on here. Life is ultimately a mystery that won't ever be solved no matter how big you build your bonfires. But, you can develop a relationship with life. That relationship begins by humbly acknowledging the depth of the mystery and then setting out to seek answers anyway.

Action step: When we suggest building a relationship with the mystery (or God, Goddess, the Fates, or whatever you choose to name it), we mean this literally. In the privacy of your own mind begin to have a conversation with God. Say the things you've always wanted to say. Ask the questions you've always wanted to ask. Now, like most conversations, the real key to success is *listening*. In this game listening means quietly focusing your attention so as not to be drawn into the meandering of your own mind. It means to be open to signs and synchronicities (meaningful coincidences). Answers may appear in many forms. For example, you may turn on the radio or T.V. and the next words you hear may seem to be the perfect reply to your inquiry. Or you may meet a stranger standing in a line who just happens to say something particularly meaningful to you at that moment. Unexpected feelings of contentment or joy may flow through you without warning. And, it is possible to hear "the still small voice" that is spoken of within metaphysical literature. Meditation is one key skill in quieting the mind. Some suggested readings in this area would be:

The Search for the Beloved	By Jean Houston Ph.D.
Journey of Awakening	By Ram Dass
The Meditative Mind	By Daniel Goleman

Therefore, life is uncertain.

Things change. Get used to it. Be thankful for it. This is the one thing you can be certain of, that things will change. This is true not only in the world of work, but in all aspects of your life. You may ask yourself, "will my life ever calm down, become stable and predictable? Will I ever get caught up?" The answer is yes and then things will change. When things are going bad, things will change. When things are going good, things are going to change. Peace seems to lie in realizing and accepting this fact. It is about reassuring yourself that *when times are bad, that this too shall pass.* Repeating that phrase to yourself is one of the most effective stress reducers. Thus, you can be grateful for the changes you know will carry you out of difficult times and be appreciative for the good times, because all good things will ultimately change or come to an end.

Action step: Cultivate an **attitude of gratitude**. One of the authors did a year long internship on a spinal cord injury ward. The most important thing that he drew from that experience was a constant appreciation for having an intact body and being able to walk, something that we regularly take for granted. We recommend that whenever you feel particularly mistreated by life that you consider the ramifications of losing one of your senses, or the function of some part of your body. Remember the last time you were ill or had a toothache, or headache, and appreciate just how wonderful normal is.

Everything is connected.

One of the most profound illusions of our being is the essential solidity of the objects around us. Science, particularly physics, assures us that in spite of appearances, things are more empty space than solid matter. What appears to be solid is really a vibrating group of particles, most of which have no mass. These particles seem to be influenced by the people who try to study them (i.e. the Heisenberg Uncertainty principle). These particles retain a relationship with one another over astronomical distances. Furthermore, all beings constantly exchange particles with one another. The science of ecology demonstrates that change in one part of a system necessarily provokes change across the system. Chaos theorists have demonstrated that profound changes can be induced by minor perturbations in a system, as minor as a butterfly flapping its wings. We are ultimately not separate from anything. Therefore be careful and consider the actions you take on every level including your thoughts. Whatever you do, you do it to yourself. Do not burn your own house down. This is the fundamental truth that underlies the various versions of the Golden Rule. It makes sense to treat others how you would like to be treated. After all, they are you!

Action step: Reinforce this belief by reading about cutting edge discoveries in science. Paradigms for understanding the mystical/spiritual view of life are becoming more and more accepted and are supported by experimental data. Some reading to whet your appetite includes:

The Holographic Universe	By Michael Talbot
Recovering the Soul	By Larry Dossey M.D.
A New Science of Life	By Rupert Sheldrake
The Conscious Universe	By Dean Radin, Ph.D.

Life is trouble.

To again quote Zorba the Greek, *"Life is trouble. Only death is not. To be alive is to undo your belt and go looking for trouble."* Now before you seek out a barroom brawl, let us suggest that it is the attitude that is important here. Life very often involves dealing with problems. We have a choice. We can whine about them or we can deal with them. We have tried whining. Sometimes, even very dedicated whining! It doesn't help. We recommend taking the challenge, jumping into the fray and solving problems.

Action step: You really don't have to worry about an action step here. Trouble simply cannot be avoided. Those who have tried to elude it report that it comes looking for you!

Death is a great therapist.

"I don't believe in life after death, but I am bringing a change of underwear."

Woody Allen

" The question is not whether we will die, but how we will live."

Joan Borysenko

Whatever comes after this life, the apparent rule is that we will all get the opportunity to find out (i.e. everybody dies). This is your shot at *this* lifetime. Scanning the literature and lore on death and dying you will probably find very few people who on their deathbed said, *"I wish I had spent more time at the office"*. Death has a remarkable ability to clarify our thinking about what is important.

Action step: Suggested readings include:

Tuesdays with Morrie   By Mitch Albom

Journey to Ixtlan   By Carlos Castenada

When faced with difficult choices, when you find yourself resistant and unwilling to take a risk, try having a conversation with Death. When you find that Death has no guarantees to offer other than, "I'll be back", you may discover a new intensity permeating your actions in any moment. After all, this may be the last time you make love, sip some tea, hug your children, teach a class, etc. Give yourself fully to those moments because . . .

Here and now is better than there and then.

Effective individuals are adept at placing themselves fully in the moment. This is also one of the best antidotes for stress. Losing yourself in thoughts of what has happened and what will happen is a fine way to create anxiety and depression. These don't seem to exist in the fully experienced moment.

Action step: Suggested readings include:

Be Here Now   By Ram Dass

The Power of Now   By Ekhardt Tolle

Any activity which carries you into a profound awareness of the present moment is a worthy practice. The writings and recordings of Thich Nat Than on mindfulness are very inspirational. Any meditation discipline is a fine approach but so are pottery, poetry, painting, or playing at anything in which you lose track of time and become fully involved in the moment. As to what will fully involve you, you need to consider the next section.

Are you getting what you really want or what you are supposed to want?

"Thinking at its highest level is asking the right relevant question."

Walter Pauk

"Follow your bliss."

Joseph Campbell

The questions you ask go a long way towards shaping the possible answers you will find. Questions like, "What should I do with my life?", have an inherent appeal to look outside of yourself for answers, for validation, for reassurances that you are doing the right thing. Yet all wisdom traditions suggest that it is knowing and trusting yourself, that is looking inside of yourself, that leads to the best and most fulfilling answers.

The Sufi mystic Rumi once said, *"Start a large and foolish project, like Noah. It makes absolutely no difference what people think of you."* If you don't take the time to seek answers, if you don't make the effort to really get to know yourself and what really moves your heart, you risk living somebody else's life. Yes, life is difficult, full of choices, seemingly unfair at times. But life is also beautiful, effortless and involving when you do the things you love, the things that come easily to you. When you find ways to serve others while doing what you love, success is virtually inevitable.

Action step: You need to spend more time with your dreams and fantasies. Take quiet time to remember times that have made you smile, warmed your heart, filled you with compassion, excited you, put you at peace. While you are feeling any of these feelings, follow the flight of your thoughts. Your heart is a compass that will point to your path. In this respect it can be said that the successful life requires constant questioning and attending to how you answer those questions moment to moment and day to day until you die and get the answers to the ultimate questions. Here are some questions to live with and by. Put them on your mirror or in your notebook and check them regularly.

WHO AM I?

WHAT DO I LOVE TO DO?

WHAT IS MY PURPOSE?

HOW CAN I HELP? (Instead of "What's in it for me?")

WHAT IS LIFE? (A dance, banquet, seasons, game, comedy, etc.)

HAVE I LAUGHED TODAY?

WHAT IS SUCCESS FOR ME?

IS THERE ANOTHER WAY OF LOOKING AT THIS? (Of course there is!)

IS THIS THE DAY I'M GOING TO DIE?

AM I LEADING THE LIFE I WANT TO LIVE?

AM I THE PERSON I WANT TO BE?

DO I KEEP MY WORD? (Especially to myself)

HOW WOULD THE PERSON I'D LIKE TO BE DO THE THINGS I'M ABOUT TO DO?

It has been said that at the end of our lives we will be concerned with the answers to only two questions:

WAS I LOVED?

DID I LOVE WELL?

MIND, BODY, SPIRIT—SEEK YOUR BALANCE

The universe is a perfectly balanced ballet of opposites, light and dark, cold and heat, pain and pleasure, chaos and order, etc., etc. The perception of any form necessarily involves the presence of a background. Ultimately, we are physical, mental and spiritual creations, and our well being depends on balancing the needs of all these different aspects of ourselves. Oftentimes, when people question what they want in their search for fulfillment, they neglect to consider this vital issue from a balanced perspective. One way to remedy this situation is for you to consider the multiple roles you fill in your daily life. Besides being an individual you may also be a mother, father, son, daughter, brother, sister, student, teacher, employee, employer, professional, friend, and so on and so forth. Thus, as you explore the path towards which your heart steers you, seek to set goals for all the roles of your life. To totally ignore or short change any role is to invite regret to haunt you later.

It is in fact very difficult to consider an aspect of our lives where balance is not a consideration. When our breathing and attention are focused in the area of the diaphragm, our center, we feel relaxed and balanced. All athletic prowess requires balance. Effective communication is a balance between being committed to listening and courageous enough to make certain that you are also heard. Our decisions are based on balancing what we know with certainty against what we cannot know with certainty (i.e. the future). And still we need to act in life based on our deeply held convictions. Yet, we need to be peaceful and unattached to the outcomes of our actions. Perhaps Mark Twain said it best when he wrote, *"Moderation in all things . . . but don't miss anything."* Being balanced means all things have their place in life including, at times, extremes. Thus, sometimes seeking balance looks a little unbalanced. If you are aiming for a target and consistently missing to the right, you may need to aim to the left, and not directly at the target itself in order to hit the mark.

Action steps: (1) Imagine attending your own funeral. Consider what you would want those in attendance to say about you. Choose to listen in on people from many areas of your life and imagine how you would like to be eulogized. (2) Learn to juggle. This is a deceptively challenging task which teaches you to gracefully and playfully keep many things in the air at once. It requires physical and mental balancing that can give you an intense involvement in the here and now. Whose life hasn't felt like a juggling routine from time to time!

When in doubt, do something different.

Doing the same things you've always done and expecting to get different results is a kind of madness. A more useful madness is to be willing to break out of the rut of established routines that are not working for you. It can be as simple as driving home in a new way, or trying the dish on the menu that you've never tasted. It can be as daring as returning to school after years in the work force or taking time off to go on a spiritual retreat. The same old thing gets you the same old things. Someone once said, "You can either have what you want in this lifetime or have all the excuses why you didn't get it."

Action step: Try something different. Go on . . . **DO IT** !

Get comfortable with confusion.

Understanding occurs when we discern a pattern in our experience of the world. Confusion is what happens just before we begin to understand. Getting upset over your confusion simply doesn't help. Better to breathe, relax, pay attention and wait until understanding comes around. Relaxing facilitates understanding for it makes it far easier for you to access your intuitive wisdom. What you need to attend to is right in front of you. If you take your attention away from it, it will simply take that much longer to come to an understanding. Also, remember our first premise: **life is a mystery**. Some confusion is part of the tour package. We suggest that breath and attention can transform confusion into wonder in the same way they transform fear into excitement.

Love yourself while you discover that love is the answer.

> *"You might as well like yourself. Just think of all the time you're going to have to spend with you."*
>
> Jerry Lewis in *The Nutty Professor*

The wisest teachers throughout history assure us that life at its core is found to be an ocean of love of which we are all a part. We are never really separate from this love even though the trials and tribulations of life seem at times to be anything but loving. We choose to believe this premise simply because it seems to work for us. To us it means that we are all as good at our center as the best of us. Be patient and loving with yourself along the way. Trust the intuitions of your own heart. Have Fun! Learn to forgive yourself, again, and again, and again.

SELF EXERCISES

This section is filled with suggestions, ideas, and recommended readings to assist you in finding the balance that characterizes effectiveness. Don't just skim the action steps or blindly read through them while forgetting them a second later. Make a commitment to invest in yourself and follow those that ring true for you. Even more difficult but potentially rewarding and illuminating would be to experiment with those actions steps about which you may be skeptical. Be an adventurer and explore those steps which elicit your resistance. The most profound learning experiences are waiting for you there.

KEY TERMS

Vision Quest	Representational Systems	Meditation
Wishstorming	Auditory	Beginner's Mind
Visualization	Visual	Mantra
Unconscious Mind	Kinesthetic	Mindfulness
Modeling	Gustatory	Tai Chi
Observational Learning	Olfactory	Qi Gong
Transpersonal Psychology	Attitude of Gratitude	Self-Regulation
Collective Unconscious	Synchronicity	

CHAPTER 6 QUESTIONS

True or False (T or F)

1. _____ State your goals in negative terms so that you won't be disappointed later on if you don't achieve them.

2. _____ When goal setting, it helps to be as specific as possible.

3. _____ Athletes who practice their sport with mental rehearsal (visualization) typically find it to be a waste of time.

4. _____ Visualization promotes healing.

5. _____ For world-class athletes in the U.S. and Russia the rate of performance improvement directly corresponded to the percentage of time spent in mental rehearsal.

6. _____ Sacred texts warn you to avoid visualization practices.

7. _____ Humans often learn how to do things by observational learning or modeling.

8. _____ Relaxation is irrelevant to the visualization process.

9. _____ Negative visualizations are more powerful than positive visualizations.

10. _____ When meditating it is important to try as hard as you can to achieve a meditative state.

11. _____ Mindfulness is the cultivation of awareness by practicing awareness.

12. _____ Tai Chi and Qi Gong are Eastern methods for improving your sexual performance.

13. _____ You create your reality with your thoughts, your words and your mental images.

14. _____ One thing you can be certain of is that things will change.

15. _____ Change in one part of a system provokes change across the system.

16. _____ You are separate from your environment.

17. _____ The Golden Rule is an outdated principle which no longer applies in our modern world.

18. _____ Your effectiveness will be undermined if you allow yourself to be fully in the moment.

19. _____ Effective people consistently look outside of themselves for reassurances that they are doing the right thing.

20. _____ If what you are doing isn't working, just try harder.

21. _____ If what you are doing isn't working, try something different.

ESSAY QUESTIONS

1. What is the purpose of examining the *goal of your goal?*

2. Describe the steps for securing your goals.

3. What is the relationship of modeling to the effects of visualization practice?

4. How does relaxation facilitate the process of visualization and the effects of such?

5. What is the relationship of visualization practice to effectiveness?

6. Distinguish between participant and observer imagery.

7. Summarize the attitudes necessary for successful practice of mindfulness meditation.

8. What is the purpose of a focal point in meditative practice?

9. What is Transpersonal Psychology?

10. Describe an attitude of gratitude.

7

Manage Yourself in Time

When we think about "effective" people what typically comes to mind are individuals who are very productive, who not only do most things competently, but who do them in a timely manner. Effective people respect deadlines and usually finish tasks on time, sometimes with time to spare. But effectiveness is much more than just producing a lot of work. Effective people are typically well organized, and have learned to juggle multiple responsibilities, projects, and tasks while still making time for rest, relaxation, enjoyment and personal relationships. Success in our current world usually requires an ability to see the big picture followed by a sustained focus on the critical details for getting it done. What enables effective individuals to develop and maintain competence and maximize their chances for success is that they are adept at culling out what is important, and then they use their time wisely. Indeed, good time management skills are typically a hallmark of effective individuals. But, you need to be wary of the common tendency to confuse efficiency with effectiveness. While effective individuals are typically well organized and they may be efficient, an over emphasis on efficiency will actually diminish your effectiveness, but more on this later.

Have you ever spent a day, at work or at home, where you were busy almost non-stop, but by the day's end you felt as though you had accomplished nothing? Perhaps this was because you put your focus on tasks, concerns, projects or undertakings that were really not very important. You may have spent your day doing busywork, trivial jobs that were easy, or tasks that other people requested of you, but which were of very low relevance to your own agenda. Or perhaps you felt you had accomplished little because nothing was finished, or because you were immersed in multiple tasks in a disorganized fashion, flitting back and forth from one to another and never really making any headway on any. Every one of us has had at least one day like this, but if you find yourself fitting this pattern on a regular or even a semi-regular basis, it is time to take a look at how you manage time and experiment with more effective strategies for managing yourself in time. Even if you consider yourself to be adept at utilizing time, you may find at least a few tips or tools in this chapter that will refine or add to your skills.

THE EIGHT STRATEGIES FOR SUCCESS

If you follow these central strategies for everyday success, you will increase your productivity, your effectiveness, and as a side benefit, you will lower your stress level.

1. Focus first on high priority items.
2. Group related tasks and do them together.
3. Get organized.
4. Break it into doable chunks.
5. Develop and use timetables.
6. Focus on one thing at a time.
7. Finish it fully.
8. Do it when you think of it.

1. Focus First on High Priority Items

Think in terms of the **Pareto principle**, which is also called the **80/20** rule. The Pareto principle teaches that 80% of the benefit comes from doing 20% of the work. Figure out the most important and beneficial 20%, and make that your priority to tackle first. Completing the important 20% often expedites or simplifies completion of the remaining 80% of the work.

But how is it that you determine what is or should be a high priority? How do you know what is really important? Obviously, this is not cut and dried. Tasks, jobs, or things you have to do are rarely either important or unimportant. Importance lies on a continuum ranging from low to high. Steven Covey recommends that you determine importance based on how closely an activity is tied to your life goals and desired results as defined by your personal mission statement (explained in more detail later in this chapter). In a similar but more simplistic schema, Dru Scott, Ph.D. advises ordering the time demands in your life into three categories arranged as concentric circles. The outer circle is reserved for what she refers to as "marginal matters," which consists of the hundreds of relatively trivial demands that use of chunks of time each day (i.e., washing dishes, looking through mail, running errands, updating your files, etc.). Many people try to get these little tasks out of the way first so as to make time to focus on the important stuff. But too often the small, bothersome, marginal tasks end up consuming your whole day, and before you know it, nothing of lasting value is accomplished. Give these tasks the lowest priority. That does not mean that you ignore them or never do them (after all, these tasks do have their place in the scheme of things), just do them last when possible.

The middle circle or "secondary matters" consist of tasks that are certainly valuable, but they do not contribute to your long term goals or bring you much in the way of rewards or satisfaction. They are meaningful tasks but are not of the highest importance. Dr. Scott suggests that if you are investing a lot of time in "worthwhile activities" but are getting minimal joy or sense of accomplishment, then you are probably stuck overemphasizing secondary matters. For example, what if you are knocking yourself out, spending one to two hours daily preparing gourmet dinners for your family. You do this because you think that is what a good wife/mother should do. Meanwhile, let's say you really don't enjoy cooking, your kids would much rather go to McDonalds, and your spouse barely notices your efforts. Is this then the best use of your time? Cooking delicious, nutritious meals is a very worthwhile and essential task, but only if you enjoy it (if it relates to your life goals), and/or your efforts are rewarded (i.e. appreciated). If you love cooking and experimenting with new recipes, then by all means continue, but if you don't then consider ordering out and spending your time in ways that make your heart sing.

Put your main focus on the center of the circle, the bull's-eye, which should consist of the highest priority items. This relates to your central concerns—what you most want and value in your life along with essential activities which you must do in the course of the day to stay healthy and support yourself financially (i.e. pay your rent). Your central concerns relate to your long and short term life goals. Your essential activities often refer to maintenance tasks such as paying your bills, grooming, eating, exercising, getting a decent night's sleep, etc. These two categories represent the tasks you should focus on accomplishing first. These are the activities that will result in the most fulfillment and/or keep you on track for having your life in order. When these, or most of these, have been handled then put your focus on secondary matters. Leave the marginal stuff for last.

2. Group Related Tasks and Do Them Together

It is common sense that when you group similar jobs together you can accomplish them faster than if you did each one separately. For example, if you have three errands to run, it is certainly more efficient to do all three at once rather than take the time to drive your car three different times. If you have three letters to write it may make sense to do them all in a row when you are in the writing mode and have all the necessary equipment in front of you.

3. Get Organized

Lack of organization contributes to ineffectiveness because when you approach your work in a disorganized fashion tasks generally take longer to accomplish and the finished product often is not as good. Experiment with the following tips for improving your organization.

A. Things To Do Lists

Making a list of Things to Do on a daily or weekly basis is an excellent way of getting yourself organized, and helping to remember small items or tasks that are easily forgotten unless you take the time to do a daily inventory. Post your list in a prominent place (like the bathroom mirror or the refrigerator door) where you will be likely to see it often, or keep it in your appointment book if you refer to it regularly. Scratching items off your list once they are finished becomes quite rewarding, leading to a sense of relief and accomplishment each time an item is crossed off. Some people prefer using a checkmark to indicate completion. Pick the one that feels best to you or, like one of the authors, use a combination of both (a checkmark for items in progress and the scratch off for what is finished).

B. Create a Realistic Schedule

Things to Do lists are very useful, but they have their limits. In particular, avoid getting caught in the trap of spending all your time accomplishing unimportant, marginal items and scratching those off your list, while ignoring important, more difficult and time consuming tasks. Without some sort of schedule, you can create stress by wasting time, working inefficiently, and missing opportunities because you didn't plan ahead. But over scheduling yourself is stressful as well. There is an art to creating a workable daily, weekly and monthly schedule. Start by compiling a list of all you want and need to accomplish over a certain time period, say a month. Begin your daily schedule by arranging time for any appointments or meetings scheduled for that day. Then block out chunks of at least an hour for high priority projects that required sustained work over time. The earlier in the day you can get to these, the better you will feel. Next, build in time for secondary items. Then complete your schedule with the routine, quick or easy, marginal tasks that need to be completed that day. Make your schedule flexible. Build in time for interruptions, unexpected events, problem solving, and travel time, as well as for breaks and relaxation. If you can't finish everything (and this may occur often), postpone the lowest priority items. Following a schedule will not guarantee that you always get everything done that day, but if you have made progress on your high priority goals you will feel more in control. Engaging in this type of planning may seem time consuming at first, but it will actually increase your time in the long run.

C. Get Rid of Unnecessary Papers

Are you swamped with papers? Is your desk at work or at home piled high with stacks of papers waiting for your attention, be it unopened junk mail, bills to pay, periodicals to read, forms to fill out, etc.? Do you feel overwhelmed just looking at the paper piles? If so, following these guidelines will help you eliminate the piles easily. Handle each piece of paper only once, if you possibly can. Each time you handle a piece of paper do something to move it along (i.e. pay that bill, toss out junk mail, file that important paper, fill out that form). Most importantly, when in doubt, THROW IT OUT. If you don't it is likely to just sit there on your desk, collecting dust and adding to your pile. Once you have made sufficient headway on clearing the pile, keep your desk cleared of everything except the highest priority items.

4. Break It into Doable Chunks

Many tasks, particularly if complicated or time consuming, can appear overwhelming leading to avoidance, delays, or disorganization (approaching the task in a piecemeal manner). We can't emphasize enough how helpful it can be to break big jobs into workable steps. Taking time to initially subdivide the project into steps, listing those steps, and then putting them in order will save you time later on. It will help you proceed more smoothly, and often with less frustration. You will be approaching the task in an organized fashion which will minimize chances of forgetting an important step, allowing you to feel a sense of task accomplishment as each step is completed. Remember, a skyscraper may look huge, but it was built one brick at a time.

5. Develop and Use Timetables

We humans are much more likely to begin and to complete something when we have committed to a deadline. Deadlines bring home the reality that we have to get moving. The best way to develop a workable timetable is to work backwards. If you do not have a deadline from an external source (i.e. boss, teacher), then set your own target date or time for completion. After breaking the task or assignment into doable chunks, estimate how much time each chunk will reasonably take to finish. Then give each chunk its own target date or time for completion. Doing this gives you an opportunity to plan accordingly so as to leave yourself ample time for task completion. This will help you avoid the stress of last minute rushes or the kind of slip-shod work you have to settle for if you run out of time.

For example, if you are a student facing a big assignment, such as a term paper that is due in two weeks, you could chunk the job in a format such as the following:

a.	Get relevant articles and books from the library	2 hours
b.	Do Internet search	2 hours
c.	Read through sources and pick out relevant information	4 hours
d.	Organize report into 3 sections	1 hour
e.	Write introductory paragraph	½ hour
f.	Write section one	2 hours
g.	Write section two	2 hours
h.	Write section three	1 hour
i.	Proofread report	1 hour

You would next assign each chunk to a date and time of day that you work in between your class and/or work schedule. You have nine chunks to be divided over fourteen days. The four hour preparatory chunk might best be sub-divided into two, two hour chunks scheduled for consecutive days for continuity. This schedule takes a large intimidating project and makes it doable.

The same strategy works well even when you are faced with a complicated, last minute task that is due by the end of today. Like those times when your boss rushes into your office and drops a big job in your lap that is due by 5:00 p.m. Or when old friends call you to say they are in town for a short trip, and want to drop by your house to visit you this evening. Meanwhile, your house is a total mess. In situations such as these, work backwards and figure out how much time you need to fully complete each step. Add together all the time frames, taking into account time for meals, and a few short breaks for unavoidable interruptions. That will give you your estimate of how long the entire job will take. From there you can determine when you have to start, if you need to get up earlier than usual to begin, or if you need to postpone something else (i.e. that mid-afternoon haircut may have to wait) in order to finish.

6. Focus on One Thing at a Time

It often helps if you can focus on one task at a time. People with problems managing their time often flit from one project to another, or try to do several things simultaneously. The end result is often delays, mistakes and disorganization which wastes rather than saves time. Uninterrupted concentration on a task, when possible, produces a better product in less time. Arrange your work space to minimize distractions. This does not mean you can only do one thing at a time. It is certainly possible to type your term paper while your clothes spin in the dryer. And you can let dinner simmer while you make that important call. The key here is **not to try to do two or more things that require concentration or focus at the same time**. Once your laundry is in the washer, you can focus on your term paper.

7. Finish It Fully

*"It's not how much you push along the way,
   but it's having something within you to finish."*
                                       Michael Jordan

Effective individuals finish what they start. No matter how much work you may do in the course of a day, if you don't finish anything, you may end up feeling frustrated and your effectiveness is diluted. You will be far better off with three finished projects as opposed to six half finished jobs. Finishing will boost your personal satisfaction and motivation, lower your stress level, and enhance your ability to concentrate because you have less tasks with which to be concerned (i.e. only three to finish rather than six). Finishing tasks on a regular basis has a large impact on how others view you as well, whether you are perceived as effective, dependable, successful. Starting many tasks or projects and leaving them unfinished wastes time and energy, contributes to disorganization, and also makes mistakes or careless errors more likely (due to lack of concentration or forgetting because you have too many irons in the fire). Working to focus on one task at a time sets the stage for completing a task before moving on the next one. We certainly realize that in the real world this is not always possible. At work, phones ring, colleagues barge into your office with pressing concerns, meetings must be attended, equipment breaks down and must be repaired, etc. But when it is possible to finish one task, as opposed to starting or working on another that is not pressing or vitally important, we recommend that you opt for task completion.

8. Do It When You Think of It

Oftentimes it is just the sheer volume of tasks which makes you want to delay. By doing the task immediately, if possible, you can avoid the inefficiency involved in relocating the necessary materials which saves time and effort. You also prevent yourself from forgetting to handle it.

COMMON TIME-WASTERS AND EFFECTIVE ANTIDOTES

There are always a myriad of potential time wasting or time consuming influences which can interfere with accomplishing what you have planned. These influences may be external or internal, but either way it can be useful to know how to creatively turn potential time wasters into opportunities for personal growth, and/or getting something done in spite of the obstacles. Review the following roadblocks, and think about which have or currently do apply to you. Consider how you might put these suggestions to good use.

Slow Decision-Making

Many people slow themselves down considerably because they can't make up their minds. So much time is spent going back and forth between choices that there is no time left to take action. This can be just as problematic with minor, everyday decisions (i.e. What should I wear today?) as with major, life affecting choices (i.e. Should I accept that promotion?). According to time management expert Dru Scott, Ph.D.,

> *"When you are spending too much time making up your mind, review what you most want to accomplish before you begin comparing alternatives."*

Dr. Scott advises that you first consider your goals and all relevant aspects of those goals, with respect to the decision. Then compare each alternative with your goal or goals before comparing choices to each other. Some choices will dissolve quickly because they are not conducive to achieving those goals. Once you have appraised the extent to which each choice could potentially meet your goals, only then compare the alternatives to each other. Insertion of this extra step will typically facilitate swift decision-making and short circuit back and forth ruminations.

But remember that decision making takes time. Don't be afraid to make snap judgements regarding inconsequential, everyday matters (i.e. Should I have chocolate or vanilla ice cream for dessert?). If nothing of any significance is riding on your decision, then just pick because either way it will not matter very much.

Worrying

Do you ever find yourself spending a lot of time worrying about everything you have to do or all that you would like to do, rather than doing it? Rumination can be a major time waster, for worry in itself is neither a productive nor rewarding use of your time. But trying not to worry is destined to fail. Telling yourself not to worry is the equivalent of giving yourself the command, "Don't think about pink elephants". What happens? Of course, the first thing you think of is a pink elephant! The key is not to try to stop worrying, but rather to schedule it, to literally set up a time devoted exclusively to worry, but at a time that is convenient for you, a time that does not interfere with your work. Effective individuals worry just like everyone else, they just limit the distracting influences of nonproductive worry by scheduling it.

If you tend to worry on a daily basis then set up a daily fifteen minute period to worry to your heart's content. You may want to arrange this time for after work or school to help plan your next day's agenda. Avoid scheduling your worry time right before or at bedtime because this could disturb the relaxation and winding down essential for sleep. If you do not worry on a daily basis but have difficulty letting go of worries when you ruminate, schedule a weekly half hour worry appointment with yourself. Scheduling such worry times helps put your mind to rest. If worries, fears, or obsessive concerns pop up in your mind, remind yourself that you will definitely consider this concern later at your worry time. Sometimes we worry because we fear that we will forget to do or handle something unless we remind ourselves with worries. Or we worry because we don't know how something will turn out. The value of scheduling worry time is that it makes it much easier to let go of those worries because you know you will get to them later. This frees you to focus on your work. Many people find that once they keep the date with themselves for the worry time, some concerns have already evaporated and others can be dismissed quickly. You may end up finishing your worrying even before your time is up.

Attempting To Do Things Perfectly

Don't try to do things perfectly, just focus on doing them well. Striving for perfection typically leads to fear of failure, procrastination, or difficulty with getting it finished (i.e. you keep delaying until it is "perfect"). Effective individuals strive for excellence—not perfection. In most cases an 80% job is all that is necessary to accomplish the task appropriately. Does that inter-office memo or weekly housecleaning really have to be perfect every time? Is it really the end of the world if there is some dust on top of the TV? There are some rare tasks that are worth doing as close to perfect as you can. Determine what those are, and typically they should relate closely to your high priorities. If these tasks are of low priority then reevaluate whether you really need to devote the effort to do it perfectly. Abandoning the need for perfection on unimportant tasks will save you valuable time and energy. Invest that time and energy saved on what is really central and important.

Working Against Your Body Rhythms

Sometimes we slow ourselves down or lower our effectiveness by failing to heed the rhythms of our bodies. If you are a morning person, have you ever tried to finish an important report late at night to meet a deadline? Remember how hard it was to stay awake and focused? If you are a night owl, can you recall how difficult it can be to try to effectively plan your day at the crack of dawn when you are groggy even after two cups of coffee? So pay attention to your body rhythms. Schedule difficult, challenging tasks for the times when you are most alert and energetic. If you are a morning person, do the difficult, energy consuming tasks early in the day. If you are a night person, save the challenging projects for the evening. Save the easy, routine tasks for times when your energy is at a low ebb (i.e. mid-afternoon for many people).

Failing To Recharge Your Batteries

Effective individuals work hard, play hard and know when to relax. Rest and relaxation are essential to keeping your energy level up so you can be productive. Working until you burn out will only slow you down and limit your effectiveness. Take short breaks to refresh and revitalize, particularly if you notice your concentration faltering. Sometimes engaging in a **power nap,** shutting your eyes for five to ten minutes and reclining in your chair, is all you need to perk up. Or take a five minute walk around your workplace and step outside for some fresh air. Likewise, all work and no play is a sure way to maximize stress and risk damaging effectiveness. Make time for relaxing activities and fun. Don't be afraid to occasionally take a day off to recharge and revitalize yourself. We refer to this as a "mental health day", taking a day off so as to prevent yourself from getting sick. Your energy for your work will increase as a result and you will therefore make much better use of time allotted for work.

Feeling That You Are Responsible for Everything

Is your motto, "If you want it done right, then do it yourself"? If so, you may often find yourself bogged down by insignificant tasks that you could easily delegate to others. If it is possible to hand over some tasks at work, invest time now in training others how to properly complete these jobs. This is an investment that could really pay large dividends of time later on. And what if your colleagues or supervisees don't do those tasks perfectly or as well as you can? If there are no major consequences to your organization as a result then don't sweat it. Give them feedback to help them improve and put your focus on the important aspects of your own work. Remember, perfection for the sake of perfection is a total waste of time.

At home it can also be very beneficial to delegate. Even young children (ages six to ten) can learn to wash dishes, set the table, vacuum, or use the microwave or prepare simple meals, and they often revel in the feeling of being "grown up" that accompanies having household responsibilities. Oftentimes younger children are much more motivated to help around the house than teenagers. However, whatever the age of your children, giving them household chores saves a lot of time for you and helps them learn the skills to live in the real world. It goes without saying that if you are married, you should work out a fair division of labor between you and your spouse for household and maintenance tasks.

If you can afford it, hire out as many household jobs as you can financially manage. If you cannot afford a maid weekly then hire one to come every two weeks; either way it is a big help. Employ a lawn service. Arrange to have groceries or dinner delivered on occasion. Some high paid, extremely busy individuals even hire personal shoppers to do their Christmas shopping or even personal shopping. If you love to shop or truly delight in mowing your lawn, then we don't advise that you give up your pleasures, but do consider hiring services when possible.

But what if you are a student, unmarried, without children, and living either alone or with your parents. You may say that you have no one to whom you can reasonably delegate any of your tasks. That may very well be true, but you still should consider that effective individuals have the ability to say "No" to low priority items or requests from others which distract them from completing work that is really important. They know that they cannot possibly take care of everything, so they have learned to delegate if possible, or at other times to refuse. Remember that spreading yourself too thin detracts from your effectiveness.

Getting Stuck Waiting

One of the most notorious wastes of time is getting stuck waiting. Whether you are waiting at the doctor's office, the checkout line at the store, or stuck in traffic, these common, insidious little delays add up. They rob you of time that could be better spent accomplishing something or better enjoyed in a relaxing or pleasurable pursuit. When you run short of time, have you ever wished to find an extra hour in your day? Using waiting time constructively or finding ways to reduce it can help you find that magical "25th hour" in your day.

Sometimes it is possible to reduce or eliminate waiting time. For example, you could call ahead to your dentist or doctor's office before a scheduled appointment to check whether the Dr. is on time, or, as is usually the case, behind schedule. If the latter is the case, you can ask for an estimate of how delayed your session may be, and then adjust the time you leave accordingly. Or you could choose to purchase groceries when the supermarket is not crowded. One author regularly shops for food at 8:00 a.m. on Sunday when the supermarket is empty and she can zip through the aisles and the checkout lane. Grocery shopping at this time saves anywhere from thirty to forty five minutes every Sunday, compared to shopping just a few hours later.

Waiting may be a fact of life but wasting time while stuck waiting is not. If you anticipate that you will need to wait, come prepared. Use that time to work on something that counts for you. Small chunks of time often offer great opportunities to complete quick, routine tasks. For example, while waiting at the dentist's office, use that fifteen or twenty minutes to pay bills, read your mail or write that letter. If waiting in line, pull out a sheet of paper and make a necessary list or plan. If you are at work and are waiting for someone else to show for a meeting, or for a particular telephone call or report to be faxed before you can complete part of your work, then switch to other tasks, rather than watching the clock in frustration while you fume over the inaction of others. If you are in a similar situation, but cannot spend potential waiting time in your own office, then come prepared. Bring portable work with you that you could do while waiting. It could be reports you need to read or edit, figures you need to re-check, etc. Laptop computers and cellular phones are the perfect tools for this situation.

Many people who habitually come prepared to make constructive use of waiting time often end up appreciating those extra minutes, that extra hour or two, so to speak. One of the authors found ways to utilize waiting time at her daughter's monthly orthodontist checkups, sessions that would normally last thirty to sixty minutes. Every month she would come prepared and use this time to balance her checkbook, and catch up on journal reading. She came to look forward to those quiet times to catch up. Remember, found time is like found money. The time you save in one venue will free you to spend more time enjoying yourself, or have more time to earn your living.

Starting Your Day Off on the Wrong Foot

How you begin your morning sets the tone for the rest of your day. If your mornings are spent in chaos, full of last minute rushing, stress and aggravation, it takes a good deal of energy to put this behind you, energy that is better spent working on your priorities. Streamlining and de-stressing your mornings can only add to your effectiveness and your productivity. If your morning routine could use an overhaul try following these steps.

1. Create a fantasy of your ideal, but realistic morning complete with what you need to accomplish, the optimal pace for this, and including time for any desired amenities such as a relaxed cup of coffee or a good nourishing breakfast. Then determine what tasks or chores absolutely must be completed before you leave in the morning (i.e. feed pets, shower and shave, make school lunches, water plants, daily exercise routine, etc.) Add to this your desired amenities, which you have deemed essential to your well being, such as listening to the radio for fifteen minutes prior to getting out of bed. Design your mornings to accomplish your essentials by creating a timetable. Figure out how much time you need to complete all the essentials and then work backwards to determine when you should wake up.

2. As you review your essential morning tasks, consider how many of them could be done the night before, such as preparation of school lunches, which you could even delegate to your kids. If picking out clothes often bogs you down, then do it the night before and lay everything out. That way you won't get waylaid by a last minute missing button, a lost sock, or a shirt that needs to be ironed. If you should need to switch your clothing plan you can do it the night before without the time pressure of coming up with another outfit at the last minute. Make sure you examine your children's homework the night before, rather than getting stuck checking math problems on your way out the door to work. If you are a student and have classes to attend in the morning, make sure you gather all of your textbooks, papers and required paraphernalia the night before, so you don't waste valuable time searching for your calculator or trying to track down your favorite pen.

3. Give yourself suggestions for a relaxed, enjoyable morning before you drift off to sleep. Suggest to yourself that you will be well rested and have the energy and motivation to do that which you need to do.

4. Build flexibility into your morning routine. Make a habit of getting up ten to fifteen minutes earlier than you need to just to have the slack time to handle those last minute, mini-domestic crises that always seem to crop up (i.e. your cat missed the litter box, your son just spilled a whole bowl of cereal in his lap, your car keys are misplaced, your tire is

low on air, etc.). And if you should happen to enjoy a calm, uneventful morning, then use those extra few minutes to read the paper, savor your breakfast, play a computer game, or whatever pleases you.

5. Why waste time making new decisions every morning about non-daily but recurring events such as watering your plants or washing your hair. Come up with a workable schedule for those tasks and stick with it. This saves you the time and trouble of, for example, having to decide every morning whether you should shampoo your hair. If you know beforehand that Wednesday and Saturday are shampoo days, then that is one less issue to consider. Of course, you need to be flexible—your schedule should not be etched in stone.

6. Be aware of what you need in the morning to start your day off on the right foot. Typically this is beyond what you want to accomplish, but relates to the tone or ambience you want to set. This could involve having certain music on in the background or inspirational tapes. It might involve watching the sun rise as you drink your morning coffee. One couple discovered that their morning amenities clashed. He enjoyed listening to a rousing sports talk show while he showered and shaved. His wife loved having an hour of quiet time to drink coffee and plan her day. She deliberately got up earlier than necessary just to have that unhurried, quiet hour before waking her children for school. It was well worth it to her to miss a few moments of sleep to have that peaceful, morning time. But her husband's need to listen to men grumble loudly about football violated her silent space, and her desire for silence infringed on his enjoyment of sports talk. The dilemma was solved with the purchase of a shower radio and waterproof walkman.

THE FOUR GENERATIONS OF TIME MANAGEMENT

All of the tips and strategies presented so far are useful and have their place, but they tend to put a premium on efficiency and "getting it done". While this is certainly vital, there are other perspectives on effectiveness which emphasize not how much or how quickly you produce, but rather focus on determining what is really important, on what you want to accomplish and what type of person you want to be. This helps to address the large gap that many people perceive between they way they spend their time and what is really important to them.

The fact is, time management strategies have evolved along with the demands of the workplace. The first wave or generation consists of notes and checklists. Such lists are helpful for keeping track of what you need to do, but do not necessarily help with organizing or prioritizing. Too often you are guided merely by the next thing on the list rather than any fundamental plan. The second generation involves the use of tools such as appointment books and planners to allow for better scheduling and organizing methods. But this focus on the "schedule" can lead to perceiving other people and relationships as interruptions or barriers to efficiency. Keeping to the schedule becomes paramount rather than assessing how much of the schedule is really worth keeping. The third level includes the important idea of prioritization, goal setting and planning to guide your schedule. This represents a significant improvement but subtle flaws still exist. Operating at the third level rarely gets you beyond prioritizing pressing problems, solving new crises or keeping up with deadlines. Many people feel uncomfortable with second and third generation approaches because they feel that systems which heavily schedule them are restricting and prevent flexibility.

Third level systems are still left with the problem that they channel you to put your schedule ahead of people, no matter how much you value the relationships in your life. No matter how hard you try it is impossible (not to mention unwise and unfulfilling) to be efficient with people. You can be efficient with things, with writing reports, house-cleaning, bookkeeping, errands, etc., but being in relationship with other people is not about cutting corners, delegating intimacy to others, or setting limits on conversation. If your spouse is feeling lonely and needs to spend some quality time with you, sched-uling a ten minute appointment to fit him or her into your schedule isn't the way to pro-ceed. If your child is very upset because the family pet was hit by a car, you wouldn't delegate the job of comforting her solely to your babysitter.

Basically, the first three generations are focused primarily on the skillful manage-ment of time. Steven Covey, in *First Things First,* further describes the inadequacies of previous systems, reminding us that,

> "Time management itself is a management, not leadership, perspective. Management works within the paradigm. Leadership creates new paradigms. Management works within the system. Leadership works on the system. You manage "things"; but you lead people. Fundamental to putting first things first in our lives is leadership before management. "Am I doing the right things?" before "Am I doing things right?"

The Fourth Generation

So, traditional time management methods assist you in working harder, smarter and faster with the implication that this will help you gain control over your life, leading to increased success and personal satisfaction. Due to the obvious drawbacks of the first three levels, a fourth generation has emerged which is not about the managing of time per se, bur rather about managing yourself in time more effectively. Rather than focus-ing on time and things, newer fourth generation approaches focus more on results and relationships. The fourth generation system put forth by Steven Covey in his landmark books, *The Seven Habits of Highly Effective People* and *First Things First,* emphasizes effec-tiveness rather than just efficiency. Covey approaches time management from a whole different perspective than traditional systems. He recommends that you organize your schedule around priorities rather than prioritize your schedule. But the first step in doing this is to compose what Covey refers to as your "personal mission statement"or philoso-phy, which can serve as a beacon to guide you in determining not only your current pri-orities, but in deciding what is really important to your life and the level of importance. This will naturally assist you with managing your time more effectively.

Your Personal Mission Statement

This mission statement needs to focus on the kind of person you want to be (your character), and what you want to contribute or accomplish, along with the values and principles upon which you desire to base and guide your life. This philosophy is akin to your own personal constitution and can function as the basis for making major life decisions as well as everyday decisions. It can empower you with a guiding set of values in the midst of change. Your mission statement needs to reflect your uniqueness as a person. Covey reminds us that one important aspect of effectiveness is to have a changeless core, or sense of who you are and what you are about, and what you value. This enables you to flow more easily with change, and to determine what directions you should take and what is important. Having a sense of mission creates a lynchpin of your own proactivity. It gives you the vision and values from which to guide your life, and helps you to set your short and long term goals. Refer back to Chapter 6 if you need help with determining your goals.

Composing your own personal mission statement also involves taking into consideration all of the major roles you play in your life. This could include your role as a husband or wife, as a parent, or as a family member. It would include your occupational role or roles in your job or career, and your role as a student if you are in school either full or part time. It should also include your role in any other pursuit or hobby that takes a reasonable amount of your time and/or interest (i.e. golfer, sculptor, skier, boat owner, guitar player, gardener, etc.). Make sure your mission statement addresses each of the major roles you play. However, many people feel torn between their various roles which always seem in constant conflict and competition for their limited time and attention. This conflict is often most pronounced between work and family roles. Finding balance is not always easy and goes to the heart of effectiveness. Composing your mission statement with all your vital roles in mind, and then committing to live by it can assist you in finding that balance. Refer back to Chapter 6 for more guidance and suggestions on finding this balance in your life.

One strategy for composing a mission statement is to use the 100th birthday technique which helps you adopt a useful perspective on long range accomplishments. Imagine that you have made it to your 100th birthday and you are still well and lucid. A newspaper reporter comes to interview you, to write the story of your life, and asks you to name your most important contributions in terms of accomplishments and roles you have played. How would you answer? Would you want to say that you were a good parent or loving wife/husband, that you made a million dollars, that you wrote a best-seller, climbed Mt. Everest, invented a new household appliance, became CEO, achieved a black belt, mastered gourmet cooking, broke par when golfing, ran a marathon, operated your own successful business, etc. Of course, the list is endless, limited only by your interests and imagination. But be realistic. Do not set goals you cannot possibly achieve.

Your goals do not need to be tied to world records, fame, or monetary success to be valid for you. And be wary of setting all your goals in one arena (i.e. work) and ignoring the other roles you want to play in your life (i.e. spouse, parent, friend, etc.).

URGENCY VS. IMPORTANCE IN TIME MANAGEMENT

Steven Covey recommends that you divide your work tasks and projects into four categories (or quadrants) as illustrated next:

Quadrant I Urgent and Important	Quadrant II Non-Urgent but Important
Crises	Proactive activities
Pressing problems	Long-range planning
Projects with deadlines	Networking
Some meetings	Relationship building
Some preparations	Prevention/Maintenance

Quadrant III Urgent but Not Important	Quadrant IV Neither Urgent nor Important
Interruptions	Busywork, trivia
Some phone calls	Some phone calls
Some meetings	Some mail/junk mail
Some reports/some mail	Pleasant activities
Many pressing matters	

The two aspects that define any activity are its urgency and its importance. Things which are urgent, such as a ringing phone, demand to be attended to immediately, or at least very soon. Urgent matters are often popular or important to others, but they may or may not be important for you. Covey further recommends that you define importance based on how closely an activity is tied to your goals and desired results, as well as to your personal mission statement in life. Urgent activities call for a quick reaction. Tasks that are important, but not urgent, typically require more initiative and proactivity. If you have not defined your goals and therefore are unclear as to what is important to you, it is very easy to be swallowed up by urgency. That is why it is so important to develop your mission statement and attempt to live by it.

Quadrant I tasks, both urgent and important, typically take the form of crises or problems which require immediate attention. Although we all have some Q I activities in our work lives, many people are consumed with Q I work and are beset with problems all day long. While the demands of any quadrant could potentially be stressful, clearly it is Q I activities that contain the greatest potential for raising your stress level. It is not surprising that individuals mired in Q I activities are more prone to burnout. And the more time spent in Q I, the more it appears to expand because you are not taking the time to be proactive and prevent future problems. When overly immersed in Q I work, the tendency is to escape to the more mindless, easy Quadrant IV activities. While that might provide a temporary breather, it does little to set the stage for a meaningful decrease in Q I and its inherent stress.

When people spend a lot of time in Quadrant III activities, urgent but not important, it is usually because they assume these tasks are really important and lie in Q I. This is based on being influenced by the expectations of others, because the matter is urgent or important for them. That does not necessarily mean that it need be urgent or important for you unless it fits with your goals. Quadrant IV activities, often termed busywork, are often pleasant and offer an opportunity to take a break. Be wary of spending the majority of your time in Q III or Q IV for that leads to irresponsibility. Successful, effective people minimize time spent in Q III or Q IV, saving that for mini-breaks, because, urgent or not, they are not important.

The key to effective personal/time management is to maximize time spent on Q II activities which are important but not urgent. This involves work which is proactive and preventative such as long term planning, networking and building business relationships, establishing a business plan and personal mission statement, preventative maintenance and preparation, (along with maintaining your health and personal relationships.) etc. These are all things we want to do, and know we should do, but tend to put off because they are not deadline driven. But it is only by engaging in Q II activities that you can shrink the stressful Q I, by preventing crises and problems in the first place, thereby increasing your effectiveness.

Initially, the only way to spend more time on Q II activities is to subtract time from Q III and IV. Increasing your emphasis on Q II requires that you practice proactivity, that you make it a priority to attend to important tasks that relate to your life goals, even if these tasks are not deadline driven or urgent. Obviously you cannot ignore Q I, but it will begin to diminish once you increase your Q II proactivity. In order to lessen time spent in Q III and IV you have to learn to say, "No" to some activities (even if important or urgent to others), or to delegate. This may require that you strengthen your assertive skills (refer to Chapter 10).

A ringing phone is a typical example of a Q III situation. It urgently demands that you interrupt your work to answer and respond, but often the calls are only important to the caller. The perfect example of this is telephone solicitation. This author has lost count of how many times my work has been interrupted by someone trying to sell me something they think I desperately need, be it a new long distance phone service, a new credit card, computer supplies, etc. These sales people are fast talking and know every trick in the book to keep you on the phone. I am amazed by how many of my colleagues patiently sit through sales pitches and then list all the reasons why they are not interested. Meanwhile, five to ten minutes were wasted. Our method for handing such calls is short and sweet. We nicely and diplomatically state, "Sorry, we don't accept telephone solicitation", and then hang up immediately without waiting for a response. Over the years we have probably saved days worth of valuable time by ducking such time wasters.

PROCRASTINATION

Earlier in this chapter we discussed a variety of influences that contribute to mismanaging your time. But this book would be incomplete if we did not address what, for many people, is the most notorious enemy of personal effectiveness: procrastination. "Never do today what you can put off until tomorrow". That is the motto of the procrastinator. We all procrastinate to one degree or another. It becomes a major problem in your work or personal life when important tasks or responsibilities are left undone or are completed in a slipshod manner because inadequate time was left to complete the task properly. Procrastination lowers anxiety in the short run due to the relief we feel from task avoidance. But it greatly increases our stress in the long run as tasks pile up or time runs short. Meanwhile, you are sabotaging your effectiveness the longer you delay.

The main and most direct cause for procrastination is **low frustration tolerance** (Ellis & Knaus, 1977). You need to accept the fact that in order to receive future rewards, you often need to undertake present discomfort. In essence, you need to be able to **defer gratification**. *Just so you don't underestimate the profound impact of being able to defer gratification, consider the results of this landmark study.* Back in the 1960's researchers Walter Mischel and Phillip K. Peake (1990) offered four year olds at a preschool at Stanford University (children of faculty, staff, and graduate students) a simple choice. They could receive one marshmallow at the start of class, or, if they waited until the end of class, they could get two marshmallows. A longitudinal study of these children years later, once they had graduated high school, revealed that those who opted to wait for two marshmallows later were far more successful and effective in their lives, in general, than those who had opted for one marshmallow now. The implications of these results were discussed at length by Daniel Goleman in his 1995 book *Emotional Intelligence* where he stated:

> *"The emotional and social difference between the grab-the-marshmallow preschoolers and their gratification delaying peers was dramatic. Those who had resisted temptation at four were now, as adolescents, more socially competent: personally effective, self-assertive and better able to cope with the frustrations of life. They were less likely to go to pieces, freeze or regress under stress, or become rattled and disorganized when pressured; they embraced challenges and pursued them instead of giving up even in the face of difficulties; they were self-reliant and confident, trustworthy and dependable; and they took initiative and plunged into projects. And, more than a decade later, they were still able to delay gratification in pursuit of their goals."*

Low frustration tolerance is based on the irrational notion that present pain or discomfort is "too hard to bear". This belief that you cannot stand present pain for future gain invites and practically commands you to continue your delay tactics. This can be a very debilitating cycle. Again, everything hinges upon what you tell yourself about the "onerous task". In order to overcome a tendency to procrastinate you need to begin by learning to identify your irrational thoughts (Ellis & Knaus, 1977), and then replacing them with thoughts that promote productivity. If your frustration tolerance is adequate, you will take the temporary discomfort in stride and conclude that, indeed, the task may be aversive, boring or anxiety provoking, but, "So what!" Where was it decreed that you have to like everything you do? After all, the task will not go on forever, particularly if you start now. If you tell yourself that it may be unpleasant, but so are many things that you easily survive, it will help you to persevere. If you remind yourself that there actually may be aspects to the task that will even intrigue you or benefit you, it can give you the wherewithal to get started.

For example, if you are avoiding beginning and/or completing a certain project at work it is likely that you are thinking (on either a conscious or unconscious level) one or more of the following irrational and ridiculous thoughts: (1) that you will be totally miserable the whole time you are working on this task; (2) that you cannot possibly bear the torture of this duty; (3) that it is entirely unfair and sadistic for your boss to foist such a terrible assignment upon you; (4) that you cannot possibly enjoy any part of this project; (5) that you are destined to fail horribly at this task; or (6) that if you rebel you will get a hero's acclaim down the road. In place of these self sabotaging statements you can choose to substitute the following: (1) that you can choose not to be miserable; (2) that you certainly won't die from working on this task so of course you **can** stand it (no doubt you have endured much worse); (3) your boss' goal is not to ruin your life but to make the business succeed; (4) perhaps some aspect of the work will prove reasonably interesting; (5) there is no guarantee you will fail, and it is not the end of the world if you don't succeed in everything; and (6) the one you hurt the most by delaying is yourself.

Many people believe that if they wait until they feel more like doing the avoided task, then they will be able to finally get moving. But actually, it is the reverse that is more often true and certainly more efficient. That is, if you wait around for your feelings to change, you could wait forever. But if you change your behavior, your feelings will change to match your new actions. This follows the tenet "**attitude change follows behavior change**". When you behave differently you will tend to feel different as emotions tend to shift to fall in line with your actions. Therefore, acting in a timely, efficient and productive manner (even when you don't feel like it) will actually create the motivation to continue working and may even, in some cases, lead to increased task enjoyment. At the very least, you can enjoy the fact that you have completed the task and it no longer hangs over you.

Six Steps to Overcoming Procrastination

1. The Bits and Pieces Approach

One of the best antidotes to procrastination is to break tasks or projects down into doable chunks. Are you prone to letting tasks pile up until you feel overwhelmed and/or indecisive as to where to begin or how to prioritize the task? You might feel as though you need to accomplish an entire task once you get started, and this can become an overwhelming undertaking. Giving yourself permission to do just one small piece can get you started, and provide the necessary momentum for completion of the whole project in time. By using the bits and pieces approach you can whittle down unfinished tasks and finish parts of projects (and eventually the whole project). Once you start a small part of a task and get into the swing of it you might discover that you feel like finishing the whole thing, especially if it goes faster or smoother than you had anticipated. Or you can use your energy to switch over to another avoided task which may prove to be easier once you have built up positive momentum from the former, especially if the tasks are related.

2. Getting Organized

Lack of organization contributes to procrastination for when you approach your work in a disorganized fashion tasks feel more overwhelming and generally take longer to accomplish. Follow the suggestions from earlier in the chapter regarding:

a. Things to do lists

b. Create a realistic schedule

c. Do it when you think of it

In addition, consider these tips:

d. *Modify your work environment*

Your work environment can be conducive to getting down to business or it can promote procrastination depending on how you arrange your work space. Remove as many distractions as possible from your work sphere. Take an hour to clean up your desk or work space. Throw out all unnecessary papers or paraphernalia.

e. *Block off escape routes*

Unplug the telephone, close your door, turn off the TV. Arrange your work station so you have all the materials you need to get started. That way you avoid getting up, and possibly getting distracted, to get various items.

3. The Five Minute Method

You can use this technique to start a wave of positive momentum. Pick that task or project that you have been delaying starting and then agree to start and work on it for just five minutes. At the end of this time period you can stop or you can ask yourself whether you are willing to invest another five minutes. Do this as a non demand procedure and follow your sincere inclinations. You do not have to work beyond the first interval, but if you are like most people, once you have gotten past the first five minutes (getting started is often the hardest part), you will probably find that you can easily continue. So you can work for another five minutes, and perhaps another, and before long you are working steadily. Many people find that once they get started it is far less onerous or aversive than anticipated. Once a significant amount has been done the drive for completion kicks in as you desire to get the task finished and behind you. Likewise, when you begin or complete one task it is often easier to switch over to other long postponed activities (particularly if related to the first task), due to the build up of positive momentum.

4. Don't Wait for Inspiration

"Genius is 1% inspiration and 99% perspiration."
Thomas Edison

People who procrastinate when faced with a creative endeavor often delay in order to wait for that moment of "inspiration" to overtake them before they begin. Instead of putting off your project, use probability theory to help you begin. When you begin a project, with or without any particular inspiration, you stand a good chance of perhaps stumbling into a streak of spontaneous brilliance and producing extremely good work. Or at the very least, you greatly increase your chances of getting some very good ideas for that task or future projects. The more you produce the greater the probability that some of it will be very good.

But what if your work or creation fails to live up to your standards? It is perfectly OK if some of what you turn out is not very good. Do you really think that every canvas turned out by Picasso was ready to hang in the Louvre? And do you honestly believe that Mozart never wrote a sour note, or that your favorite author doesn't have a wastebasket filled with crumpled, rejected pages? As consumers of artwork or books we see only the finished products which usually have been refined countless times. Successful artists and writers thrive by giving themselves permission to make mistakes and produce a certain amount of garbage in the process of doing good work.

Playing the probabilities also gives you the opportunity to hone your skills through experience and practice. If your work requires creative projects or writing, or if you are an artist, musician or writer who is not currently inspired, forcing yourself to work at the very least will improve your level of craftsmanship. So when inspiration does come you will be far better prepared to perform.

5. Reward Yourself

All human behavior is motivated by reward or by the expectation of reward in the future. A reward is anything that feels good, be it money, praise, awards, a new car, a vacation, a back rub, etc. Humans can often sustain unrewarded behaviors for long periods of time as long as there is some hope for reward down the line. Procrastination persists because it is reinforced by the immediate reward of relief from task avoidance. Tasks that you dread and delay may often have rewards associated with them, but typically they are in the future or you need to wade through discomfort first to get those rewards. Even though procrastination carries with it many long term punishments (including lowering your effectiveness and increasing your stress level), the short term rewards motivate you to keep delaying. To counterbalance the rewarding aspects of procrastination, it is important to find ways to make the "dreaded task" also rewarding in the short run. Peruse these suggestions for ways to reinforce yourself and see which ones appeal to you. Try them out the next time you put something off.

a. The Premack Principle

One way to build in rewards for getting it done is to utilize the **Premack Principle**, postulated by David Premack. The principle states that if two behaviors differ in their likelihood of occurrence (i.e. you are more likely to do one rather than the other) the less likely behavior can be reinforced by using the more likely behavior as a reward. In layman's terms, this strategy capitalizes on the fact that any activity you find enjoyable can be used as a reward or incentive for working on a task you tend to put off. Here you give yourself permission to engage in rewarding activities contingent upon doing the tasks you tend to put off (i.e. you could schedule a massage for yourself after finally completing that report).

b. The Profit-Penalty System

Rewarding yourself works when you make the rewards meaningful and present them only upon completion of the desired task (or chunk if you are using the bits and pieces approach). In general, punishment is a very ineffective way of inspiring change. You have already been exposed to the negative consequences of procrastination many times, and if that worked you wouldn't continue to delay! Punishment as a way of modifying behavior can be useful, however, when it is done strategically and in combination with a reward system.

In the **Profit Penalty System** you use both a reward and penalty in tandem. You start by breaking a project into doable chunks and set up a reward contingent upon successful completion of the piece. At the same time you can also penalize yourself for non-completion. In the **Double Profit Penalty System** you create a no-lose situation for yourself. You make a contract with yourself where non-completion of one specified task is linked up with the need to complete another avoided task. With such a plan you cannot lose, for whenever you delay, you must compensate for this by being productive in another area. Therefore, you "win if you do and win if you don't".

6. Viewing Mistakes as Feedback

Perhaps you procrastinate for fear of making a mistake or doing something poorly. However, it is quite irrational to think that leaving yourself even less time to complete something will make you less likely to make mistakes. And where is it written that it is catastrophic or even necessarily bad to make a mistake? Mistakes are feedback, nothing more and nothing less. Both forms of feedback, correct and incorrect, are equally vital for the learning process. Without both we learn more slowly.

Research reveals a strong link between procrastination and perfectionism (Flett, Blankstein, Hewitt & Koledin, 1992). Perfectionism goes hand in hand with fear of failure. If you maintain a perfectionistic attitude you will be more prone to stall until you can "do it right", or you avoid because you fear that you can never do it right. So what if you do it and part of it is wrong? Is the world going to come to an end? If you delay, that is the equivalent of doing it wrong anyhow. At least, if you go ahead and complete it, you stand a chance of getting part or all of it right. We have no quarrel with striving for excellence, but that is not the same as holding out for perfection.

You cannot achieve excellence without making mistakes along the way or risking making other errors. In short, making mistakes is an essential part of improving yourself. What is necessary is to adopt a healthy attitude about being in error. It means learning to laugh at yourself and not take yourself so seriously all the time. Oftentimes, what endears you to others are memories of those times when you made a funny mistake. We recognize that not all mistakes are funny, but the vast majority of errors are harmless and ultimately can be humourous or neutral if viewed from the proper perspective (refer to reframing in Chapter 2).

THE EFFECTIVE STUDENT

The fact that you are reading this book and/or taking this course indicates that you are a student, if not in school per se, then at least a student of your own life, interested in learning how to function more effectively. Whether you are a full time or a part time student, whether you are fresh from high school or returning to college after years in the workplace, it pays to master the techniques and strategies that can enable you to achieve academic success. The ability to mange your time wisely and stay on task will serve you well in this context. While a comprehensive review, or an in-depth exploration of the myriad ways to develop and improve your study habits is certainly beyond the scope of this text, in the pages that follow we will offer you a sampling (a smorgasbord if you will) of tips that we have found to be the most crucial for promoting academic effectiveness. These tips fall into three basic categories: (1) improving your memory; (2) mastering a good study method; and (3) mastering test taking strategies including overcoming test anxiety and developing test taking sophistication.

Improving Memory Retention

While there are many gimmicks and so-called herbal panaceas for supercharging your memory, the fact remains that you first have to learn something, and often learn it well, before you can expect to remember it. There are no magic substitutes or reliable short cuts for the memory enhancement steps outlined below, but if you follow these strategies we guarantee significant improvement in your retention skills.

1. **Pay attention.** If you are not paying adequate attention, information will never be properly encoded and thus never transferred into either your short term or long term memory. This is why popular sleep learning products rarely work (i.e. tapes to learn a foreign language while you sleep). It's likely you can remember a time when you went to class but were so distracted or preoccupied with other matters that you were clueless as to what was presented. Just showing up is not enough.

2. **Learn the material very well.** Contrary to popular belief, overlearning aids in retention.

3. **Organize the material.** Create an organizational structure that makes sense to you. One way to do this is to rewrite your lecture notes in outline form while it is still relatively fresh in your mind, or outline a chapter in your textbook. To the extent that you can make information meaningful to you by relating it to other concepts or experiences with which you are familiar, it will be much easier to remember. This occurs because it promotes the kinds of associations which facilitate memory retrieval.

4. **Use rehearsal.** The more you rehearse information you are learning, the stronger your ability to retrieve and recall it. But this doesn't mean that you should just reread the same material over and over again, rather, what is more effective is to paraphrase the information by putting it in your own words, or even better, attempting to explain it to another person.

5. **Minimize rote memorization.** The rote method, where you attempt to just memorize information without any organization, has only limited utility. As stated above, we tend to remember that which is meaningful to us, so rote memorization is only helpful if and when you create a meaningful structure and attempt to commit that to memory.

6. **Write it down.** Taking notes or writing about material you are attempting to learn (particularly if you paraphrase) is a powerful tool for transferring information into long term memory. This is also important for remembering day to day, practical information as discussed earlier in this chapter. That is why Things to Do lists, reminder lists, appointment calenders etc. are so helpful. Among researchers in the field of memory enhancement, these are the most frequently used memory aids.

7. **Use memory aids when appropriate.** These techniques, called **mnemonics**, are very helpful, particularly for remembering strings or lists of information. These systems work by making material more meaningful by adding a structure, such as making it into a song or rhyme, or linking it with other entrenched memories (like the letters of the alphabet).

8. **Reduce interference and distractions.** One of the biggest factors causing you to forget is the role of interference. Competing information, both related and unrelated, that you have learned before and after you

study, can interfere with memory retrieval. When new learning interferes with previous learning, this is termed **retroactive interference**. When old learning inhibits retention of new material, this is called **proactive interference**. Smart timing of studying can minimize interference factors. For example, studying just prior to going to sleep helps to prevent interference. Also, be careful not to study similar topics within the same study interval. Confusion between topics can lead to retroactive and/or proactive interference. By the same token, limit distractions while studying (i.e. a TV or radio in the background) because this too can create interference and disrupt later recall. Save watching TV or listening to music for your study breaks, or for a reward for staying on task for a specified work period. There can be some individual variability, however, as some people concentrate better with some background noise or music.

9. **Sleep on it.** As mentioned above, going to sleep immediately after studying minimizes interference with new learning because you are limiting your mental activity after studying. There is also evidence that sleep allows for the consolidation of newly learned material.

10. **Distribute learning sessions.** Avoid cramming by spreading your study periods over spaced time intervals. Data indicates that two or three shorter study periods interspersed with breaks are usually more effective than one long, unbroken, exhausting study session. When studying more than one subject, be sure to take breaks between subjects so as to reduce the potential for interference effects. To further inhibit interference, make sure you engage in activities unrelated to your studying during your breaks (i.e. Kick back and have some fun!). But if you must study several subjects in one day, try to vary the topics as much as possible, again to decrease the potential for interference.

11. **Exercise.** Research appears to indicate that physical exercise facilitates memory in humans as well as animals (Samorajski, Delaney, Durham, Ordy, Johnson & Dunlop, 1988). The reasons for this are still unclear, but researchers believe that increased levels of oxygen and brain nutrients stimulated by exercise are responsible for the boost in memory acuity.

12. **Test yourself.** Periodically obtain self feedback about what you have and have not retained by testing yourself. There are numerous ways to do this including end of chapter questions, practice exams, listing the important points you've learned from memory and cross checking this with your notes, etc. Keep in mind that, just because you felt that you understood the material presented in class or in your textbook, this does not guarantee that you will remember it the next day without practicing the steps outlined above.

13. **Be aware of the influence of learning contexts.** It helps with information retrieval if you can learn the material in a situation similar to the one requiring recall of that same information. This applies to the physical environment you are learning in (i.e. the room, the seating arrangement, the lighting, etc.) as well as your emotional state. In other words,

if you study in the library and it is very similar to your classroom, then it is easier to remember. And did you know that interference can be reduced just by studying two different subjects in two different rooms (Higbee, 1988)?

An Effective Study Method—The SQ3R

In the Introduction we mentioned a particular study strategy that we recommended for approaching this textbook. Actually we advocate that you use this method for studying in general. To reiterate, many educators laud a study system known by the acronym of the "**SQ3R**". If you use this technique for studying any textbook, you will find that it will greatly enhance your understanding and retention of course material. The SQ3R method consists of the following:

- **Survey:** Before beginning the book thoroughly survey the Table of Contents to get the big picture of what is covered. Then before reading each chapter, look it over to get an overview of the information covered in that particular section.

- **Question:** Before reading each chapter in full, briefly skim it and jot down any questions that occur to you about the material.

- **Read:** Carefully read the chapter and find answers to the questions that you previously asked while skimming the chapter.

- **Recite:** Paraphrase what you have learned. To reiterate, putting material into your own words greatly enhances your ability to understand and retain information. One helpful hint for doing this is to explain the material to yourself as if you were attempting to explain it to a friend or younger sibling.

- **Review:** After each chapter, go over the material carefully, including answering the end of chapter questions and making sure you know the definitions to all key terms.

The Art of Taking Tests

In your role as a student you are inevitably faced with that sometimes onerous task of taking tests, often multiple exams in each course you take. Unlike in high school, in college your test scores may determine most, if not all, of your grade. One of the most frequent student complaints center around an inability to do well on tests despite adequate preparation. Meanwhile, other students breeze through tests, getting high grades with minimal preparation. Is this just a function of the **survival of the smartest**? No—not at all. Psychologists have long recognized that certain students possess a set of skills, along with an emotional equilibrium, that contributes to passing and doing well on tests. Of course, adequate preparation lays the solid foundation, but test taking skills can confer an added edge. These test taking skills fall into two main categories.

Mastering Test Anxiety

Recall from Chapter 2 when we talked about the Yerkes-Dodson law, the fact that you are more likely to perform well when you are moderately aroused. In test taking terms this means that having some anxiety before an exam is actually a good thing, because it heightens your mental alertness and acuity. But very high anxiety levels can interfere with performance, particularly on difficult tasks such as a hard or confusing exam. Have you ever failed or done poorly on a test for which you thought that you were well prepared? Have you ever been so anxious about a test that you totally blanked out, unable to think straight or recall information you knew well just hours before? If you suspect that test anxiety is a problem for you, fill out the following brief self test to check this out.

TABLE 7.1 Measuring Test Anxiety

Read the following statements and rate how they apply to you, using the following scale.

0 = Never   1= Sometimes   2 = Often   3 = Always

_____1. I do not feel that I study properly for tests.

_____2. I typically begin to feel nervous several days before a test.

_____3. My nervousness increases on the day of the test.

_____4. I believe that I will do poorly on tests.

_____5. If I do not know an answer, I begin to panic.

_____6. I get confused when taking rests.

_____7. Even if I have prepared adequately, I feel unsure of my answers.

_____8. I forget information that I have studied.

_____9. While I'm taking a test, I tell myself that I do not know the answers.

_____ Your Score

Interpretation:
A score of 12 or higher indicates you suffer from test anxiety. The higher your score beyond 12, the more debilitating your test anxiety will be. If all or even most of these statements frequently apply to you, pay particular attention to and follow the guidelines in the next section.

If your test anxiety level is high, there are a variety of techniques that can enable you to reduce your anxiety prior to and during test taking. **Remember—the goal here is not to be cool as a cucumber, but to get your anxiety down to that moderate, manageable level which will enhance your performance.**

Practice Active Relaxation—To help yourself unwind, do Progressive Muscle Relaxation just prior to your exam. You needn't even go through the whole sequence if you are pressed for time or in a setting not conducive to the technique. Just focus on tensing and relaxing the muscles in your shoulders, neck and head. Engage in diaphragmatic breathing at least 6–10 times prior to the test, and use it during the test if you need to calm yourself (Review Chapter 5 guidelines for these procedures).

Use Cognitive Restructuring—Following the instructions in Chapter 2, identify your irrational thoughts and fears regarding the test. Challenge your assumptions about failure and humiliation. Substitute rational, reassuring messages reminding yourself of past test taking successes, and about how well prepared you will be (based on heeding the study tips in the last few pages, of course!).

Visualize Success—Using the teachings on visualization in Chapter 6 as your guide here, first vividly imagine yourself in a relaxing scene. Pick a scene that you typically associate with calmness and tranquility, and put yourself there in your mind's eye. Once you are feeling mellow, then fantasize that you are about to start the test. Imagine yourself remaining tranquil, reading each exam question thoroughly and calmly, recognizing that you do know the right answers and then envisaging yourself getting fully absorbed with putting down your answers. Allow yourself to recall previous times of test taking success. Clearly remember those scenes and that sense of flowing with the exam. Visualizations of this type will boost your self confidence and help you to relax during the test. Remember that being able to vividly imagine a realistic scene makes it far more likely that you can realize that goal.

Testwiseness

Developing **testwiseness**, which is also called test sophistication, involves learning strategies for guessing that can help increase the likelihood of picking the right answer, particularly on multiple choice exams. Many studies have demonstrated that these methods can be learned, and that utilizing them improves test performance (McClain, 1987). McClain's work also revealed that high test scorers as a rule, carefully read and consider each test question and answer alternative, and that "A" students often try to come up with the correct answer prior to reading the answer alternatives. But being testwise is much more than just using tricks to improve guesswork. It involves:

* using your time during exams wisely
* mastering strategies to minimize your errors
* applying deductive reasoning (i.e. proceeding from the general to the specific)
* recognizing cues inherent in the tests which point to the right answers

We must stress, however, that **learning these strategies is not a substitute for studying**. Don't fool yourself into thinking you can go into a test totally unprepared, armed only with this system, and walk out with a good grade. These strategies can enhance your performance, to elevate a C performance to a B, or a B to an A, but no amount of cleverness in test taking can replace studying and learning the subject matter.

Testwiseness involves recognizing that many multiple choice tests have built in flaws within the questions that can help you determine or deduce the right answer, or, at the very least, help you eliminate certain alternatives. The common flaws are as follows:

1. Information in earlier or later questions can reveal the right answer. If you are stumped, skip a question for the time being because information that turns up in other questions may hold the key to the correct answer.

2. Alternatives that are highly implausible or improbable are likely to be incorrect and should be rejected. Options that contain flippant or overly judgmental words or phrases often fall into this category.

3. If two answers are equivalent or basically the same then neither can be correct, and both can be eliminated. On the flip side, if two answers are contradictory, then one is likely to be the correct option.

4. Correct answers are likely to be more detailed, longer and specific. When in doubt, pick the most detailed option.

5. Beware of all-inclusive words. Incorrect answers are far more likely to include words such as always, never, every time, everyone, etc.

6. Look for the greatest similarity in terminology between the question and the answers. The answer most similar to the question is more likely to be correct.

7. Be aware of grammatical inconsistencies between questions and answers (i.e. changes in verb tense, or singular to plural nouns, etc.). Exclude answers which contain such inconsistencies, and pick the options which match grammatically.

8. When questions have answer alternatives that include dates or numbers that are ordered, avoid picking the first or the last. The correct answer is usually somewhere in the middle rather than at the extremes.

9. If you have no idea as to the right answer, and there are no hidden clues anywhere in the question, select option C. For some reason, exam writers seem to slightly favor the third position (option C) for the correct answer.

10. Don't be afraid to change your answer. A myth has been perpetrated that your first guess has the greatest chance of being right. This is not necessarily the case. Several studies have demonstrated that regarding answer changes during tests, wrong to right changes outnumber right to wrong changes (Benjamin, Cavell, & Shallenberger, 1987).

Conclusion

Ultimately, managing your time wisely is about making choices for your life. No one is born a wizard at time management. Competent individuals recognize that a fundamental aspect of effectiveness involves being well organized, focused on important goals, productive, punctual, and able to study and prepare adequately when necessary. But accomplishing this often does not come naturally; it requires some effort and choice. To achieve this end you need not be perfect. It is not the end of the world if you occasionally waste your time; sometimes you need to just kick back and do nothing. And you are not an abject failure if you are not the epitome of organization at every moment. Effective individuals are adept at balancing, at knowing when to be organized, productive, and efficient, and when to rest and have fun. There are other areas of life where effective people are faced with important choices, most notably in the area of relationships. The next chapters focus on how to make choices that can facilitate satisfying interpersonal relationships.

SELF-EXERCISES:

1. Take the time to compose your personal mission statement. Really give it some thought and follow the suggested exercises for thinking it through. You will find that the effort you put into this will be well spent.

2. Pick two or three of the myriad suggestions for managing time that appeal the most to you, or are the most relevant for your particular situation. Make a commitment to experiment with using them for a two week period. Pay careful attention to the effects in your life.

3. If you have never experimented with using the SQ3R study method, try using it to prepare for your next upcoming exam and evaluate whether it was useful for you.

KEY TERMS

Pareto Principle (80/20 Rule)	Mnemonics
Premack Principle	Retroactive Interference
Mission Statement	Proactive Interference
Procrastination	SQ3R
Low Frustration Tolerance	Testwiseness
Profit-Penalty System	Defer Gratification
Double Profit-Penalty System	Power Nap

CHAPTER 7 QUESTIONS

True or False (T or F)

1. _____ Effectiveness is only about being efficient.

2. _____ Effective individuals focus on getting trivial busywork finished first in order to have time to focus on important tasks.

3. _____ Tasks which other people think are important should always be designated as your high priority items.

4. _____ Essential activities and central concerns should comprise your high priority items.

5. _____ Making Things to Do Lists is a total waste of time.

6. _____ Effective people tend to be disorganized because that contributes to their creativity.

7. _____ Breaking a large project into doable chunks or steps is an excellent strategy to avoid feeling overwhelmed.

8. _____ Effective people spread their focus and do multiple important tasks simultaneously.

9. _____ Effective individuals always strive for perfection.

10. _____ It helps to schedule tasks to correspond to your personal body rhythms.

11. _____ Unfortunately, it is impossible to make productive use of time you spend waiting.

12. _____ Effective people spend most of their time dealing with tasks that are urgent but not important.

13. _____ Attitude change follows behavior change.

14. _____ Memory enhancement strategies work well even if you are not paying attention.

15. _____ Long, unbroken study sessions are superior for learning and retention over study periods interspersed with short breaks.

16. _____ Sleeping after studying helps consolidate the material you have reviewed.

17. _____ Paraphrasing your study notes only contributes to interference with memory.

18. _____ In order to do well on a test you need to be completely calm and relaxed.

19. _____ On multiple choice tests, correct answers tend to be longer, more detailed and specific.

20. _____ Never change a test answer because your first impression is usually the correct one.

21. _____ Using testwise methods can help you do well on exams without studying.

Short-Answer Questions

1. Composing a _____ helps you determine what is important in your life and serves as a guide for decision making.

2. Covey recommends ordering your work tasks based on _____ and _____.

3. In order to maximize time spent in Q II activities you must be _____.

4. The main cause of procrastination is _____.

5. When new learning interferes with old learning this is referred to as _____ _____.

6. _____ refers to approaching test questions in a way that facilitates picking the correct answer.

Essay Questions

1. Define the 80/20 rule.

2. Describe two common time wasters and how to counteract them.

3. What is a power nap?

4. According to Steven Covey, what kind of tasks (in terms of their relative importance and urgency) help us to be proactive?

5. What kinds of irrational beliefs contribute to procrastination?

6. Describe the Five Minute Method for combating procrastination.

7. Which of the six techniques described for overcoming procrastination would you use if you found yourself delaying unnecessarily on something?

8. Describe the five steps of the SQ3R method.

9. What are some methods you can use to decrease debilitating test anxiety?

10. Explain the role of interference factors in disrupting retention of learned material.

11. Why does organizing study material make it easier to learn and remember?

SECTION TWO

*Interpersonal
Effectiveness*

Develop Your Emotional Intelligence

Build Trust as You Communicate—Part I

Build Trust as You Communicate—Part II

8

Develop Your Emotional Intelligence

This textbook has spent a lot of time talking about effectiveness. But what do we really mean by effectiveness? To define it as success in school, or in a career, or in terms of income level, is of course, far too narrow a definition to be meaningful. In general, effectiveness refers to competency in skills for living in your personal life, in your relationships, and in your chosen occupation, hence the overall organization of this book to address those three broad areas. This book has been designed to foster the development of building blocks for effectiveness. Acquisition of various skills build in a cumulative fashion which will become evident as you read further.

THE CONCEPT OF EMOTIONAL INTELLIGENCE

In his groundbreaking 1995 book, *Emotional Intelligence,* psychologist Daniel Goleman summarizes a body of theory and research emphasizing the fundamental role of **emotional intelligence** (termed the EQ) in effectiveness and life success. Dr. Goleman reminds us that high intelligence (as measured by IQ tests, SAT scores, G.P.A.'s. etc.) is a very poor predictor of who will succeed and/or be effective in life. So the good news here is that you don't need to be a rocket scientist to be an effective human being. But why is it that, among individuals with relatively equal potential in terms of levels of intelligence, education, and opportunity, only certain ones excel while others flounder? For example, a longitudinal study (Valliant, 1977) was conducted with a sample of Harvard graduates from the 1940's, following them over several decades of life. Back in the 1940's there was much greater variability in admission testing scores for Harvard enrollees than exists today. Those with the highest SAT scores actually tended to be less successful than their lower scoring counterparts with regard to career success, income and even more importantly, in their interpersonal lives, as measured by marital satisfaction and quality of social life. In a similar vein, an ongoing study of valedictorians and salutatorians graduating from high schools in Illinois in 1981, as reported in the Chicago

Tribune, revealed that while this group continued to achieve academically in college, they did not necessarily excel later on in their careers. Ten years after high school graduation, only 25% of this group had risen to the higher levels of their chosen professions. Another study, (Felsman & Valliant, 1987) conducted with hundreds of boys who grew up in a slum in Massachusetts, many of whom had low IQ's, found that IQ level was not a good predictor of employment stability. The researchers concluded that other factors such as frustration tolerance, ability to control emotions, and to get along well with others were far more important.

Goleman concludes that IQ contributes at most about 20% to the factors leading to success in life. The other 80% is due to other factors, and Goleman makes the convincing case that many of these other characteristics comprise that set of attitudes, skills and behaviors that we have come to know as emotional intelligence. So what exactly is this *"emotional intelligence"*? It includes such skills as being able to motivate yourself and persevere in the face of frustration, to delay gratification, to control your emotions and impulses (i.e. think before you act), to empathize with others, and to think positively. EQ is a relatively new concept, but what psychologists are discovering is that it is just as important, if not more powerful than IQ, in contributing to your effectiveness. And while IQ is a relatively stable attribute, your EQ can be modified and improved far more readily.

Gardner (1983) was one of the first to attack the notion of an overall IQ, preferring to break intelligence into a wide spectrum of intellectual abilities. Initially he posited seven types of intelligence, with the first two representing the traditional academically based abilities of verbal and mathematical aptitude. Along with this he described spatial intelligence (relating to artistic abilities), kinesthetic intelligence (related to athletic ability), musical intelligence, and two levels of emotional intelligence characterized by leadership skills and people skills. Later Gardner subdivided emotional intelligence into four components: (1) leadership skills; (2) the ability to make friends and nurture relationships; (3) the ability to resolve conflicts and (4) emotional perceptiveness. He emphasized the role of what he termed intrapersonal intelligence, that is, knowing and understanding yourself and your emotional reactions, and interpersonal intelligence, the ability to read and understand other people along with how to work cooperatively with them.

Goleman takes this one step further and divides emotional intelligence into five domains:

1. **Self Awareness**—the ability to know your own emotions. This involves being able to adopt the witnessing stance so as to master self understanding and insight into your own needs and feelings. Knowing and understanding your feelings gives you more direction for wise decision making. (See Chapters 5 and 6.)

2. **Managing your emotions**—the ability to master stress, control anger, overcome depression and anxiety, and remain optimistic, etc., all contribute to skills in being resilient so as to bounce back from life's inevitable setbacks. (The lessons from Chapters 1 through 5 are relevant here, along with the section on managing anger in the later part of this chapter.)

3. **Self-motivation**—the ability to persevere, to delay gratification and wait for rewards (i.e. Remember the marshmallow study!), and to stay focused and on task is essential in most life endeavors, particularly those that involve long term goals. (Chapter 7 on time management, in particular the section on overcoming procrastination, is very applicable here.)

4. **Perceptiveness**—the ability to perceive and correctly identify the emotions of others along with skill at recognizing the impact of your behavior on others. The cornerstone of this is the ability to empathize with others, to literally be able to put yourself in the shoes of another person, along with the ability to read and understand nonverbal cues. (This chapter and the next will help you acquire and sharpen these important skills.)

5. **Handling relationships**—skill in relating to others and managing their emotions. It involves listening skills, conversational skills, being able to resolve conflicts, and knowing how to be appropriately assertive. It also subsumes the ability to establish rapport with others along with leadership skills. (Once again, this chapter and Chapters 9–10 will hone your abilities in these areas. In this chapter we focus on helping you learn effective methods for managing conflicts with others and mastering your own emotional responses.)

EFFECTIVENESS IN RELATIONSHIPS

When you were a child, you were dependent on your parents for all your basic needs. You needed them to feed you, look after your safety, educate you, and generally make sure that you survived (You even needed them to wipe your behind!). As you grew and matured you became increasingly less dependent on others for meeting your basic needs, but you still remained dependent financially and emotionally. Your goal, if you are like most Americans, is to become independent. Indeed, independence has been glorified by our culture and by the media. History books pay homage to the rugged individualists who helped tame and expand our country from coast to coast. These were individuals who depended primarily on themselves and the land for their survival. Popular culture lionizes figures like the Lone Ranger who personified the qualities of independence and courage. The current drive to own a car (no pun intended) is partly an outgrowth of this need for independence, the ability to rely on yourself to get where you want to go.

From Independence to Interdependence

In the previous chapters we have explored what we believe to be the essential elements of personal effectiveness. If you practice these and incorporate them into your life you will find yourself becoming a truly independent person, someone who recognizes that his life is his own responsibility, who sets a direction for his life and then can make things happen. But truly effective people realize that independence, while certainly a worthy goal, is the not the end of the road. You see, we really are not islands onto ourselves. Personal effectiveness is not enough. To be genuinely effective, you have to learn to become

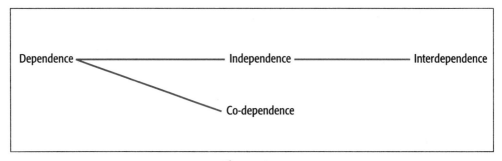

Figure 8.1

interdependent. **Interdependence** is the relationship that ensues when two or more independent individuals decide to come together to achieve a common goal. They recognize that by working together they can achieve much more than the mere sum of their individual accomplishments. This has been referred to in the literature as **synergy**. Healthy marriages are characterized by interdependence, resulting from two spouses working as a team to satisfy mutual interests, such as paying the bills, raising the children, cleaning the house, etc. In fact, interdependent relationships, whether in a marriage, a business partnership, or a friendship are typified by mutual respect and a workable division of labor.

Unfortunately, many individuals in our society go from being dependent to being **co-dependent**. Co-dependent individuals depend on each other because deep inside they feel they could not survive on their own. Rather than give support to each other's growth, they seek to create situations which assure them that they will not be left alone. That is, they seek to make the other person dependent on them, just as they are dependent on the other person. The classic example is that of an alcoholic husband and his co-dependent wife. Although she professes that she wants her husband to stop drinking, she dutifully buys his six packs so that he won't be angry at her. While co-dependency can masquerade as interdependence, the difference lies in that true interdependence can only be achieved after you have successfully become independent. Figure 8.1 visually represents the continuum from dependence to interdependence with co-dependence as an offshoot which bypasses independence.

While we are saying that the road to interdependence, that is, interpersonal effectiveness, goes through independence, we are not implying that you must be perfectly independent. Becoming independent and interdependent is an ongoing, life long process. It not a static goal that you achieve, but rather one which you continually move towards.

THE WIN-WIN FRAME

Just as personal effectiveness required adopting a frame of proactivity, interpersonal effectiveness begins by embracing the paradigm of win-win. To be interdependent, and therefore interpersonally effective, you must set out looking for win-win outcomes. According to Adler and Towne (1993), when you approach an interaction within the framework of win-win . . .

"the goal is to find a solution that satisfies the needs of everyone involved. Not only do the parties avoid trying to win at the other's expense, but they also believe that by working together it is possible to find a solution that goes beyond a mere compromise and allows everyone to reach their goals."

This might be obvious, but we are here to tell you that it is easier said than done. We often introduce this concept to our students by engaging in a simple demonstration. We ask for two volunteers to come up in front of the class and arm wrestle with each other. The rules are that each time one participant pins the other, he receives a dollar as a reward. We tell them that they have one minute to get as many pins as possible. What would you do if you were one of those students? What typically happens is that the two struggle against one another, trying with all their might to pin the other whom they perceive as their opponent. As a result, very few pins are recorded and very little money is earned. If they approached the task with a win-win outlook, they would quickly realize that the way to maximize earnings is to offer no resistance, and merely take turns quickly pinning one another. With this frame of mind they could conceivably pin each other as often as once per second and each walk away with a bulging wallet.

The Prisoner's Dilemma

There is a experimental research design in social psychology known as the **prisoner's dilemma**. Imagine that Jose and Tashara have been arrested for robbing the Vanguard Savings Bank and placed in separate cells, unable to communicate with each other. Both care much more about their personal freedom than about the welfare of their accomplice. The prosecutor assigned to the case makes each the following offer. "You may choose to confess or remain silent. If you confess and your accomplice remains silent, I will drop all charges against you and use your testimony to insure that your accomplice does serious time. Likewise, if your accomplice confesses while you remain silent, he will go free while you do the time. If you both confess, I will get two convictions, but I will see to it that you both get an early parole. If you both remain silent, I'll have to settle for token sentences on firearms possession charges. If you wish to confess, you must leave a note with the jailer before my return tomorrow morning."

The "dilemma" here is that each gains the most if one confesses and the other does not. Yet the outcome obtained when both confess is worse for each than the outcome they would get if both remain silent. So if both cooperate, they both end up winning, but if they both compete, they both end up losing. This research paradigm has been extensively studied under numerous conditions. In fact, more than a thousand journal articles about it were published in the sixties and seventies. This design has three possible outcomes: (1) one subject wins by betraying a partner; (2) both win by cooperating; or (3) both lose by competing and betraying each other. In a classic series of experiments utilizing this research design, Robert Axelrod (1984) submitted results which clearly indicated that the biggest winners in the long run were the ones who cooperated, demonstrating that win-win outcomes are not only desirable in theory but also in practice. Yet most subjects assumed that by competing and betraying their partner, they could maximize their winnings. Sound familiar? This is reminiscent of the arm wrestling experiment done with our students.

Win-Lose or Lose-Win Outcomes

The model that has been ingrained in almost all of us is one of competition, not cooperation, leading to **win-lose outcomes** where (hopefully) you win and they lose, or **lose-win outcomes** where you lose and the other person wins. Think about it. Sports are based on win-lose. Card games and board games are also based on win-lose. Similarly our educational system is based on a win-lose paradigm where students are compared to each other, with some coming out on top with A's and B's, and others winding up on the bottom with D's and F's. Admissions to universities, and access to scholarships and grants are dependent on how you stack up against your fellow students on various measures. So it is not surprising that we hang a frame of win-lose when approaching most situations, even when such a frame does not yield the most effective results. We often fail to realize that other frameworks even exist.

If you are playing tennis, or chess, or any other competitive event, we recommend that you still put your focus on beating your opponent. After all, it would get really boring to shoot hoops if you let each other score without playing defense. However, we strongly recommend extreme caution in trying to win in the arena of interpersonal relationships, whether at home or at work. If someone asked you who was winning at your marriage or at your relationship, we hope you would recognize the absurdity of this question. Yet most often, spouses with troubled marriages enter marital counseling with the hope that the therapist will choose sides and explain to their partner how wrong they are. You see, they are hoping the psychologist will declare them the winner and their partner the loser. Perhaps this helps to explain why over fifty percent of marriages end up in divorce. It is explained rather early on in the process of marital therapy, that in interdependent relationships if you are both not winning, you both end up losing in the long run.

Lose-Lose Outcomes

A **lose-lose** outlook is one which assumes that none of the participants can get what they want and neither side is satisfied with the outcome. It's hard to imagine how anyone could deliberately go for a lose-lose outcome, yet this is a fairly common way of failing to resolve conflict. Since both parties have their focus solely on winning they fail to realize that as a result of their struggle they often both end up losers. Perfect examples of this on the global scene are the many wars which have been waged throughout history. On an interpersonal level most of us have witnessed battles of pride where both parties dig in their heels and end up losing in order to save face.

Other Possible Outcomes

Steven Covey, who teaches us to *"Think Win-Win"* in his popular 7 *Habits* book, also lists two other possible outcomes. One alternative is to go for **Win** without concern for whether the other party loses or wins. Here the outcome for the other party is irrelevant. You don't necessarily want to defeat the other person, your only concern is whether your needs get met. Another possibility is what Covey refers to as **Win-Win or No Deal**. Here the parties agree that if they cannot find a solution that is mutually beneficial then there is no deal. The parties walk away agreeing to disagree. This is more common in the context of a business deal where parties negotiate and discover that a mutually beneficial arrangement is not possible so they agree not to enter into the deal. Covey points out that this is a far better outcome than if the parties entered into a business relationship, deal, or contract which later turned out poorly, leading to disillusionment and conflict.

Win-Win Outcomes

Good relationships embody the ability to compromise, to find ways that allow each party to get some of what they need. Great relationships embody the ability to synergize. That is, they find ways for both parties to collaborate and create means that allow for the needs of each to be met. In other words, they find a way for everyone to win. As Steven Covey has said, *"this requires courage and consideration"*. Courage helps us stand up for what we need. Consideration allows us to honor the fact that others feel their needs as deeply as we feel ours. Consider this story for a moment . . .

> Two young girls are fighting over a single remaining orange. Both simply insist that they need it. In a win-lose relationship one of the children will end up with the orange, and one will end up with nothing but bad feelings and a desire to win the next time. In a good relationship they will cut the orange in half and share it. They will compromise and this is better than one of them losing. Neither, however, is completely satisfied. In a great relationship they speak to one another about why they want the orange. As it turns out, one of them needs the peel for a recipe and the other simply wants some orange juice. Both can have everything they want because they had the courage to speak up for themselves and the consideration to listen.

Barriers to Win-Win

It is obvious that win-win resolutions to conflict are superior to win-lose and lose-lose solutions. Why is it then that win-win outcomes are rare? There are three basic obstacles to win-win solutions with the first being that often people are oblivious to the possibility of a win-win solution. As mentioned beforehand in the arm wrestling example, and extensively supported by the research on the prisoner's dilemma, we are all socialized to be competitive and to mistakenly define winning as defeating our opponent.

A bigger barrier that prevents many people from seeking win-win solutions is anger or resentment. Disagreements and conflicts are often emotional affairs where people get so caught up in their emotions, in their need to be right, to win, or come out on top, that they reflexively resort to a combative approach without stopping to consider other alternatives. The latter part of this chapter deals with handling anger. Learning to work through negative emotions constructively will help put you in the frame of mind necessary to think clearly and be open to win-win possibilities.

Lastly, win-win outcomes are unusual because they require the cooperation of the other person as well. No matter how creative and open you are to generating a win-win outcome, it can be difficult to do so if the other person's primary agenda is to defeat you. In this case the challenge is to persuade the other to see how a spirit of cooperation is in his or her best interests as well as yours.

Mental Sets Essential for Win-Win

Effective individuals operate from a model of looking for win-win solutions to disagreements or conflicts, whenever possible. As stated before, not all situations lend themselves to win-win outcomes, but in the arena of interpersonal relationships, most conflicts can be approached from a standpoint of cooperation. There are three mental sets that you will need to incorporate into your way of thinking that are prerequisites to generating win-win options and win-win solutions.

Making Deposits into the Emotional Bank Account

In order for win-win to be possible, both parties need to trust one another. But how do you build trust? Stephen Covey coined the concept of an **emotional bank account** which we hold with each other just by virtue of being in a relationship. We continually make withdrawals from and deposits into this bank account. The amount of trust experienced in a relationship is directly proportional to the balance in this account. Consider a romantic relationship. When you first meet the person, you make numerous deposits into the emotional bank account. You are attentive, complementary, you listen because you really want to get to know the other person. You call them often, spend time with them, maybe exchange gifts. Perhaps you might even put the object of your desire up on a pedestal. But as so often happens, after the novelty wears off, you begin to take the other person for granted. You stop making as many deliberate deposits. There is a tendency to assume that the balance will stay static. After all, you have made many deposits. You forget that you make withdrawals just because you have different needs or because you may, at times, act in an insensitive fashion. As time passes, all the little withdrawals add up, and you no longer have funds in the account. That is when the relationship gets into trouble.

Our ongoing relationships, like marriage, parenthood, or business partnerships, require frequent, ongoing deposits. Old deposits evaporate if you don't replenish them. If you run into an old friend that you haven't seen for years, it is often possible to pick-up right where you left off because your earlier deposits are still there and there have been no withdrawals. But with people that you interact with regularly, more frequent investment is necessary. Remember, you are likely oblivious to some of your withdrawals. Covey recommends six types of deposits that help build the fund in your emotional bank account with another:

- **Understand the Individual**—In order to make deposits, you must first know what the other considers a deposit. You can only do this by learning to really listen to learn a person's needs or interests. Remember that what may be a deposit for you, may be meaningless, or even a withdrawal for someone else.

- **Attend to the Little Things**—Oftentimes it is the little things that count the most. Small insensitive things that you do or forget to do, add up to be large withdrawals. On the other hand, those small niceties or favors that you do for another are often the purest proof that you care. In fact, frequent small deposits typically lead to larger balances than the occasional huge deposit. In relationships, the little things are the big things.

- **Keep Your Commitments**—Remember the power of your word. Keeping your promises constitutes a major deposit and is an essential element of trust. Breaking your promises, particularly if this happens regularly, constitutes a major withdrawal.

- **Clarify Your Expectations**—You can create many problems and potential withdrawals by assuming that your expectations are self-evident and understood by the other person. *Keep in mind, other people are not mind readers.* It is a major deposit to make your expectations explicit and clear right from the beginning.

- **Show Personal Integrity**—Integrity embodies many things, all of which are essential for trust to develop. Integrity is more than just being honest or keeping your word. It is also about being loyal and fair. One of the best ways you can show that you are loyal and fair is by acting this way towards those who are *not* present. If you are two-faced and criticize or gossip about others behind their back, those present can't help but wonder if you will do the same to them.

- **Apologize Sincerely When You Make a Withdrawal**—Those with integrity admit when they have been wrong and apologize from the heart. It takes courage and high self-esteem to do this. Yet a genuine apology is a major deposit into any relationship.

Giving up Being Right

When relating to others, one of the strongest barriers to cooperation is our incredibly strong need to be right. It seems that human beings are the kind of beings who just need to be right. And this seems to be the case only with humans. Think about it, animals clearly do not display this tendency. For example, if a stray dog was used to frequenting a certain restaurant to feast on leftovers and steak bones in the garbage, and then suddenly the restaurant discontinued the practice of having easily accessible leftovers, Rover would no doubt return several times to check it out, but he would then roam elsewhere in search of a good meal. Rover is able to forget about being right. He just switches his behavior to something else that works. Animals don't care about being right; they just want to be happy. People, on the other hand, are a different story. If a group of people was used to eating a certain favored dish in a restaurant and it was taken off the menu, they would first complain bitterly. If the restaurant did not capitulate, they then might form a committee to investigate the problem further. They might decide to picket the restaurant or call for a boycott. Perhaps they would even sue the restaurant for denying them their constitutional right to their favorite meal. But all the time they were being right they would be hungry!

Interpersonally effective individuals realize that always needing to be right does not lead to satisfying relationships. Instead they operate from the premise that they would rather be happy than right. We suggest that when involved in interpersonal struggle, you ask yourself the question: Would I rather be right or happy? You see, being happy often requires giving up the need to be right. Please understand that giving up being right does not necessarily imply you are wrong. It just means that you switch your focus from winning the argument or disagreement to accepting that there are probably valid aspects of each viewpoint. Remember the lessons from Chapter 1? There is no substitute for your willingness to experiment with different pairs of glasses and notice what happens when you do. In other words, *there is no right way to see things.* Of all the possible ways of looking at the world, the one most guaranteed to impede your effectiveness and create conflict is the one that insists that your way of seeing things is the right way.

Giving up trying to always be right is a really hard thing to do. Why? We all love being right. Right? We've been taught since our youngest days to do the "right thing" according to the authority figures that surround us. We are rewarded for it. We feel good about ourselves for doing it. We try to figure out what the right thing is because we want to succeed, to win. Our culture worships winning. We remember the winners and display their names prominently in our stadiums, magazines and commercials. Winners generally make a lot of money. The losers don't get the endorsements, the high praise. When you win you typically feel good about yourself. Losing often hurts. And losing can be stressful and threatening to your self esteem. The key is to remember that in the long run, in interpersonal relations, if all parties involved do not win, then you all lose.

Stepping Into the Shoes of the Other

But practically speaking, how do you give up the need to be right, to win in your personal relationships? When we are trying to be right, by definition we see the other as wrong in their point of view, in their way of thinking. In order to go for a win-win solution to a problem it helps to be able to *step into the other person's shoes and experience the world through their eyes.* To accomplish this we suggest that you use the skills of visualization and imagination that we have discussed earlier. Start the process by doing your relaxing breathing, and then begin to allow a sense of the other to form in your mind. See them in detail. Notice their expressions. Pay attention to the language they communicate through their body, their nonverbal communications. Hear not only the words they speak but the tone, tempo and volume of their speech. Speculate about what they are feeling. As you do this imagine that you can step into their body and look out of their eyes. Hear yourself saying the words and thinking the thoughts they might be thinking until you can feel what they are feeling. Do this until you can feel their sense of being right. Then step back into your own body and notice if you feel any differences. Could they possibly feel as strongly as you do? Is it possible that their position has merit as well? Remember, the idea is not necessarily to give up your position and adopt theirs (though that might happen). The idea is to move yourself to a place where you can work towards both of you meeting your needs, where both of you can win. Allowing yourself to feel, think and experience the other person's viewpoint is a powerful way of facilitating the process of win-win.

When Not to Try for Win-Win

Given that not every situation will lend itself to a win-win outcome, despite your best intentions, how do you know beforehand whether to approach a conflict from a win-win standpoint? Adler and Towne offer some guidelines to help you tailor your approach. They recommend that you:

1. Consider giving in to the other person and accepting a lose-win outcome when . . .

   ❀ you discover that you are in the wrong.

   ❀ the issue is very important to the other person and of minimal importance to you.

   ❀ other people need to learn a valuable lesson by making a mistake.

   ❀ the long term cost of winning outweighs the short term gains of such.

2. Consider a compromise when . . .

   ❀ sufficient time does not exist to forge a win-win solution.

   ❀ the issue is not important enough to spend time in further negotiation.

   ❀ the other person is definitely not open to a win-win outcome.

3. Consider competing and going for a win-lose outcome when . . .

   ❀ the issue is very important to you, the other person is certain to take advantage of you if you approach the situation in a noncompetitive fashion, and you are really not concerned with establishing a long term relationship.

4. Consider cooperation and trying for a win-win outcome when . . .

   ❀ the issue is too vital to settle for a compromise.

   ❀ a long term relationship between you and the other is at stake or in jeopardy.

   ❀ the other person is willing to cooperate.

CONFLICT RESOLUTION

When conflicts or disagreements erupt between friends, lovers, spouse or relatives, typically the problem is approached in an informal fashion. Ideally, all parties discuss their positions and needs, possible options and solutions are discussed, and eventually a consensus is forged. Giving up being right and being willing to step into the shoes of the other make it far easier to create a climate for effective problem solving and the possibility of a win-win outcome.

When conflict or disagreement exists between people who do not have emotional bonds with each other, the steps to effecting what has come to be called in the literature as **conflict resolution** tend to become more formalized. Many authors have put forth useful guidelines for conflict resolution. There is a lot of overlap between each of the different systems, yet each one has few unique elements. What follows is our synthesis of several systems which we have broken down into seven major steps. In theory, this format can be used by any individuals for resolving conflict, even if they have a close personal relationship, but in practice it is more likely to be used in more formalized situations such as business deals or conflicts, mediation to resolve lawsuits, etc. However, it is also often used to facilitate divorce agreements.

In reality the steps may not flow as smoothly as presented here. You may find it necessary to jockey back and forth between steps as snags develop in the process, or if you encounter resistance on the part of the other side. But in any event, it is important not to skip any of the steps. They all build upon one another. You can't have a building without a foundation, and you can't have a fourth floor without a third floor.

STEP ONE: Acknowledge/Identify the Problem or Conflict to Yourself

Don't run away from the conflict or attempt to avoid it with a premature resolution like immediately giving in, or insisting on your way or the highway. Admit to yourself that there is a problem, and recognize that some conflict is an unavoidable part of life, particularly among people who live or work together. What is important is how it is handled. But you also need to recognize that the problem that is causing the conflict belongs to you. Why? Because you are the one who is dissatisfied; you are the one who therefore needs to "own" the problem as yours. This is not the same as saying that it is all your fault or that you are to blame, but rather that it is your problem because it causes discontent for you. Recognizing this important fact will make a difference when the time comes to approach the other party involved. Instead of ranting or raving or being judgmental, it can help you state your concerns in a descriptive fashion, which will likely be more accurate and objective, and will minimize the possibility of eliciting a defensive reaction on the part of the other party. Part of acknowledging what the problem is for you is to identify to yourself what needs you have that are not being met as a result of this problem or conflict.

STEP TWO: Agree on a Date and a Procedure

It may be pointless to try to resolve a conflict unless all parties are prepared to do so and have set aside the time to do so. Fights often ensue because one party confronts another who isn't ready at that moment to deal with the issue at hand. It is very useful to set aside a time beforehand to deal with the issues, whether it is a conflict between spouses, a dispute between landlord and tenant, a clash between co-workers, or a disgruntled student seeking a meeting with his teacher. Request that a meeting time be set up at a mutually agreeable time and date. Make sure enough time is allotted to complete the process or at least to make some headway for more complicated issues. Decide the appropriate place where the meeting should take place. In business deals or legal disputes where negotiations may take place over several meetings, it may be wise to alternate locations since most people feel more comfortable on their home turf. Or it may be best to have the meeting in a neutral location. Another important procedural issue involves who will attend the meeting. If more than two parties are involved in the dispute, agree beforehand on who can and should be included in the meeting.

STEP THREE: Describe Your Problem and Your Needs

Even though your position may be different or in conflict with that of the other party, that does not mean that you do not have some shared or compatible interests. If you didn't have some shared interests you probably would not be sitting at the bargaining table to begin with. For example, if you have a dispute with your landlord, no matter what the nature of the conflict, it is in your landlord's interest to retain you as a tenant (assuming you pay your rent on time!), and it is in your interest to have your living conditions be up to par. Your landlord can only satisfy his need for a renter if he accommodates you in some fashion.

Describing your position has several aspects to it. The first aspect involves stating your position and your needs clearly and forthrightly. Following the guidelines for assertive responses presented in Chapter 10 will allow you to present your side effectively. Whenever possible use "I language", meaning that you state your position by describing what you want, what you need, how the situation creates difficulties for you, etc., rather than making "you statements" which place blame or shift responsibility for the situation onto the other party. In order to present your position effectively, it is important to do your homework. By this we mean plan what to say after thinking about it carefully. Feel free to use prepared statements, even charts or tables of figures if appropriate to highlight the salient points of your position.

After stating your wants and needs it is then often strategically useful to define the conflict in terms of a mutual problem to be solved, building on the notion of shared interests. This "we are in this together" approach helps to tap the motivation of all involved parties to cooperate in reaching a mutually satisfactory agreement, i.e. a win-win outcome. It can also be very helpful if you work to separate the people from the problem. Endeavor to consider the situation or the conflict separately from the personalities involved. It helps if you are willing to be at least somewhat flexible in your position, and that you enter the negotiations with the mind set that both you and the other party are basically reasonable people who want to reach a fair resolution to a problem in which you both have legitimate interests. Notice that we never refer to the other person or persons as your "opponent" or "adversary", but rather simply as the other party. This helps to foster a climate where a win-win outcome has a chance.

Recognize that you begin creating a climate for either cooperation or contention from the moment the negotiations begin. To create a cooperative atmosphere begin the meeting with ice-breaker conversation. If the negotiations are prolonged, lasting over many hours or several days, it can be useful to have meals together so as to promote an opportunity to view each other as people apart from the conflict and build rapport.

It is also very important that you manage your emotions appropriately. If you didn't have strong emotions regarding the issue at hand it is unlikely that you would be going through a complicated process like conflict resolution. It is important to control your anger for it will not serve you well in this process. Direct expression or indulgence of anger will likely lead to defensiveness on the part of the other party and may cause them to dig in their heels. And anger will cloud your ability to think rationally and be flexible in your own best interest. So we advise you to avoid ranting and raving, or giving ultimatums in an effort to assert your power negatively. Rather, exert your positive power by being assertive and using I language, but avoid trying to bully your way into an agreement—that is not the way to forge a win-win outcome. Positive power thrives on a willingness to believe that the problem can be solved and a commitment to being persistent.

Once you have presented your position you need to check whether the other party has understood what you said and what you meant. Given that this may be an emotionally charged situation, it is certainly possible that there have been some miscommunications or misunderstandings. Before proceeding make sure that the other party has fully understood your point of view, not that they need to necessarily agree with you at this point in the process, but at least that they comprehend your message, what you want, what you need, and why this is so for you.

To facilitate this, just ask the other party to tell you their understanding of your position. If they have misunderstood some aspect of it, then take this opportunity to correct their misconceptions before moving on.

STEP FOUR: Seriously Consider the Other Party's Point of View

Now it is time to give the other party their say on the issues. Give their point of view serious consideration. That means listening fully and attentively, using the skills for active and empathic listening which are laid out in full detail in the next chapter. Do your best to step into the shoes of the other party, to see the situation or conflict from their eyes. Remember the value of being willing to give up being right. Just as you asked the other party to feed back to you their understanding and interpretation of your position, do the same for them and share your understanding of their point of view. Give them the opportunity to clarify their position on issues or correct any misunderstandings you may have developed about where they stand and why.

It is just as important for the other party to have their say as it is for you. It is also helpful to try to equalize the amount of time that both parties get to present their sides. Why? First of all, because that is what is fair. The other party has just as much right as you to get their needs met and find satisfaction. If you expect them to cooperate in meeting your needs, it is reasonable to expect that you will behave in a fair fashion. Secondly, it is essential if you want to achieve a win-win outcome, or any solutions for that matter. If the other side has difficulty expressing themselves, then ask questions to draw them out and help them to clarify their position. Ask about the feelings and experiences that led to their current position. The more you understand about them and the more they understand about you, the more likely you can arrive at a win-win solution.

STEP FIVE: Explore Possible Solutions

Once a mutual understanding of positions, wants and needs has been established you are ready to move on to problem solving. This is best accomplished by generating as many potential solutions as possible and later evaluating them to decide which one best meets everyone's needs. As you begin the process of looking for solutions, it helps to adopt the attitude that there may be more than one solution that is mutually satisfying. The advice of McKay, Davis and Fanning, from their book *Messages: The Communication Skills Book*, is especially relevant here. They enjoin you to . . .

> *"Get rid of the notion that there is only one best way to divide up the pie, that the pie is only so big, and that you absolutely must get the biggest piece. These are all self-defeating ideas. There are actually several good ways to cut up a pie. You may even find a way to make the pie bigger. And ending up with the biggest piece isn't always ideal, especially if you antagonize people and end up getting your pie in the face."*

Depending on the situation it may be very important to do homework beforehand to determine what is fair, especially in a business negotiation or some type of deal involving merchandise and/or money. Tracking down precedents or benchmarks will help you generate proposals that are reasonable.

One of the best methods for generating options or potential solutions is to brainstorm with all interested parties or on your own. **Brainstorming** involves the uninhibited offering of ideas and suggestions by all members of a group. All interested parties should be encouraged to participate. All suggestions, no matter how outlandish or unrealistic, should be listed on a blackboard or large writing pad without being judged, evaluated, or associated with anyone's name. Do not, at this stage, criticize, praise, or in any other way evaluate the suggestions. Just list them all, no matter how ridiculous or unworkable any might be. The goal is to generate as many ideas as possible for further exploration. Remember that even a seemingly crazy idea may lead to another great idea. Try to come up with as long a list as possible, the more and the wilder the better. Approach the problem from every angle. Try to go beyond the 9 dots. To facilitate this process try looking at the problem through the eyes of imaginary experts. How would a judge solve the problem, or a cop, or a psychologist or a school principal? What about your mother, or your brother? How would a banker approach the problem? How would a priest, minister or rabbi attempt to resolve this issue? Oftentimes shifting to the mind set of another can free you of your blinders and help you see possibilities that had eluded you beforehand. This last suggestion is especially helpful if you are stuck brainstorming all by yourself.

While brainstorming also consider time honored methods for resolving issues or forging compromises. The classic way of dividing disputed assets or property is splitting it down the middle, if possible. In buying or selling, the equivalent solution is to split the difference. Consider the ways you could soften aspects of your position that are not critical to you in order to make your proposal more palatable to the other party. Permanent changes can be proposed as temporary ones to see how they will work out. Major changes can be done in steps. Unconditional demands can be made contingent upon something important to the other party.

STEP SIX: Evaluate and Negotiate

When you reach this stage of the process it is useful to set a reasonable deadline that is agreeable to all parties involved, otherwise negotiations could go on forever. Setting a deadline spurs each side to be flexible so as to bring the matter to a conclusion. Many people become willing to budge when they see the deadline approaching. Of course you can always extend the deadline if necessary, but having one in place helps to move things along.

Now that you have your list of potential solutions it is time for all parties to begin to evaluate each option. Some will be easily identified as unworkable or unrealistic and quickly discarded. At first glance, some will be acceptable to one side but totally unacceptable to the other side. Discuss these using the guidelines for clear communication and effective listening, and eliminate those that will never, under any circumstances, be considered by one side or other. At this point the list should have been whittled down to those solutions which are potentially acceptable to each side, although many might only be acceptable with reservations, and others only acceptable with changes or modifications.

At this point, if you have communicated your position effectively and been a good listener, you should have developed a good working relationship with the other side, or at least an improved working relationship. You are now ready to turn the option or options that you favor into proposals. Approach the proposal slowly and describe your favored solution in detail. Then move on to your second or third choice, if such exist. Listen to what option or options are favored by the other side. This creates a cycle of proposal/counter proposal that may be repeated several times, including discussions and time-outs to consider various propositions. Discuss the difficulties that you each have with aspects of the proposals on the table. As the proposals and counter proposals evolve, it is likely that their terms will keep moving ever closer together. Look for the overlap between your proposal and that of the other party. What adjustments can be made to make the non-overlapping parts of the proposals more aligned with one another, keeping in mind what needs to happen to generate a win-win solution, based on your needs and your knowledge of the needs of the other party. By offering choices, being flexible, and open to new information, you create a cooperative climate that makes this type of back and forth negotiation possible. Do not offer your proposal as an ultimatum for that is guaranteed to fail.

While this negotiation is ongoing, if you sense that the other party is in an agreeable frame of mind, this is the time to present a "**yesable proposal**". A "yesable proposal" is an aspect of your position that, if stated as a direct question it would be easy for the other side to answer yes. For example, if you are negotiating for a pay raise you could ask whether such a raise would be forthcoming if you agreed to making it contingent upon an agreed-upon increase in productivity on your part. If you know that improved productivity is important to your boss, then you are offering to meet his/her needs in exchange for what you want (a win-win solution).

If a win-win solution is just not possible despite all your best efforts, then you need to begin to negotiate a compromise so as to get at least some of what you want in exchange for giving up at least some of what the other side wants. Even in this case the process of working toward win-win has not been in vain. You likely have, as a result of this process, forged a better working relationship with the other party. The resulting atmosphere of goodwill may prevent future conflicts or may help in solving further dilemmas down the road.

To reach an agreement, of course there must be a consensus. It is usually quite clear when this has been achieved when only two people are negotiating, but if there are more than two participants, especially if the issues at hand are important, it may be best to take a more formal vote. Usually a hand vote will suffice, but in a business negotiation involving many individuals it may be useful to do a confidential written vote to minimize group pressures and allow each party to vote freely.

Herb Cohen, in his book *You Can Negotiate Anything*, recommends that you write what he terms a **memorandum of agreement**, which is also called a **letter of intent** or a **memo of understanding**, detailing all aspects of the agreement. This written record is there to remind all parties of the exact nature of the agreement you have reached. All parties should sign it. It can prevent misunderstandings later on if one party insists that the agreement was different from your memory of such. It also builds on the fact that people are more likely to follow through after they have entered into a more formalized, signed arrangement. This memorandum should be written in straightforward, common-sense language. In a more formal negotiating situation such as collective bargaining, such agreements need to be written in legal language and may need to be composed by an attorney.

STEP SEVEN: Enact the Solution and Follow-Up

To put the plan into action everyone involved needs to be clear about what is to be done, when, where, and who is responsible for what. It helps to include this information in the written agreement. It is also useful to begin implementing the plan as soon as possible to avoid the resistance or suspicions that delays could arouse.

Until you have enacted the plan and given it some time to see how it is working, you cannot reasonably evaluate whether the solution has worked. As you close your negotiations decide when and how to evaluate the plan. How long to wait and how to conduct the evaluation process depends on the nature of the plan and how complicated it is. After a reasonable amount of time has passed to test the viability of the solution, have another meeting and discuss the results of the follow-up evaluation. If there are difficulties with implementation then brainstorm how to adjust or modify the plan. If it is a total disaster you may need to scrap it and start from scratch.

PATHWAYS THROUGH ANGER

As mentioned above, one of the biggest barriers to a win-win outlook is your anger. Anger motivates you to want to win, to defeat others whom you view as opponents or adversaries. Effective individuals have learned to cope with anger, to work it through and manage it constructively rather than destructively. This is essential to adopting a win-win framework. But how do you do this? To answer this question, you first need to understand the nature of anger.

The Nature of Anger

Have you experienced times when you were quick to anger, either in the workplace or at home, as if your fuse had become significantly shorter? Unless you are a yogi master and have achieved perfect balance and enlightenment, of course you have. All of us have had periods when we were more irritable and less tolerant. Have you noticed that there is a direct relationship between these periods and the level of stress in your life? Undoubtedly, a very common response to stress is anger and irritability. But why? Remember, stress is your body and mind's response to perceived threat. If you consider, that for our ancestors "threat" typically took the form of attacks by animals or other tribes, then anger was an adaptive reaction which mobilized them to take defensive action. Therefore, anger had survival value because typically, for our forebearers, the appropriate response was to physically fight for their lives. But in today's world physical confrontations are no longer useful in most situations. Yet, you are left with this holdover, emotional baggage of anger. Verbal expression of this anger, particularly if unmodulated, is certainly not much more adaptive, either in your work environment or in your personal life.

Violent, unrestrained expression of anger, both rational and irrational, has been at the forefront of national headlines and at the core of many of the most serious problems faced by today's society. As population swells, often leading to over crowding or congestion, and cultural shifts appear to occur at an ever quickening pace, many individuals become overwhelmed and resort to violence. The recent attacks on the World Trade

Center and the Pentagon focused everyone's attention on the profoundly tragic consequences of violence, while highlighting the need to understand the underpinnings of
anger and to develop methods to prevent future bloodshed. Meanwhile, we all struggle
to understand why adolescents have engaged in countless school slaughters over the last
few years, and why adults bring firearms to work and shoot co-workers and innocent
bystanders. Has our world become more violent, or is it the ever present media coverage
which gives this impression? By the same token, is domestic abuse, of both children and
spouses, on the rise? Or is domestic violence just more routinely reported and publicized? Either way it is clear that violence is a serious problem with which we must all
contend, so as to avoid either becoming a victim or a perpetrator of such. Learning to
co-exist is of paramount importance, and the prevention of violence first involves learning to handle anger.

But anger is a basic human emotion that we all experience from time to time, sometimes to the level where we can lose control of our behavior and/or resort to aggression.
According to a study by Averill (1983) most people report being angry, at least to the
point of getting mildly annoyed, several times weekly. Researcher Diane Tice (1993)
found that anger is the emotion that people have the hardest time controlling. Making
it even harder is the fact that for some, anger can be energizing or even exhilarating at
times, leading to something akin to a rage addiction in certain individuals.

Many theorists have attempted to explain the root causes of anger and aggression.
An early theory, the **frustration-aggression hypothesis** (Dollard, Miller, Doob,
Mowrer, & Sears, 1939) focused on the role of frustration (as a result of being blocked
from reaching a goal) as a primary factor. Most psychologists readily acknowledge the
role of frustration in the development of anger, but agree that other variables are equally
important. Freud postulated that humans have an inborn aggressive drive which contributes to personality formation. Furthermore, Freud recommended pursuing an emotional release, which he called **catharsis**, by venting or acting out anger. There is also
some evidence that testosterone levels are related to levels of aggression, but this is based
on correlational studies so causation cannot be conclusively inferred.

Currently there is a greater emphasis on the role of learning histories as the primary
factor in the etiology of anger. That is, an individual will exhibit anger and hostile behaviors to the extent that anger has been rewarded and modeled for him or her. Likewise,
to the extent that anger was punished and inhibition of such was modeled, an individual will display the ability to control anger and restrain aggression. Statistics appear to
indicate that merely observing violence can trigger heightened aggression as demonstrated by the increased incidence of domestic violence each year immediately following
the Super Bowl. As a result, there is a lot of controversy today over the role of observational learning (modeling) on the expression of anger, particularly in children. Consequently, the debate rages over the extent to which children should be allowed to watch
violent movies or TV programs. There is research which suggests that long term viewing
of violent TV shows can cause children, particularly boys, to behave more aggressively.
One study found that eight year old boys who preferred violent programs were more
aggressive at that age, as well as at age eighteen, as compared to a group of boys who preferred less violent entertainment (Lefkowitz, Eron, Walder, & Huesmann, 1977). But
because this was correlational research, again it is unclear whether this was a cause or an
effect. That is, was their preference a function of a more violent bent, or did watching

violent shows create more violent kids? The debate continues as this question still has not been conclusively answered.

When is anger likely to lead to violence? There is no foolproof method for predicting who will become aggressive and when violence will occur, but there are factors which are associated with the likelihood that an individual will engage in violent expression of anger including:

- a previous history of violent behavior
- having been physically abused in childhood
- having witnessed violence in the home as a child
- a history of harming animals as a child
- heavy exposure to violent TV programs or video games
- absence of remorse over hurting others
- family history of mental illness or violence
- brain damage (which can interfere with the brain's inhibitory mechanisms)

Road Rage

One common situation where many individuals experience anger, often to irrational levels, is while driving. Does this ever happen to you? This common phenomenon, dubbed **road rage**, is on the rise, reportedly increasing by 7% yearly since 1990. A leading researcher in this area, Jerry Deffenbacher, surveyed 1500 college drivers and identified the following six situations likely to trigger road rage emotions and behaviors:

- hostile gestures from other drivers
- other drivers breaking traffic laws
- the presence of a police car
- another driver driving too slowly
- driver discourtesy (i.e. being cut off, slow driving in passing lane, etc.)
- traffic jams or obstructions

Everyone feels aggravation on the road sometimes, but for some individuals, driving to work every day is an never ending exercise in fury. To determine whether you have a problem with road rage, fill out the questionnaire in Table 8.1 which will compare you with other college students. High scorers are three times more likely to experience road rage than low scorers. High scorers experience road rage because they are likely to personalize the mistakes or behaviors of other drivers, to view these incidents as personal affronts.

THE PHYSIOLOGY OF ANGER

So what can you do about learning to control your anger and modulate your expression of it? First, it is important that you understand the physiology of anger. Goleman (1995) offers an illuminating explanation of why certain individuals sometimes "go off the deep end" and respond impulsively and explosively with anger. He refers to such outbursts as

---

TABLE 8.1 Road Rage Scale

This test describes common, potentially anger provoking situations that occur during driving. Imagine that each of the situations described is actually happening to you while driving. Then rate the amount of anger that would be provoked in each situation using the following rating scale:

1 Not at all   **2 A little**   **3 Some**   **4 Much**   **5 Very much**

_____ 1. Someone makes an obscene gesture toward you about your driving.

_____ 2. You pass a radar speed trap.

_____ 3. Someone runs a red light or stop sign.

_____ 4. Someone honks at you about your driving.

_____ 5. Someone is weaving in and out of traffic.

_____ 6. A police officer pulls you over.

_____ 7. You are driving behind a large truck and cannot see around it.

_____ 8. A bicyclist is riding in the middle of the lane and slowing traffic.

_____ 9. Someone is slow in parking and holding up traffic.

_____10. A truck kicks up sand or gravel on the car you are riding in.

_____11. Someone speeds up when you try to pass them.

_____12. A slow vehicle on a mountain road will not pull over and let people by.

_____13. Someone backs right out in front of you without looking.

_____14. You are stuck in a traffic jam.

_____ Total Score

Interpretation: The higher your score the more likely you are easily provoked and angered while driving. Compare your level of driving anger with that of other college students on the chart below. The percentile tells the percentage of students who scored at or below your level.

Score	Percentile	Score	Percentile	Score	Percentile
21	0	41	25	52	72
26	1	42	28	54	79
30	3	43	32	56	86
32	5	45	40	57	89
35	10	47	50	59	93
38	17	49	60	60	95
40	22	50	64	64+	99

---

emotional hijackings and explains this in terms of brain circuitry as outlined in the work of LeDoux (1992). Our brains have two basic neural response systems, one governed by a brain structure called the amygdala (a center in our primitive brain) and the other controlled by the neocortex, the thinking brain or seat of higher reasoning and planning. Emotional explosions, particularly anger, occur when the amygdala perceives what it thinks is an emergency and bypasses the neocortex. In an instant the amygdala triggers the fight/flight response before the neocortex has a chance to process any information, let alone determine how to respond appropriately. This capacity to act before you think does have survival value for it gives you the potential to react instantaneously in an emergency so as to avert danger, when taking the time to evaluate the situation might waste precious seconds and endanger your life. The problem is that, for some people, this neocortical bypass occurs in many situations where it is not only unnecessary but harmful. Here the brain interprets danger not just from physical threats but also from symbolic threats to our dignity and self esteem, but the failure to activate the neocortex typically results in behaviors we later regret. This direct amygdala circuit accounts for those instances when our emotions totally overwhelm our rational minds.

The work of psychologist Dolf Zillman (1989) is also relevant here. In a series of studies Zillman demonstrated how rage reactions develop. Typically, once the fight/flight reaction is activated even mildly, the body remains in a state of heightened arousal (or edginess) for awhile. Then, if later stimuli should mobilize the amygdala and trigger an emotional hijacking, the subsequent emotional response (whether it takes the form of anger or anxiety) is of especially great intensity. This cumulative reaction helps explain why people sometimes greatly overreact to what appears to be only mild provocation.

Physiologically, anger is arousal. When you are angry the fight/flight response has been activated preparing your body to either fight or flee. Clearly, anger helps you if you need to fight. The problem is that when we are stressed we tend to look around to see what is making us angry. That is, we tend to externalize the sources of our anger and/or stress. We assume that something out there is causing our arousal. This is true, not just with humans, but with our animal cousins as well. For example, imagine a lab rat in a box whose floor is covered with an electric grid. If that rat is alone and we shock it, the rat will jump, look for an escape route, and will manifest clear signs of arousal. If we put another lab rat in the box with our first rat, and then shock them both, the rats will attack each other. It's as if the rats are blaming each other for the shock.

The Role of Attribution in Anger

Often, we behave just like our friends the rats. We look around for who is to blame for our uncomfortable feelings and sensations without being consciously aware of what we are doing. Yet even more problematic, paradoxically, those with whom we feel most comfortable are the most likely targets of our direct aggression. The old saying *"you always hurt the ones you love"* is really true. Don't get us wrong. We also get angry with people with whom we are not close or comfortable, but we are more likely to express our anger towards them indirectly. This is particularly true if they are in a position of authority over you. So instead of telling your boss how angry you feel, you might just complain to your cronies at the water fountain or over lunch. Then when you go home at the end of the day and your spouse or significant other does something even mildly annoying, you are ready to literally bite their head off.

But physiological arousal, in and of itself, does not produce your emotions. *It is how you label this arousal that determines what you feel.* This point was driven home in a classic experiment (Schacter & Singer, 1962) which changed how psychologists viewed emotions. In this study the researchers injected subjects with adrenalin, which can cause powerful arousal reactions, but told them that they were only getting a vitamin shot. The subjects were then exposed to a confederate who supposedly received the same injection, but who then behaved in either an angry or an euphoric fashion. Subjects exposed to the angry confederate became angry, and those exposed to the euphoric person became happy. However, subjects injected with a placebo and also exposed to the same confederates did not have any strong emotional reactions. Schacter, in formulating his **Attribution theory**, concluded that emotion is much more than a physiological event. If humans are faced with physiological arousal of unknown origin they will search their environment for an appropriate explanation or label for this arousal.

Thus, emotions are created by your evaluation of your internal and external environment. The subjects in Schacter's study attributed their arousal to either anger or elation depending on what appeared to be the case in the environment. If exposed to an angry confederate they interpreted their own arousal as anger and therefore reported being mad. In a similar vein, Berkowitz & Turner (1974) were able to elicit angry behavior from subjects merely by telling them that they were angry. In this study subjects were exposed to the mildly provoking behavior of two confederates and then given false feedback about their arousal levels. How the subjects subsequently behaved toward the confederates was directly tied to the level of feedback they received—to how angry they thought they were based solely on inaccurate feedback.

This tendency to attribute the source of your uncomfortable feelings to an external agent further aggravates the problem because "putting it out there" lowers your control. If you perceive that you are not in control in a particular situation, then you are being reactive. And as we mentioned in Chapter 2, we feel we are in control when we believe we have a choice. Well, the fact is that whether or not you get angry, or stay angry is really *always* your choice. Being able to recognize this gives you control. You see, it is not the event out there that causes you to flare; it is your interpretation of the situation which ultimately leads you to be, or not to be, angry.

The fact that we have choice as to whether we feel anger, or any feeling for that matter, is the reason why two people can be faced with the same situation yet respond in ways that are diametrically opposed. For instance, imagine that you are driving in your car and someone cuts you off, almost causing an accident. The common response is to react with immediate anger and to grumble or even scream at the inconsiderate son of a gun who dared to intrude on your sacred vehicular space. You tell yourself, or them, what an idiot they are, perhaps questioning how they ever obtained a drivers license or commenting on their dubious parentage. The incident may even become an indictment of all the drivers in your city, none of which are as skilled as you. Meanwhile you are stewing in your own juices and continuing to aggravate yourself. You are well on the way to experiencing road rage.

Can you see how the meaning you gave this situation led to your angry response? Is it possible that another meaning, that also explains the other driver's behavior, could lead to a different response? What if, instead of assuming incompetence or inconsideration on the part of the other driver, you said to yourself, "poor guy, he must have a lot on his mind. I wonder what is going wrong for him?" Undoubtedly, were you to ask yourself these questions, your response to the same event would be quite different. Once again we are reminded of Steven Covey's motto, *the way you see the problem is the problem.* Not surprisingly, the solution invariably lies in changing the way you view the situation.

Anger and the Type A Personality

But you might be sitting there saying, "Why should I change? I have a right to be angry!" The truth is, you are correct. You do have a right to be angry, but are you happy with the results? Persistent or frequent anger has serious deleterious effects on your emotional and physical well being, as well as on your ability to be effective. There is no doubt that anger and resentment damage your health. A convincing example of this comes from what we have learned about the **Type A personality**. In the 1970's cardiologists Meyer Friedman and Ray Rosenman noticed that their patients tended to share certain personality characteristics. They called this cluster of behavioral traits the "Type A personality". Type A individuals tend to be very hard driving, achievement oriented, compulsive, overly concerned with time pressure and easy to anger, as compared to **Type B** individuals who are laid back, easygoing, and less concerned with time. A strong relationship was discovered between the Type A orientation and cardiac problems. But, later research revealed that the only aspect of Type A behavior that was really related to heart disease was the "hostility" component. That is, one could be hard driving and compulsive without incurring a greater risk of heart disease if hostility was not present. In one study (Barefoot, Dalhstrom, & Williams, 1983) conducted with physicians who are typically a very Type A group, 250 doctors were administered a hostility scale. Twenty five years later the mortality rate of the high hostility scorers was several times higher. This has led health psychologists to conclude that of all human emotions, hostility is the deadliest. Anger is particularly harmful to your health when it is repressed or when it is turned back onto yourself. But inappropriate expression of anger towards others is also dangerous to your physical well being as well as your interpersonal relationships. Hostility that

---

TABLE 8.2 Hostility Scale

Answer the following questions true or false.

_____ I often get annoyed at checkout cashiers or the people in front of me when I'm waiting in line at the supermarket or other stores.

_____ I usually keep an eye on the people I work or live with to make sure they're doing what they should.

_____ I often wonder how extremely fat people can have so little respect for themselves.

_____ Most people will take advantage of you if you let them.

_____ The habits of friends or family members often annoy me.

_____ When I'm stuck in traffic, I often start breathing faster and my heart pounds.

_____ When I'm annoyed with people, I always let them know about it.

_____ If someone wrongs me, I'll get even.

_____ I usually try to have the last word in an argument.

_____ At least once a week, I feel like yelling or even hitting someone.

If you answered "true" to five or more of these questions, you may qualify as excessively hostile.

is characterized by brooding resentment, suspicion and frequent angry outbursts is extremely damaging to your health (Smith, 1992). Take out a moment to fill out the Hostility Scale to help determine if anger and hostility are a problem for you.

The fact that anger is a risk factor for heart attacks is well documented. Anger sets off a physiological mechanism that makes your heart beat faster, your blood pressure rise, your coronary arteries constrict, and your blood get stickier. A recent study of more than 1.000 patients at Mount Zion Medical Center who had survived heart attacks, found those who had counseling to reduce their anger, aggression and hostility had half the rate of recurring heart attacks as those who received no such help dealing with anger.

Catharsis Is Not Always the Answer

There is a mistaken belief that a good way to release anger is to immediately vent it. George Bach, in his seminal book *The Intimate Enemy*, describes this as the **Vesuvius effect** when you explode just like a volcano. Often, after such a cathartic expression you do feel better, as if a load has been lifted of your shoulders. While this might work if you are alone in your room hitting your pillow, can you imagine just letting go with your boss? It is safe to say it probably wouldn't be the most effective strategy. In addition, research indicates that such expressions tend to reinforce the anger, making you quicker to anger in the future. Diane Tice (1993) concluded that giving vent to anger typically failed to dispel it and often only intensified it. She found that it was far more effective for individuals to first cool down and then later, in a constructive, assertive fashion attempt to settle the conflict. Thus, psychologists no longer recommend the catharsis approach espoused by Freud because, in many instances, acting angrily can lead to further anger and perhaps even aggression. The situation in the Middle East between Israel and the Palestinians is a perfect example of this. Both sides justify escalating violence with their *"eye for an eye, tooth for a tooth"* philosophy. The bloodshed may not end until everyone left alive on both sides is both blind and in need of dentures.

LEARNING TO CONTROL ANGER

Is anger always bad for you? Actually, the answer is no. Anger is a normal human reaction. It becomes problematic when it is chronic, persistent and unresolved. There are in fact, instances when anger can be useful. Anger can be helpful for mobilizing your energy so that you can take appropriate action. If you were never able to get angry you might become so complacent that you would never seek to resolve issues in your life.

The task is not to always prevent anger, but to learn how to move through it efficiently and effectively. A former mentor of ours, Jacqueline Small, teaches that "the only way out is through". **You need to be aware of your anger** and rather than getting mired in it, recognize it as a signal that something is amiss and must be addressed. Then you can use the energy it creates to mobilize you to take appropriate action. Many other authors and psychologists recommend various systems and methods for avoiding, controlling and redirecting anger. In his book, *The Trusting Heart: Great news about type A behavior,* Redford Williams lists a series of strategies for reducing your hostility level. It is likely that you will find these strategies to be familiar, combining methods outlined in previous as well as upcoming chapters, the only difference being that anger management is the focus. This list represents a good summary of ways to combat hostility.

- Become self aware. Adopt the witnessing stance (See Chapter 5) and monitor the self talk which fuels your anger (See Chapter 2)

- Interrupt angry thoughts. A method called **thought stopping** is very useful here. To use this strategy, wear a rubber band on your wrist and snap it whenever you become aware of engaging in hostile, irrational self talk. The mild pain you experience from the snap should help interrupt your negative thought patterns and provide an opportunity for you to use cognitive restructuring techniques (See Chapter 2).

- Cultivate empathy by stepping into the shoes of the other (Refer to that section in this chapter).

- Learn to laugh at yourself. Don't take yourself so seriously (See section on reframing below).

- Practice active relaxation techniques (See Chapter 5). Counting to ten before you respond and/or practicing diaphragmatic breathing can help you calm yourself and prepare to respond appropriately instead of impulsively to anger.

- Improve your listening skills (See Chapter 9).

- Take the risk to trust others.

- Practice the art of forgiving others (See the last page in this chapter.).

Zillman (1989) recommends two main strategies for defusing anger. The first method basically involves using cognitive restructuring and reframing techniques to challenge anger provoking thoughts, in order to facilitate a reevaluation of the original interpretation that triggered anger in the first place. However, he points out that timing is absolutely crucial in this process. The earlier in the anger sequence this occurs, the more likely it is to be useful for defusing or reducing anger. He refers to a "window of opportunity" for this to work. If anger has already escalated to the point of rage, efforts to think rationally often will not work because of what he terms a state of "cognitive incapacitation", where individuals literally cannot think straight because they are so blinded by rage. Can you ever recall a situation when you were beyond rational thinking because you were so enraged?

Zillman also advises that you pursue a cooling off period to defuse anger, that you allow yourself to cool down physiologically by seeking out a setting devoid of further triggers for anger. There are various ways to promote cooling off. Engaging in physical exercise (i.e. walking, jogging, etc.) can be very useful because it works off the physical tension built up in fight/flight arousal, and can provide time for you to reflect on the situation and engage in rational thinking. Likewise, involvement in active relaxation techniques such as breathing exercises or progressive muscle relaxation is an excellent way to facilitate cooling off. Or it could be as simple as getting some space from another person during an argument to prevent a unproductive escalation of hostilities. In general, Zillman stresses that distraction is vital to allow for cool down. Many of the above activities allow for distraction as well as direct tension reduction. Zillman further emphasizes that this cooling down period will backfire if that time is used to pursue a train of anger inducing thoughts, for in that case the anger will continue to build rather than dissipate. The power of distraction is that it can derail an angry train of thought. Diane Tice surveyed strategies people use for handling anger, and found most people do find distractions such as watching TV, movies or reading useful for interfering with angry thoughts. But interestingly, she found that common indulgences such as shopping and eating proved to be ineffective distractions as individuals tended to stew in angry thoughts while engaging in these pursuits.

REFRAMING REVISITED

To quote Daniel Goleman:

> "The train of angry thoughts that stokes anger is also potentially the key to one of the most powerful ways to defuse anger: undermining the convictions that are fueling the anger in the first place. The longer we ruminate about what has made us angry, the more 'good reasons' and self justifications for being angry we can invent. Brooding fuels anger's flames. But seeing things differently douses those flames. Tice found that reframing a situation more positively was one of the most potent ways to put anger to rest."

We totally agree and have found the most effective way of beginning to use anger rather than be used up by it, is to remember to consider the frame through which you are viewing the particular situation. Take a couple of deep diaphragmatic breaths and then shift your attention to your muscles, particularly those muscles in your shoulders, neck and jaw. Take a moment to relax these. Then assume the witness/observer stance. Look at the situation from the outside. Ask yourself, "How can I look at this differently?" We talked about reframes in Chapter 1. Reframing is a powerful method for dealing effectively with anger. We would like to offer you a couple of reframes we have found particularly useful for working through anger.

Look for Comedy

One approach involves viewing your life as a sitcom in progress. It asks that you think of yourself as a comedy writer of your own life. In almost all situations an element of humor or absurdity can be found if you look at it from a different perspective and seeing the humor inherent in a situation effectively defuses much of the anger. Think for a moment, if you were an objective, uninvolved bystander witnessing your situation, is there any aspect of your circumstance that could be seen as humorous? Who is your favorite stand-up comedian? If that person was observing what was happening to you, what pithy or funny remarks would he/she make about you or your dilemma? You can probably remember times when you witnessed an event where a friend, colleague, or relative became angry, while you had a hard time keeping a straight face because you could see the absurdity in the situation. You can do this with yourself as well. As a matter of fact, almost any situation will seem funny when you are looking back at it after the passage of time. Realize that you have the choice to imagine that time has already passed when you are involved in your particular dramas.

The "Grand Drama" Viewpoint

Another useful reframe involves looking at your situation from a frame of reference where you view your life as an unfolding drama for the benefit and entertainment of a higher being. And why not? Your life is God's gift to you. How you live it is your gift to God.

A Chapter in Your Life

A related reframe is to consider that your life is a novel in progress, and what is happening to you at any moment can make for a fascinating chapter in the book that is your life. How can you write this chapter taking into account what you will ultimately learn from the experience? We find that any of these perspectives will help to get you unstuck from the anger of the moment. If none of these appeal to you, can you think of others that would serve you better? Take some time to reflect on this now.

Viewing Criticism as Feedback

One of the things that often triggers your anger is criticism. It goes without saying, that no one really likes to be criticized. But some individuals handle criticism better that others. Why is it that some people seem to take negative feedback in stride and even appear to benefit from it, while others are overwhelmed with anger and self-doubt? Again the answer lies in the meaning attributed to the criticisms. One of the main reasons is that often people tend to equate criticism with themselves rather than about their actions. Therefore, negative feedback is viewed as a statement about self worth rather than an observation about behavior. When viewed this way criticism tends to remind you of your inadequacies.

However, if you are able to adopt the reframe that it is not you but your actions that are being critiqued, it becomes easier to consider the possibility that there is validity to the complaint. You no longer need to feel as though there is something wrong with you, that you are a bad or worthless person, rather you need to focus your attention on the appropriateness, effectiveness or worthiness of a particular behavior.

You need to recognize that in any situation where you receive criticism, three possibilities exist: (1) your behavior is definitely out of line and the other person's complaint is valid; (2) your behavior is questionable but the criticism is also a reflection of biases, difficulties or neuroses on the part of the critic; or (3) your behavior is fine and it is the critic who has the problem (i.e. remember the old saying, *"criticism reflects the critic"*.). It is important to take a good look at your behavior, but how you respond will depend on which possibility you decide best fits the situation.

If you decide that your behavior has been inappropriate, you must be careful not to fall into the trap of taking this as evidence that you have done something wrong and should feel bad about it. This trap is avoided by remembering to look differently at your mistakes. As discussed in Chapter 3, you *can* decide to view mistakes as *"feedback"*— important feedback which helps train you how to do things properly. It is when you realize that your mistakes are invaluable teachers that you will cease to repeat them.

Case Study in Anger Control: Road Rage

Sally is a high powered executive who works downtown in a major metropolitan area. She enjoys the excitement and cultural amenities of the big city, but she prefers to live in a more rural atmosphere. To accomplish this aim she purchased a home on the outskirts of the suburbs in an area that still feels like country. The price of this is that she has a very long commute, in rush hour traffic, to and from her job. On a good day it takes her 45 minutes to get to the office, and most days it takes over an hour to reach work. She hates the drive, but she is very satisfied with her job, and has no desire to move closer to work and lose the country environment she cherishes. Lately Sally has found herself frequently engulfed in road rage, getting furious at bad drivers or inconsiderate motorists who cut her off. She found herself often screaming in her car, leaning on the horn unnecessarily long, flipping the bird to other motorists, and then feeling agitated throughout the drive and even after she reached her destination. She was very concerned about her feelings and her behavior. She feared that she might anger strangers with her offensive gestures, who might then attempt to retaliate in some fashion. Mostly she was upset about the holdover agitation she felt even after getting out of the car. Her blood pressure was up and she was getting frequent tension headaches during her drive home which lingered all night.

Assisting Sally to work through road rage to achieve road peace first involved helping her to recognize that she had a choice whether to respond with anger to difficult driving situations. Sally was encouraged to identify the underlying assumptions that were fueling her anger. She believed that she had no control in the situation, for after all, she couldn't stop lousy drivers from making driving mistakes, going too slow, or cutting her off. But the thought that triggered the bulk of her anger was her assumption that, "they got away with it". That is, the person driving like a madman got away scot free while interfering with her and/or putting her in danger in the process.

Sally was able to overcome her road rage by being willing to shift her thinking. She began to acknowledge that, while she certainly had absolutely no control over the driving behavior or competency of other motorists, she always had control over how she chose to respond to any given driving situation. She then searched for a way to *reframe* the trigger assumption: that bad drivers get away with it. She recognized that if a given driver was really that unskilled, then it was just a matter of time before that person was either ticketed by police or hospitalized from a traffic accident. The next time she witnessed a bad driver (a speeder weaving dangerously in and out of lanes on the expressway), she fantasized that driver got a speeding ticket later that day. She further realized that if a person wasn't an incompetent driver but just inconsiderate (i.e. the guy who cuts you off because he is in a hurry), then this inconsideration would catch up with him/her in other areas of life, particularly in interpersonal relationships. A person who always puts his/her needs above others rarely can sustain lasting relationships. So the next day, when a dapper businessman in a new Mercedes almost ran her off the road to cut into her lane, Sally imagined that he returned home that night and discovered that his wife had left him for being such an insensitive cad.

Sally was amazed at how adopting these alternative perspectives, these reframes, and engaging in these reframed fantasies defused her anger. Remembering to *breathe slowly* from the diaphragm when the driving got tense helped her to keep her mind open to new perspectives, rather than engaging in knee jerk reactions of rage. She also began using her time in the car more constructively. She began listening to Books on Tape, rather than complaining that she didn't have time to read. She also began carrying a tape recorder in the car, and periodically dictating reports that didn't get finished at work. Using her time more productively lowered her stress level, and reduced her feeling that she was wasting two hours a day in the car. The *distraction value* of these activities was such that she stopped spending time searching the landscape for bad drivers or driving errors as she had before. Within two weeks of adopting this change in perspective Sally was free of road rage.

Case Study 2: Workplace Anger

Carlos had been working at his sales job for a mid-sized manufacturing company for two years and had enjoyed phenomenal success. He had quadrupled his earnings in that time due to his high sales figures and the companies commission structure. He was the top salesman in the company. His forte was in developing new accounts and generating increased orders from existing customers. Rather than enjoy his success, Carlos became even more driven and began having inappropriate temper outbursts at work when other workers did not meet his expectations. He became enraged when other workers made minor errors which delayed the processing of orders for his customers. He would often yell at these co-workers and insult them. What upset him the most was what he perceived as the meddling behavior of the sales manager, his immediate boss. When his boss would attempt to assist him on an account (to help with paperwork), Carlos took offense. He assumed that his boss was implying that he couldn't handle it by himself. Mostly he was worried about getting fired either because of his temper outbursts or because he was disliked. He feared that the bosses wanted to can him so they could hire someone else at a much lower salary level. He knew he had to deal with the situation when his boss took him aside and told him that he needed to work on his attitude. Carlos was having problems sleeping at night, and relaxing on the weekends with his family because he was so caught up in anger and worry.

Carlos was encouraged to use *diaphragmatic breathing,* and wait ten minutes before responding to any mistakes made by co-workers or perceived slights by his superiors, so he would have time to *cool down.* Using *cognitive restructuring* he confronted his irrational expectation that people should always be perfect and never make mistakes. He was encouraged to identify the other assumptions that were underlying his anger. The first assumption was that he was soon to be fired despite his success. To find a *reframe* to combat this, he was encouraged to think of everything his company had to lose by firing him. He quickly realized that the company stood to lose a lot of money and business if he was let go, even if they did hire a lower paid replacement. He had to admit that it would be a very foolish move for his employers to fire him, even if they did find him to be a "pain in the butt". The second assumption involved his belief that his boss's efforts to help him with paperwork implied that he was not competent. When reflecting upon alternate explanations for his boss' behavior, Carlos realized that when his boss helped with paperwork it freed him up to do that which he did best (i.e. develop new accounts and increase orders from existing accounts). Therefore, his boss' assistance could help both Carlos and the company increase earnings.

When Carlos returned to work he practiced breathing techniques and taking a ten minute breather to walk around the office if hassles arose. Using the guidelines in Chapter 10 for practicing *assertive* (as opposed to aggressive) behavior, he approached his co-workers diplomatically and calmly. When his boss came to assist with his paperwork, rather than resenting it and glaring at him as he had done previously, he thanked him. Within a week he and his boss were on much better terms. They had a heart to heart talk, and his boss confirmed that he wanted to pitch in so as to enable Carlos to focus solely on selling. Carlos suggested a brainstorming meeting between the sales and shipping departments to foster improved communication and problem solving to expedite timely shipment of orders. At the meeting Carlos practiced *empathic listening* and began to understand why his co-workers made many of the errors. This meeting was very productive, and as a result numerous suggestions were made to help fix the existing problems. Carlos acknowledged that mistakes would still occur, but he was hopeful that the frequency could be significantly reduced by implementing the ideas offered at the meeting. Lastly, Carlos kept reminding himself that he was a very valuable employee who had control over whether he was fired by how he chose to behave in the workplace. Several weeks after his change in attitude his bosses took him aside and praised his work and the improvement in his attitude. From the discussion it was abundantly clear to him that he was, indeed, a very valuable employee with a secure job. Within two weeks he began to enjoy going to work again. His sleep normalized and he began to relax and have fun on his weekends.

Self-Exercise: Developing your own plan to defuse anger

Take a moment and think about a situation or a person that often triggers your anger. Notice that we did not say something or someone who *makes* you angry—*no one can make you angry,* for whether you respond with anger is always your choice. Now, take a few moments to practice diaphragmatic breathing, and consciously release the tension from your muscles to better prepare you to deal with the stress of these thoughts. If it is a situation that you are thinking about, what alternate perspective or reframe can you create to help you view things differently? Are you harboring any irrational ideas which contribute to your anger and could be challenged? Spend a few minutes pondering the situation from this new frame of reference? What happens to your anger? Do you find it diminishing or perhaps even fading entirely? If you have been thinking about a person who often triggers your anger, make your best attempt to put yourself in the shoes of that individual. What feelings or motivations might that person have that led them to behave in ways that anger you? This does not mean that you have to agree with that person or condone his/her behavior, the only requirement is that you spend some time viewing the world from his/her eyes. Do you notice that it is harder to generate anger when you understand where someone else is coming from, even if you don't agree with them? Does that person's point of view have any validity, given that person's experiences or beliefs? Now that you have likely attenuated your anger by thinking differently, are there any other alternative behaviors you could adopt that might help you cope? For example, would being more assertive help you to deal better with the person or situation? If your answer is yes, pay special attention to Chapter 10.

Forgiveness

Since anger and resentment are damaging to your health and can undermine your effectiveness with others, then clearly, the ability to forgive and let go of past hurts and disappointments is a desirable goal. Let's be clear about what forgiveness is and is not. Forgiveness is not forgetting what happened, thereby placing yourself again in a situation where you could be mistreated. It is certainly not about condoning behavior you find offensive or hurtful. It is the process of letting go of the energy invested in past hurts or disappointments so that you can free that energy for more productive, growth oriented activities. The decision to forgive stems from the realization that anger and resentment have a damaging effect on you. There is an old Chinese saying, *"When setting forth on a mission of revenge, first dig two graves"*. We wonder if you or anyone you know has ever said, "I don't get mad, I get even!" As cool as that statement might sound, you must realize the eventual toll such an approach will take on you.

Although forgiveness begins with a decision to do so, it is important to remember that it is a process. As such, it takes time and a willingness to go through the particular emotions involved, whether hurt, anger or even depression. The problem develops when you get stuck in this process because of righteous indignation. Do not get caught in the trap of believing that you can only begin to forgive when an apology is offered or amends made. When and how you forgive is totally up to you, whatever the circumstances. **Ultimately, forgiveness is more for yourself than for others.** It is abut freeing yourself of negative emotions to benefit you.

Assertiveness

Some situations that anger you certainly call for some type of response beyond letting go of your anger. Many times you will need to respond to individuals who have angered you so as to rectify the situation or prevent future occurrences of whatever is provoking your hostility. This is best accomplished by dealing diplomatically and assertively with the other person or persons rather than passively avoiding conflict (and allowing your resentment to build and take a toll on you), or responding aggressively (where you risk alienating others, making the situation worse and later being ashamed of yourself). A comprehensive treatment of effective and responsible assertive behavior is included in Chapter 10.

KEY TERMS

Interdependence	Lose-Lose Outcomes	Brainstorming
Synergy	Win-Win Outcomes	Yesable Proposal
Co-dependency	Win	Type A Personality
Prisoner's Dilemma	Win-Win or No Deal	Type B Personality
Win-Lose Outcomes	Emotional Bank Account	Vesuvius Effect
Lose-Win Outcomes	Conflict Resolution	Catharsis
Letter of Intent	Attribution theory	Road Rage
Frustration-Aggression	Emotional Intelligence	Thought Stopping
Hypothesis	Emotional hijacking	

CHAPTER 8 QUESTIONS

True or False Questions (T or F)

1. _____ IQ is more important for success in life than EQ.

2. _____ Independence is always superior to interdependence.

3. _____ In order to be interdependent you must be co-dependent.

4. _____ Cooperation is the key to the prisoner's dilemma.

5. _____ Interpersonal effectiveness is characterized by going for win-lose outcomes.

6. _____ It is not always possible to get a win-win outcome.

7. _____ To be interpersonally effective you need to prove to other people that your way is the right way.

8. _____ When attempting to resolve conflict it helps to approach the other party when they are not expecting it an try to get them to agree to your proposals.

9. _____ In conflict resolution it is important to try to intimidate the other party into submission.

10. _____ After reaching a consensus it helps to write down the agreement in clear language and have all parties sign it.

11. _____ Your learning history has no impact on how you express anger or how short your fuse will be.

12. _____ An emotional hijacking occurs when your neocortex is bypassed by your amygdala.

13. _____ The best way to deal with anger is to have a catharsis and immediately vent.

14. _____ You always have a choice whether to be angry.

15. _____ Anger is always bad for you.

16. _____ Physical exercise can help defuse anger.

17. _____ Never pay attention to criticism under any circumstances.

18. _____ Forgiveness is as much for you as for the other person.

Short-Answer Questions

1. Skill in understanding yourself and reading the emotional reactions of others is an important component in _____ _____.

2. _____ refers to the fact that individuals working together can achieve more than the sum of their individual accomplishments.

3. A person who enables or supports the problems of a significant other out of fear of angering that person is said to be _____.

4. According to Covey, in order to go for a win-win outcome you need both _____ and _____.

5. In order to really understand and appreciate another person's point of view you need to _____.

6. A formalized procedure for resolving disputes is referred to as _____ _____.

7. The process of generating as many solutions to a problem in an uninhibited fashion, free of judgement or criticism is called _____.

8. During a negotiation, if the other party is being very agreeable and cooperative, that is the time to present them with a _____ proposal.

9. A tendency to have angry outbursts while driving is termed _____ _____.

10. Emotional explosions, particularly anger, occur when the _____ perceives what it thinks is an emergency and bypasses the _____.

11. Unrestrained expression of anger has been termed the _____ effect.

12. _____ individuals tend to be very hard driving, achievement oriented, compulsive, overly concerned with time pressure and easy to anger, as compared to _____ individuals who are laid back, easygoing, and less concerned with time.

13. Cognitive restructuring techniques are more effective if used _____ in the anger sequence.

Essay Questions

1. What are the components of emotional intelligence?

2. Describe the barriers to going for win-win outcomes.

3. What do you need to do to keep a positive balance in the emotional bank account? What behaviors lead to deposits and which to withdrawals?

4. Given an example of a situation where you would be well advised to not try for a win-win outcome.

5. When is anger most likely to lead to violent behavior?

6. What is the relationship between your perception of a situation, the meanings you give to it, and anger?

7. Describe and discuss the theory you think best accounts for the development of anger or rage reactions.

8. Persistent anger and hostility have been linked to which physical problems? How does anger lead to ill health?

9. Describe the initial steps that are helpful for working through anger.

10. List some useful reframing strategies for defusing anger.

9

Build Trust as You Communicate

Part I: Listening Skills

Communication can be most simply defined as the transfer of information among individuals. What are the means by which human beings communicate? Basically, we share information with each other in one of four ways: (1) speaking, (2) writing, (3) reading, and (4) listening. These are obviously not abilities which are inborn, but skills you learn and develop through experience. However, most of us have not received an equal amount of instruction in all these areas. From infancy you began the process of learning to speak, both in terms of mastering the words and the particular gestures characteristic of your language. As a young child your parents and other care givers would repeat words and sounds and encourage you to mimic them. Later in school, you likely received more formal training in how to speak appropriately. Over the years you expanded your vocabulary and learned proper grammar. In fact, most colleges currently include a speech class as one of the general educational requirements. Similarly, your education in reading may have began even before you attended school if your parents read to you. By the time you reached your school years you were taught how to translate the symbols on the page into meaningful sounds and words. Throughout your school career you took formal classes in reading, learning to refine your skills in this area. Your training in writing also began at an early age, from first scribbling your own name, to printing simple words, until you finally mastered cursive writing sometime in elementary school. Throughout your educational career you were exposed to numerous courses in writing, often called English classes, including multiple required courses in college.

Yet how many of you have ever received formal instruction in listening? If you are like most people, the answer to this question is that you have spent virtually no time or very minimal time actively learning how to listen. You might remember your parents

209

saying, "shut up and listen", or your teachers admonishing you to stop talking to your classmates and listen to the lecture. But listening involves so much more than just being quiet.

LISTENING VS. HEARING

It is important to realize the difference between listening and hearing. If we were able to emerge from these pages and stand before you clapping loudly, you would surely be able to hear the sound of the palms of two hands forcefully colliding against each other, unless of course you had a severely disturbed hearing apparatus. Hearing, you see, is automatic. It can occur passively. It is very possible to hear what someone says, but not really listen to it. Your auditory membranes process the sound waves, but your brain could be oblivious to the message or meanings being transmitted.

Listening, on the other hand, is much more active. It is something you consciously choose to do. It cannot occur without your effort, your attention, and your concentration. Really listening requires a proactive decision to do so, followed by internal and external behaviors aimed at maximizing the probability of receiving an accurate message. Yet despite our inadequate training in this area, a study conducted with college students found that the majority of their time, up to 53%, was spent in listening activities (Barker et. al., 1981). This same study revealed that students spent approximately 14% of their communicating time writing, 16% reading, and 17% speaking. Another study showed that employees of major corporations spend about 60% of their workday listening to others. It is very ironic that the communication skill we use the most is the one for which we are least prepared.

The Epidemic of Poor Listening

Communication is very much a two way street. It does not matter how well you speak if no one is there to listen. Studies of the listening ability of thousands of subjects reveal that most people fail to listen well (Atwater, 1986). Some of this is tied to memory. Research indicates that after hearing a ten minute presentation, the average person understands and retains only about half of what was said. After two days another one-half of the information is forgotten. Thus, you can expect to remember approximately one-forth of what you heard someone say two days before.

We have even more disquieting news about how poorly most of us listen. How well do you think college students listen? Not very well according to Paul Cameron, a professor at Wayne State University (cited in Adler & Towne, 1993), who assessed the thoughts of students in his introductory psychology class at random intervals during his lecture. Much to Professor Cameron's dismay the vast majority of his students were not necessarily listening to him. He found that 20% of his students, both male and female, were enjoying erotic thoughts! Another 20% were reminiscing about something. Only 20% were actually paying attention to his lesson, and of those only 12% were really actively listening and thinking about the lecture material. The other students were busy daydreaming, yearning for lunch, worrying, or, surprisingly, thinking about religion. Now perhaps Professor Cameron was a boring lecturer, but it is much more likely that students' sexual fantasies were just more compelling than anything taught in class.

To add to the problem, when attempting to improve communication skills, many people overlook the importance of strengthening listening ability (Chiasson and Hayes, 1993). Although most of us agree that listening is important, the overemphasis on sending skills and the underemphasis on receiving skills cause many to fail to recognize the vital nature of effective listening. This is not surprising. Our society stresses the value of speaking your mind, of being able to clearly state your position, feelings or needs. Think about it. When you picture an effective individual, don't you imagine someone who is not afraid to say what they think? Yet, as Stephen Covey in his previously cited book *The Seven Habits of Effective People* astutely observes, interpersonally effective individuals "***seek first to understand, then to be understood***". When your first emphasis is on truly comprehending and appreciating the other's paradigm or frame, you are building rapport. When people really feel understood, they are much more likely to develop trust in you. No wonder listening is a skill that is essential to making and keeping relationships. It involves making a commitment to understanding how other people feel, how they see their world, getting a sense of their particular map. It is about making the attempt to see the world thorough their eyes. Listening is arguably the most important deposit you can make into the emotional bank account you hold with someone. It is a compliment to others because when you truly listen it directly implies that you care about what is happening to them, that their life and experiences are important enough that you will pay attention to them. It is a way in which you can join in their world.

How well do you listen? Fill out the following questionnaire as straightforwardly as possible to assess your listening ability. This questionnaire lists behaviors involved in good and bad listening. Using the scale, objectively rate how you typically behave by checking the appropriate response. Don't feel badly if your score is not what you want it to be. Most people are not good listeners for reasons explained in the next section. This inventory may help you identify some listening behaviors you can begin working on to improve your listening skills.

EFFECTIVE COMMUNICATION—LISTENING SKILLS

As mentioned earlier, true listening is more than just being quiet while someone else is talking. In *Messages: The Communication Skills Book* the authors (McKay et. al.) point out that true listening requires that you have at least one of the four following intentions in mind.

1. To understand someone.
2. To enjoy someone.
3. To learn something.
4. To give help or solace.

So real listening does not occur unless you have at least one of the intentions stated above, and you act on it by paying attention and concentrating on what the other person is saying. Steven Covey's motto speaks eloquently about the importance of this intention to understand another human being, and the value of accomplishing this first before communicating your own needs or message.

TABLE 9.1 Listening Questionnaire

1. Making eye contact with the person who is speaking.

Never	Seldom	Sometimes	Often	Always
1	2	3	4	5

2. Judging the subject as uninteresting.

Never	Seldom	Sometimes	Often	Always
5	4	3	2	1

3. Letting personal feelings and thoughts of prejudice interfere.

Never	Seldom	Sometimes	Often	Always
5	4	3	2	1

4. Keeping an open mind about the speaker's ideas.

Never	Seldom	Sometimes	Often	Always
1	2	3	4	5

5. Faking attention.

Never	Seldom	Sometimes	Often	Always
5	4	3	2	1

6. Listening just for the facts.

Never	Seldom	Sometimes	Often	Always
5	4	3	2	1

7. Resisting internal and external distractions.

Never	Seldom	Sometimes	Often	Always
1	2	3	4	5

8. Judging the speaker's delivery.

Never	Seldom	Sometimes	Often	Always
5	4	3	2	1

9. Using your thinking speed to reflect on the message.

Never	Seldom	Sometimes	Often	Always
1	2	3	4	5

10. Interrupting the speaker or jumping to conclusions.

Never	Seldom	Sometimes	Often	Always
5	4	3	2	1

Your score can be interpreted as follows:	
25 or below:	You need to work on your listening skills. Your difficulties in this area may be causing problems in your interpersonal relationships. Pay careful attention to the guidelines in this chapter and you can improve significantly in this area.
26 to 35:	You are an average listener. With more attention to the fundamentals explained in this chapter, you should be able to improve your skills dramatically.
36 to 43:	You are a good listener. Follow the suggestions outlined in this chapter and you can become an excellent listener.
44 to 50:	You are an excellent listener. Keep it up. This chapter should help you refine your skills even further.

Pseudolistening

Pseudo or fake listening occurs when some other intention is being satisfied, according to McKay et. al.. There are many reasons why you may fail to listen. You may not feel like putting in the effort required to listen. Or you may avoid listening because someone is saying something you don't want to hear or that threatens you, so you manage to block it out, either by not hearing it in the first place (selective attention) or forgetting it immediately (repression). Or you may listen poorly because you never learned how to listen effectively. Unfortunately, people sometimes pretend to listen when they really are not, and many pseudolisteners are adept at appearing attentive. This may even be true for you, for each of us is guilty of occasionally acting as if we are listening when our attention is elsewhere. We may look at the person, nod our head in encouragement as if we agree with what the person is saying, even murmur "Mm-hmm" occasionally, but if asked to repeat or explain what was being said, we would be at a total loss.

When you are pseudo-listening you are pretending to listen; your intention is not to listen but to meet some other need, such as:

1. Pretending to listen to make people think you're interested in them so you will be liked.

2. Being vigilant to watch for signs of potential rejection.

3. Listening for one specific bit of information and ignoring everything else.

4. Focusing on your rebuttal or the next thing you want to say rather than on anything the person is saying.

5. Pretending to listen so someone will listen to you.

6. Listening to uncover someone's vulnerabilities or weakness in order to take or gain an advantage.

7. Looking only for the weak points in the speakers line of reasoning so you can come out on top, i.e. listening to get ammunition for your counterattack.

8. Checking only to see how the speaker is reacting, to make sure you produce the desired effect.

9. Half-listening because that is what a nice person would do in the same situation.

10. Feigning listening because you don't know how to get away without hurting someone's feelings or offending them. Or your willingness to listen falters because the other person is boring you, and you are unsure how to make a graceful exit. In other words, you pretend to listen to be polite.

BLOCKS TO EFFECTIVE LISTENING

Even when it is our sincere intention to listen there are factors which interfere with our ability to do so. The most common reason is that you may be preoccupied, so caught up in your own thoughts, fantasies or emotions that you cannot give sufficient attention to the other person. Or the other person may overload you with information, or speak so quickly that you cannot process it all at once. Sometimes there are so many distractions in the surrounding environments, such as loud noise, that it is hard to pay careful attention, even when you want to do so. By the same token, you may be behaving in ways that may give the other person the impression that you are not listening. It will be very useful for you to familiarize yourself with the most common barriers to effective listening and communication which are summarized as follows:

1. **Judging**—Our natural tendency to judge, to define things as good or bad, cool or uncool, can be an enormous barrier to effective communication. If you prejudge someone in a negative way it will influence your ability to listen. Negative labels have tremendous power. For example, quickly labeling someone as stupid or crazy makes it highly unlikely that you will pay much attention to what that person has to say. Other types of judgmental responses include moralizing, advising, warning and ordering. When you are judgmental, other people are put on the defensive and typically turned off.

2. **Mind Reading**—Rather than paying attention to what the person is really saying you are busy operating on the basis of your assumptions about what the person is thinking and saying. Once in a while, if you are very perceptive, your efforts at mind reading may be on target, but for the most part mind reading usually leads to mis-communications and misunderstandings. Remember the old joke, *"When you assume you make an ass out of you and me"* (i.e. ass/u/me).

3. **Stereotyping**—When you operate on the basis of your widespread generalizations about a person based on group membership or some physical characteristic, rather than getting to know that person for who he or she is, you are setting the stage for poor listening and distorted communications.

4. **Interrupting**—Frequent or needless interruptions disrupt communication and interfere with the flow of the conversation. When a speaker is interrupted repeatedly he/she will often become distracted (i.e. lose his/her train of thought) and feel frustrated. And if you are the one chronically interrupting, then rather than listening you are obviously

attending more to what you want to say than to what is being said. Giving the other person the time and space to talk is more than politeness, it is the essence of true listening. And the other person owes you the same respect. Interruptions are more likely to be made by persons in positions of authority over you like parents, teachers, bosses etc. And men tend to interrupt more than women, particularly in male-female conversations.

5. **Comparing**—You are listening for the purpose of seeing how you measure up to the other person, drawing comparisons and contrasts in your head. The end result is that you are so busy feeling either inferior or superior that minimal attention is given to the speaker.

6. **Advising**—You put yourself in the role of the problem-solver and put your attention on searching for the right advice for the speaker. In the meantime, you don't hear what is most important, how the speaker is feeling and, consequently, you fail to acknowledge these emotions. Of course, there are many times when people will ask for your advice. In this instance we are referring to the tendency to take on that role even when your advice has not been solicited. Sometimes all the speaker wants is an opportunity to vent, to have someone listen sympathetically, and he/she is not looking to have the problem solved at that moment. This is a common occurrence in male-female conversations. Oftentimes women just want to be listened to, while men feel a compulsion to solve the problem rather than empathize.

7. **Rehearsing**—You are busy concentrating on and reviewing what you want to say next which detracts from your ability to listen to the speaker.

8. **Stage-Hogging**—Stage hogs, also called conversational narcissists, listen with the primary intent of changing the focus of the conversation back onto themselves. At every opportunity they shift the topic back to what happened to them, their feelings, etc.

9. **Filtering**—This occurs when you only listen to what you want to hear and ignore or forget the rest.

10. **Dueling**—You are so invested in arguing and debating, perhaps to show off your verbal or intellectual prowess or just to prove you are right, that you fail to listen to any valid points made by the speaker. You argue for the sake of the argument.

11. **Derailing**—You keep changing the subject or making jokes to create detours in the conversation. This prevents the discussion from reaching any closure. The speaker may end up very annoyed with you.

12. **Daydreaming**—This occurs when something the person has said triggers off a chain of private associations, and before you know it you are attending to your fantasy and not the speaker. This is more likely to happen if you are bored or anxious. Be aware that this often ends up communicating that you do not value what the speaker has to say.

13. **Placating**—You are so invested in being "nice" or "polite" that you agree with everything the speaker says, either ignoring your true opinions or feelings, or pretending you feel differently.

14. **Hidden Agendas**—When you enter a conversation with special interests or needs that are not evident on the surface and about which you are not forthcoming, the resulting communication is often distorted. It becomes difficult to really listen because you are looking for openings to further your agenda.

15. **Overreacting**—In this case you allow yourself to get caught up in emotion over a word or words that you find offensive or insulting, and your emotional reaction prevents you from hearing or being open to the main message being conveyed.

THE BUILDING BLOCKS OF EFFECTIVE LISTENING

We have been given two ears but a single mouth,
in order that we may hear more and talk less.

—Zeno of Citium

Active Listening

Active listening, also called **reflective listening**, is a process of giving the speaker non-judgmental responses as a way of checking the accuracy of what you have heard, and whether you fully understand the message the speaker is attempting to communicate. Psychologists, clinical social workers, and marriage counselors, who are professional listeners, have long practiced this type of listening as a way of truly understanding and helping troubled individuals. It has become apparent that everyone could benefit from learning how to listen in this fashion to facilitate effective communication. Pay careful attention to these elements for active listening. If you make a sincere attempt to practice and incorporate these we guarantee that your listening skills will improve dramatically. Reflective listening has three essential components which are typically used in conjunction with one another, but which we will present separately for purposes of explanation.

1. Paraphrasing

This involves stating in your own words what you think someone has just said. This gives the speaker the opportunity to find out if you have really understood what he/she was trying to convey. In the event that you have misunderstood, partially misunderstood, or missed an important point, the speaker can then clarify matters so that your understanding more nearly matches the intended message. It is important to paraphrase in your own words so that you do not fall prey to "parroting". Paraphrasing involves highlighting the main points of the speaker's message, rather than getting mired in exhaustive repetition or minor details. This technique is ideal for establishing rapport and really making the other person feel like you have heard him or her. Paraphrasing usually begins with phrases such as:

"It sounds like you are saying . . ."

"As I understand you . . ."

"What I hear you saying is . . ."

"You mean . . ."

"Correct me if I'm wrong, but are you saying . . ."

"You think . . ."

"From your point of view . . ."

If the speaker's message is long or complicated it is best to summarize in your own words your understanding of the communication. Summarizing helps you to tie the various parts of the conversation into a meaningful whole. It lets the speaker know that you have heard the overall message and that you haven't just focused on one salient point. The use of summarization is especially useful when you are trying to resolve differences, defuse an argument, or problem solve. Summarizing responses could start with:

"Summing up what you've said . . ."

"Your main points, as I understand you, are . . ."

"Recapping what you have been saying . . ."

2. Clarifying

When you clarify you are basically asking questions to facilitate your understanding of the speaker's message, to get background information, additional relevant facts, or to fill in gaps in the narrative. This enables you to get the big picture. It is important to ask for clarification in the context of what the speaker thought and felt, from his or her relevant personal history. Of course, there is no right or wrong way to ask a question (as long as it is phrased in a nonjudgmental way), and the tenor of the query will depend on the message being questioned. But some common clarification questions include:

"What do you mean?"

"I'm confused, could you clarify that?"

"Could you repeat that?"

"How did it happen?"

3. Feedback

This involves sharing your reactions to what you have heard the speaker say. There are three rules for giving feedback. It should be:

1. Immediate
2. Honest
3. Supportive

For example, if your gut reaction is that the speaker has left something out of the message you could say, *"I get the feeling that there's something you are not telling me"*. This invites the speaker to open up more if this is the case, to disagree if you are in error, and to feel as though you care enough to want to hear the whole story. If you had responded with non-supportive comments such as *"You're holding out on me"*, or, *"You're lying"*, you would likely only elicit defensiveness on the part of the speaker.

Feedback can also involve sharing whether you agree or disagree with the speaker, particularly if the speaker is looking for your opinion. Imagine a scenario where a friend recounts to you a story of a foolish thing he has done, and he is asking you to confirm or deny this. A supportive but honest remark might be, *"I think there is a real possibility that you did make a mistake."* If you had responded with judgmental comments like, *"You've been a total fool"*, or *"You are such an idiot"*, this would only serve to hurt his feelings and make him think twice about sharing his weaknesses with you ever again.

Empathic Listening

This type of listening goes further than reflective listening because it involves putting yourself in the shoes of the other, as discussed in the previous chapter. Reik (1972) refers to this as "listening with the third ear", where you listen not just to the words but to the meanings behind the words (i.e., to what the speaker is feeling and thinking). When you listen empathically you do your best to literally get inside of the other person's frame of reference, to attempt to see the world through his or her eyes, to understand his or her particular paradigm, and to understand how that person feels. Perhaps, to go even a step further, to feel his or her pain. One requirement for empathic listening is that you recognize that everyone is trying to survive the best that they can. Here many of your reflective comments are focused on the feeling or emotional tone of the speaker's message, gleaned from the speaker's words and your reading of the speakers body language (more on this in the next section). That is, you paraphrase and reflect or mirror back the speaker's feelings, attitudes and emotions. Reflective comments that focus on feelings could begin with phrases such as:

"I sense you are feeling . . ."

"You feel . . . (angry, sad, frustrated, etc.)"

"Do you feel . . . ?"

"It appears that you feel . . ."

"You seem really . . . (sad, hurt, angry, etc.)"

Empathic listening is a powerful tool for enabling you to get accurate data from which to understand another person. Instead of projecting your own assumptions and feelings, based on your personal history, and making interpretations, you are getting in touch with the reality inside another person's head and heart. Empathic listening generates deposits in the Emotional Bank Account. That is, because you are taking the time to really listen and understand, by virtue of this process you become supportive. When you listen empathically you are communicating, *"I value you"*, and this, in and of itself, is one of the most important emotional bank account deposits you can possibly make.

When you first practice active or empathic listening it may feel somewhat artificial or phony, like you are talking in a way that is unnatural for you. Remember that the acquisition of any new skill usually feels awkward in the initial learning stages. Do you recall how awkward you felt when you were first learning to drive a car? But over time and with practice, driving became automatic and second nature to you. The same is true with reflective or empathic listening. Over time and with practice, it will become a natural part of you.

The rewards of being a good listener will make the effort you put into developing this skill well worth it. It can be very gratifying to be told, *"Thank you so much for listening to me"*.

SELF EXERCISE: EMPATHIC LISTENING

Consider this story. For years you have been close friends with a woman, Maria, who has a habit of getting involved with men who treat her poorly. She had a rough childhood. Her father abandoned the family when she was a child, and her mother was so busy working to support Maria and her siblings that she had very little time for them while Maria was growing up. Maria has been involved with a man, Donald, who is an alcoholic. Although he treats her adequately when sober, when drunk he becomes verbally abusive and on one occasion he was physically abusive to her. She forgave him. Recently Maria lost her job, and when Donald invited her to live with him she jumped at the chance because she was broke. Late one night Maria knocks on your door, distraught and weeping. Her lower lip is swollen and bloody and her arm is bruised. She explains, "Donald came home drunk and flew into a rage because the apartment wasn't spotless. He said if that if I am at home and not working, the least I could do was clean up. I tried to explain to him that I was feeling sick today so I rested, but he wouldn't listen. He started screaming at me, calling me awful names, and then he grabbed my arm really hard and punched me in the mouth. I'm so afraid to go home, but I'm even more afraid to leave him. I can't make it on my own. It was my fault. I drove him to this. I should have cleaned up today and I didn't. I don't know what to do. But I don't have any choice; I have to go home to Donald."

Think about this event. Now take a few moments and rewrite the episode from the point of view of this woman. Before you give any consideration to how you might advise her to deal with this situation, imagine you are her, seeing the world through her eyes, walking in her shoes, and write down the thoughts, feelings and conscious experiences you have as Maria during the situation described above. In other words, try to experience the incidents just as Maria did. The goal here is not to condone Maria's decisions to stay in abusive relationships, but to try to understand and empathize with her from her point of view. If you do want to have an impact on her future decision making, empathizing with her first will help pave the way. If you are *unable* to put yourself in Maria's shoes you may have written something like this:

> What is wrong with Maria? How can she let herself be abused like that? If she had any sense at all she'd leave him immediately and never speak to him again. But she is obviously too stupid to do that. She's obviously very insecure and she clings to him because she is too cowardly to stand on her own two feet. She was abandoned by her father so she is trying to win the love of another man who is "no good" to compensate.

Here you were not putting yourself in Maria's shoes.

1. You were evaluating—she is stupid.
2. You were analyzing—she is insecure and cowardly.
3. You were explaining—she is trying to compensate for paternal abandonment.

Listening with Openness

It is very difficult to listen, to really hear what another person is telling you, if you are busy finding fault with the speaker or his or her words. When you adopt a judgmental stance you filter information and focus on whatever seems false, silly, or foolish, meanwhile you are ignoring any valid points or expressions of feeling.

Nearly everyone has trouble listening openly at least some of the time, particularly when the speaker is saying something that disagrees with your point of view, or contradicts your beliefs. Why is this? Because all of us, at least to some extent, fear being wrong. Your opinions and beliefs are closely tied to your self-esteem. You may equate being wrong with being stupid, bad or worthless. And it can be very threatening to witness your sacred cows being chopped into mincemeat. How different the world would be if everyone could view their beliefs and opinions as temporary hypotheses, held until disproved or modified. The resulting openness to other paradigms or contradictory information would be a major step forward in interpersonal and international relations.

Adopting an accepting attitude is critical for creating a favorable climate for communication. Acceptance does not mean that you automatically agree with what the speaker is saying, or that you condone improper behavior. Acceptance refers to maintaining a basic attitude of positive regard towards the speaker, regardless of whether you agree with his or her words or behaviors. When people feel accepted it is much easier for them to be honest and open with you, and to put more stock in what you have to say. Adopting a judgmental stance puts others on the defensive and practically insures that they will be very guarded in what they say and reveal to you.

SELF EXERCISE: In order to practice listening with openness, deliberately choose to listen to a radio or TV talk personality who espouses a view contrary to your own, be it political, religious, moral, etc. Take the time to listen with openness and find just one statement you can agree with, or fact that shouldn't be ignored. The point here is not to give up or forsake your whole philosophy on life, but to recognize common ground and the fact that even individuals with views diametrically opposed to yours will, from time to time, make valid points.

Listening with Awareness

This involves listening with your eyes as well as your ears by paying as much attention to **nonverbal behavior** and voice tones as the words themselves. A good listener "reads between the lines", listening and watching for more than the speaker's words. Attending to this dimension will give you valuable insights beyond the words and greatly enhance your ability to listen empathically.

In particular, pay attention to whether there is congruence (i.e. a match) between the speaker's body language (i.e. actions/nonverbal behaviors) and his or her words. Does the person's tone of voice, emphasis, facial expression, posture, and body movements fit the content of his or her communication? For example if a speaker nods his or her head while saying no, or the reverse, subtly shaking the head no when agreeing to something, then obviously the person has ambivalent feelings. Or for a more extreme example, let's say someone tells you that his mother has just died, but meanwhile he is grinning and leaning back comfortably with his legs propped up on his desk. Here you are getting mixed signals, also referred to as "**double messages**". There is no congruence between his words and his actions thus the message is very confusing.

If the person's body language, facial expression, tone of voice, and words don't match, your job as a listener is to clarify and give feedback about the discrepancy so as to deduce what the speaker is really feeling, or what is really going on. If you ignore the incongruity, you are settling for an incomplete or confusing message. It is important for you to realize that incongruity does not necessarily negate the veracity or sincerity of the spoken words. Resist the temptation to over interpret nonverbal behavior. There typically are many potential explanations for incongruent body language. For example, in the case that someone smiles when telling you how sad he is that his mother has died, you should not necessarily assume that the person is secretly thrilled about the death. Sometimes people smile out of embarrassment over intense emotions, or as a way of distancing themselves from strong feelings. Similarly, if someone fails to keep eye contact when telling you she cares about you, that doesn't necessarily mean that she is lying. Can you think of other reasons why she would behave in such a manner? Remember, truly effective communicators always seek to clarify the message, without assuming that they already know the meaning of the message.

UNDERSTANDING NONVERBAL BEHAVIOR

One of the main reasons why we are sometimes confused by what people say is because so much of what is being expressed is nonverbal. It has been estimated that only 7% of the meaning of a face-to-face communication is conveyed by the words alone! That is a staggering figure. Up to 93% of meaning is communicated nonverbally. It has been estimated that 38% of the emotional impact of our words is communicated by the vocal aspects of the message. This is referred to as **paralanguage**, which is a term given to how something is said rather that what is said. This includes characteristics such as the tone and pitch of voice, vocal inflections, emphasis on certain words, and the length and frequency of pauses. The other 55% of meaning is conveyed by facial expressions, bodily movements and gestures, duration of eye contact, and posture (Mehrabian, 1986). The reason why it is so important to pay close attention to nonverbal signals is that much of nonverbal behavior is unintentional and unconscious, thereby revealing deep, underlying feelings or attitudes. A good listener also attends to paralanguage, to those clues in voice tone, changes in pitch and tempo, and how quickly someone speaks. When anxious or excited people tend to talk faster, but when depressed, grief-stricken, or overtired, speech generally is slower than normal.

Facial expressions are especially revealing, particularly the mouth and the lips. Smirking usually accompanies sarcasm. While in deep thought many people purse their lips, but when tense they may bite their lower lip. Most people recognize how revealing their faces are and may try to mask their emotions by putting on a face (i.e. smiling to hide anger). To a trained observer such forced expressions seem strained or put on, but an untrained eye could be fooled. The eyes have often been referred to as the "windows to the soul" because of what they can reveal. Our eyes are a good barometer of our level of social comfort. Avoidance of eye contact often reflects shyness, guilt or disinterest. Maintaining good eye contact communicates openness, interest and comfort. In addition, we tend to unconsciously perceive pupil dilation as an indication of attraction (often sexual) or interest. Too much eye contact (staring) can reflect aggressiveness or prurient interests.

Body postures, bodily movements and gestures also reveal volumes about attitudes. If someone leans toward you it usually indicates interest and involvement in what you are saying, but if that person leans back it may reflect disinterest or a desire to get away. When people feel threatened there is a tendency to cross their arms over their body, a response known as body armoring. We get clues as to whether a person likes us or not by reading nonverbal cues. The kinds of nonverbal behaviors which can denote that someone likes you include smiling, head nodding, touching you, gesturing freely, raising the eyebrows, moving closer to you, and facing you squarely. On the other hand, body language that indicates dislike could include frowning, yawning, moving away, standing at an oblique angle to avoid facing you, shaking one's head and self grooming actions (Kleinke, 1986).

Another important aspect of nonverbal communication is expressed through touch and the distance with which we choose to stand when interacting with others, which is referred to as **personal space**. Touching is perhaps the most intimate kind of physical closeness, which communicates different meanings depending on who does the touching and under what circumstances. Touch can reflect affection, sexual interest, dominance, caring, and sometimes aggression. The message that touch conveys will depend on how gentle or rough the touch, the length of the contact, whether it occurs in an appropriate context, whether it is a friend or a stranger doing the touching, and whether it is from the same or opposite sex. In an acceptable context, touch usually is well received. Touching behavior can also be an indicator of status and dominance. A higher status individual often feels free to touch a lower status person, but the reverse rarely happens. In addition, cultural factors play a very important role here, because touching is considered more acceptable in some cultures than in others. For example, Latins are much more comfortable with touching than say, the British. Cultural factors also play a focal role in acceptable distances for personal space. Intimate distance (0 to 18 inches away from the body) is reserved for family members, lovers, and very close friends. Personal distance (1 to 4 feet) is the space we earmark for conversations with friends and coworkers. Social distance (4 to 10 feet) is used for impersonal business and casual conversations. Public distance (10 feet and beyond) is reserved for speaking to a group. Carrying on personal or private business at public distance would likely be considered very inappropriate, cold and aloof. Significant ethnic differences are apparent in the amount of personal space needed for comfortable interpersonal interactions. Americans, Germans and the English like more distance while Arabs, Greeks, Latin Americans, and the French prefer to interact at closer distances. Touching or standing too close to another person too soon can be perceived as an invasion of personal space.

The distance from which we stand from others when interacting can be very revealing about the nature of the relationship. One study demonstrated that couples in troubled marriages stood or sat significantly farther away from each other during conversations than those who were happily married (Crane, Dollahite, Griffin, & Taylor, 1987). A skilled marital counselor can learn volumes about a new couple presenting for marital therapy just by noting how far they sit from one another in the waiting room prior to their first appointment.

Detecting Deception

What about nonverbal indicators of deception? How can you know when someone is lying to you? Individuals who are adept at lying are masters of making their nonverbal behaviors match their untrue words. Great actors and actresses act with their bodies as well as with the delivery of their lines (i.e. their body language comes across as genuine). But fortunately, not everyone is a skilled liar. Nevertheless, although most people think they are usually capable of detecting when someone is trying to deceive them, research indicates that is not necessarily the case. The work of Paul Ekman (1985) is particularly illuminating in this regard. His research teaches us that **there is no one reliable indicator of deception**. For example, although it is commonly believed that shifty eyes or fidgeting are signs of dishonesty, these signals are only dependable indicators of discomfort, but don't always reflect deception. Most people are unskilled at detecting lies because the cues that we typically look for (i.e. in words and facial expressions) are often poor indicators, because good liars can talk a good game and mask their emotions. But we can learn to detect whether a person is unprepared to lie, and whether discrepancies exist between verbal and nonverbal behaviors. Ekman claims that with the proper training you could learn to discern when someone is lying to you 85% of the time (Ekman, O'Sullivan, Friesen, and Scherer, 1991). Careful observation of signs of emotional arousal, bodily movements and speech patterns can improve your ability to determine whether someone is trying to deceive you. Ekman recommends that you pay attention to the following:

1. **Signs of autonomic nervous system (ANS) arousal.** Lying is usually accompanied by a certain amount of ANS arousal which can manifest in various observable ways. For example, ANS arousal is often characterized by an increased and/or irregular respiration rate, pupil dilation, blushing, and an increased frequency of swallowing and blinking. Since these are involuntary responses often occurring out of an individual's awareness, they are harder to inhibit, thus the presence of these signs can indicate lying. But we caution you to consider that these are signals of emotional arousal, and may only indicate discomfort or embarrassment as opposed to lying.

2. **Body movements.** When lying, people tend to gesture less, but there is often an increase in self touching behaviors such as scratching or rubbing one's self. Be aware, however, that skilled liars may actually decrease the frequency of self touching behaviors to elude detection (DePaulo, 1994). The closest thing to a dead giveaway of deception we have found is when a person touches or covers his or her nose or mouth when speaking.

3. **Speech patterns.** Liars are more likely to give evasive or indirect answers, overly detailed or complicated explanations, or to respond with defensive tirades (e.g. the stereotypical response of the unfaithful spouse confronted with evidence of infidelity). (You need look no further than former President Clinton's infamous statements denying his relationship with Monica Lewinsky for examples of such). False statements are also often peppered with an increased frequency or duration of hesitations

or pauses, and pause words (such as ah, um, uh) along with stuttering. And interestingly, dissimulators are more likely to make "slips of the tongue".

What about when an individual's words and overt behaviors do not match, even when words and nonverbal behaviors appear to be in synch? For example, let's consider a situation where someone appears to sincerely express interest in having a relationship with you, but continually makes excuses why he/she cannot spend any time with you. Or a situation where someone insists that engaging in a certain activity is very important to him, yet when the time comes to follow through he consistently fails to show up or do anything that is required. Oftentimes we are faced with dilemmas such as these, where people's words and overt behaviors do not match. As in the case with non-matching verbal and nonverbal cues, your job is to point out the discrepancy and ask for clarification. For both of these cases you can use the Perception Check (covered in Chapter 10) as a method of seeking clarification. If you have already done this and the discrepancy persists despite your best efforts, then the best rule of thumb is to believe the overt actions over the words.

The Rules for Effective Nonverbal Communication

Learning to accurately read nonverbal signals is a valuable skill that will greatly improve your ability to be perceptive and responsive to other people. As an added bonus, picking up on nonverbal cues will assist you in knowing when to adjust your own behavior (i.e. if you are doing or saying something that offends or hurts another person) before the situation gets out of hand, as it might if you are oblivious to your impact on others. To summarize, we have synthesized this information into what we call the five rules for effective nonverbal communication:

Rule 1 Maintain good eye contact but be careful not to stare at others.

Rule 2 Use your body language appropriately to communicate interest in another, if that is your intent. Face the person squarely, lean forward, smile, gesture freely, keep your arms open, and nod your head at the appropriate times.

Rule 3 Speak clearly, fairly rapidly, and modulate your tone of voice and vocal inflections to keep your speech interesting.

Rule 4 Use the power of touch appropriately. Touch can be a potent tool for establishing rapport, but be careful. Strangers typically do not want or expect to be touched. Men often are not comfortable being touched by other men, except for close friends.

Rule 5 Respect the personal space of other people. Be sensitive to the cultural differences in what is perceived as an acceptable amount of personal space.

The subject of body language is fascinating and complicated. If you are interested in learning even more about nonverbal cues and how to accurately read them, some suggested readings include:

Body Language by Julius Fast

Manwatching by Desmond Morris

Nonverbal Behavior for Effective Listening

Just as you the listener will be attuned to the body language of the speaker to help pick up feelings or underlying attitudes, the speaker will also react to the nonverbal aspects of how you listen. Nonverbal behaviors associated with good listening skills include:

1. Maintaining good eye contact
2. Leaning forward slightly
3. Nodding or saying, *"Uh huh"*, to let the speaker know that you are listening and to continue.
4. Keeping your arms open

A Final Note on Effective Listening

The ancient Greeks had an enlightening philosophy which was reflected in three sequentially arranged words: **Ethos**, **Pathos** and **Logos**. The first, **Ethos**, refers to your personal credibility, your trustworthiness, the faith people have in your integrity. It also refers to your balance in the emotional bank account. **Pathos** refers to your empathic side. It means that you are capable of perceiving and attuning yourself with the emotional content of another person's communication. **Logos** is the logical, reasoning aspect of your character and your communication.

The sequence of these is important. First Ethos, then Pathos, then Logos. Your character first, then your relationships, and then your logic. This is a paradigm shift for most people who tend to go straight for the Logos, the left brain logic, in communicating. That is, they immediately resort to their logic without first taking the Ethos and the Pathos into consideration. This brings us back to Steven Covey's essential precept regarding the need to *"seek first to understand before attempting to be understood."*

KEY TERMS

Pseudo Listening	Clarifying	Personal Space
Active Listening	Feedback	Ethos
Reflective Listening	Empathic Listening	Pathos
Paraphrasing	Nonverbal Behavior	Logos
	Paralanguage	

CHAPTER 9 QUESTIONS

True or False (T or F)

1. _____ Listening happens automatically without any conscious effort on your part.

2. _____ It is important to be judgmental so people know where you stand.

3. _____ Good listeners are careful not to interrupt needlessly.

4. _____ Good listeners don't ask questions, they just keep quiet.

5. _____ 93% of the meaning of a face-to-face communication is conveyed by nonverbal behaviors.

6. _____ Words are a much more valid and true expression of a person's feelings than nonverbal behaviors.

7. _____ If someone has their arms crossed over his/her body it may indicate that he/she feels threatened or angry.

8. _____ There is no one reliable indicator of deception.

9. _____ Cultural differences do not play an important role in personal space.

10. _____ In effective communication logos should precede ethos and pathos.

Short-Answer Questions

1. The communication skill we use the most is _____.

2. After two days the average person remembers _____ of what you heard someone say.

3. Reflective listening involves _____ what you have heard the speaker say so he/she can let you know if you have understood.

4. _____ listening focuses on reflecting back feelings and attempting to truly understand the other person's frame of reference.

5. We give _____ when our verbal behavior is not congruent with our _____ behavior.

6. _____ is the term given to how you say what it is that you say.

7. _____ refers to your integrity, _____ to your empathy, and _____ to your logic.

Essay Questions

1. Name and describe the important elements in being a good listener.
2. How does being judgmental influence the communication process?
3. Describe the three elements of reflective listening.
4. How does empathic listening differ from reflective listening?
5. Why is it sometimes so difficult to detect deception? What cues would you look for to try to determine whether someone is being dishonest?
6. Discuss the rules for effective nonverbal communication.

10

Build Trust as You Communicate

Part II: Communicating Effectively with Others

Effective communication is a two way street. It requires good listening skills *and* good conversational skills. The foundation of successful interpersonal relationships, whether in your personal life or in the workplace, depends on your ability to communicate your thoughts, feelings, concerns, and needs. But just as hearing and listening are not the same thing, talking and communicating are not always the same. True communication only occurs if the speaker clearly expresses, and the listener attends to and understands the message being conveyed.

HOW TO BE A GOOD CONVERSATIONALIST

People who are popular and well liked tend to be good at making conversation. But being a good conversationalist is much more than just talking a lot. We have all had the experience of being in the presence of someone who talked a lot, but bored us to death or made us uncomfortable with sustained self-absorption. Fontana (1990) offers these tips for expressing yourself effectively in conversations:

1. **Keep your message interesting.** Avoid rattling on incessantly about minor details, unless you know for sure that the other person sincerely wants to hear this minutia (*i.e. If someone asks you what time it is, don't tell them how to build a watch*!) Pay attention to nonverbal cues from the listener to discern if he or she is getting bored and adjust your speech accordingly.

2. **Show your sense of humor.** This doesn't mean you have to tell jokes or be a stand-up comedian. Allow yourself to make humorous or witty remarks when appropriate, and by all means, demonstrate that you have the capacity to laugh at yourself. Poke fun at yourself by making occasional self-deprecating comments. This puts people at ease by demonstrating that you don't take yourself too seriously.

3. **Show an interest in the other person.** Refrain from being nosy, but do ask questions to draw the other person out. Most people will enjoy talking about themselves if given a chance, so you will make a good impression if you show a genuine interest in another person.

4. **Avoid monopolizing the conversation.** This includes interrupting the other person.

5. **Stay focused on the topic at hand.** While everyone occasionally goes off on tangents (and sometimes this helps keep the conversation interesting), resist rambling or bouncing from subject to subject without completing your point.

6. **Offer sincere compliments when appropriate.** Everyone loves positive feedback.

7. **Refrain from engaging in annoying mannerisms such as fidgeting, or using irritating expressions** (such as punctuating your statements with "you know" or "whatever").

8. **Talk fairly rapidly.** A quick speech rate coveys enthusiasm, intelligence, confidence or expertise. If you notice signs of impatience in your listener, or if people are often finishing your sentences for you, this a good tip-off that you are talking too slowly.

Rapport Building

There is yet another aspect of being a good conversationalist, which is more sophisticated than the tips mentioned above. This has to do with being able to develop **rapport** with another person. Two people are said to have a good rapport when they are comfortable with one another and can get on the same wavelength, either emotionally, intellectually or both. To the extent that you can develop a good rapport with someone you will increase the probability that you can put that person at ease and/or develop a friendship. Rapport building is affected by many variables. For example, it is often easier to establish rapport with someone if the two of you have very similar interests, backgrounds, values, or ways of thinking or expressing yourselves. Then rapport builds naturally. Likewise, if you are engaged in an activity together (i.e. working on a project for a class or at work), or have frequent contact with that person (i.e. by virtue of living next to one another, or working side by side, or sitting next to the person in class day after day) this commonality can help lay the groundwork for rapport. Psychologists have long known that this **propinquity** (that is, having frequent contact with a person because you live close by or work nearby at the same workplace) is a big factor in who we develop as friends. But just being around a person a lot is no guarantee of friendship or rapport; propinquity only provides ample opportunity to develop rapport.

So how do you go about trying to establish rapport with another, be it a stranger or an acquaintance you would like to know better? To a great extent, developing rapport is about putting someone at ease by *mirroring their nonverbal and verbal behavior*. What does this mean? It requires that you must be willing to be flexible in your presentation of self. This does not mean you need to be phony, but rather you need to mirror back those aspects of that person's behavior that you feel comfortable with. For example, if the person is very down to earth and uses salty language, feel free to let your hair down (if you feel comfortable with that), but if the person is rather formal and uses a lot of big words, trot out your best vocabulary. If the person talks very fast, speed up your rate of speech, likewise, if the person talks slowly, speak in a more languid way to mirror him or her. If the person gestures a lot, gesture back, but if he/she is more stiff, hold back on your gestures. Why does this work? Because most of us are most comfortable with people we perceive as being like us, at least in some ways. Mirroring is a one way of accomplishing this and putting another at ease. Used in conjunction with empathic listening (the other rapport building skill) you will have the skills necessary to establish relationships. Charismatic and well liked individuals do this unconsciously.

Making a Good First Impression

If you want to make a good initial impression when speaking with someone for the first time, heed these verbal and nonverbal tips from Mary Mitchell (1998).

- Refrain from discussing controversial topics such as religion or politics. Also, no one wants to hear about your health problems at a first meeting (i.e. keep the constipation report for your loved ones).

- Jokes are fine, but avoid any that are off-color, could be perceived as prejudicial, or that are very lengthy and involved.

- Face the person squarely, lean forward, stand upright and maintain good eye contact.

- Keep your arms open, don't touch your face, and resist shifting your weight between your legs (which could make it appear that you want to get away as soon as possible.).

The Art of Small Talk

Although small talk is often dismissed as superficial or unimportant, nothing could be farther from the truth. This idle chitchat or "how's the weather" banter often serves as the ice breaker or lead-in to more meaningful encounters and interactions. Bernardo Carducci reminds us that just about every romance, or friendship, or business deal began with small talk when the people first met each other. In his 1999 book, *The Pocket Guide to Making Successful Small Talk*, he offers tips for how to master the art of small talk. If you are shy or uncomfortable with meeting strangers, you might find these suggestions particularly relevant.

- Begin with a simple statement. This does not necessarily have to be a witty or brilliant comment. Often it can just be the proverbial remark about the weather (i.e." It's so windy out today").

- Introduce yourself. Offer some non-private personal information about yourself (e.g. telling the other person where you work) which gives that person a hook upon which to ask you a question, or make a personal comment so as to continue the exchange.

- Select a topic that is of general interest. Don't worry about whether it is superficial, most small talk is about relatively trivial or mundane matters.

- Keep the conversation moving by making associations to other subjects or asking questions.

- Pay attention to the other person, and follow the guidelines for effective listening from Chapter 9 (including the tips on how to listen well non-verbally).

- Make a graceful exit. Polite statements such as "It's been a pleasure meeting you", "Have a great day", or "I hope to run into you again", allow you to end the conversation smoothly.

ASSERTIVE SKILLS

Effective communicators are adept at listening, but also skilled at expressing their own needs and desires. As mentioned earlier, effective communication is a two way street. It isn't enough to be a great listener if you cannot express yourself effectively in return. Oftentimes, the type of verbal expression that is hardest to master is the art of being appropriately and effectively **assertive**. Consider the following scenarios which may resemble situations that you or someone you know has had to face. These scenes were derived from stressful work situations presented by participants in our Assertiveness Training workshops.

Scenario 1

You are a full time student and also employed part time to cover your expenses. A close friend of yours lost his job and was broke. Since you had a small savings you offered to lend him several hundred dollars to meet his bills until he could find employment. He enthusiastically accepted your offer, and promised to pay you back as soon as he got a new job. A few weeks later he landed a job but made no mention about repaying the loan. You decided to wait a few weeks to let him get paid and caught up with his bills. A month passed and still no word from him on loan repayment. Then he invited you over to his home to see the brand new stereo system he just bought. You are feeling angry and thinking he may have taken advantage of your generosity by buying a luxury item before paying you back. Meanwhile, your car breaks down and you are now falling into debt without your savings to fall back on.

Scenario 2

You have developed a reputation at your company for being an excellent worker. As a result of your competence your boss keeps adding to your responsibilities. Although your workload has increased significantly, your boss has not offered you a raise. In order to keep up with your rising workload you have to work overtime several times a week. Since you are a salaried employee you do not get paid for overtime. You are growing increasingly resentful and stressed out. You worry constantly about keeping up with your work, but you are afraid to turn down new assignments and disappoint your boss.

Scenario 3

You have a long standing friendship with someone whom you often get together with on the weekends. However, your friend has a habit of frequently canceling plans with you at the last minute, sometimes with good reason and other times not. You have been very understanding about this and have not wanted to complain for fear of jeopardizing the relationship. It is Saturday night and you have special plans with this friend. You are all dressed and ready to leave when the phone rings and, once again, your friend has to cancel your plans. You feel very angry and disappointed.

Scenario 4

You are a legal secretary working for a high powered attorney in a large law firm. Your boss, Mr. Reynolds, has a habit of strolling into work late in the morning and wasting time until the afternoon when he goes into high gear and is quite productive. But because of his delays in getting down to work, paperwork that needs to be finished and filed that day is often not completed at the end of the workday at 5:00 p.m. You routinely work overtime for up to one full hour on almost a daily basis in order to complete paperwork that must be filed that day. Although it is inconvenient for you to stay late, the extra money you earn from overtime pay comes in handy and makes it worth your while. One day the firm's top managers announce that due to dwindling profits, all overtime work and pay will be indefinitely suspended. Your boss is not in agreement with this new policy, but has no power to change the mandate. You are very worried that you will be put in the uncomfortable position of having to work overtime for free in order to complete necessary tasks.

ASSERTIVENESS DEFINED

The scenarios described above represent the kinds of difficult situations that we all confront periodically. What these situations have in common is that they call for an assertive response. Whether you are a student, employee, employer, friend, parent, etc. situations will arise where you will need to assert yourself in order to deal with the situation. Assertion involves standing up for your personal rights and expressing ideas, needs, feelings and beliefs in direct, honest and appropriate ways without violating the rights of other people (Lange & Jakubowski, 1976). When you are assertive you can accept compliments and take criticisms. You can negotiate for what you need, disagree with another, and ask for clarification when you don't understand. You can set limits when necessary, and you are able to say, *"No"*.

The basic message you are communicating when you are assertive is: This is what I think. This is what I feel. This is how I view the situation. This message expresses who you are and is said without dominating, humiliating or degrading the other person. Assertion involves respect for others, but not deference. Deference is acting in a subservient manner as though the other person is right, or better simply because they are older, more powerful, experienced, knowledgeable or in an authority position over you. When you express yourself in ways that are self-effacing, appeasing, or overly apologetic you are showing deference. Two types of respect are intimately involved in assertion: (1) respect for yourself, that is, expressing your needs and defending your rights and; (2) respect for the rights and needs of the other person or persons.

Assertive self-expression is a hallmark of effective communication skills. It is a prerequisite for satisfying interpersonal relationships. Being assertive will not give you an iron clad guarantee of having things go your way, but you maximize your chances of success while minimizing the chance of alienating others. Assertiveness contributes to interpersonal effectiveness, higher self-esteem, lower levels of stress, and more satisfying relationships (Davis et al., 1988).

Differentiating Assertiveness from Passivity and Aggression

Non-assertion, also called **passivity**, involves violating your own rights by failing to express honest feelings, needs, thoughts and beliefs and consequently permitting others to potentially take advantage of you. It also involves expressing your thoughts and feelings in such an apologetic, diffident, or self-effacing manner that others can easily disregard you and/or your message. Nonassertion shows a lack of respect for your own needs. It can also imply a subtle lack of respect for the other person's ability to handle disappointments, to shoulder some responsibility, to handle his or her own problems, etc. The goal of passivity is to appease others and to avoid conflict at any cost. And often there is a high price to pay for routinely avoiding conflict. Part of the price paid for passivity is that it renders you ineffective.

Aggression involves directly standing up for your personal rights and expressing thoughts, feelings, needs, and beliefs in ways which can be dishonest, usually inappropriate or intimidating, and always violates the rights of other people. The usual goal of aggression is domination and winning by intimidation, forcing the other person to lose, or at the very least, to lose face. Winning is assured by humiliating, degrading, belittling, or overpowering others so they become weaker and less able to express and defend their needs and rights. You need not get physical in order to be aggressive. Individuals who are aggressive directly compromise their effectiveness by alienating others.

We can think of assertiveness, passivity and aggression as being on a continuum with assertiveness representing the effective middle ground between aggression and nonassertion. It represents a balance of respecting the rights of others while also respecting your own rights. It represents the effective middle ground of diplomacy between the deference and self-effacement characteristic of passivity, and the intimidation and bullying characteristic of aggressiveness. Put simply, when you are assertive you can set up a win-

win situation. When passive you create a lose-win scenario and, obviously, when you are aggressive you produce a win-lose situation.

There is another ineffective option to assertiveness, and that is what we refer to as **passive-aggression**, which may sound like a contradiction in terms, but represents a form of behavior which we have all, at one time or another, demonstrated. Passive-aggressiveness is an indirect form of aggressiveness where we literally get back at someone, not by what we directly do or say, but by what we fail to do or say. The classic example is when you give someone the silent treatment when you are angry at him or her. This cold shoulder approach allows you to get back at the person by what you fail to do (i.e. talk and be friendly). Or for another example, take the case of a formerly dedicated employee who feels that his boss is too demanding and eventually adopts an "I don't care attitude", deliberately working slowly and finding excuses to take time off work.

Negative Consequences of Failing to Be Assertive

Failure to handle situations in an assertive fashion can have very negative consequences for you and for your personal and business relationships. In the short run, a passive stance helps you avoid anxiety producing conflicts. However, in the long run, if you are frequently passive you will feel a growing loss of self-esteem and an increasing sense of resentment or anger. This increases your stress level which can lead to anxiety, depression and/or psychosomatic difficulties (e.g. headaches, ulcers, hypertension, etc.). On the other hand, handling situations in an aggressive manner also works in the short run because you may achieve a temporary emotional release and get your needs met through intimidation. But in the long run, the negative consequences of aggressiveness are obvious. Highly aggressive behavior at work may ultimately cost you promotions or even your job. Bullying your employees (if you are the boss), supervisees or co-workers leads to poor interpersonal relationships and literally invites passive-aggressive retaliation on the part of your colleagues. For example, a tyrannical boss may find that his subordinates react to his aggressive, authoritarian stance with work slowdowns, deliberate mistakes, property damage, theft, backbiting, etc. In your personal life, aggression can lead to failed relationships, high blood pressure, fights and even potentially trouble with the law. People who are frequently aggressive eventually feel deeply misunderstood, unloved and unlovable because they fail to recognize the impact of their behavior on others, and how such alienation is inevitable.

Benefits of Assertion

Being assertive maximizes the likelihood that your needs and the needs of others will be met, therefore increasing your effectiveness. It will definitely lower your personal level of stress and help ward off illness. One of the greatest benefits of assertiveness is that it will definitely increase your self-respect and self-confidence, as well as garner respect from others.

Why People Fail to Behave Assertively

There are many reasons and not all of them will apply to you. Ponder those reasons that are relevant for you and be aware of the misconceptions that often underlie your line of reasoning.

- Fear of loss of approval from others or of getting an angry response.

- Failing to distinguish between assertiveness and aggression. That is, mistaking assertiveness for aggression. This is a particular problem for women in our culture who are given so many double messages (i.e. encouraged to be strong and outspoken and then vilified for being bitchy or masculine).

- Mistaking nonassertion for politeness or consideration. How can you learn to differentiate non-assertion from graciousness or politeness? A good rule of thumb is to listen to your body. Certain body signals will cue you when your response changes from politeness to nonassertion. Tension and discomfort will arise that typically are not present when you are being polite. If you are confused as to whether to assert yourself or whether to keep quiet and "be polite", you need to ask yourself the following questions:

  > Am I likely to bring this up later?
  >
  > Will my relationship with this person suffer or change if I keep silent?
  >
  > Is there a hidden expectation present?
  >
  > That is, will I feel used because I have unexpressed expectations about reciprocity that may go unfulfilled?

- Mistaking passivity for being helpful because agreeing to do things you really don't want to do might help another person. In genuine helping you eventually make yourself obsolete. In rescuing you end up in the victim role with feelings of being used or taken advantage of by someone with an expectation that you will always be there to bail him/her out.

- Aggression is often an outgrowth of feelings of powerlessness, where a person believes that he will be controlled too easily by others unless he behaves aggressively. Here there is a tendency to behave aggressively as an overreaction to past emotional experiences.

- A maladaptive belief that aggression is justified and the only way to get through to other people can also fuel aggressive behavior.

- Aggression also often results from feelings of anger or hurt that have built up to a boiling point leading to an explosion. If the situation had been dealt with assertively in the first place, the aggressive episode could have been prevented.

- Failure to accept your personal rights. It is hard to be assertive if you do not believe you have the right to express your reactions, take care of your needs and stand up for yourself. Some people not only feel they shouldn't express their needs, but think they should not even have them in the first place.

The foundation of improving your assertive skills involves understanding and believing that you have certain rights an individual and that it is not only OK, but healthy and useful to yourself and others to stand up for your rights. Individuals who are appropriately assertive and self confident have internalized the following tenets.

THE ASSERTIVE BILL OF RIGHTS

1. I have the right as a human being to have needs, and my needs are as important as the needs of others. I have the right to ask (not demand) that other people respond to my needs.

2. I have the right as a human being to have feelings and form opinions. Furthermore, I have the right to express these in ways that respect the feelings and opinions of others.

3. I have the right to expect respect from other people. It is incumbent upon me to also show the same respect for others. Respecting others does not mean that I allow them to take advantage of me or disregard my needs

4. I have the right to choose whether, in a particular situation, I want or can reasonably meet other people's needs or expectations.

5. I have the right to say, "No."

6. If I frequently compromise my needs or sacrifice my rights, I am teaching others to take advantage of me.

7. If I live my life in such a way as to always avoid conflict or the possibility of hurting someone under any circumstances, I will end up hurting myself and others in the long run. It is only through the honest (and timely) expression of needs, feelings, reactions and thoughts that I can ultimately develop satisfying interpersonal relationships. When I am assertive everyone will benefit in the long run.

8. If I stand up for myself while simultaneously showing respect for others, I will gain self-respect as well as the respect of others.

9. By being assertive with others and explaining how their behavior affects me, I am giving them the opportunity to change their behavior and respecting their right to know where they stand with me.

10. I do not have the right to demean, intimidate, or manipulate other people into meeting my needs. I do have the right to ask, however, and to attempt to persuade while respecting their right to refuse.

A USEFUL FRAMEWORK FOR ASSERTIVE BEHAVIOR

When learning to become more assertive or to polish your assertive skills, it can be very useful to have a framework or steps to follow in order to know how to construct a potentially effective assertive response. This applies on the job or in your personal life. What follows is a four step framework that you should find helpful, especially at those times when you may be tongue-tied, for you can always fall back on these steps. This framework is not the gospel; you don't always have to follow this format, and this is not the only effective way to proceed. But nonetheless, this is still a very useful summary of how to construct an assertive response.

Step One: The Problem Behavior

The first step is to identify the problem behavior. It is important to keep your language to specific discussions of observable behaviors; do not address personality characteristics. For example, it is much more effective to say, "I am aware that you have not completed several reports that were due", rather than, "lately you have been so lazy!" The first sentence is merely a description of behavior (or lack of behavior) you observed, wherein the second sentence includes value judgements. If you make value judgements or comment on personality characteristics, particularly in a derogatory fashion, you are just likely to anger the other person, even if your description is totally accurate. You stand a greater chance of resolving the issue, and getting the other person to listen to you if you limit your descriptions to observable behavior. If you merely tell someone they are "an idiot", it only demeans them and gives absolutely no information about what they did or did not do behaviorally to have merited that insult. Whenever possible, your language should include "I statements". I statements refer to what you have observed, witnessed, felt, etc., so that you are taking responsibility for your feelings, experiences and observations. This is in contrast to "You statements" which typically involve pointing the finger at another person. It is the difference between saying "I feel hurt when you say . . ." rather than "You hurt me".

Step Two: Effects

Next you identify what effects the problem behavior has on you. There are two types of effects. The first refers to the difficulties or inconvenience that the problem behavior causes for you or your organization, and the second is how you feel about the problem behavior (e.g. angry, confused, hurt, disappointed, etc.). In some cases only difficulties are involved, in others only feelings, and in some instances both occur. In some cases where both are involved you may opt only to mention the difficulties and keep the feelings to yourself, such as in situations where you are dealing with strangers or peripheral acquaintances. This can often apply in a business situation as well, where it might be far more appropriate to deal with the problem behavior at hand than to express personal feelings.

Step Three: Consequences (Optional)

It is very important to note that this step is optional. Here you identify the consequences of the problem behavior if it persists. Basically, you are saying what will happen if the person does not stop the problem behavior. It is not always appropriate or possible to specify consequences, and that is why this step is optional. Sometimes the situation only calls for you to express how you feel about something and specifying consequences would be overkill. At other times it may be more strategic to wait to specify consequences and determine whether there is a need for escalation later on if the person refuses to change or acknowledge that there is a problem. Never specify a consequence that you are not throughly willing or able to follow through with, for then you run the risk that the other person will call your bluff and your credibility and clout will be damaged. If there are no consequences you can readily state and follow up on, then skip this step entirely.

Step Four: Alternatives to the Problem Behavior

The last step involves specifying alternatives to the problem behavior. What is it that you would like the other person to do instead of or in addition to the problem behavior? You may think that this should be obvious and you don't need to spell it out, but many times, just because it is obvious to you what the person ought to be doing, it may not be obvious to him or her. Other people are not mind readers. If you are going to give feedback, give it fully and let others know clearly and diplomatically what your expectations are. Once you have elucidated your expectations and have some inclination from the other person that he/she is receptive, you need to ask for a commitment for change. Do not be afraid to ask people to commit themselves to behaving differently. If they verbally agree to change they are more likely to follow through.

Fine-Tuning the Assertive Steps

When asserting yourself it is often very helpful to incorporate a style known as **empathic assertion**. Here you convey sensitivity to other person over and above expressing your feelings or needs. When it is possible to proceed in this fashion, it is often highly effective because it helps to establish rapport and minimize defensiveness on the part of the other. It involves making a statement, usually in step one, that conveys recognition of the other person's situation or feelings followed by another statement where you stand up for your rights and suggest other alternatives. It requires that you put yourself in the shoes of the other, and let him/her know that you have at least some understanding of his/her situation or feelings, but you still have your own needs to take into consideration.

Likewise, there are times when your initial efforts to be assertive are discounted and you will need to escalate. **Escalating assertiveness** describes a situation where you start with a minimal assertive response and, for whatever reason, it does not work. At this point, you do not back down but rather become increasingly firm and escalate without becoming aggressive. It is here that you may opt to include step three (consequences), because the other person has not responded appropriately to less firm statements on your part. Here you can gradually increase from a request to a demand. Or when someone is asking something of you, increase from stating a preference of "no" to an outright refusal. Or it could represent switching from an empathic assertive approach to a more firm, cut and dried approach.

In the course of asserting yourself there are a variety of tactics that others will often use to derail you before you get your point across. The most common tactic involves the other person interrupting you to tell their side of the story. Do not allow this. Firmly speak up and say, "Excuse me, I'd like to finish what I am saying". If they persist with interruptions, escalate and say, *"Please stop interrupting me. I will give you plenty of time to reply, but now I would appreciate it if you would let me finish"*. Another side tracking tactic is deflecting. Here a person responds to your assertion by bringing up things from the past, often irrelevant, that you have done to aggravate them. The best way to handle this is not to take the bait. Refuse to let the conversation be drawn in another direction, even if their complaint is valid. If it is valid you should promise to deal with it after your issue is resolved or thoroughly discussed. For example, you could say, *"That is not relevant. If you want we can discuss that after we get through this."*

Using the Four Step Framework

If we return to the scenarios at the beginning of this chapter we can construct assertive responses using the four step framework and I statements. Study the following examples.

Scenario 1

Step One. "Several months ago, when you were in a financial jam, I lent you $ 300. I was glad to help out. Over a month ago you got a new job but so far you have not paid back anything towards the loan. I recall that you had promised to pay me back as soon as you got a job. It has been over a month since you got hired at your new job."

Step Two. "I am feeling angry and disappointed that you chose to buy a stereo before paying me back. Right now I have gotten in debt because I had to pay for a costly car repair."

Step Three. "I am concerned that if this persists it will hurt our friendship."

Step Four. "I would appreciate it if you could pay me back as soon as possible. If you cannot pay back the whole lump sum at once, could you pay it in two or three installments? Can I have a commitment from you to pay back at least $ 100, if not the whole amount, by the end of this week?"

Scenario 2

Step One. "I have been with this company for four years now and I am very pleased that you are happy with the quality of my work. Several times over the last few months I have, at your request, taken on increasing volumes of work. In order to finish I have to work overtime and/or bring work home for which I do not get paid because I am salaried. And I have not gotten a salary raise in two years."

Step Two. "Given all the extra work I have taken on, I am easily doing the work of two employees. Although I have been willing to do the extra work, out of loyalty to the company, I do not feel I am being adequately compensated for the work I am doing."

Step Four. "I truly feel I deserve at least a 10% raise. My taking on extra work, over and above my job description, saves you from hiring someone else full or part time. I deserve to get some of that savings to you back in terms of increasing my salary. Can I receive a raise at this time?"

Note: If this should fail and the boss refuses then escalate and include step three.

Step Three (option 1). "If you cannot see clear to raise my salary at this time then I have no choice but to refuse to take on any more extra work. My job description does not indicate that I am responsible for those tasks."

Step Three (option 2) *This option is designed to use your leverage (i.e. the fact that you are a highly valued worker) to persuade your boss to give you a raise.* "If you cannot see clear to raise my salary at this time then I may have to begin searching for a new job. If I am going to be doing work at this level, then I deserve to be paid for my efforts. I know I can make significantly more money at other companies. My preference would be to stay here, but I may have no choice if you cannot raise my salary. Can I count on you for a good reference? By the way, keep in mind that if I have to leave, you may need to hire two people to handle the load that I have worked. So I believe it is in everyone's best interest for you to give me a raise."

Scenario 3

Step One.   (Empathic assertion) "We have been friends for many years, and over this time there have been numerous occasions when you have canceled your plans with me, often at the last moment. I understand that sometimes things have come up for you that were out of your control and you had to change our plans. But this has happened so often that I now feel I must speak up."

Step Two.   When you cancel our plans at the last minute it leaves me in the lurch because it is usually too late for me to make other plans, like tonight. And I feel irritated and disappointed, as if I cannot count on you. I fear our friendship will suffer.

Step Four.   "I would greatly appreciate it if you could give me more advance notice when you are unable to keep our plans."

Step Three.   (optional) "If you cannot commit to this then I may decide not to make plans with you again."

Scenario 4

Step One.   "Mr. Reynolds, it is very important that we discuss the new rule about working overtime. (*Empathic Assertion*) I know that you had nothing to do with the new ruling. I do not blame you in the least. But this is creating a problem for both of us. Your work habits are such that you come to the office late and don't really begin getting down to business until the afternoon. As a result, I have had to stay overtime on almost a daily basis in order to get all the paperwork finished and filed on time."

Step Two.   "If I do not stay late then important papers may not be filed on time. Our clients and your reputation will suffer and I will feel as though I am not doing a good job. I am now concerned that I will be put in the difficult position of having to work overtime for free which I feel is unfair to me. Working overtime takes away from my time with my children and makes it hard for me to keep up with responsibilities at home. I was willing to do it when I could earn a significant amount of extra money."

Step Three.   "I am not willing to work overtime on a regular basis unless I am compensated for my time. I may have to leave the office at closing time without completing important papers."

Step Four.   "But I have some ideas about how we can resolve our mutual dilemma. First of all, you could agree to pay me out of your own pocket for overtime work and then I will be glad to continue as before. If that is not acceptable to you then we need to work together on time management. You need to come to the office by 9:00 a.m. and use your morning time more productively. If you are able to get the paperwork to me earlier in the day, then I will have no difficulty in completing and filing all necessary papers by 5:00 p.m. I am willing to meet with you early each morning to help you organize your morning time more efficiently. We have to do something different because clearly we cannot continue functioning the same way. Which of these alternatives would you prefer?" *When asserting yourself with individuals in authority over you, it can be very effective to offer several options and ask them to pick one. That way they retain the illusion of being in control, (i.e. they get to choose) and will often admire your ingenuity in developing solutions.*

THE PERCEPTION CHECK

Effective individuals are also adept at communicating in many situations, not all of which require an assertive response. There is an offshoot of the assertive response which has been called the Perception Check (Adler & Towne, 1993). This involves situations where there is not a need to assert yourself, per se, but when you note something that concerns or confuses you about another person, and you want to check out what is really happening. A classic example, one that all of us have experienced at some point in our lives, is a situation where someone you care about is acting differently towards you, perhaps uncommunicative or standoffish. You don't have a clue as to what is going on. Is the person angry with you? Have you done something to hurt or anger him or her? Is the person upset, and if so, is that person just upset for reasons that have absolutely nothing to do with you? The perception check is a useful, caring method for finding out and answering questions like those above.

The perception check is a three step method which has similarities to the four step framework for assertiveness, but with several fundamental differences. Here your aim is to be empathic, to elicit a honest response, and to listen so as to truly understand what is going on with the other person. Of course, you do not always have to follow these steps, but if you are unsure how to proceed this framework will come in very handy.

Step One. Identify what you have noticed about the other person by referring to observable behaviors. When possible use "I statements".
Step Two. Give two possible alternatives or interpretations of what the person's behavior might mean or might be about.
Step Three. Ask for clarification.

Using the situation mentioned above as an example of how to use the perception check, you might proceed like this:

Step One. "Sandy, lately I've noticed that you have been very quiet around me, not like your usual talkative self. And you have also seemed so distant. At the party last night you didn't even come over and say, 'Hi' to me. And whenever I looked at you, it seemed like you looked away."
Step Two. "I'm worried that perhaps I have done something to hurt you. Or perhaps you are just upset or worried about something else."
Step Three. "Please tell me what is going on. Are you angry with me?"

Now Sandy is free to tell you what she is feeling and why. Your job now is to really listen without getting defensive, and to put yourself into her shoes in order to understand her behavior.

NONVERBAL ASPECTS OF ASSERTIVENESS

How you say what you say is just as important as what you say. That is, the body language you display has a profound effect on how your words will be interpreted and on the responses you will get. No matter how well crafted your assertive response may be or how appropriate your words, if your nonverbal behaviors are not congruent with your verbal communication you can totally sabotage your message, and greatly reduce the likelihood of getting the reaction you seek. If your nonverbal behaviors reflect passivity, deference, self-effacement, timidity, or lack of confidence you will undermine your message and invite others to discount your words. On the other hand, if your words are assertive and appropriate but your demeanor is intimidating or aggressive it will also detract from your message. Other people will respond with fear or resentment rather than accommodation. Effective communicators are congruent in words and body language.

Basically, you want to present a demeanor that is consistent with assertiveness. It is neither timid nor aggressive, but rather forthright, confident, and matter-of-fact. One of the most effective ways to present a confident demeanor is to maintain eye contact. When you look directly at someone's eyes while talking to them it conveys confidence, self-assurance, and that you mean what you say. A passive stance usually involves minimal eye contact or looking down which conveys lack of confidence or uncertainty about your position. An aggressive stance often involves staring a person down, which is not what we mean when we suggest making eye contact. Sometimes it is hard to maintain eye contact, particularly if you have trouble with being assertive, because it may make you uncomfortable. Despite this, we encourage you to force yourself to do so for several reasons: (1) it will make your assertive responses more effective, and (2) keeping eye contact gets a lot easier once you practice doing it.

Posture is also important when delivering an assertive response. You can maximize your effectiveness if you stand up straight, face the person squarely, and lean forward slightly. This conveys a sense of confidence. Likewise, if you are sitting down it is useful to lean forward slightly. Leaning back conveys fear or lack of confidence. People tend to lean back and look down when they are unsure of themselves or afraid. Obviously, getting too close to someone or getting in their face is an aggressive posture that you would want to avoid. It is always wise to respect the personal space of other people.

What you do with your arms reveals a lot about your internal state. For example, have you ever seen two people sitting across from each other in a restaurant, both with their arms folded across their body? Even though you might not overhear the content of their conversation you can usually tell, just from their arm postures, that they are either arguing or annoyed with each other. How do you know this? Remember from the section on nonverbal communication in Chapter 9 that arms crossed over the body is referred to as a "body armoring" response, an unconscious way to protect or hug yourself when feeling threatened. When threatened, most people will immediately adopt this posture unconsciously. Thus, it is very important not to cross your arms over your body or you will convey that you feel intimidated by the encounter. Rather, make a point to leave your arms open. Open arms communicates that you are confident, comfortable and that you mean what you say. Incidentally, when on the receiving end of feedback maintain the open arm posture. In this way you will come across as non-defensive and open to feedback, qualities that are respected by others.

Also, allow yourself to gesture freely while asserting yourself. People tend to gesture and use their arms when they are comfortable. When you gesture you communicate comfort and confidence, and people are much more likely to take you seriously. But, there is one gesture we recommend that you definitely avoid: pointing at someone. People hate it when you point at them like a scolding parent or an angry schoolteacher. They will tune you out and resist you if you resort to finger pointing.

Perhaps the most important nonverbal aspect of assertiveness is your tone of voice. So much is conveyed by the volume, pitch and rhythm of your voice. Avoid shouting which is perceived as aggressive. Also avoid being so soft-spoken that you come off as timid. It is best to speak in a firm, consistent voice tone where you pause for emphasis, and also emphasize key words by slowing down your voice tempo and increasing your volume slightly. Do not talk fast or swallow your words when asserting yourself. It may be useful to talk a little slower, particularly if you are a fast talker, and a little louder than usual for emphasis. Table 9.1 summarizes the differences between assertive vs. passive or aggressive communication styles.

	PASSIVE	ASSERTIVE	AGGRESSIVE
TABLE 10.1 Differentiating Communication Styles			
Verbal Behaviors	Apologetic Indirect statements Rambling Not saying what you really mean Giving up easily	Direct statements Honest expression of feelings Describing objective behavior "I" statements Straightforward Good listener Talking slowly Emphasize key words	Accusations, threats Insults, put-downs Blaming "You" statements Sarcasm Failure to listen Manipulative comments
Nonverbal Behaviors	Incongruencies Poor eye contact Soft, timid voice Looking down Fidgeting Leaning back Slumped posture	Actions congruent with words Good eye contact Firm, calm voice Assured manner Gesturing Leaning forward Erect posture Open arms Face person squarely	Staring Yelling, shouting Loud, hostile voice tone Arms crossed over body Finger pointing Getting too close Clenched fists Breaking things
You Are	Scared, anxious Helpless Manipulated Ignored Resentful	Confident Effective Respectful Valued Relieved	Angry, full of rage Indignant Misunderstood Controlling Guilty
Others Feel	Frustrated Puzzled Unsure of your needs	Respected Valued	Intimidated Alienated Angry, resentful Humiliated, hurt Defensive
End Results	Stress Depression Low self-esteem Helplessness Failure to solve problem Resentment Lost Opportunities Health problems	Problem solving High self-esteem Self-respect Respect of others Satisfaction Good relationships Less stress Improved health	Interpersonal stress Guilt, remorse Low self-esteem Loss of self-respect Loss of respect from others Passive-Aggressive responses Frustration Failure to solve problems Broken relationships Loneliness Hostility from others Potential legal problems

Asserting Yourself with Aggressive People

It can be difficult and stressful to have to deal with aggressive, unreasonable, or nasty individuals, whether in your personal life or at your workplace. When dealing with such people it is common to feel as if you have no control, and to become angry and aggressive yourself. The following pointers should prove useful for handling encounters with aggressive people.

* Make ample use of empathic assertion. Try paraphrasing what you have heard the person say or commenting on the feelings that are being expressed in their demeanor. For example, simple comments such as: *"You sound like you are feeling very angry"*; or, *"This is obviously very upsetting for you"*, can help an angry person to feel understood, and in some cases can help defuse their anger. It is also helpful to ask questions to get the person to clarify the problem and work towards a solution.

* Keep your focus. Aggressive interactions, particularly with people you know well, often get sidetracked from the original issue with laundry lists of everything else that is a problem. Work to bring the focus back to the issue at hand. Use phrases such as, *"We've gotten off the subject. You were talking to me about . . ."*

* Postpone the discussion until cooler heads prevail. If you and/or the other person are enraged, and it does not look as though either of you will cool off soon, it may be wise to suggest discussing the matter later when both of you have calmed down. If the other person refuses to delay, explain that you need time to think about the issue and make a definite appointment to discuss it as soon as possible.

* Try the **broken record technique**. In an ordinary situation calling for an assertive response, the broken record technique could come off as obnoxious. But when dealing with an aggressive person who refuses to listen to your assertive response, and who fails to respond to your efforts at escalation, this technique can come in handy to reinforce your request. Basically it involves repeating your request over and over, like a broken record, even if the other person is arguing, or ranting and raving. You just calmly continue to state your request, even during their protestations. It often involves being willing to interrupt. All parents have had to rely on this method at times when dealing with resistance or disobedience from children.

In summary, we urge you to practice using the four step framework the next time you find yourself in a situation that calls for an assertive response, whether this happens or in your personal life or on the job. These principles apply to all situations calling for effective assertiveness. Pay careful attention to how you feel after you assert yourself. Although you might experience some fight/flight activation as you initially engage in assertive behavior, the resulting relief and surge in self confidence you are likely to feel afterwards will go a long way towards enhancing your effectiveness, boosting your self-esteem, and lowering your stress level.

PERSUASION

In your role as a student or an employee you may be required to participate in meetings of various types. Many people are concerned about how to insure that their voice will be heard, that their ideas and input will be taken seriously by the group, the teacher, the boss, or the supervisors or supervisees. Getting lost in the shuffle can contribute to feelings of loss of control. It is important to learn how to be influential in groups, at work and in your personal life, and how to maximize your impact without being perceived as aggressive or overbearing. Basically this is about being persuasive, which is related to your assertive skills. Effective communicators know how to be persuasive when necessary. There are two principles which can maximize your ability to persuade others when giving your opinion at work, in meetings, on committees, etc. The two principles concern how to use **timing** and **tact** when expressing honest opinions.

Timing involves several issues. First of all, you have to decide where your priority or priorities lie. Otherwise you run the risk of being assertive just for the sake of being assertive, and talking too much and too long. The end result could be that others would view you as being on an ego trip and tune you out. You want to save your assertive efforts for those points that are really important to you. Observations of groups indicate that it is usually more effective to express an opinion after ⅓ to ½ of the group participants or committee members have already voiced their positions. By that point the members have a good sense of the group's general position and can address themselves to the points being raised, but this timing reduces the chance that group members will have already made up their minds before you speak up.

To be maximally persuasive when expressing an opinion, you need to state your thoughts clearly, concisely and without self-deprecating remarks. For example, saying, *"I just don't understand. Maybe there is something wrong with me but this proposal doesn't feel right to me"*, implies that you are inadequate; that there is something wrong with you. It is generally more persuasive to express yourself as a capable person. It is more effective to say, *"The way I see it, there seems to be a flaw in this proposal that is hard to pin down. Does anyone else sense that too?"* Needless to say, the non-verbal behaviors accompanying opinions are extremely important in determining how that opinion will be received.

Tact is also very important when taking a position that is in opposition to the rest of the group or a powerful group member such as a boss, supervisor, or teacher. Here it is often most effective to use empathic assertion in order to "stroke" or warm up the group to your opinion. This stroking does not mean using flattery or making ingratiating comments, but rather finding something that is genuinely good about the group consensus or another person's point of view. For example, *"Susan, your point is really well taken. But despite the obstacles we face, I believe we need to take action rather than do nothing."*

Other Aspects of Persuasiveness

While timing and tact certainly help create an environment conducive to persuasion, there are other variables you need to take into account in order to maximize your ability to convince others, whether at the workplace, in academic debates, or in your personal life. The following pointers summarize the characteristics of effective persuaders and the ways in which they enhance the impact of their message.

Aspects of the Communicator

- ❖ Effective persuaders work to establish their knowledge and/or expertise on the subject, as well as their credibility. A wealth of research, along with common sense, indicates that if you are perceived as a credible expert, your opinion will be valued more highly. And, if you act like you know what you are talking about (i.e. making sure you display confident/assertive nonverbal behaviors), your persuasiveness will be amplified.

- ❖ Speaking rapidly also appears to enhance persuasiveness. Advertisers discovered this fact long ago, hence the tendency for commercial messages to be so fast paced.

Aspects of the Message

- ❖ Emotional messages or appeals tend to be more convincing than dispassionate speeches.

- ❖ When attempting to persuade others (particularly if they hold views opposed to yours), it is useful to present both sides of the argument, to elucidate the pros and cons of both sides. The fact that other arguments are acknowledged up front and defused will increase the impact of your message.

- ❖ Repeat the key points of your position in various ways. Messages that are repeated ultimately will become familiar. Most people are more likely to be persuaded by that which they find familiar, because familiarity breeds comfort (and not always contempt).

Aspects of your Audience

- ❖ To be effective in influencing others, you need to take into consideration the characteristics of your audience. Try to tailor your message to fit the demographics of your listeners.

- ❖ A highly educated or intelligent audience or listener will respond better to a more sophisticated or complex argument. A less educated audience may respond better to a less complex message.

HOW TO RESIST BEING MANIPULATED BY OTHERS

And now for the other side of the coin, when others are successful in persuading you. At various times in your life you may have found yourself in situations where you were deftly maneuvered into doing something, or going along with something which you did not agree with. Sometimes you may not have realized this until after the fact, but in other situations you may have sensed that you were being conned, coerced, manipulated, or guilted into something, yet felt powerless to resist. Perhaps this involved getting sold something by a high pressure salesperson and later regretting the purchase or the price you paid (*Remember that used car you bought way back when?*). Or it may have involved getting manipulated by a friend or relative out of a sense of obligation or guilt. In any event, you were pressured (either subtly or overtly) into compliance when that was not what you wanted.

None of us is completely immune to manipulation, but effective individuals are less likely to get manipulated by others in their environment. What is it that gives certain people that strength of character to both recognize attempts at manipulation for what they are, and the will to refuse to comply? How can you learn to avoid being coerced into doing things you don't want to do? Obviously, the lessons about assertive behavior will serve you well here. **You always have the right as an individual to say "No". And it is not your job, nor your duty to always please the other people in your life (particularly salespeople).** However, in order to successfully resist techniques that others may use to get you to comply, you also need to be able to identify these up front, so you can be less prone to falling prey to them. Robert Caldini (1988) has offered various tips to help you counteract these attempts at manipulation, which can be roughly subdivided into two broad categories: (1) sales techniques, and (2) miscellaneous compliance techniques.

Sales Tactics

⊛ The most famous of these is the *"low ball technique"*, a favorite of new and used car salespeople. Here, merchandise or services are initially offered at an unbelievably good price (a deal you just can't turn down), but once you've made the commitment to buy, all these new costs (i.e. taxes, surcharges, special fees, etc.) suddenly appear. According to Caldini, **if you would not have agreed to make the purchase if the revised price had been offered initially, walk away from the deal.**

⊛ Another common tactic employed by salespeople involves invoking the *"scarcity principle"*. In this scenario you are told either that this is the only one left, or that the sale price is only available for a very limited time (usually only today!). They are hoping to take advantage of the fact that most people will perceive objects or opportunities as somehow "more valuable" when they are scarce, and thus will comply more readily with a request to buy now so as to not lose this golden opportunity. Caldini advises that you take time to assess whether you *really* want the goods or services. He asks you to **consider that just because an item is scarce or at a low price, it will not necessarily feel, sound, taste, or work any better than if it were more readily available.**

⊛ Salespeople (often of the telemarketing or door to door variety) frequently use the *"door in the face technique"* where they make a large request (e.g. for a big donation to a cause) followed by a much smaller request. They fully expect you to refuse the big request, but anticipate you will agree to the smaller one, which many people do out of guilt over having already turned them down. **Remember, you can say "No" twice.**

⊛ In what is referred to as the *"foot in the door technique"*, salespeople will go out of their way to befriend you, or chat at length with you to establish rapport and get you to like them, *before* making a request. Caldini advises that you be on guard if you find yourself being sweet talked or overly charmed by a person prior to them making a request or trying to get you to buy something. **Just because you like someone does not mean you have to comply.**

  In the *"that's not all technique"*, a salesperson will throw in all sorts of extra goodies to sweeten the deal, before you have a chance to say no. This tactic is very common in TV commercials asking you to call in and buy a product (*"and if you do it today I'll throw in this handy, dandy. . . . you can't live without at no extra cost . . ."*). The bottom line here is that **if you don't really want or need the main product nor the extra goodies, then just say no.**

Miscellaneous Compliance Situations

  By far the most difficult situations to resist occur when the *"rule of reciprocity"* is brought into play. Here someone has done a favor for you, made a concession of some kind or gone out of his or her way for you, and you feel obligated to repay in kind. Just as we had discussed in Chapter 8, reciprocity and compromises in relationships are crucial and healthy, and we urge you to honor your obligations to family members. But if you suspect that the original favor was merely a ploy to get you to reciprocate, then by all means feel free to refuse. **Do not feel guilty if you can avoid being exploited.**

  Many people try to use their *"authority"* to throw their weight around and get you to do their bidding. Caldini cautions us that just because someone claims to be an authority, this is no guarantee as the trappings of authority can easily be falsified. Certainly, it is wise to take the advice or recommendations of true authorities into consideration, but ***do not be afraid to question authority.*** Caldini advises you to ask yourself two important questions: (1) *Is this person truly an expert* (i.e. ask for credentials)? and (2) *Does this authority have a vested interest in my compliance* (e.g. Will they benefit if I buy this product?)? If there is any doubt on either of these fronts, protect yourself and refuse to comply.

  Modeling also affects our compliance behavior. If we see others doing something, we are likely to follow suit, even if we are unsure. This is a natural human tendency (part of how we learn) and is usually benign and often helpful. But, if you sense that what is being modeled is somehow phony or a false set-up to elicit your compliance, that's your cue to take a strong stand and say no.

SELF EXERCISE

We can virtually guarantee you that sometime in the next few weeks a situation will arise where you will feel the need to assert yourself, to express your needs, to say "No", or to check out a discrepancy you observe in the behavior of a friend or significant other, etc. The situation may be as mundane as asking for a refund on damaged merchandise, or asking the noisy people behind you in the movie theater to be quiet. Whatever the situation may be, practice using the four step framework and see the difference it will make. Some people find it useful to rehearse the four steps in their mind prior to beginning the assertion, provided of course that you have the time to do so.

KEY TERMS

Assertion	Empathic Assertion	Timing
Passivity	Escalating Assertiveness	Tact
Aggression	Broken Record	Rapport
Passive-Aggression	Perception Check	Propinquity

CHAPTER 10 QUESTIONS

True or False (T or F)

1. _____ Talking and communicating are always the same thing.

2. _____ When in conversation you can avoid boring another person by going into minute details.

3. _____ The best way to make a good first impression is to say something controversial.

4. _____ People are more likely to feel at ease with you if you establish rapport.

5. _____ It is easier to develop a rapport with someone who is similar to you.

6. _____ Small talk should be avoided at all costs.

7. _____ During conversations, refrain from asking questions of other people because they will usually find it annoying.

8. _____ When you are assertive you are respectful of your own rights and needs as well as the rights and needs of the other person.

9. _____ Assertiveness and aggressiveness are the same.

10. _____ When asserting yourself it is recommended that you make "You statements" instead of "I statements" whenever possible.

11. _____ When asserting yourself it is important to inhibit all gestures.

12. _____ The broken record technique should be used as often as possible, preferably any time you need to assert yourself.

13. _____ You should never question authority as authority figures always deserve respect.

14. _____ In the *"low ball technique"* salespeople offer you a free ball if you purchase their product today.

15. _____ The most difficult type of manipulation to resist occurs when the rule of reciprocity is brought into play.

16. _____ You always have the right to say "No".

Short-Answer Questions

1. Most relationships begin with _____.

2. _____ exists when you have frequent contact with someone by virtue of living or working close by.

3. Expressing your anger towards someone indirectly, by what you fail to do, is called _____.

4 When dealing with highly verbally aggressive individuals the _____ technique may prove useful.

5. Persuasion involves elements of _____ and _____.

6. In order to maximize the impact of your input during a meeting you should express your opinion about _____ of the way through the meeting.

7. To maximize your ability to be persuasive, you need to take into consideration aspects of your _____, your _____ and you as the _____.

Essay Questions

1. Describe what you need to do to carry on a conversation in an effective fashion.

2. Explain the tips for making small talk.

3. How does assertiveness differ from passivity and aggression?

4. What benefits are possible as a result of assertive behavior?

5. Identify the four steps for assertive communication. Why is step three optional?

6. Explain empathic assertion.

7. Why is your nonverbal behavior so important when you are delivering an assertive response?

8. What are three important nonverbal behaviors that should accompany your assertive responses to maximize your effectiveness?

9. Describe some tips for increasing your ability to be persuasive.

10. Discuss at least three common sales tactics geared towards manipulating you to buy something and the mental set necessary for resistance of such.

SECTION THREE

*Occupational
Effectiveness*

Know the Workplace

Design Your Own Career

Be People Smart

Make Work Fun

11

Know the Workplace

Do you remember when you started college? You had to get yourself registered for classes. The campus was full of buildings that housed, among other things, classrooms . . . and you had to find the rooms where your classes would be held. You had to figure out where the bookstore and cafeteria were. You were probably not able to function comfortably or effectively until you got "the lay of the land." It also helped to learn the lingo used by other students to describe things related to college life. Understanding what "credits" are and how they relate to completing a degree was also useful information. Once you became familiar with the college environment, things made more sense. You could move around, make choices and decisions and figure things out a lot easier.

Likewise, when you first enter your work life, you could find yourself in a similar situation. To "get around" better in the career world, you need to know some of the basics. Consider what is going on around you, what you will be experiencing, and why there is an expected conformity in the way you behave professionally and personally. Knowing these basics helps you anticipate things, adapt more easily and in general be more "with it" in your career behavior. This sophistication makes you more confident in your decision-making processes and work habits, making the quality of your work more rewarding. Even if you are a more seasoned worker with years of experience returning to college, you still have to orient to a new college experience and/or the possibility of a new work environment as your professional career changes.

The average worker has typically worked eight hours a day, five days a week, 50 of the 52 weeks in a year. That's most of your year right there! Add to that the trend with technology to expect workers to be available 24/7 and it is even more consuming. When you consider that you may work thirty or more years of your adult life, it becomes clear that the most of your life is spent in your career. Get the picture? And what if your career is not rewarding? How many people do you know or hear about who hate their work. You don't want to be one of them, right? It is probably not a coincidence that most heart attacks occur at 9:00 a.m. on Monday mornings! Could this be related to work? So there's something to be said about getting some basic information about the dynamic environment in which we fulfill our career aspirations. So let's find out what's happening in the world of work.

OCCUPATIONAL TRENDS

One trend that is obvious to everyone is that the workplace is constantly evolving. Alvin Toffler (1971), a sociologist, pointed out decades ago that change was changing. It is speeding up like a boulder coming down the mountainside. Unlike the lives our parents or grandparents lived, things now are changing so fast it is mind-boggling! We have moved from an agriculture-based economy to a manufacturing economy to a service economy. Now we seem to be moving into a knowledge economy. Add to all of that the influence of computers and WOW what a profound change.

It may be difficult for you to imagine that there was life without computers. Computers have changed the way things happen in so many arenas. To name a few, consider business, government, education, communications, and automobile operations. We depend on computers to operate practically everything in life. What would happen if the computers suddenly stopped? At the turn of the century in 2000, there was great concern about computers and Y2K. Experts pondered the potential chaos and disaster that could result from failed computers. Now, since 9/11, there is concern that chaos could be caused by terrorists' attacks on computer systems which could greatly damage our economy. Since computers are so important to keeping things running there is a new term for experts in computer systems. We call them **"gold collar workers."**

It is estimated that well over 80% of the world's technological advances have occurred in the last hundred years. Technology feeds on itself—one breakthrough leads to a host of other advances which then spur on even more developments. This cycle is never ending and will keep accelerating. Additionally the Internet is changing the way we do everything from shopping to research to communicating. This is related to the information explosion that we are experiencing. There was more information produced in the 30 years from 1965 to 1995 than had accumulated in the entire previous history of civilization, in the roughly 5000 year period spanning 3000 B.C. through 1965! It now appears that the amount of available information is doubling every five years. This information is available to us instantaneously, not only from the Internet, but TV, and satellites or we may read about it in our handheld PDA's while we are waiting in line somewhere. The more we learn and discover, the more we must change or risk falling more and more behind.

Other changes are happening today. These include diversity in the workforce; global competition and interdependence; new organizational patterns, uncertainty following the terrorist attacks of 9/11, the blending of work and non-work in employees' lifestyle; and how one views work security.

Increased Diversity

One of the changes we see in society is the increasing diversity in the workforce. Unlike previous decades where white males dominated the work force, the Bureau of Labor Statistics projects that those entering the workforce between 1992–2005 will include greater representation of diverse groups.

By 2004, it is estimated that Hispanics will become the largest minority group in the United States. Although there are high concentrations of Hispanics in several states, this population is dispersed throughout the nation. More than half of all immigrants coming here in 2000 were from Latin America. Within the Hispanic population are subgroups with cultural and socioeconomic differences. Asian Americans, with their many subgroups, are a smaller total number, but comprise the fastest growing ethnic group in the U.S. African American and Native American growth rates are higher than the growth rate for Caucasians. More than ten percent of our population is made up of persons born outside the United States (Patel, 2002).

We see the rising numbers and influence of women who are projected to comprise 47.9% of our civilian labor force in 2010. This is an increase of 15 percentage points in the decade from 2000. This means a variety of ethnic, social, and cultural customs and attitudes among workers who co-exist in the same workplace. Additionally, more disabled workers, who comprise the fastest growing minority group in the workforce, are broadening the scope of workplace differences. The potential for misunderstandings and conflict is obvious. Learning to interact positively with people of varied backgrounds, cultures and characteristics brings a growing challenge.

Often we are unaware of our prejudicial attitudes or behaviors. When describing a group of people involved in an activity, how many times do we hear someone refer to a particular person in the group as "this Black guy" when no one else's skin color is mentioned. It's irrelevant in any case; isn't it? Why is this person's skin color singled out? Why can't he just be referred to as "a guy" as the others were? And what goes on in the minds of those who heard that man so described. What stereotypes do we carry around relating to African Americans? Hispanics? Women? Asians? Persons with disabilities? To work well with a variety of people whose personalities and attitudes are formed from environments different from the one we know, suggests we have an open mind. We must be willing to respect differences and to learn about and appreciate a broad array of perceptions and behaviors in the workplace. Remember empathic listening? The extent to which we can understand what it is like to be in that person's shoes impacts our sensitivity and level of respect. Further, if we learn to value and appreciate diversity as a richness that surpasses homogeneity, it increases our chances for success in our careers. Remember, not only the workforce, but the clients, customers, patients, or students you count on for your work are also diverse. Relating effectively with a mix of people is necessary for success.

In addition to the diverse groups mentioned above, another source of diversity in the workplace is the growing age gap found among present day workers. Workers are living longer and working longer. Life expectancy for the U.S. population reached 76.9 in 2000. Eighty percent of baby boomers say they plan to work at least part-time during their retirement (Roper Starch Worldwide, Inc, 1999). DeCenzo (1997) breaks age groups into three separate eras, (1) those born pre-1946, (2) those born between 1946-1964, and (3) those born after 1964. He labels these groups and summarizes some of the differences in the following chart:

	Mature Workers born pre-1946	Baby Boomers born 1946–1964	Baby Busters/Generation X born after 1964
Value Most	Family	Careers/Money	Personal Gratification
Want from Job	Security	Advancement	Control own destiny
Favorite TV Show	"60 Minutes"	"ER"	"The X Files"
Ideal Vacation	Trip to town of ancestors	Disneyland	Deserted Caribbean island

The differences in these generations' values and attitudes are obvious. The **mature workers** lived during or close to the time of the Great Depression. In that era resources were scarce, unemployment abounded, and people learned to be exceedingly frugal to survive. It makes sense that this group desires security from their jobs. It is also no surprise that this group wants to be informed of what's happening on a news magazine type of TV show. They do not want to be caught unaware as in the stock market crash of 1929 or the Pearl Harbor of 1941.

The **baby boomers** evolved in a great era of building. The space program, the rapid advancement of technological innovation such as TV and other communications networks evolved. These post-World War II babies had a more plentiful life than their parents. They came to see careers as central to their lives and value advancement and the money it brings. Many workers of this era are "workaholics."

The **baby busters** or **Generation X** group born after 1964 are seeking personal gratification and want work to allow them the freedom to pursue their own interests. They are looked upon as selfish and intolerant by the other two age groups.

More recent studies have reported on the group following the Generation Xers. This group is referred to as **Generation Y**. These persons are born between about 1977 to 2000. There are about 70 million who comprise 26% of the U.S. population. These group members grew up in an era of prosperity, expanding technology, and are more ethnically diverse than any previous generations. They are expected to outnumber the large number of baby boomers that made up that generation. Gen Y individuals have grown up with computers, they are astute in computer use, about 75% have computers in their homes, and half have internet access at home. They are less cynical, more optimistic, self-confident, and expect to be better off financially than their parents. They are the most educationally oriented generation in history, recognizing that education is the key to their success. "They are more open and tolerant as products of biracial and multicultural marriages, and rail against sexism and homophobia. They are the best hope we've had so far for a more open, tolerant society" (Tulgan and Martin, 2001). They are socially conscious and are spurring a trend of volunteerism with a concern for the environment, poverty, health status, the elderly and other community problems or issues. They want their careers to offer them meaningful roles at work where they feel they are making a contribution. They want to be a part of a very motivated work team and develop an open-minded workplace. They have high monetary and personal goals. Their self-confidence has prepared them to make the moves necessary from one job to another to fulfill their goals.

How do you imagine these diverse groups might interact together in the same workplace? What types of conflicts can you envision? Have you had any experiences with this issue in your work history?

Global Competition

People say we live in a shrinking world. And yet, we know the world hasn't really shrunk. Today interacting with people around the world has become so easy and accessible. The marketplace is no longer just *our* community, our state or even our country. For example, less expensive labor in other countries has caused many manufacturers to move abroad for their workforce. So called "American" cars today are built from car parts made all over the world. McDonalds and Burger King are now operating world-wide. We are driving cars, using tools and household items, and devouring medicines and foods from countries all over the world. We are used to seeing American companies expand and have branches in other parts of town or another state. Now we see "branches" in other countries. Transnational corporations are now tailoring their products and marketing strategies to fit the citizens of the countries in which they are located. Many of these corporations earn more than half their income from foreign countries.

To succeed in a global corporation, it is imperative that one has respect for diversity and culture. A consideration for political values, moral patterns, as well as social and economic conditions is also necessary.

A further global concern is the interdependence of the political and economic status of countries. How many American products are produced in China? What would the result be on our economy if China changed their production practices? How has the changing economy in Latin American countries recently impacted the United States? Look at the concerns for the U.S. regarding oil production and availability and how that has influenced economic and political outcomes. And then there is the ongoing war on terrorism and the political and economic issues there.

Changes in Organizational Structure

In addition to working in a global economy, another continuing trend is businesses seeking more economical practices to improve profits. We see changes occurring both among and within organizations. In the corporate world, we see businesses grouping together, merging with each other, buying out others and otherwise combining forces. We see companies being swallowed up in takeovers, resulting in long standing firms going out of business. We've seen this in Miami with airlines that have shut down and banks that have been taken over leaving people displaced from work. Another business issue is that of the gap in earnings between corporate executives and workers, as well as concerns regarding ethical practices within corporations causing losses to shareholders of stocks.

One continuing trend is **downsizing**, which is one example of organizational change within the company. The process of downsizing means doing more with less as positions are cut from the payroll to reduce costs. Once the workforce within the company is leaner, companies begin to expect workers to cross-train, meaning learning the work of another employee. For instance, we see respiratory therapists and nurses cross-training in hospitals; we see financial aid and registration clerks cross-training on a college campus.

Further, technology is being implemented to increase efficiency and minimize the need for personnel. Personnel costs, by the way, are the most expensive items in the budget. Robots or computers are also being used to replace humans in doing tasks.

This "reduction in the workforce" has led to two categories of workers . . . (1) full time or **core workers** and (2) part-time or **contingent workers** (DeCenzo, 1997). Historically we have expected that most people would be "core" workers. However, since change is so common in organizations, the best way to be prepared for changing personnel needs is to hire people for projects or short-term temporary work. Then when there are seasonal changes, changing needs for expertise, or different priorities and projects, there is no need to retain them. Tourism companies, hospitals, colleges, and a host of other businesses use these hiring practices. Full-time workers usually have benefits not offered to part timers and full-time employees have more job stability. Part-time workers may receive higher salaries, but generally do not receive health insurance, retirement packages, and other benefits.

The advantages to working full time includes the security of a paycheck, job stability, position or rank, and benefits, such as paid vacations, retirement packages, sick leave and others. The advantages of being a contingent worker include flexibility in work schedule, extended time off, possibly higher salary and opportunity to change work environments frequently. With the increased use of technology, workers are "connected" electronically to their work through cell phones, pagers, PDAs, cyber cafes, and the like. This is having implications for the nature of the work day or work week. As mentioned earlier, there is an increasing expectation among managers that their employees will be available 24/7 to solve problems that could impact profits. This is causing a blurring between work and non-work time. The portability of technology has a growing number of workers working at home, telecommuting, and trouble-shooting from remote locales.

The self-confidence, technological expertise, interest in continued learning, and optimism of the Generation Y group has produced self-reliant, self-competent, flexible individuals who are better able to deal with the changes in organizational structure than their older counterparts. Continuing change has been a greater part of their lives and they not only cope, but *seek* new challenges and opportunities for career fulfillment.

Occupations in Demand

With an ever expanding, aging and more and more diverse population we will have a changing mix of goods and services being demanded. Workers' skills will have to change to meet these changing requirements. Employers will continue increasing the use of technological developments and revised business practices to enhance their production at lower costs. Data from the Bureau of Labor Statistics indicates that total employment is expected to increase 15% in the 2000–2010 period. The fastest growing occupations will be those that require more education and training. However, there is also an increase in the number of occupations that involve short-term training, which accounts for over one-fourth of all new jobs expected to be created in the decade to 2010. It is an important issue to be aware of what "hot" new jobs or steady old ones are in demand. For example, suppose you wanted to be a blacksmith. These workers make the metal shoes that horses wear. That dream would have been easy to fulfil a hundred years ago, when horses were used for transportation, but today you will find very limited opportunities.

What **career areas** are projected to have the fastest growth in the decade from 2000 to 2010? The ten businesses or organizations with the fastest wage and salary employment growth are listed here in order from highest to lowest:

- Computer software engineers, applications
- Computer support specialists
- Computer software engineers, systems software
- Network and computer systems administrators
- Network systems and data communications analysts
- Desktop publishers

- Database administrators
- Personal and home care aides
- Computer systems analysts
- Medical assistants

What career areas are projected to have the most employees? In 2010, the following industries will employ the most workers. Here is where most people will be working:

- Non-farm wage and salary
- Service producing
- Services
- Goods producing
- Retail trade
- Government
- Manufacturing
- Unpaid family workers
- Transportation, communications, utilities

Although this information is current for the latest report from the Bureau of Labor Statistics, these data were collected prior to the September 11th attack which has had an impact on the stability and hiring in many industries. For example, costs to industries for increased security, insurance, shipping and delays at borders could be as high as $150 billion just for the year 2002 (Bernasek, 2002). It is difficult to envision the impact on the predictions developed prior to 9/11, but the most recent data and projections can be found on the Bureau of Labor Statistics web site at *http://stats.bls.gov.* This site has a variety of information topics and recent news releases.

LEADERSHIP IN THE WORKPLACE

In small businesses or offices as well as large organizations, there is a "climate" that reflects the personalities of the people there, especially the person or persons in charge. This may vary from place to place depending on such things as the nature of the work, the type of organization, but especially important is the style of leadership provided by those with administrative responsibility. The setting may be very structured and formal, or it may be loose and casual, depending on the type of work and the size of the organization. For example, if you work in a small automotive repair shop with a single owner/operator, you may have few employees and a casual climate. If you work for the county court system, you may have hundreds of employees in specialized jobs. There may be strict job expectations, highly structured procedures, policies, and a great deal of formal documentation.

In every work setting, the type of organization is summed up in the basic mission or purpose that the organization exists to achieve. The more the members of the organization understand and agree with the mission, the more likely people will work as a team to accomplish the purpose. However, there are other things besides the purpose that affects how employees work together.

A major consideration is the type of leadership that is demonstrated in the work environment. Think of the leaders you have known in organizations or jobs. Perhaps you can see differences in the styles of behavior different people in charge have shown. Obviously, in any work setting you are going to be affected by the leadership operating in the environment. So let's take a look at leadership. Let's consider what it means. Then, let's examine variations in style that produce differing results. Finally, let's ask about the possibility of leadership in your future.

What Is Leadership?

There are endless definitions, but they all seem to come down to the idea that **leadership** means influencing people to think and/or act a certain way. Leadership implies there is a goal or desired outcome, and that communication is used to guide members of a group to accomplish that goal or achieve that outcome.

Many people use the words "leader" and "manager" to mean the same thing, but many researchers and writers distinguish between these terms. In general, the main difference between a leader and a manager is that the leader is concerned with people. The leader focuses on the attitudes, reactions, motivations and the behaviors people exhibit toward accomplishing the mission of the organization. Leaders also usually have a broad long-range vision of where the company is headed. Managers, on the other hand, are more concerned with the details of the tasks to be accomplished in a work group. They keep the operations going smoothly. Their focus is directed on day-to-day processes. Some distinctions between **leadership** and **management** are summarized below:

Management	Leadership
Appointed to role	Emerge from group
Formal authority	May have no formal authority
Efficiency	Effectiveness
Systems	Innovation
Controls	Creativity
Policies	Adaptability
Procedures	Flexibility
Structure	Vision
Look to bottom line	Look to horizon
Reward and punish	Inspire

Warren Bennis (1989) illustrates the difference in function between a manager and a leader as follows:

Manager	Leader
Is a copy	Is an original
Asks how and when?	Asks what and why?
Accepts the status quo	Challenges the status quo
Is the good classic soldier	Is his or her own person
Does things right	Does the right thing

The role of a manager and leader may exist in the same person in an organization but often do not. Managers may or may not be leaders; leaders may or may not have management skills. Some people consider leadership a part of management; others see leadership and management as very different functions. What do you think?

Variations and Outcomes

Remember in Chapter 1 when we talked about how reality is all in your head? And how perceptions influence how you think, react, and behave? Douglas McGregor (1960) stated that leader behavior is a function of how a leader perceives workers. McGregor determined two general ways leaders might see reality. In what he called **Theory X**, the leader views workers as people who dislike work, have to be closely supervised or pushed because they are basically lazy, irresponsible, or self-centered with little concern for the organization. However, McGregor's **Theory Y** leaders see workers as people who consider work as a pleasurable, natural part of life. They are internally motivated to be productive, accomplish goals, and are willing to learn and accept responsibility. These people are looked upon as creative and capable of contributing ideas to the organization.

Leadership styles can be categorized in three major categories (1) autocratic, (2) democratic, and (3) laissez faire. They fall on a continuum from the *power* being concentrated in a single person (**autocratic**), concentrated on the group and its leader (**democratic**), or to the group operating rather independently from the leader (**laissez faire**). The relationship of the leader to the group is visually depicted in the figure below:

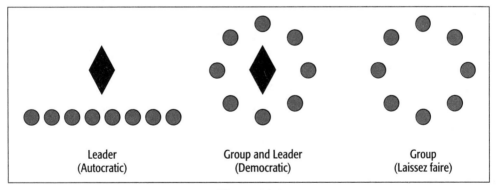

Leader	Group and Leader	Group
(Autocratic)	(Democratic)	(Laissez faire)

Figure 11.1

In the **autocratic** style, the information flows from the leader to the group in a one-way direction. The leader is like a dictator who makes the decisions and maintains control. Workers are told what to do and they do it. Workers are in a submissive relationship to the leader. Some autocratic leaders are "benevolent dictators" who make decisions with the interests of employees in mind and are supportive of employees. But there is no gathering of information from employees in determining decisions.

In the **democratic** style, also called participative style, the leader embraces employee involvement in decision-making and gathers opinions, information, suggestions and preferences from employees. The participative leader may or may not actually implement the employee's recommendations, but at least considers the employee input in arriving at a decision. If the decision of the leader were different from the group, the democratic leader usually explains his or her rationale for the decision made and indicates how the employee opinions played into the outcome. Valuing employee input is believed by the leader to make the workers feel more a part of the process and therefore keeping them more committed. This typically is the case. For the best results with the democratic style, the group needs to have an appropriate amount of interest in common with the leader, and the necessary knowledge and skills to contribute significantly to the decision making process.

The **laissez faire** style of leadership places the power for decision making within the group. The leader is more of a liaison between the work group and outsiders and secures needed resources for the group to meet its goals. **Empowerment** is a term heard frequently in discussions of work settings; this means providing the group with the authority to make decisions as a group. Of the three leadership styles, the laissez faire approach imparts the most power to the group.

Is there one best style of leadership? Not really. It all depends on the context in which the leadership occurs. There are times when an autocratic approach is most definitely the best way. Consider this . . . What if a fire broke out in your classroom? You would not want your professor to say, (while the room is filling up with smoke!) "Now students . . . let's brainstorm ideas together and discuss how we should respond to this fire alarm that's sounding." Clearly autocratic orders given to vacate the room are the most efficient and appropriate response.

Laissez faire leadership works best when the work group is highly knowledgeable about their work and highly motivated toward the goals of the organization. Physicians doing research in a laboratory, for example, probably need very little direction to do a good job. Professors in a college are rarely told by their deans how to teach a course. Having the freedom to work independently has traditionally been reserved for the highly educated and knowledgeable professions. Now in the workplace we have a trend for self-managed teams that have no traditional boss or supervisor. Rather, the responsibility for planning, organizing, and overseeing their work is carried out by the team members. Large American companies with fifty or more employees have half of their employees working in self-managed or problem-solving teams (Boyett and Snyder, 1998). Soshona Zuboff, a Harvard Business School psychologist noted that

> corporations have gone through a radical revolution within this century, and with this has come a corresponding transformation of the emotional landscape. There was a long period of managerial domination of the corporate hierarchy when the manipulative, jungle-fighter boss was rewarded. But that rigid hierarchy started breaking down in the 1980's under the twin pressures of globalization and information technology. The jungle fighter symbolizes where the corporation has been; the virtuoso in interpersonal skills is the corporate future. (Goleman, 1995).

Although democratic leadership is the best balance of power by involving more people in the decision making process, there are times when a more autocratic or laissez faire approach may be the most appropriate. Leadership doesn't occur in a vacuum and the context of the leadership determines which is the best method to follow.

Numerous researchers have referred to this "it depends on the situation" idea as contingency leadership, situational leadership, or contextual leadership. In fact, it is suggested that the truly effective leader can vary his or her style to match the needs of the situation at hand. In this case the leader should consider not only the situation, but also the type of followers and the leader's own preferred style. These are qualities embedded in what Daniel Goldman calls **emotional intelligence** (1995). When people are anxious or upset, they cannot focus, remember, or make good decisions. As Goleman states, "leadership is not domination, but the art of persuading people to work toward a common goal." For our own careers, recognition of our core feelings about what we do and what changes might make us more satisfied is basic to our own emotional intelligence and therefore our success. Goleman suggested in 1995 that three applications of emotional intelligence in the workplace are (1) being able to air grievances as helpful critiques, (2) creating an atmosphere in which diversity is valued rather than a source of friction, and (3) networking effectively. As discussed earlier, these skills are reflected in the characteristics of Generation Y individuals now entering the workplace in huge numbers.

Is Leadership in My Future?

Are you already a leader? Are leaders born or made? There are ideas and research for both sides. Perhaps you can develop leadership skills just like any other skills you acquire with work and practice, like how to drive a car, how to write a paragraph, or how to play a musical instrument. Some research has suggested that there may be some inborn traits that characterize an effective leader such as emotional stability; dominance; enthusiasm, conscientiousness, social boldness, being somewhat emotionally detached, self-assured and compulsive. Whether evolving from nature or nurture, to be effective as a leader, people need to have skills in several areas. Specifically, there is a need for (1) technical knowledge related to the area of work, (2) interpersonal effectiveness and (3) critical thinking skills.

Management consultants Frigon and Jackson (1996) suggest that successful leaders should be able to do the following:

1. Share power and authority
2. Build mutual trust and respect
3. Use team building, problem solving and process analysis
4. View all tasks as cooperative undertakings
5. Decentralize decision making
6. Stop finger pointing
7. Believe that everyone has good ideas
8. Chase fear out of the workplace
9. Cooperate with organized labor
10. Recognize that this is a long-term commitment

Dubrin (1999) lists the following behaviors and skills as those of an effective leader:

1. Develop appropriate self-confidence (not too weak; not too confident)
2. Practice strong ethics
3. Develop partnerships with people (emphasize power sharing)
4. Help group members reach goals and achieve satisfaction
5. Make expectations known
6. Set high expectations
7. Give frequent feedback on performance

8. Manage a crisis effectively

9. Cultivate a strong customer orientation

10. Ask the right questions

Gardner (2002) notes that the advantages of leadership include financial and status rewards as well as a sense of satisfaction from successfully leading a group to a common goal. On the down side, leaders must invest a huge amount of time and energy and may be the brunt of criticism from others such as questioning the motives and integrity of the leader. He notes that leaders typically have a strong desire to use power over others or a strong need to accomplish great things. Other characteristics of a leader are ambition and the ability and willingness to work extremely hard.

Kirkpatrick and Locke (1991) enumerate the following leadership the traits:

1. Drive

2. Honesty and Integrity

3. Self-confidence

4. Creativity

5. Expertise

6. Cognitive ability

7. Leadership motivation

8. Flexibility

and of these traits flexibility may well be the single most important trait in order to recognize the most appropriate approach or actions to take in a given situation.

Many psychologists believe that charismatic leaders (those who intensely inspire individuals toward change) are born out of the difficult times and social crises that the followers are experiencing. Bass (1998) has listed four essential components of charismatic leadership as (1) *idealized influence* where leaders are admired and trusted, followers identify with them and believe they have high capabilities and standards; (2) *intellectual stimulation* where leaders encourage innovation and creative thinking; (3) *inspirational motivation* where leaders create a team spirit, exhibit extraordinary enthusiasm and optimism and clearly communicate goals; and (4) *individual consideration* wherein leaders pay attention to and communicate with each individual follower's needs.

Gender differences continue to be seen regarding leadership . Few women hold leadership positions in government, fewer than five of the Fortune 500 major corporations have a women heading the company. The idea of a woman, the nurturer, as a corporate head has not been the traditional thinking in American society. However, as Jean Lipman-Blumen (1992) points out, the concept of female leadership is no longer an oxymoron. Considering global interdependence, the trends toward team-driven work patterns in corporations, and the technologically networked world, the traditional leadership of the past based on competitive, controlling, aggressive, self-reliant individualists is not well suited for the world ahead. What she calls "connective leadership," an integrative model of leadership that creatively revitalizes individualism with the female perspective, sees the world as a system of interconnected uniquely important parts, rather than as independent, competitive, isolated and unequal entities.

The leaders of the 21st Century must have the essential elements of effectiveness we have been learning throughout this text. These include knowing how to reframe and be flexible, being proactive, self-confident, able to master stress in the midst of constant change, think ahead as a visionary, and managing oneself in time. Further, leaders for this century must be emotionally intelligent, be good at listening to and expressing thoughts and feelings, and be knowledgeable about workplace trends.

As you prepare for your future and your contributions as a leader in the workplace, keep this in mind. A good place to continue developing your skills in the areas listed above is in your role right now as a student in your college career. You are a potential leader in your classes, in your peer groups, on your campus, in your jobs at this moment.

As a Chinese philosopher stated in the 6th century B.C.:

> To lead people, walk beside them . . .
> As for the best leaders, the people do not
> Notice their existence.
> The next best, the people honor and praise.
> The next, the people fear;
> And the next, the people hate . . .
> When the best leader's work is done the
> People say,
> "We did it ourselves!"
> —Lao-tsu

PERFORMANCE EVALUATIONS

Many of us have a reaction when the term "performance rating" comes up. It certainly gets our attention . . . like when a teacher says, "This is going to be on a test" . . . and we start writing down this now *important* information! We may have been taught that we should not be judgmental about other people and most of us get a little anxious about someone officially "judging" us. Of course our reaction to the idea of having our work performance evaluated in writing depends on many things. First, our level of self-esteem comes into play. Secondly, our reaction is based on how we perceive we are doing in the job. Additionally, the level of trust we have for the evaluator and the process also impacts our reaction.

In our careers, we can count on there being a formal evaluation process that documents our work performance. **Performance reviews** in a large organization may be more formal than in a small business. The process is usually done at least once annually, with shorter periods involved during a probationary period. Performance appraisal is used in all kinds of organizations to make decisions about employees. These decisions could include getting a raise or promotion, identifying a need for training or development, or even being terminated. Performance evaluations are something you need to be aware of when you first start a new position. In fact, keep in mind the ideas from Chapter Six and create a vision of yourself as you want to be in this new position. This provides the basis for setting your goals to achieve that vision.

Why Are Performance Reviews Important?

Basically, performance reviews are formal methods for giving you written feedback about how you are doing your job, identifying your strengths and weaknesses. If you need to improve or need more training in some aspect of your work, identifying this is the first step to enhancing your performance. The "documenting" part of the process is important to the organization and to you. This begins a permanent part of your personnel file and "follows" you throughout your work history at this organization, and perhaps beyond! It is important, not only to the organization, but to you as a record of your work. Suppose you perform years of excellent work. Then you encounter a supervisor who may have inappropriate or capricious reasons for wanting to terminate you. Your documented excellence becomes your basis for raising questions in this situation.

The Review Process

Ideally, the performance evaluation process is a joint activity that involves your supervisor and you. The expectations for the work that is being evaluated should have been established in the beginning. Goal setting with your supervisor is the first step. If formal goal setting is not a part of the review process, then a set of standards, job description, or written expectations should be the *a priori* (or before the fact) basis for rating your work behavior. It's pretty hard to know if you are performing well if it's not clear what you're supposed to be doing. Some specific expectations communicated before you begin the evaluation period should become the basis for comparison or rating of your work. DeCenzo (1997) describes the performance appraisal process as including the following steps:

1. Performance standards for your job are established by the organization
2. You and your supervisor set measurable goals
3. Your performance is evaluated using some type of evaluation form
4. Your performance is compared to the pre-established measurable goals (You may be asked to evaluate yourself)
5. You and your supervisor discuss the formal appraisal
6. You performance is "rewarded" or corrective action taken

You wouldn't be satisfied if you sat in a class for a whole semester and didn't get any feedback on your progress until you got your final grade. Likewise, you wouldn't want to work for a whole year without any feedback on your progress. There's a saying that "no news is good news" meaning if something were wrong, you'd hear about it. That is not a good rule to apply in your work evaluation. If you have not received any indications from your supervisor regarding the level of your performance, remember the buck starts and stops with you . . . ASK! You might say to your manager, "I've been working here for about two months now and I wanted to ask you about how you think I am doing. If you have a few minutes to share your feedback, I would really appreciate it." Feedback should be a continuous yearlong process that gets documented in the annual performance review. There really shouldn't be any surprises for you or your supervisor if there has been communication throughout the year.

What your performance is judged by may be individual goals that you and your supervisor have set. If not, there may be a list of expectations that appear on the standard company evaluation form. The format for the written document may also vary. It could be essay, or short answer, or checking a rating form. The categories of description of your performance may vary. Some have only two ratings, satisfactory and unsatisfactory. Others may have a broader range of ratings such as Outstanding, Above Expectations, Met Expectations, Below Expectations, Unsatisfactory (this sounds like an A,B,C . . . situation, doesn't it!)

Although ideally, the final judgment of your performance will involve input from both your supervisor and you, the supervisor is the final word in rating your performance. Many appraisal systems allow for the employee to register differing opinions in writing. This does not change the supervisor's official rating of you as an employee nor the copy of that in your file. However, the employee's rebuttal may become a part of the documentation for that evaluation.

The annual evaluation should be a quiet, private, un-rushed meeting between the supervisor and the employee. This may be one of the few times or even the only time that you and your supervisor have a one-on-one discussion of this significance. It is an opportunity to confirm mutually known information and discuss information about work that is new to either the supervisor or the employee. For example, an employee may share that he or she is taking a college course related to work that the supervisor was not aware of. Likewise, the supervisor may know of resources to help an employee that were previously unknown. It may also be a time to discuss goals for the next evaluation period. Some people report that their formal work appraisal is just a quick going over of a checklist. This may leave the impression that such sessions and the documents are not really that important. Don't be misled. It still goes in your personnel file as a formal record of your year's work. Look over the document carefully and discuss any points you think are inaccurate or incomplete. Use all the human interaction and conflict resolution skills learned earlier in this book to assertively communicate any areas of concern with your supervisor.

How Can I Use the Performance Review?

You should keep a file of your performance reviews for several reasons. First, they comprise a record of your work performance over time from which you can find patterns in your behavior. This is extremely significant information for your career development. You may note that more than one supervisor has commented upon an area of strength. You may also see a pattern of observations about areas in which you need to improve. This can be useful in helping you identify your passions as well as those areas that need development.

Secondly, your compilation of performance reviews serves as a reality check regarding your own self awareness and self assessment. It is helpful to receive feedback from others about what you excel in, even if you already feel you are skilled in the area. It confirms for you aspects that increase or affirm your strengths. Although it may "sting" momentarily, it is also an opportunity to discover places where you need improvement.

A third reason for hanging on to your performance reviews is that it provides you with information that you may want to use to update your resume every year. Even though you don't expect to be "job hunting" every year, the process of updating your resume when the information is fresh will keep you ready should the need or the opportunity present itself.

Performance rating forms are found in many and varied forms. Some are open ended for supervisor comments; some have specific topics and ratings. Items taken from an actual performance rating form are shown below. These are only sample items and not a complete employee evaluation form.

Purpose: To assist in accurately appraising employees, to improve performance, to enhance the supervisor/employee relationship, to improve the motivational climate, and to serve as a useful tool in the growth and development of employees.

Instructions:
1. Evaluate employee's work performance for the evaluation period under your supervision (refrain from basing judgments on recent events or isolated incidents). Do not allow personal feelings or personalities to govern your evaluation.
2. Check the appropriate rating that best describes the employee's performance; Check ALL categories.
3. After the employee signs this evaluation, no changes may be made without the employee's knowledge.

QUALITY OF WORK Consider standard of workmanship, accuracy, neatness, skill and thoroughness of work accomplished

Makes frequent errors, needs improvement	Makes recurrent errors, needs improvement	Usually accurate	Is almost always accurate	Is exact and precise

QUANTITY OF WORK Consider use of time, ability to meet schedules, and productivity levels expected of this position

Does not meet minimum requirements	Does just enough to get by	Volume of work is satisfactory	Very industrious, more than required	Superior work and production

JOB KNOWLEDGE Knowledge concerning work duties which an individual should have to accomplish a satisfactory job performance rating

Poorly informed, lacks work experience	Lacks knowledge of some phases of work	Moderately informed, good potential	Understands all phases of work	Has complete mastery of all phases of assigned work

ATTITUDE Consider cooperation with supervisor, co-workers and other groups with whom this employee associates in accomplishing his/her work

Problems in working with others in office/ outside contacts	Occasionally has problems in working with others	No problem working with others	Cooperative, tolerant, able to work with others to accomplish tasks	Exceptional, effective in personal relations at all levels

If you were designing a performance rating form, what descriptors or characteristics do you think you would want to include? From the items on the form above, which, if any, do you think are not clear, or not appropriate?

POLICIES AND PROCEDURES—THE RULES OF THE GAME

Another area that matters in knowing the workplace is being familiar with policies and procedures. Imagine that you are driving in city traffic and there are no traffic signs, no traffic lights, and no stop signs. Everyone is driving however and wherever he or she wants. Some people are on the left side of the street; some are driving on the right side. What a mess . . . total chaos! It's pretty obvious, we need some "rules of the game" to bring direction and order to driving (in fact, it's hard enough with rules!).

Suppose you enroll in a college course and there is no course syllabus. This leaves the student with no explanation of what the course is about, requirements and expectations, or the grading policy. How secure would you feel? How would you be able to predict what is going to happen? See the point? We really DO want rules! It helps us know what to expect and how to succeed.

When we look at it this way, it is easy to see that we need some level of conformity. It helps groups of people accomplish their mission. There is a need for structure and organization. We really do need to know the "rules of the game."

In order to bring consistency and order to the workplace, companies have rules that are usually called "Policies and Procedures." These explain how things are supposed to work. The **policies** describe the general guidelines or rules for governing activity; the **procedures** tied to them indicate how these guidelines are to be carried out.

Policies and Procedures—Written and Unwritten

Policies and procedures are documented in some written volume and/or available through an on-line network. The length, detail and formal presentation of the rules can be voluminous or brief.

At the College where this author is employed, there are two huge volumes, one for policies and a second for procedures. The policy manual contains sixty-five separate policy statements and for each policy there is a list of procedures found in the second manual. Fortunately, all these policies and procedures are accessible to employees on-line for ready reference.

Usually a handbook and/or a formal orientation session will serve to highlight the policies and procedures that are relevant for specific employees. These explain such policies as work hours, benefits, safety issues, absenteeism, and disciplinary procedures. It is important to read your employee handbook and keep it for future referral. If you violate a policy or procedure you weren't aware of, but you've been given the information in writing . . . well, you can see how this could affect you at the workplace.

In addition to the formal written company or organization policies and procedures, there are endless "unwritten" practices, norms, ways of doing things that are not written down anywhere, but like so many social conventions in life, that are known and followed by the majority of workers. In society, for example, if we walk into a restaurant and all the tables are empty except for only one person sitting at one of the tables, we would not walk over to toward that table and sit next to that person. In fact, we would probably select a seat that is some distance from that only other customer. This is an example of a social convention regarding selecting seating in a public place. This "rule" of behavior is probably not written down in an etiquette book anywhere, but it is one that most people learn with experience. So how do you, as a new employee get the scoop on these office practices that are not recorded anywhere? The answer is to find a mentor.

A **mentor** is a senior or experienced employee who serves to assist a new employee through advising, role modeling, explaining normative behavior, introducing contacts, and generally being available to answer questions and give support. Several studies have examined the effect of having a mentor and found that employees with mentors tended to make more money at a younger age and were more likely to follow a career plan than those employees without a mentor (Gomez-Majia, Balkin, and Cardy, 1995) Many companies and organizations have formalized mentoring programs where a new employee is assigned a mentor to help him or her integrate into the workplace. Such mentoring programs should have specific goals, clear role definition of the mentor and the protégé, training for mentors, and should encourage the new employee's independence and self-reliance (Newby and Heide, 1992). If you are not assigned a mentor when joining an organization, it is important to seek out an experienced employee who appears to be successful as a mentor. Professional and trade associations are another area where mentoring from experts in the field is available. Not only educational aspects are valuable from such associations, but the social connections and networking opportunities are important to members (Dansky, 1996).

Advantages of Policies and Procedures

Since we like to be in charge of our lives, sometimes rules and regulations seem confining or controlling and even something to be ignored. But, in the workplace we need to recognize there are some advantages to having clearly spelled out rules. Some of the advantages include:

1. Clear understanding of expectations and responsibilities
2. Understanding of consequences of behavior
3. Predictability of the work environment
4. Security of knowing how to succeed
5. Fairness and equity in rules applying to all employees

If we are unfamiliar with the "rules of the game" and have not received any information as a new employee, we should find out information by asking and by seeking a mentor. Develop your own "employee handbook" as you collect information if you receive little or no orientation to a new position.

STRESS IN THE WORKPLACE

We have addressed stress earlier in this text in order to understand what it is (Chapter 4). Further, we learned methods for keeping stress at levels that allow us to remain in charge of ourselves (Chapter 5). Since recognizing the potential for stress is important to knowing the workplace, a few more words on the topic are in order.

There are some things that are a given. One is that the stimulation from events in most any workplace today sets the stage for a stress epidemic. The potential is there. A second given is that one of two things will happen. You will either

(1) Succumb to stress at work and suffer the consequences of physical, psychological, and spiritual drain, or

(2) Master stress at work and keep your body, mind, and spirit balanced and productive in meeting your goals and enjoying the rewards.

To address this choice, let's add to our arsenal of "stress preventers" two more ideas. The first is to hone in on **stress awareness** at **work (SAW).** If you took a look at what's happening in you and those around you at work today, it is quite possible you **SAW** it. And like a "saw," you can cut it off at the pass. Just as we have said place colored sticky dots in strategic places to remind you to breathe deeply, you can also use that reminder to draw into yourself and spend a few seconds answering the questions, "How do I feel right now? What emotions am I experiencing? Fear, frustration, anger, or other distressing feelings? Or the pleasant, happy, elated, excited feelings of eustress? Then remember to elicit the "relaxation response" as Herbert Benson calls it to help us calm ourselves inside.

To help you in the process of discovering how you are experiencing your workplace, the following Workplace Stress Test may provide insight and stir your thoughts on the matter. Take a moment to complete this exercise. Perhaps ask a co-worker or friend to complete it, too. Then talk it over and be sure to include ideas for bringing things into physical and psychological equilibrium. Remember to push the button on your SAW when you feel yourself getting tense!

WORKPLACE STRESS TEST

If your score is 35 to 55 you are moderately stressed.
If your score is 55 or more you are definitely stressed.
1= Never   2=Rarely   3=Some of the time   4= All of the time

1. I feel tired at work even with adequate sleep	1	2	3	4
2. I feel frustrated in carrying out my responsibilities at work.	1	2	3	4
3. I am moody, irritable, or impatient over small problems.	1	2	3	4
4. I want to withdraw from the constant demands on my time and energy.	1	2	3	4
5. I feel negative, futile, or depressed about work.	1	2	3	4
6. My decision-making ability is less than usual because of work.	1	2	3	4
7. I think that I am not as efficient at work as I should be.	1	2	3	4
8. I feel physically, emotionally, or spiritually depleted.	1	2	3	4
9. The quality of my work is less than it should be.	1	2	3	4
10. My resistance to illness is lowered because of my work.	1	2	3	4
11. My interest in doing fun activities is lowered because of work.	1	2	3	4

12. I feel uncaring about the problems and needs of my
    co-workers, customers, clients, patients, etc., at work.   1   2   3   4

13. Communication with my co-workers, friends, or family
    seems strained.   1   2   3   4

14. I am forgetful.   1   2   3   4

15. I have difficulty concentrating on my job.   1   2   3   4

16. I am easily bored with my job.   1   2   3   4

17. I feel a sense of dissatisfaction with my job, that there's
    something wrong or missing.   1   2   3   4

18. When I ask myself why I get up and go to work, the only
    answer that occurs to me is "I have to."   1   2   3   4

A second point on stress is the issue of **pacing**. Work environments may be super busy, or slow and laid back. You may not be able to control the pace of the atmosphere at work, but you surely can control yourself, right? The whole notion of "pacing yourself" on the job to lower stress is a good idea, but only if you pace yourself in the right way. Pacing yourself properly can enhance productivity and lower stress. Pacing yourself wisely is not a matter of slowing down, but rather using strategic planning for structuring your time. Here are some pacing tips that will enable you to recharge your batteries, revitalize yourself and ultimately be more productive and creative.

Tips for Pacing Yourself

❀ Pay attention to your natural body rhythms to determine at what times you function at your best. Are you a morning or a night person? When possible, schedule your most difficult tasks for your peak performance hours. Try to avoid tackling difficult or exhausting projects during that part of the day when your energy is at its lowest.

❀ Shift between pleasant and unpleasant tasks. After finishing a difficult piece of work shift to something mindless, easy and/or pleasant.

❀ Allow some time each day, even when you are swamped with work, for pleasurable work tasks, even if they are not highly productive.

❀ Use your breaks and lunches to relax. Do not work over lunch unless it is absolutely essential.

❀ Take mini-breaks for three to five minutes throughout the day to de-stress and balance yourself. Talk to a co-worker, have a refreshing drink.

❀ Choose leisure activities that balance the unique stresses in your line of work. For example, if you deal with people's complaints all day long then choose solitary, peaceful pursuits, or if you are cooped up in a windowless office all day then choose outdoor activities. If you work alone make sure your leisure time includes social activities with friends.

❀ Take vacations. Carefully consider the length and type of vacation you plan in order to balance work stresses. If your work is very sedentary, plan an active vacation. If your work is physically exhausting, plan a vacation where you allow a good amount of time for just kicking back and relaxing. If you work alone and feel lonely, visit friends or family or vacation with others.

❈ If possible take a break during your workday to exercise, do relaxation practices, or run an errand. Back in Chapter 5 we talked about the importance of stretching your muscles for decreasing stress and physical strain. Take a moment several times during the day to stretch one or more of those muscle groups when you feel tense or fatigued.

SUMMARY

In this chapter we have been examining aspects of the work environment that are important for you to recognize, anticipate, and confront. We have prepared you with strategies to enable you to "move around" with ease. We have looked at trends in the world of work such as change, globalization, new organizational patterns, diversity, and leadership styles. We have reviewed some of the administrative realities of the workplace such as policies, procedures and performance evaluations. These topics were presented to give an overview of what to expect in today's workplace. We have closed with added suggestions on how to master the stress that looms in the work environment. Having looked at the workplace, you are now ready to move on to examining your role in this milieu as you create it for yourself.

SELF EXERCISES

1. Pick three people in your life (present or past) that represent each of these three major styles of leadership: autocratic, democratic and laissez faire. How did you respond to each of these leaders? If you are or were a leader, which type would you aspire to be most of the time?

2. Design a performance appraisal form for a job you have done or now doing. Consider the main areas of work. Imagine that you are the owner of the company or the chief operating officer (CEO) of the organization. What would be most important to the organization?

KEY TERMS

gold collar worker	Theory X	procedure
baby boomers	Theory Y	SAW
baby busters	autocratic	Generation X
downsizing	democratic	Generation Y
core workers	laissez faire	leadership
contingent workers	empowerment	management
manager	mentor	emotional intelligence
leader	policy	performance appraisal

CHAPTER 11 QUESTIONS

Short-Answer Questions

1. Alvin Toffler wrote that change is _____.
2. It is estimated that well over 80% of the world's technological advances have occurred in _____ years.
3. The workforce of the future will no longer be dominated by what group of employees? _____
4. By 2004, the largest minority group will be _____.
5. The age group referred to as mature workers (born before 1946) want _____ from their job.
6. Persons born between 1977 and 2000 are a group called _____.
7. Reducing personnel in organizations to cut costs and increase profits is called _____.
8. Workers who work part-time or temporarily on a given project are called _____ workers.
9. The most job openings found in the fastest growing industries are in the _____ field.

10. If your boss sees you as lazy, not liking work and irresponsible, he/she is following Theory _____.

11. If a leader behaves like a dictator, we would say the leadership style is

    _____.

12. Being sensitive to the impact a decision may have on employees is what Daniel Goleman would call _____ _____.

13. A formal written evaluation of our work performance is called a

    _____ _____.

14. The "rules of the game" in work settings are called _____ and _____.

15. One way to pace yourself is to _____.

Essay Questions

1. What is the historical progression of technological change?

2. How is the workforce composition changing to become more diverse?

3. How have corporations changed the way they are organized to cut costs?

4. Compare and contrast the core worker to a contingent worker.

5. Compare the role of manager to the role of leader.

6. Compare and contrast autocratic, democratic, and laissez faire leadership styles.

7. Describe the advantages of performance reviews.

8. Outline the ideal process for a performance review.

9. What are the advantages to policies and procedures?

10. Describe three strategies you could use to reduce stress in the workplace.

12

Design Your Own Career

Suppose you were going to build a house. You would have a lot invested in your home, right? And you wouldn't want a house just "put together" on a whim. No, you'd want an architectural drawing carefully planned showing the details of the whole project. The house plan would be based on information about your needs, limits, and preferences. Houses are a lot like careers . . . a lot is invested and you may live in them a long time. Yet, in your educational experience I'll bet that you have not (in a decade or more of schooling) had a meaningful experience of learning about occupations, how to choose one, how to plan your work life, or how to achieve career success. Career education is just not a priority for our K–12 school curriculum. For a decision and an area of our lives that we spend so much time in, and that has such an impact on our lives, it is extremely important to select a career as an informed choice rather than in a casual way or by default.

THEORIES ABOUT CAREER CHOICES

Many psychologists have studied and developed theories about career choice. Some wrote about stage theories saying we move from childhood fantasies of career toward more realistic ideas. There are some people who determined as a child they wanted to be in a certain profession and remained committed to that goal through their life career. In contrast, there are many students who know they want a college degree, but they're not sure in what area or how this relates to their career life after college. Some students have decided on a career, but may actually know very little about what is required to enter that profession, or what life in that career means in terms of day to day activities or demands, salary, availability, work locations or the like.

Psychologist John Holland (1985) developed a theory regarding vocational behavior that considers six basic personality orientations. He described the six types as

1. **Realistic**—These people apply scientific principles in things that they do. They may have mechanical abilities; they like doing or making things. Examples of occupations in this category would be pilot, electrician, engineer, or construction worker.

281

2. **Investigative**—People in this group like abstract thinking, discovering new knowledge, testing hypotheses, solving problems. Examples of workers in this category would be a research scientist such as a physicist, chemist, medical researcher, college or university professor.

3. **Conventional**—People in this category enjoy working in structured situations. They are usually very self-disciplined, orderly, like organizing and can work comfortably at routine, repetitive tasks. Occupations in this area include clerical worker, accountant, bank teller, data entry or billing clerk.

4. **Enterprising**—This group includes people who are persuasive, like to influence other people, are risk-takers, and enjoy business ventures. Sales managers, real estate brokers, and business owners would fall in this category.

5. **Social**—Individuals with this orientation like to work with people especially in helping relationships. Occupations in this area would include social worker, counselor, teacher, health care worker, and clinical psychologist.

6. **Artistic**—This group includes people who are creative, imaginative, emotional, and who hold unconventional perspectives which they like to express in artistic forms such as painting, sculpting, music, writing, and dance.

Holland noted that everyone has some of all these inclinations, but we could rank order them in terms of preferences for ourselves. Review these six types and place them in order from the most to least preferred orientation as you see yourself. Completing an interest inventory such as the Strong Interest Inventory, the COPS-P, or the Self-Directed Search can help you in determining the order of these orientations. Occupations that combine your top two or three of Holland's orientations may be the ones that fit your personality best.

Anne Roe (1972), another psychologist and occupational theorist, identified an array of variables that relate to vocational behavior. She sees these components interacting for each of us changing in importance as we move through our career development. The elements she discusses include the following:

State of the economy—the general state of things . . . war, peace, inflation, depression, labor markets, trends for specific businesses. Expansion or failures of specific business areas.

Family Background—Family origin, culture, socio-economic circumstances, values, educational levels, aspirations and expectations.

Chance—Unexpected events such as running into someone who knows of a position that just became open, being "in the right place at the right time." One's reaction to the chance event, however, is not a matter of chance! Also, many so called "chance" events are not really random . . . they are influenced by the person's behavior.

Marital Situation—If not married, nor aspiring to be, the effect of this variable will be different than for someone married. Particularly with two partners having careers in today's world, the degree of willingness to re-locate to accommodate a partner's promotion, the concern for care of children, and the amount of time available for family life all affect careers.

Physical—Refers to physical capacities, not only appearance and strength, but additionally sensory and perceptual capacities.

Intellectual—Cognitive abilities of a general nature as well as special abilities of all sorts. The more recent ideas of multiple intelligences relates here.

Temperament and Personality—Natural or acquired patterns of behaviors, preferences, styles, ways of taking in and responding to stimuli in the environment.

Interests and Values—What activities, environments, and events capture our attention and liking? What values are basic to our lives? What is most important to us.

Learning and Education—What we know from general education and experience.

Acquired Skills—Special skills and techniques learned through organized training.

Roe suggested that the further from the average that any of these variables may be at any given time, the more significance that element will have in influencing career behavior. For example, in time of economic extremes—war, depression—the economy becomes a large factor; if a physical handicap develops then physical becomes a looming factor. The advantage of Roe's theory is that it goes beyond the individual in looking at career decisions and planning to family issues and other environmental realities. Since none of us operates in isolation, this is a reminder that our careers occur in the social context of which we are a part. Consider the variables from Roe's theory of vocational behavior. What insights can you gain about yourself in relation to the factors listed above?

Focusing on Strengths

A new philosophy about personal satisfaction and professional development has been inspired by Buckingham and Clifton, both from the Gallup Organization, based on hundreds of thousands of case studies and careful analysis. This is presented in their recent book, *Now, Discover Your Strengths* (2001). These authors say most organizations are built on two flawed assumptions: (1) that each person can learn to be competent in almost anything, and (2) that each person's greatest room for growth is in his or her areas of greatest weakness. Instead, they contend, the best managers in corporations and organizations assume that (1) each person's talents are enduring and unique, and (2) the greatest room for growth is in areas of greatest strength. They note that training and development in companies that focus on "improving weaknesses" are doing damage control . . . not development. A *strength* is defined as "a consistent, near perfect performance in an activity." From over two million interviews, these authors extracted 34 themes that in combination help capture the unique themes in each person's life. Questions they would ask a person include: "What are your strengths?" How can you capitalize on them?" "What are your most powerful combinations?" "Where do they take you?" "What one, two or three things can you do better than 10,000 other people? Related to the idea of putting our talents under a bushel, these writers affirm the notion that instead our **talents** are what we must develop and let shine, instead of focusing on our weaknesses. They provide numerous case examples from anonymous individuals in the world of work as well as some famous people like Tiger Woods and Bill Gates. Tiger Woods has learned to maximize his strengths in driving his golf ball, rather than focusing on his weakness in getting out of sand traps. Gates is not talented in running a business, so he has a partner who is. This allows Gates to focus on his talent and strengths in software development and to excel. In this new philosophy of career decisions and development, some of Buckingham and Clifton's 34 specific themes will become apparent in a combination that helps capture the unique themes in each person. Among these, the five most dominate themes form a cluster they would call one's "signature theme." This signature theme is then related to career areas. Three principles of living a life of strength include (1) being able to do consistently, over and over the same work happily and successfully; (2) not needing strength in every aspect of a role to excel; and (3) that you will excel only by maximizing your strengths, never by "fixing" your weaknesses. These authors have developed an inventory called the StrengthsFinder, an on-line questionnaire that yields your five dominant themes. To use this resource, one must purchase their book to obtain an identification number for access to this inventory. Talents are considered to be any recurring pattern of thought, feeling or behavior that can be productively applied. Reviewing the physiology of the brain in early development, these writers note that recurring patterns evolve from early years. Since the brain retains connections that are related to these evolving talents and discards neural connections not being used, it is not possible to switch to a new design of talents after a certain age. Therefore, our talents are enduring qualities that must be developed if we are to excel in the workplace. The positive tone of this philosophy is similar to the work of researchers discussed in Chapter 14 who have studied professional reward and satisfaction in the workplace, discovering a connection between (1) people who are passionate about their work and find it fulfilling and (2) the success of the companies for whom they work. As more and more workers become passionate, the company's productivity increases. It is important to discover your natural talents and build them into strengths to be used in your career life. Centering on building our strengths rather than worrying about "weaknesses" is a relieving thought for many of us!

Self-Assessment

Whether it is deciding on a specific career, deciding where to complete your studies for that career, or determining your goals and long-range objectives for your career life, the place to begin is looking at yourself. Self-awareness is the first step. How well do you know yourself? How can you find out about yourself? Where do you begin?

Looking inward at ourselves is referred to as **introspection**—the process of discovering what is going on inside ourselves and noticing patterns in our behaviors, feelings, and attitudes. It is an interesting journey, one we are often too busy and too caught up in the day to day demands to do. Introspection takes time, quietness, reflection.

You might be wondering, "So how do I 'introspect' myself?" Well, you could stand before a mirror and have a conversation with yourself. Ask yourself questions about what you think is important in life, your personality characteristics, your interests, dislikes, and on and on. (If you take this approach, do it when no one else is home . . . you don't want someone calling the psycho squad to come and get you!) We discussed earlier in the text the "witness stance" where you psychologically step outside yourself and view yourself as a witness, attempting, as much as anyone can, to be objective. Some other approaches to self-awareness include writing, getting feedback, completing assessment instruments, and portfolio development.

Writing

Whenever we are trying to figure out what we do think about things, writing can be a helpful tool. Having to write down your thoughts often allows you to crystallize your thoughts and discover your own ideas. Writing diaries or journals of various types can help you to expose patterns in your life. Keeping a career related journal where you capture information about yourself related to your work life might be a useful way to enhance your self-awareness.

Feedback

Gathering feedback from other people is another way to learn about yourself. What kinds of impressions, personality quirks, strengths, hang-ups, habits others see in you is useful . . . and sometimes surprising. You can gather information from others informally and verbally by asking them what they see you doing, how they would characterize your personality, what they see as your strengths and weak areas. Many times getting unsolicited feedback is a part of our interaction with others. Our bosses, teachers, co-workers, friends give us feedback regularly by their comments to us, their requests of us, the referrals they make to us, suggestions they give us, questions they ask us. Sometimes their relationship with us requires written feedback of a more formal nature. Work supervisors and teachers evaluate us regularly and their feedback of our behavior is documented in our personnel file or the grade roll. Reviewing such feedback may expand your awareness of self.

Assessment Instruments

Many inventories, surveys, and rating scales exist for helping people to assess themselves. Many of these assessment tools are available through campus career counseling centers, testing centers or through faculty. Popular inventories include the Strong Interest Inventory, COPS-P and the Myers-Briggs Type Indicator. The Strong inventory asks questions about your preferences and provides a profile of your interest patterns. This inventory has integrated the Holland theory of six orientations into the interpretation of the interest information.

The COPS-P Interest Inventory provides interest scores referencing the COPSystem Career Clusters. With a focus on professional occupations, the COPS-P can be used to explore college majors, help college students conquer career indecision and assist adult professionals with career issues. The inventory heightens self-awareness while providing access to the most current occupational information available. The Myers-Briggs is a personality instrument built on Jungian theory of human behavior. It is one of the most researched instruments in existence. This inventory yields a "personality type" (one of 16 possibilities) which helps you see the way you take in and process information and your style of decision-making. The National Career Development Association maintains a web site (*http://ncda.org*) that lists internet sites for career planning. Included here are a variety of free instruments by type of assessment such as interest, values, ability/skill, and personality. Readers are encouraged to visit this site and others to explore ways to gain assistance in self-assessment.

Other written information is available by reviewing your performance on aptitude or achievement testing. In high school, what was your profile of scores on the achievement tests you took? Did you take the SAT or ACT examinations? Are there other tests you have taken such as course placement tests? Your patterns of scores on these tests are another piece of information to plug into the "Who am I" equation.

On-line Assessment Opportunities

In addition to published inventories and surveys, as mentioned above, there are numerous websites that contain self-assessment inventories or surveys that can be answered on line. Many of these ask that you complete questions which are then analyzed and feedback given you as to the "fit" for certain career groups. Robert Reardon, Program Director of the Career Center at Florida State University as a test author and researcher considers test validity, reliability, standardization procedures, theory base and quality of work as areas to be concerned about in using on-line assessments (Hansen, 2002). Richard Bolles (2001, 2002) author of a career classic book, *What Color is Your Parachute* lists seven rules about taking career tests as follows:

1. There is no test that everyone loves.
2. There is no one test that always gives better results than others
3. No test should necessarily be assumed to be accurate
4. You should take several tests, rather than just one.
5. Always let your intuition be your guide.
6. Don't let tests make you forget that you are absolutely unique on the face of the earth—as your fingerprints attest.
7. You are never finished with a test until you've done some good hard thinking about yourself.

The Florida Academic Counseling and Tracking for Students organization and the Florida Department of Education have partnered to provide students with the internet version of Florida eChoices, a career exploration and information system from Careerware. This program allows students and adults to assess and identify interests and match those interests with occupations within Florida. The site *http://facts.org* also has extensive databases of occupations, colleges, universities and graduate schools. In addition to eChoices, this site also has available SIGI PLUS (System of Interactive Guidance and Information PLUS), a career planning product developed by Educational Testing Services. SIGI PLUS helps individuals assess their work related values, interests, skills and search for related occupations and college majors. This highly researched and comprehensive program provides students and adults with a realistic view of the best educational and career options for future success.

Portfolio Development

Artists have used portfolios—examples of their achievement—for years to apply for positions, to seek entrance into educational programs, to sell their work and ideas to others. A portfolio is a collection of representative samples of what you have done.

Some school programs have expanded portfolios to English classes and other subjects where the portfolio becomes a collection of papers written and work completed to document learning. Keeping a job or career portfolio wherein you collect evidence of your accomplishments can help you write an annual self-assessment of your work, and can help document reasons you might make requests for such things as a promotion or a raise. Such a notebook of information is most useful when you begin writing or updating your resume.

You may decide to use Holland's theory to rank personality orientations for yourself. You can use Roe's ideas to determine what you know about physical characteristics, personality patterns, family background, values, intellectual skills, interests, and the like. You may try writing or gathering feedback from people and assessment instruments. Through on-line assessments you can determine patterns in your values, interests, and skills. By whatever means you employ, it is important in self-assessment to determine the answers to questions like: "What do I **value** in life?" "What's more important—money or family—or something else?" "What are my **personality** characteristics? Am I an introvert or extrovert, organized or unstructured, quiet or talkative, dominant or submissive, emotional or not, rely on thinking or feelings to make decisions, a leader or a follower, assertive, creative, modest, tenacious, versatile, efficient, conservative, humorous, ambitious?" "What are my **skills** and talents? What are my **strengths**? Am I best at thinking, talking, creating, fixing, analyzing, learning, organizing, explaining, helping, writing, problem solving, or leading? Who Am I?" The more I can understand myself, the better prepared I am to determine the career path I plan to take.

Occupational Information

After completing your self-assessment, the next step is to gather information about careers that relate to your own personality, interests, values and aspirations. Instead of focusing on one specific career, it is helpful to look at information about **career families** such as technology, health and human services, research, business, marketing, or **categories of work environments** such as corporations, government, educational institutions, and hospitals. *The Dictionary of Occupational Titles* (DOT) classifies jobs by the focus on concern for people, for data, or for things. This is an example of a broad grouping of tasks and interest. Which of these three categories interests you most?

FINDING INFORMATION ABOUT CAREERS

There are several sources you may want to tap to find information about careers. One place you do *not* want to get your information is from television programs that portray stories of people in specific fields. The real world may not be nearly as exciting as The Practice, CSI, ER, Third Watch or other T.V. programs, nor may they realistically portray the profession. Consider the difference between the activities of policemen shown on N.Y.P.D. Blue and some of the actual footage of police work in real localities.

Using Books

There are several ways of finding information about occupations such as the nature of the work, the necessary preparation, work environments, employment outlook, and salaries. In addition to the DOT mentioned above, the *Occupational Outlook Handbook* is an excellent source of information about careers. *Careers Encyclopedia* is another book resource. There are also many books on specific career areas. Most major book stores have a career section which contains books for specific career areas. Many sources for information are found on the listing from the National Career Development Association website listed above.

Using Computers

There are several ways the computer can be an excellent resource for finding information. One advantage to computer sources is that they can be updated more quickly than book sources and therefore may be more current. On-line searches can enable you to find statistics and information especially through the Bureau of Labor Statistics (web site: *stats.bls.gov*). Many other career related sites can be found by searching on specific key words. Popular sites for students seeking career help include the following:

> Monster Board—*www.monster.com*
>
> Career Builder—*www.careerbuilder.com*
>
> Career Mosaic—*www.service.com:80/cm*
>
> Quintessential Careers—*www.quintcareers.com*
>
> Jobhunters—*www.jobhuntersbible.com*
>
> JobWeb—*www.jobweb.org*
>
> National Career Development Association—*http://ncda.com*

Readers are encouraged to explore search engines with key words such as career planning, career decisions, career development and the like to find other on-line sources.

Campus Career Centers

One of the best and most helpful things you could do for yourself is to visit the Career Center on your campus. These resource centers have tons of information from the books we mentioned and others. Further they usually have an array of computer programs designed to help you gather information. You can get help in how to use Career Finder, America's Top Jobs, Career Decision, SIGI Plus and other programs right there in the center. Also career counselors are available to assist you in sorting out the information you have gathered about yourself and occupations. They will help you in making a career decision and evaluating your decision.

Interview

An excellent way to find out about the real picture of the day-to-day activities of an occupation is to interview a person in the career. Determine questions you want that person to answer before you arrange a meeting. Be sure to ask them at the beginning of the interview how they feel about their work. Remember if they are negative about their employment, they will probably give more negative answers to your questions. Try to sort out how much of their information is filtered through a generally pessimistic lens. Conversely, if they enjoy their work, you can find out why they say this . . . again remember that an optimistic person will enjoy anything more. So be sure to ask questions about facts, hours, details . . . not just opinions.

Gaining First Hand Experience—Intern or Volunteer

Some type of opportunity to spend time at a work site is even better than an interview. Not only can you actually see the work of a person or many persons, in that occupation, but you can get a broader picture of the work environment. You can get a feel for the skills required to do the tasks, the pace of operations, organizational patterns, team versus individual work, and generalization versus specialization in activities.

If you are unable to find a formal "internship" program, you may be able to arrange to be an observer, shadow a worker for a period of time, or be a volunteer in the organization. Another role for finding placement in a work setting to learn the environment is through Service Learning assignments in college classes whereby students put in volunteer hours in businesses and community organizations. Another opportunity for learning about careers while earning college credit is through Cooperative Education courses. In cooperative education courses, students are placed in a business or organization with the opportunity to learn and gain college credits while volunteering their time. All of these methods for first hand experience not only add to your knowledge, but could be added to a resume when you seek your first position in your chosen profession.

No matter what sources of information you investigate, it is necessary to gather information about any careers you may be considering. If you have acquired a lot of information about yourself in your Self-Assessment, it is equally important to find out as much as possible about careers. These two areas of information prepare you for deciding or confirming a career choice or a career change and preparing you for designing your career life.

Making the Decision

Psychologists have studied the "decision making" processes people use to determine choices. It seems safe to say that day-to-day decisions like what to eat for breakfast, what to wear, where to study on campus are easily made in routine ways. However, when a more significant and complex decision like where to attend college, whether to get married, AND WHAT CAREER TO CHOOSE has to be made, more sophisticated methods may be called for. Researchers have identified different patterns for making complex decisions that include several variables. Most suggest that a better decision is made by use of a systematic method of comparing important factors against the alternate choices.

A planned method of making a decision requires committing thoughts on paper. It could be a simple plus or negative column for given alternatives. Or it could involve a more elaborate process such as making a table on a page listing one or several factors involved in a decision. For example suppose Maria has completed her self-assessment and determined her areas of strength, interests, personality patterns, and they point to possibilities in three careers she is considering. Suppose now she considers her values and what is most or least important. She determines that salary is less important than considerations such as growth opportunities, work schedule, "fit" with personality. To accommodate this she decides to give each factor a weighted value from 1 (lowest) to 3 (highest). She then gives a rating to each choice from one to three (low to high) regarding how she rates this career on that criterion. So she makes a matrix comparing factors with the three choices as follows:

Factors	Factor Value	Career A Law	Career B Nursing	Career C Teaching
Opportunity for professional growth	(3)	2	2	2
Work schedule	(3)	1	2	3
Location	(2)	1	2	3
Size of organization	(2)	2	2	3
Benefits	(3)	2	1	3
"Fit" with personality	(3)	3	1	3
Core position availability	(2)	2	3	2
Flexibility for horizontal moves	(2)	2	3	3
Advancement	(2)	3	2	2
Salary	(1)	3	2	2

Because the factors are not equal in her value system, Maria decides to multiply the factor value times the rating for each career choice. Then by adding the products for each career, a total is found for each of the three choices. In this case, the teaching career option clearly has the most weight and stands out as the best choice.

Factors	Factor Value	Career A Law	Career B Nursing	Career C Teaching
Opportunity for professional growth	(3)	2 = 6	2 = 6	2 = 6
Work schedule	(3)	1 = 3	2 = 6	3 = 9
Location	(2)	1 = 2	2 = 4	3 = 6
Size of organization	(2)	2 = 4	2 = 4	3 = 6
Benefits	(3)	2 = 6	1 = 3	3 = 9
"Fit" with personality	(3)	3 = 9	1 = 3	3 = 9
Core position availability	(2)	2 = 4	3 = 6	2 = 4
Flexibility for horizontal moves	(2)	2 = 4	3 = 6	3 = 6
Advancement	(2)	3 = 6	2 = 4	2 = 4
Salary	(1)	3 = 3	2 = 2	2 = 2
		47	44	61

This may seem like an involved way of trying to make a decision, but considering the importance and the consequences of a career choice, it is worth the effort. If you use the SIGI PLUS on-line program, it will automatically integrate your work values as a factor into the decision-making process and determine the outstanding choice.

Whether you determined your decision the "long way" per above or through a computer program, a final step in decision-making is to reflect upon, review, and as time goes on re-affirm the decision that is made. It is always a good idea after you make a major decision to look inside (*introspection*) and ask yourself how you feel about the decision. In this age of rapid change and with new experiences, it may be that your decisions will have to be revised or changed as you move along. Coming back to re-evaluate the decision is, in any case, a helpful last step.

Setting Goals

After deciding on a career to pursue, the next step is to set specific **goals** to get you from where you are now to entering that field and planning your career path.

This is the time to put to work the ideas we discussed in Chapter 6 about creating a vision. Your career development vision embodies the goals for your career path. As you now envision yourself in the career you have chosen, What do you see yourself doing? What is your role? What added responsibilities have you taken on? How have you grown in the profession? What you see in your vision is the basis for your long term goals.

Since it is difficult to nail down every detail of what you want your life to be at the other end of your career, you may want to be more specific with goals to get yourself from here to entering the profession. Where are you right now in your educational process? What short-range goals do you want to achieve in the next two years? In the next five years? What is the next step for your educational process? And bringing your goal setting even closer, what are the implications for your goals right now and your plans for next semester? Or this semester, for that matter!

Again, this means getting information. You may need to collect information from colleges and universities where you will possibly complete your education to enter your chosen profession. It is a good idea to review the course requirements for the completion of your degree and your reaction to taking these courses. Hopefully, you will feel eager to study the requirements of your chosen career. If you review the curriculum and discover that the list of courses really turns you off, maybe you need to revisit your decision. This doesn't mean that the advanced study should appear as a "piece of cake," but the topics should be areas you are at least interested in learning about.

When you have determined your goals, you are ready to begin a written career plan. Huge numbers of small businesses fail every year. In looking at why this occurs, one of the variables that seem to make a difference is the business plan. Most failed businesses have a poorly thought out business plan, or none at all. If you are more or less a spontaneous person and "planning" makes you uncomfortable, then you need work harder than others to develop your plan in writing. In a sense, isn't your career the "business" of your life? The better you plan based on information, the more likely it is that you will succeed.

A **career plan** should include your basic mission or goal, your long range requirements, your current skills, interests and experiences, and your short term goals. A sample career plan is as follows:

Career Goal

To become a licensed registered nurse. To provide assessment, care planning, implementation of nursing intervention, and evaluation of results with hospitalized patients.

Long-range, general abilities and requirements:

- At least a bachelor's degree in nursing
- Ability to work as part of a health care team
- Knowledge of the scientific method
- Critical thinking skills
- Capacity for record keeping
- Teaching skills
- Skills in writing care plans
- Knowledge of chemistry, anatomy and physiology, and microbiology
- License from state Board of Professional Regulations

Current skills, interests, and experiences:

- Summer employment with home health company
- High school science courses
- Experience working within a team
  (summer employment, school organizations, course projects)
- High school writing courses (four years of English, technical writing)
- Top 10% in high school class
- Problem solving ability and organizational skills
- Interest in helping others

Short-term, specific goals to make your dreams a reality:

- Complete current college semester
- Good test scores
- Acceptance to a university with a good nursing program
- Keep grades up to meet requirements for nursing school
- Continue work experience or part-time employment in local hospital
- Participate in campus organizations for nursing students
- Earn a bachelor's degree
- Consider graduate school
- Improve assessment and planning skills through courses to enhance these skills
- Determine areas of content for preparing for board examination

(Adapted from Adventures in Education, Planning a Career, Texas Guaranteed Student Loan Corporation, 1998)

GETTING THE JOB

There are many important sources you can turn to for assistance in seeking employment. The campus career center has materials that will help you. Your college may have recruitment days/weeks, job fairs and special programs for job seekers. Additionally, there is an abundance of help on the Internet for open positions and tips on resume writing, search ideas, and such. Some of these are listed above. Your career service center staff will help you find these and other sites if you need help.

Also a number of business and industry directories are found in your campus library. The librarian will help you locate and use career related directories. Contacting the human resources department of these companies will provide information on job postings. Another library resource that is helpful is the collection of professional journals. These are published by organizations for the profession and often contain employment advertising. Writing or calling the headquarters office of the organization may yield additional resources for listings of employment opportunities.

Other methods to use include:

1. Newspaper advertising—want ads

2. Developing a network of contacts—professional, family, work associates, faculty members, friends, former employers, religious or other community groups

3. Using the internet—*http://jobhuntersbible.com* and *http://ncda.org* have invaluable information on where to find job openings, how to make contacts, and website information for professional organizations.

Preparing Your Resume

Again, there are many publications that can be helpful in your campus career center, in the campus or public library and in large bookstores. Further, going on-line is an excellent way to find tips for developing your **resume** and viewing sample resumes. The best plan regarding your resume is to customize your resume for each specific position opening for which you are applying. In today's world of technology, among large companies the first "screener" of your resume may very well be a scanner, not a person. Scanners can be programmed to read and sort out specific key words in a resume that relate to the specific position. Resumes not containing those key words are never read by a person. If however, you are developing in quantity general information resumes to circulate, keep in mind that these are usually organized by (1) reversed (most recent first) chronological order or (2) function or task accomplishments. A third way to organize is by targeted information for a specific position and would be a customized single resume.

The chronological order format is the one most employers prefer even though it is rather traditional. The second style, function or task accomplishments, usually identifies a general area under which examples of achievements are listed. For example:

PROGRAM DEVELOPMENT

- Developed new employee orientation program
- Implemented weekly seminars for improvement ideas
- Wrote materials for personal finance program for employees

The third, and preferred, way of organizing is the targeted format which tailors the resume to fit a specific position or job opening. Here the information presented about you is not of a general nature. Instead it includes only those items about you that are related to the job opening. This type of resume focuses on the match between you and the requirements of the position.

Resumes are to be brief, usually only one page. Items to be included are:

1. *Who You Are*—Full name (highlighted or large type), address, zip codes, and phone area code and number(s). Be sure you can be contacted through the information given in this section.

2. *Job Objective or Goal*—This is optimal here, but could be in cover letter instead.

3. *Education*—Other educational activities such as organizations, offices held, internship or co-op experiences, scholarships, and the like may be included here.

4. *Experience and Achievements*—List in reverse chronological sequence. Don't just list title; explain responsibilities of the job in brief.

5. *References*—Three or four actual references may be given (be sure to check with the person first), or you can say "References are available upon request."

6. As a guideline, use action verbs in writing such as "managed, coordinated, developed, wrote, designed, evaluated, organized and prepared."

Following is a sample resume:

Maria Student
245 College Street
Anywhere, Virginia 24609
(480) 394-5575
mstudent@compugo.com

OBJECTIVE
A challenging position in marketing and sales management

EDUCATION
Bachelor of Business Administration, Marketing Major
Wilson University, Atlanta, Georgia
Co-op Student in Sales Director's Office
Mainstream Manufacturing Company, Atlanta, Georgia

RELATED EXPERIENCE
Sales Representative
- Full-time temporary in summers; part-time during academic year, General Warehouse Products, Atlanta, Georgia
- Handled general sales and specialized in computer-related products
- Learned sales protocol, account follow-up, and packaging
- Served as back-up to sales manager in his absence

Co-op Intern
- Assigned to assist sales director, Mainstream Manufacturing Company, Atlanta, Georgia
- Coordinated sales representatives schedules

- Monitored sales records
- Developed and presented in-service training sessions
- Received award from sales representatives for contributions as an intern

Service in University Student Business Leaders Association
- Member for three years
- Chairperson, Charity Drive Project, raised $5,000 through projects
- Recording Secretary, maintained minutes, records, agendas
- President, senior year, developed orientation program for high school students, Computerized financial and historical records systems, led development of a video program for business students

Professional Characteristics
- Highly motivated, organized
- Excellent writing, oral and presentation skills
- Positive attitude, broad perspective in planning and problem solving
- Enthusiastic and energetic
- Eager to learn, grow and develop professionally

Writing Your Cover Letter

Your **cover letter** is an original business letter that complements your resume. The purpose of this letter is to get the employer to read the resume. You may want to obtain extra plain paper of the same type your resume is copied on to match the pair for a professional look. In your cover letter you want to introduce yourself to an employer and let them know why you are sending your resume. If there is a specific opening, this letter serves as your **letter of application**; if there is not a specific job posting, this then becomes your **letter of inquiry**. The letter should be brief—one page—and to the point. It should be addressed to a specific person. If you do not know the name of the person at the company accepting applications or inquiries, call the receptionist and indicate that you are sending correspondence to the person accepting such letters and wish to know the correct spelling of the name and exact address.

1. Your first paragraph is to stimulate interest . . . to indicate why you are writing, how you found out about this company, and what position you are seeking.

2. Your second paragraph (and third, if there is one) should make clear what you have to offer the company. You should point out how your skills and knowledge and experience match those listed in the job posting and/or how your skills fit with the company.

3. Your last paragraph is designed to get a response from the employer. Indicate in this closing paragraph when and how you will contact the employer to follow up.

Following is a sample cover letter:

Maria Student
245 College Street
Anywhere, Virginia 24609

Today's date

Joshua Barker, Manager
Sales Division
BCD Corporation
2420 N. W. Major Boulevard
Atlanta, Georgia 30319

Dear Mr. Barker:

I am writing to apply for the sales manager position that you advertised in the *Atlanta Daily News.* I see in this position an opportunity to use my knowledge and skills in salesmanship and my organizational skills in management.

The enclosed resume details my education and related experience. I will receive my degree in marketing with an emphasis in management from Wilson University in April. I have worked full-time during summers and part-time in the academic year at General Warehouse Products as a sales representative. At the University I was a co-op student in the sales director's office at the Mainstream Manufacturing Company in Atlanta. As president of the Student Business Leaders Association on campus, I enhanced my leadership and organizational skills through several service projects we achieved. I am highly motivated, energetic and hard working.

I would appreciate an opportunity to meet with you personally to discuss my qualifications and your organization's needs. I will call your office next week to inquire regarding an appointment.

Sincerely,

Your full name

Enclosure

When your cover letter is successful, the employer will read your resume. When your resume is successful, you will be selected for an interview. Now let's think of some pointers for the actual meeting with a prospective employer.

Preparing for the Job Interview

How you write your application letter, fill out an application, present your qualifications in your resume, handle yourself on the telephone are all important, but the single most significant factor in the selection process is how you conduct yourself in your employment interview. One survey (Byham, 1997) revealed that 80% of respondents in a national study didn't consider interview preparation as important as having a positive attitude. Yet, recruiters and interviewers for companies report that such preparation is one of the most important factors in persuading an employer to consider an applicant for a position. You can be a happy, smiling, easy-going, perfectly positive person in the interview, but corporate interviewers indicate that if it is apparent you have not prepared for this event, you can "positively" count yourself out of the running!

The goal of your interview (that you must have firmly tattooed in your brain!) is to get an offer for a position. The interview is the prime opportunity for you to communicate what you can do for the company or organization. Your job is make clear to the employer how your skills, knowledge, experience, motivation, and work habits match what is needed in the desired position. As the saying goes, remember, *"You never get a second chance to make a first impression!"*

Preparation for your interview means doing your homework—gathering information, anticipating your response to questions, devising your own questions, rehearsing your introductions. Think through and practice giving an overview of who you are and your qualifications. You should prep for an interview with just as much enthusiasm, intensity and interest as you would for a final exam.

It is necessary to gather information about the organization or company and the position. What you should know:

a. What is the nature and purpose of the organization?

b. Who are the key leaders in the company?

c. How small or large is the organization? Number of employees? Amount of sales? Number of clients served?

d. In what other locations do branches exist?

e. What is the organizational pattern for the company?

f. Who are the major competitors for this product or service?

g. What is the organization's reputation?

h. What information about this company has been in the news?

i. What are the requirements of the position you are seeking?

j. What does the job description include as responsibilities of the job?

k. Why is the position you are seeking available?

Where you can find the information:

Corporate Directories, Annual Reports, publications circulated within and publicly by the organization, Chambers of Commerce, newspaper articles, and magazine and trade journal articles and advertisements. You can also call the company as ask questions, request brochures, and inquire about other publications or video presentations designed to provide information about the organization. Try to obtain a copy of the job description if you are seeking a specific job that is posted for applications. In learning about the company, determine the vocabulary used to describe customers, products, services and processes; in other words, learn the "lingo" of the culture.

The Five C's of Job Interviewing

There are several reminders that need to be stored in your head as you prepare for your interview. Five specific pointers to remember are the five C's. These are as follows:

1. **Challenged**—Feel the spirit of challenge as you face the task of selling yourself to an employer. Recognize that this is a "biggy," but that you can do this . . . and do it well!

2. **Communicative**—This is the time to put all your skills learned in Part 2 of this text on interpersonal effectiveness. Be sure you are listening to understand, that you clearly know what is being asked. Don't answer before you have a moment to gather your thoughts and organize your answer. Then when you have thought it out, answer clearly and concisely.

3. **Candid**—BE honest and direct and you will come across as the trustful, genuine person that you are.

4. **Comfortable**—Be relaxed and at ease. If you are tense and anxious, you make interviewers tense (a situation you don't want!). Be yourself. Don't try to put on a show or be something you are not. Imagine if you were hired yet someone other than you got the job??? That is, imagine what a mess you create if you project yourself as someone you are not and they hire that impersonator! Your troubles would just be beginning!!

5. **Confident**—Never make a clear negative statement about yourself. Even if someone asks you directly "What do you see as your weakness?" do not put yourself down. Find a way to respond that doesn't make you look compromised. For example, you might say, "Some people consider me overly concerned with facts, but others will tell you I am extremely thorough and that if I report something, you can count on it being on the money!" Your phraseology is extremely important. Consider the difference between how these two responses sound . . . "I am out of work" compared to "I am in transition in my career." When asked about your academic career contrast "My G.P.A. was 2.0" to "I experienced a variety of opportunities in college from which I learned. In addition to my coursework, I learned about teamwork, persistence and leadership as part of the baseball team, and I organized the Career Forum sponsored by the student government association."

The Actual Interview Process

1. Introductions—Introduce yourself in a friendly and courteous way. Pay close attention and remember information given as you meet your interviewer, both verbal and non-verbal information.

2. Wait to be invited to be seated.

3. Listen, respond, and ask your questions in the exchange of the interview.

4. Mentally note any follow-up requests such as supplying references or transcripts.

5. Sense when the interview is drawing to a close.

6. Clarify with the interviewer the next steps in the process.

7. Summarize your pleasure at the interview experience, what you will do as the next step, and state succinctly your enthusiasm and qualifications for the job.

8. Thank the interviewer as you prepare to leave.

9. Follow up with a written (handwritten or typed) letter of thank you.

Tips to Keep in Mind

DOs	DON'Ts
Your homework . . . gather information	Appear uninformed regarding the
Rehearse . . . practice orally	organization
Prepare questions you might ask	Talk too much
Dress a level above the job you are seeking	Pretend to be listening
Arrive on time	Interrupt the interviewer
Have a firm handshake	Put yourself down
LISTEN	Be arrogant
Show interest	Be rude
Be nice	Question about salary early
Be yourself	in the interview—do it
Think what it's like to be	at the end, if at all
in the interviewer's shoes	Be an extremist . . . moderation
Ask your questions	is the key . . . in dress and
Think before responding	ideas or attitudes
Maintain eye contact most of the time	Have a telephone interview if
Thank the interviewer when you leave	you can avoid it
Send a written follow-up expressing your	Be vague or indirect
appreciation and interest in the position	Be negative

After Leaving the Interview

Although you may feel a sense of relief and accomplishment after the interview, before you call a friend to get together to celebrate, force yourself to sit with a pad and pencil and review and jot notes about the interview. What did the interviewer ask you? Where were you more uncertain about your responses? Where did you shine? What did the interviewer say or do that gave you clues as to how you were doing in the interview? Were there areas of knowledge where you wish you had had more information?

Capture in writing as much as you can about the experience before you even leave the area. You will remember the most about the experience right after it happened. Even an hour later, your recollection will be less complete. This is hard to make yourself do, but can be very significant to preparation for a second interview . . . either at this company or at another. You have proven your ability to write a cover letter, resume and secure an interview! After you have rendered your experience to writing, pat yourself on the back!

SUMMARY

In this chapter we have reviewed the process of planning your own career and making it happen. We examined the six personality orientations of John Holland and how these relate to career fit. We considered the variables that Anne Roe believes influences our career success. We investigated the power to excel by discovering and enhancing our strengths. We noted the importance of discovering and building your strengths. We described ways you can gain information about your interests, personality characteristics, values, and skills. We explored the ways to find information about careers in order to analyze the connection between the nature of the work and your own "human nature." We reviewed methods for decision making that allowed for value differences for specific factors. We discussed goal setting and development of a career plan. We looked at the steps in getting the job, and preparation related to your resume, cover letter and the interview process. Whether you are preparing to enter a profession for the first time, or if you have years of experience in the professional world, the real value of all of this is you putting it to work in designing your own career!

SELF EXERCISES

1. Complete the *Self Directed Search* or *Strong Interest Inventory* and list three occupations that fit your orientation and that appeal to you.

2. Discuss your career goal or tentative goal with a friend using the factors in Anne Roe's vocational theory.

3. Develop a career plan using the sample in the chapter as a guide.

4. Keep a self-assessment journal, recording new insights and information as you gather it.

5. Visit your campus career center with a group of fellow students. After your visit, design a brochure for the center.

KEY TERMS

realistic	values	letter of inquiry
investigative	personality	talent
conventional	career plan	strength
enterprising	goals	career families
social	resume	cover letter
artistic	introspection	letter of application

CHAPTER 12 QUESTIONS

Short-Answer Questions

1. The psychologist who developed six basic personality orientations was _____.

2. One of these orientations is _____.

3. The psychologist who looks at marital situation as a factor in career decision is _____.

4. In assessing myself, I should focus on my _____ (areas of consistent, near perfect performance)

5. The process of discovering what is going on inside ourselves including behaviors, feelings, and attitudes is _____.

6. The popular personality inventory that includes 16 possible types is the _____ _____ _____ _____.

7. The "OOH" as a source of career information stands for the _____ _____ _____ published by the government.

8. In addition to books, interviews, and internships, an excellent first place to look for career information and job listings is on the _____.

9. After making a career choice, the next step is to develop a _____.

10. A resume should be _____ page(s).

11. A letter that responds to a specific position open is referred to as a letter of _____.

12. The goal of your interview is to _____.

13. What are the 5 C's to remember in an interview? _____

    _____.

14. After leaving the interview, you should follow up with a _____ letter to the interviewer

Essay Questions

1. Describe a position that requires three of Holland's personality orientations.

2. Discuss how family background is an influential factor in career choice.

3. Describe three ways that you can get information about yourself.

4. Discuss the advantages of visiting your campus career center to determine or explore your career choice.

5. Explain to a friend in writing how to make a decision that considers various factors of different importance. Give a written example.

6. Distinguish between a cover letter and a resume.

7. Describe to a friend how to prepare for a job interview.

8. What do the 5C's for Interviewing mean?

9. What do you plan to do in a job interview? Describe the process.

10. Explain the contents of a career plan and why each part is important.

13

Be People Smart

In the 1600's John Donne wrote "no man is an island . . . ." He was right. If you think about it, we all have to deal with people. No matter what type of career you may be in, whether you are a computer programmer, a sales manager, an engineer, an artist, a physical therapist, a teacher, you name it . . . you will be doing your work in the company of other people. Some occupations have a great deal of contact with other people; some involve minimal interaction, but *all* jobs involve working in a social context of some sort. Aristotle said centuries ago that humans are social animals. So it makes sense (doesn't it?) that if you are going to be successful and you're going to excel on the job, you will also have to be "people smart." Research shows that the reason most people are fired from their jobs is not because they lack the technical skills and knowledge to do the job, but because they cannot get along with other people . . . their bosses, co-workers, clients, customers, patients, students . . . whomever their position requires they serve. The increasing use of work teams to complete projects in the workplace further emphasizes this skill.

In fact, think about it. Is there someone you know who is really "smart" when it comes to taking a test, spewing out dates and knowledge, answering questions with the most obscure facts? They might win a million with their "final answers," *but,* how do they do on the job, working in a populated environment? Do they have a working knowledge of how to interact effectively with people? Are they just "eggheads" or "nerds," or are they also able to relate interpersonally with effective results?

WHAT DOES IT MEAN TO BE PEOPLE SMART?

When we think of being "smart" we think of having a high IQ, supposedly being very intelligent when is comes to cognitive skills. However, what we have traditionally referred to and tested with IQ tests are skills in language and analytic/mathematics problem solving. Thus, our concept of "intelligence" centers around thinking skills involving memory, logic, organizing ideas and the like. In 1983, Howard Gardner challenged this traditional concept of intelligence when he proposed his theory of **multiple intelligences.** He described seven different types of intelligence that exist in humans. The first two are familiar, like those traditionally defined as intelligence, namely *linguistic* (involving sensitivity to spoken and written language and using language effectively) and *logical-mathematic* (involving logical analysis, math operations, and scientific investigation). Gardner's next three intelligences relate to artistic areas and are musical (involving performance, composition, and appreciation of musical patterns), *bodily-kinesthetic* (using parts of or the whole body to solve problems), and spatial (recognizing and using different patterns of space). Intelligences number six and seven, according to Gardner, are personal in nature and he named them *intrapersonal* (able to understand oneself, appreciate one's feelings and motivations thereby regulating one's life) and *interpersonal* (capacity for understanding intentions, motivations and desires of other people and thereby work effectively with them). Later, Gardner (1999) added an eighth intelligence to his list, that of *naturalist* (involving recognition and categorization of features in the environment). Of these eight intelligences of Gardner's, the two of import here are the personal ones . . . **intrapersonal** and **interpersonal intelligences** which speak to our ability to be aware of our inner selves and to be effective in working with other people.

Daniel Goleman (1995), discussed back in Chapter 8 of this text, notes the significance of knowing yourself as a part of **emotional intelligence**. For him, self awareness is a ongoing attention to one's internal states that can be at best a non-judgmental consciousness of feelings or at a minimum recognition of what is happening emotionally rather than "being immersed and lost in it." In his chapter entitled "Know Thyself," Goleman discusses the anatomy of our brain and cerebral emotional centers that are involved in normal functioning. He relates a story of a man who, because of brain surgery for a tumor, lost the normal neural connections in his brain between his cognitive and emotional centers leaving his thinking devoid of emotional connections. This disability in his emotional functioning caused the man severe problems. He lost his job as a corporate lawyer; his wife left him; he couldn't handle his financial affairs; and he was even unable to make simple decisions. This illustrates how important our emotions are to normal functioning. Goleman points out that even in usual day-to-day activity, a person who is annoyed by a rude encounter in the early part of the day, but unaware of his feelings, is likely to continue for hours afterward snapping at other people and making curt responses for no good reason. As Goleman explains, once this person brings the feelings from the initial early morning rude encounter into his awareness, he can then evaluate things anew. This allows him to change his frame and his behavior positively toward others. Thus, Goleman illustrates the importance of our being able to feel emotions and to be aware of them as a basis for behaving with emotional intelligence.

Silberman and Hansburg writing about interpersonal intelligence say that those who are people smart are good at the following competencies:

1. **Understanding People**—listening actively , empathically, clarifying, interpreting beyond words to non-verbal messages, and able to read other people's styles and motives in order to work with them effectively.

2. **Expressing Yourself Clearly**—knowing how to get your message across by reading the verbal and non-verbal responses of those with whom you are communicating.

3. **Asserting Your Needs**—being your own person, having and establishing limits, and being straightforward with your wishes.

4. **Exchanging Feedback**—giving feedback easily and without being offensive as well as seeking feedback from others.

5. **Influencing Others**—being able to motivate others to action, able to connect with others, discover their needs, knowing how to reduce resistance and to make persuasive appeals.

6. **Resolving Conflict**—able to use the above mentioned skills to get the subject on the table, able to figure out what's bothering you and the other person and to suggest creative solutions.

7. **Being a Team Player**—accepting the challenge to work with others through complementing their styles, coordinating the efforts of team members without being bossy, and building consensus.

8. **Shifting Gears**—Understanding differences in people, able to make changes in one's own behavior, willing to try things new and different, knowing how to handle the risk of change.

There are meaningful rewards for developing these skills. When you understand someone else, you are appreciated; when you explain yourself clearly, you are understood; when you assert yourself, you are respected; when you exchange feedback, you are enlightened; when you influence others positively, you are valued; when you resolve conflict effectively, you are trusted; when you collaborate with teammates, you are prized; when you shift gears, your relationships are renewed. (Silberman and Hansburg, 2000)

These competencies described by Silberman and Hansburg echo the ideas of Goleman regarding emotional intelligence. By the way . . . do these eight competencies ring any bells related to the steps you've been learning in this whole text about being a more effective person? Hopefully, you are mentally connecting reframing, being proactive, listening and expressive skills and thinking about how these all play out in the workplace. In this chapter, we are going to examine the process of becoming "**people smart**," as knowing what makes people tick and what ticks them off. You need to get "sharp" regarding the people around you, and the person to begin with is YOU!

UNDERSTANDING YOURSELF

The aged admonitions from Socrates and Shakespeare to know and be true to yourself are filled with wisdom. Just as you probably can't really love someone fully if you don't love yourself first, you obviously need to understand yourself before you can become astute in knowing others. So let's start with some questions to think about.

What Do You Want the Outcome to Be?

Whether you are talking about your life, your career, your marriage or family, your grades for this semester, or your tennis swing, you have to have a vision of what the desired result is like. Covey talks about this as "beginning with the end in mind." As we discussed in Chapter 6, athletes training for Olympic feats work with psychologists to visualize their success in the perfect moves. The more specific and clear the picture of what you want appears, the more likely you are to achieve it. If you don't have a goal in mind, it's like going on a trip with no destination . . . how do you know if you're getting closer? How do you know when you're there? How can you know . . . if you don't even know where you're going? Have you ever tried to do a class project when you didn't understand the assignment? How *can* you know if you're doing a good job, if you don't have a clue what you are trying to accomplish? Or why you're doing this thing in the first place?

Goal setting is the answer to the mysteries here. If you have a clear **goal** you are trying to achieve, it gives you direction and focus. This helps you know if you are staying on track, moving in the right direction, and how well you are doing.

Imagine yourself ten years down the road. What do you see for your life? For your career life? Family life? If you said you wanted to be a successful lawyer, for example, and you wanted to be a parent who is involved with your two children, how is that going to work? Lawyers spend an incredible amount of time at their jobs, especially in the first decade or so of their work . . . how are you going to do this and still manage to spend time with your children? Suppose you want to make a lot of money in a career in demand. So you decide to be a computer engineer. But, you really enjoy outdoor sports and participating in mountain bike races with your significant other. How are you going to work those long hours and be on call at all hours when systems problems occur, yet spend a long vacation biking in France or finding time to travel for races out of town? As discussed in Chapter 6, is there a way to reconcile competing goals?

As you can see, setting a goal leads you to the next steps of planning how you are going to accomplish this. In companies and organizations employers report that the best performing employees are those that consistently set goals for themselves. Research on college students over the years has confirmed that students who complete their degrees, compared to those who drop out, are more likely to have begun their studies with a specific major and career goal in mind. It makes it a lot easier to do your assignments, prepare for tests, get yourself to those early classes and such when you know *why* you are doing these things.

You are no stranger to setting goals. You do it all the time. You had a goal in mind when you started reading in this chapter in this book. What was it? How are you progressing toward meeting that goal?

Goals are usually classified into two categories . . . long-term and short-term goals. We have many short-term goals everyday. Sometimes, just getting through the day is one of your short-term goals! Turning your thoughts toward what you want the outcome to be is an important first step. Daily goals might be in the form of a "To Do" list. For "biggies" like career related, family related, or health related issues the goals will be longer term goals. Clarifying your goals helps provide the direction, like a lighthouse blinking a steady reminder regarding your course ahead. Keep a file folder or a notebook or journal in which you discuss and record your goals . . . both long and short term. We all talk to ourselves anyway, so begin a written dialogue with yourself about what you want the outcome to be. Also, refer back to the tips for goal setting in Chapter 6 and 7.

Goals help you make choices when you're faced with behavior options. Goals help you figure out which behaviors you want to repeat, develop, expand and what behaviors you want to avoid, change, or diminish. Goals help you clarify what kind of person you want to be. It's like being a parent. The goals a parent has for the child's outcome determines the behaviors that are encouraged and those discouraged. You may say, "Well, I am not a parent so what's that got to do with anything?" But, think about it . . . in a way you are like a parent and *you* are your own child!!! Aren't you taking over the role of self-regulation that your parents once held? Obviously, if you're going to figure out if you are turning out the way *you* want to, you have to know what you want!

Developing your personal mission statement can help enormously with this process.

What Is Your Personality Like?

This second question will also help you be "smarter" about who you are. We use the word "personality" in everyday speaking. We might say, "Oh, she has such an out-going personality." What do we mean when we use that term? **Personality** refers to our characteristic patterns of behavior including our thoughts and emotions. In other words, even though we have lots of thoughts and feelings, and behave in all kinds of ways, we come to have consistency in certain ways of behaving. It is like a theme or refrain in a musical piece that comes back to repeat itself. Different theorists throughout the century have had different ideas about how personality is organized, how it develops, and how it influences our way of being. But no matter which theorist you follow, all personalities theories see the "personality" as that part of us which is responsible for our total behavior system.

Each person has his or her own collection of behavioral quirks that are unique to the individual. You and your brothers and sisters (if you have any) may have some behavior characteristics that are alike, but the whole package of how you and your brother behave is different for each one. So we each have our own personality scheme. Most researchers agree that this pattern of behaviors is formed in our early years and we probably cannot make major changes in our behavior patterns. Even though we may not be able to move from being a perfectionist to becoming a person who is the opposite and tolerates or even likes disorder, we can learn how our perfectionist pattern helps and hinders us. Then we can learn to monitor and manage our selves when our perfectionist self is operating. If we have an extroverted pattern in our behavior it is unlikely that we would ever change and become the opposite, an introverted person, but again, we can recognize how our extroversion helps and hinders us and manage our extroverted self accordingly.

In trying to develop an awareness and understanding of your personality, there are many sources or methods you could use. Numerous personality assessment instruments have been developed by theorists to determine personality patterns. One of the most popular instruments is the Myers-Briggs Type Indicator mentioned in Chapter 12. This instrument identifies sixteen different basic patterns based on the combined ratings of four different opposing behaviors. This inventory is based on the theory of Carl Jung, now considered one of the earliest transpersonal theorists. Other assessment tools have included two major factors, sixteen factors, or a new popular five-factor perspective.

Without visiting a psychologist for psychological assessment, you already have a handle on some of your patterns of behavior. You sense whether or not you are decisive, bright, shy, disorganized, out-going, competitive, calm, sad, suspicious, or quiet, for example. So besides formal psychological evaluation, introspection (looking inside yourself) is one way of discerning your personality patterns.

How Can You Get and Use Feedback?

Another way you can determine information about your personality, is to gather feedback from those who see you behave over time. Members of your family, friends, teachers, co-workers, neighbors, and bosses all see you exhibit whatever patterns are part of your personality. Ask them to describe you. Present them with a list of possible characteristics and ask them to circle the ones that pertain to you. Even though they see you in different roles you play, there will be some items that are circled by people from a variety of different relationship roles with you. The ones that are circled by nearly everyone may represent some of your strongest or primary traits.

Besides performance appraisals on the job, another place where written and verbal feedback is available is in learning settings. We have been getting "teachers' comments" on our behavior and work patterns for years in the form of anecdotal comments and in formal grading or rating systems. Think back over your report cards, and other school experiences to see what patterns in behavior are evident. Think of your interactions with your friends. How did they describe you or react to you when you were in school?

Patterns from the past will emerge at differing times throughout your history. For example, in early elementary school, this author used to consistently get a low rating on her report card in a behavior category entitled "self-control." Teachers would comment on the report card that the author "talked too much." In that setting, the extroverted me was a liability. But think about it, there are settings where being a talker is an asset. Giving a speech, teaching a class, making a presentation, and giving a toast at a wedding or a eulogy at a funeral. But if this "asset" is over-done this "strength" can change to a weakness. (Even today the author's friends and colleagues will say sometimes, "she talks too much!" . . . you see—personality characteristics **are** life long patterns!)

How Can You Keep a Balance?

Like the example above, often the very thing that we are best at, if taken to extremes, becomes our downfall. For example, if we are really good at persuasion, that can lead to a successful career in law, sales, business, or politics, but if we over-do our capacity for influencing others, it can begin to create the opposite affect. We might be self-destructive if we carry our strength too far by behaving in ways that are seen as dominant, insensitive, pushy, or overbearing. So the secret is to know our personality and find a healthy balance. This means recognizing how our personality patterns help and hinder us. A person who is suspicious may be less "accident prone" as that person may use his psychological antennae to check out the safety of things more often than a person who is very trusting. The trusting person may have more "accidents" because he puts himself, unconsciously, in more risky situations. So we can see where all of our traits can be our friend or foe.

The task for each of us is to, first of all, BE AWARE of our personality patterns. Then monitor where we are in our "balancing act" as we behave through various roles in the "high wire" of life. Learning to use our personality traits to maximize our effectiveness and monitor and manage them when they become self-destructive is a key to success.

Through thinking about yourself, reviewing and gathering feedback, and perhaps completing a personality survey, determine five adjectives that describe your personality. Decide how they are strengths and how they might be weaknesses. Keep them in mind . . . and use them well!

NEEDS

Understanding your needs is another important key to behaving in ways that move you closer to achieving your goals. You might have heard people commenting about someone's behavior by saying, "Oh, she just needs to be with people" or "he needs to always be at the top of the class," or "they always want to be in charge." These three comments reflect the work of David McClelland (1961) who pioneered in research attempting to describe and explain what drives people to behave in certain patterns. He called the first need alluded to above, the need for **affiliation**, to be in social settings, connected to other people. The second comment above describes someone McClelland would say has a need for achievement, always striving to be at the top, to accomplish a lot, to exhibit high levels of performance. The third description portrays what McClelland called the need for power. We all have some of these needs, but if you were to rank order these three from the most to middle to least in your behavior, how would you order them? Do you see examples of this ranking in your behavior? In any of your role models? What about your parents?

Another psychologist who studied needs and developed a theory was Abraham Maslow (1970). Maslow spent much of his life examining what was right with people instead of what is wrong. He was interested in determining the characteristics of extremely psychologically healthy people, extraordinary people who made a difference in this world. From his research he developed a **hierarchy of needs** that are depicted in pyramid form, since each level presumes the lower level(s) of needs is/are already met. His hierarchy is as follows:

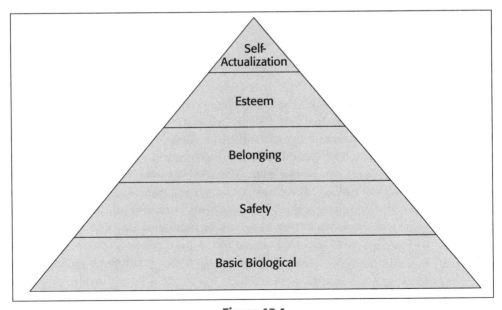

Figure 13.1

Maslow said our first level of needs were our biological needs for life, such as air, water, food, and sex. When these are satisfied, the next need level that emerges is safety which causes us to behave in ways to feel secure and safe. This would include shelter from the elements, and in today's world might include locks, alarms systems and bars on our windows! When safety needs are met, Maslow said we experience needs for connecting to other people, a need for affiliation, belonging, and social interaction. Then esteem needs would emerge and we would behave in ways to meet those needs. The final level of needs in Maslow's hierarchy is self-actualizing needs. These are needs of the highest order and include concern for things like *"the good, the true, and the beautiful."* People who are seeking to meet self-actualizing needs are experiencing a high level of fulfillment in their lives. As Maslow said, they are actualizing, or bringing to reality, the potential we all have as humans for the "good life." However, Maslow said that most people never reach functioning at this highest level. He described the characteristics of **self-actualized** people as:

> Being practical and realistic in problem solving
> Accepting of themselves and other people
> Being genuine, natural and spontaneous
> Having a need for privacy
> Being independent, self-reliant
> Having **peak experiences**, moments of exhilaration and ecstasy
> Identifying with and respecting all humankind
> Following strongly held values and ethics
> Maintaining deep, close relationships with a small number of people
> Demonstrating a broad, non-hostile sense of humor
> Being innovative and creative
> Being individualistic and resisting conformity
> Appreciating the natural and social environment

Whether we follow McClelland's, Maslow's or some other theorist's model, it is obvious that we behave in life to satisfy something that is creating motivation and the resulting behavior is to satisfy our needs. We move to change the level of tension that is created within us when unmet needs stimulate arousal.

The extent to which you can identify with your needs . . . be they for achievement, social needs, for power, for safety, and so forth, the more you can understand why you may be behaving in a certain way. Needs are often unconscious. We may realize we are hungry, but we may not realize that we have a strong social need operating. If we understood that, then we might know why we are partying or talking on the phone with a friend when our final exam is tomorrow! The idea of needs explains what motivates our behavior. This is why public schools have instituted breakfast programs for students. Administrators have recognized that if kids are hungry, they aren't going to care much about learning that one-plus-one makes two.

A good way to get in touch with what needs *are* operating in your life is to take an inventory of where you spend your time. What are you investing your efforts and energies doing? The theory says . . . there's the answer to your **motivation**. It's not a question of are you motivated or not motivated. It is a question of what needs are you motivated (and therefore behaving) to meet? What is the focus of your motivation?

We can learn a huge lesson from the advertisement industry in our country. Massive amounts of money are spent on advertising . . . and for what purpose? No, it's not to make us buy a product or service . . . it is for us to be convinced that we *NEED* it . . . then *we* take care of the buying part, sometimes even if we can't afford it! And look what a great success the advertisement industry has had . . . think of all the things we are convinced we *NEED* to live . . . cell phones, television sets, DVD players, the latest fad in clothing, toys, toys, toys!!

If we are rationally convinced that a specific degree, occupation, or lifestyle, is what we need, we will behave in ways to make it happen. So this brings us back to our goals. If we set goals and then find ourselves not motivated to do the things we must to achieve those goals . . . perhaps we "need" to work on our needs!! If we can convince ourselves, like the advertisers, that we need what those goals will bring, then we will behave to achieve those goals. This cycle of behavior starts with awareness of our need pattern that is presently operating and convincing ourselves to make changes in our priorities . . . to see our goals as *necessary . . . needed*. This will bring us to the power of commitment. Can you think of something in your life, perhaps not necessarily easy to achieve, that you decided you *WERE* going to do? You didn't say, "Maybe I'll do this," " I'll try to do this." Instead, you said *I AM* going to do this. Notice how whatever obstacles you had to overcome to do this thing, you figured a way to handle? And remember how good it felt when you could say, "Yessssss . . . I did it!"

If you convince yourself you **need** to meet that goal, you are lighting the flame of commitment which fires you into action. The intensity of this kind of energy is amazing. And you are on your way to achieving your goal, meeting your new *NEED*!

The first step to reaching success is awareness . . . then commitment . . . then comes change. Become aware of what needs are driving your behavior. Think of how can you work with those needs using them to maximize your success, override them with newly determined needs, or stop and satisfy them . . . then move on.

Triggers for Positive and Negative Behaviors

One of the smartest things you can do in learning about yourself, is to become aware of **triggers**. Triggers "set you off," either in a positive way—energized to behave in ways to be effective, or in a negative way—aroused to act out your emotions and attitudes in ways that are destructive, to others and/or yourself. In the medical world they speak of "triggers" that set off physical problems, like allergies or migraine headaches and admonish patients to become aware of trigger situations and avoid them. On the positive side, health care givers encourage the presence of trigger situations like aromatherapy, massage, meditation, deep breathing and the like that activate calming behaviors and reduce stress.

Likewise, it is important to know your personality patterns, the repeated feelings, and thoughts that when they come, cause you to become aroused and to behave intensely . . . either with positive actions and the success that brings, or with behaviors that are self-defeating.

For example, consider this scenario: A wife and husband have been married for several years. The wife has a patterned behavior in her personality. Each time her husband, a real estate agent, announces that he will be home late as he is still working with a client, she becomes angry. When he arrives home and greets her, she begins berating him. She then ignores him as if he didn't exist. She refuses to speak to him, walks out of the room, and if he tries to talk to her, she explodes with angry accusations, curse words, and blames him for the whole blow up. He withdraws and the silent treatment may go on for days. Eventually, the couple seeks counseling together where the wife discovers that her reaction to her husband's late arrivals home are tied to a sense of abandonment she experienced with her father when she was a very young girl. When her husband does not come home at the usual time, this brings back for her emotions she experienced as a child and fears that her father had left her. She learned that she could identify the triggers to this and could use her cognitive skills to re-think her response. She first felt fear that triggered anger which in turn triggered her verbally abusive reaction. This behavior was self-destructive as well as harmful to her husband whose reaction was to withdraw from her . . . ironically "abandoning" her in a sense. The husband came to understand the dynamics, too, and learned to help with the situation by assisting his wife in anticipating times when he might be late. They worked together to resolve the problem. This doesn't mean that the wife had a personality change . . . the triggers are still there in that situation. But the wife learned to be aware, to recognize the triggers, monitor her feelings and manage her behavior when the anger was set off.

The "triggers" we have come from somewhere. Are we born with them? No way. The specific events or incidents or words or situations that initiate predictable responses from us are learned associations. And we probably learned them early in our lives, perhaps long before we really remember the original incidents. These incidents involved pleasant or unpleasant consequences in our earlier times and those same feelings get generated today, even though the circumstances are different. Triggers can stir feelings that are happy, delightful, and positive as well as feelings that are sad, uncomfortable, and negative. The key is to identify the triggers that set off negative responses and avoid and monitor them, and to seek out those triggers that spark our joyous feelings.

Consider the following set of emotions and fill in the blanks for examples of patterns in your behavior:

FEELING	BEHAVIORAL RESPONSE	TRIGGERED BY
Anger		
Sadness		
Anxiety		
Power		
Compulsion		
Joy		
Calm		
Amused		
Alive		
Happy		

Warmth

Love

Exhilaration

The steps for managing negative trigger situations in your life are (1) be aware of what sets off the reaction, (2) monitor the situation, (3) use your cognitive self to explore the logic of the situation, and (4) determine alternative responses that you can employ to minimize or avoid self-destructive consequences. In the case of positive emotions, become aware of the triggers that initiate them. Then deliberately gravitate to situations that exposure you to those triggers that enhance your happiness.

Handling your personality patterns is important in moving toward achieving your goals and meeting your needs. The extent to which you become proficient in using triggers to your advantage, the more personally effective you will be. You will be "people smart" about yourself. You will also be better prepared to engage in understanding the behaviors of others.

UNDERSTANDING OTHERS

In addition to understanding yourself, your career success also hinges on your being able to understand and interact effectively with other people. Hiring and firing data shows the importance of "people skills." Research on ratings of top performers consistently rank interpersonal skills, emotional intelligence, and political skills as being more important than mental ability or intelligence (Goleman, 1998, Ferris, 1999).

In other words, no matter how traditionally "smart" you may be, it is your "people smarts" that are most significant in landing you *"excellence"* in your performance ratings. Such ratings are the bases for decisions about retention, promotion, advancement and growth opportunities in employment settings. There are many parallels between working with yourself and with others in sensing, analyzing, and behaving effectively in your work setting. These can be seen in the following model that is called the "People Smart Pagoda." In building any structure, you have to start from the ground up. The same is true in building your skills in working with people.

Awareness—of yourself and of others—stands as a foundation upon which to build skills for self-management and skills for connecting effectively with the other people in your work environment. We've discussed methods for becoming more aware of yourself. We looked at how introspection and feedback help you gather information to better understand your goals, needs, personality and situational triggers. In the same way we can develop a sharper awareness of others in our environment by examining these same factors in the people at work.

To begin, we can use careful observation of those around us. This means tuning in all our senses to gather information about those around us. Not only do we need to look at and listen as intently as we can at the behavior of those around us, but we must look at the non-verbal messages being sent. Review the sections in Chapter 9, where we discussed the skills of reading nonverbal cues and of empathic listening. In listening empathically, we attempt to understand what it is like to be in another person's skin. This enables us to gain insights into why that person is behaving as she does. In other

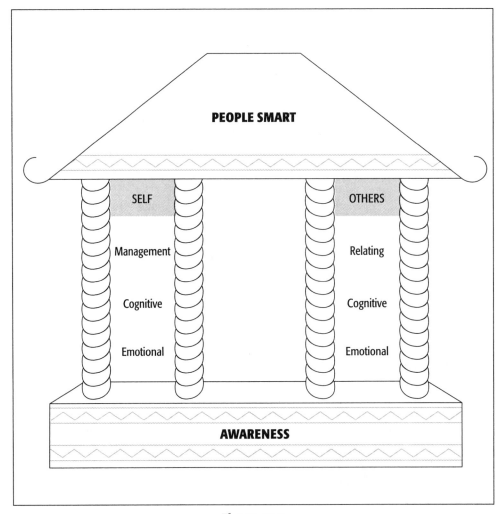

Figure 13.2

words, the best way to understand the goals, needs, personalities and behavioral triggers of others is to be a keen observer of cues and a sensitive and empathic listener.

Goals

Just as understanding how your goals direct your behavior, you can gain a sense of how the goals of group members at work influences their behavior. This will help you understand the dynamics of the group. Ask yourself, "What appear to be the goals of the group as a whole? Does a common group goal exist? Is it written down anywhere? Does everyone understand and agree on what the group is trying to achieve?"

Likewise, ask yourself, "What goals have individual members articulated for themselves as members of this group?" What is each individual person trying to achieve in addition to the common group goal? Such goals could be an opportunity to learn new things, a promotion, a chance to do something different, or a chance to make more money.

Personality

Obviously, you are not going to administer a personality assessment inventory to anyone, but through keen observation and noting behaviors you can learn something about their personality patterns. Although we all have some of all these behaviors going on from time to time . . . what consistency or patterns do we see in the actions of others? Are they:

> Extroverted or Introverted?
> Rigid or Flexible?
> Organized or Free Flowing?
> Happy or Sad?
> Stable or Moody?
> Secure or Insecure?
> Decisive or Wishy-Washy?
> Conservative or Liberal?
> Confident or Uncertain?
> Energetic or Laid Back?
> Positive or Negative?

Think of three of your closest friends. You could probably describe patterns you perceive in their personality. Write them down. Now, think about a teacher you have had that you really liked. Describe that favorite teacher's personality. How would you describe the personality of your parents? Bosses you may have had? See … you are probably already thinking of patterns in the personalities of people you know or have known.

You become more expert in "reading" other people's behavior from a process that simulates the method scientists use to find out new information. It begins with experience in being a detective of sorts in a work group. First you observe carefully, trying to gather evidence of actions, comments, and body language that give you a hunch about that person. Then "test out" your hunch or hypothesis about that person's personality by future observations, even predicting what that person will do and discovering you are either (1) right (maybe this **is** a pattern), or (2) you're wrong (mistaken impression . . . back to the drawing board!). We do this sort of thing at some level each time we meet a new person and form impressions. Usually we are not aware we are doing this. But if we work consciously at being a better observer of behavior, both verbal and non-verbal, this can help us develop expertise in "psyching" out people in our work environment.

When we get a better sense of the personality patterns of those we work with, we are better able to understand their behavior. This allows us to think and chose approaches that are more effective in dealing with that specific person. For example, in working with a person who has "dominance" as part of their personality, when making suggestions for change at work, you might make a special effort to express your suggestion in a way that doesn't threaten that person's perceived authority. Compare these two approaches:

Scene 1

"Hi Steve, how's it going?"

"Pretty busy. Hey Roger, I thought I told you to be here at 7:30. It's almost 7:45. We're going to be slammed with customers today."

"Well, instead of your always making up the schedule like we are just robots, why don't you let us pick when we want to come in. I'm not a morning person. If we did the scheduling a different way, maybe things would go better."

"I am the manager, and don't *you* forget it! I know how we need to staff this place! Now get busy!"

Scene 2

"Hi Steve, how's it going?

"Pretty busy. Hey Roger, I thought I told you to be here at 7:30. It's almost 7:45. We're going to be slammed with customers today."

"Sorry I got here late. Listen, I was thinking about my being late sometimes, and I know you have a handle on what would work and what wouldn't. I was wondering what you might think of this thought I had about scheduling. When things are less busy, maybe we could talk and I could share my ideas to see what you think about them. Okay?"

"That sounds okay for later. Right now we have to get going."

"Right, we'll talk later. Thanks for listening. I'd better hustle."

In the first scene, Roger does two things that tick Steve off. First he tries to put the blame on Steve, his manager, for his being late. This means he is not being **proactive** as we discussed in Chapter 2. Secondly, he is attacking Steve's competence and authority in how he does the staff scheduling. Especially if he knows that Steve has a dominant personality, do you see what a mistake this is? The first scene will probably continue to go "down hill" from there.

In the second scene, Roger takes responsibility for his lateness. He recognizes that Steve has a need to be in control, and acknowledges his "competence" in knowing what will work or not before Roger indicates he has an idea about scheduling. He asks, doesn't tell, Steve about sharing his idea. He is also sensitive to the reality that there is a lot of work to do as the place is busy and he has contributed to the stress with his lateness. He doesn't expect that things will stop here and now so he can discuss his idea. He does, however, plant a seed . . . that he wants to share an idea, and he solicits some agreement from Steve to listen later. Wisely, he doesn't press for a specific time at the moment as he needs to address the need to pitch in and get to work. He can come back to Steve's agreement to talk at another less busy time and try to set up a specific time to talk.

Being aware of Steve's personality, as well as being proactive, helps Roger to achieve his goals in this situation. In the next three days, carefully observe interactions you see in your work environment. Try to look at the dynamics of how what one person says to the other and how they say it, leads to a type of response, which then leads to the next person's answer, and so forth. If you spend time observing these interactions, you can begin to see *how* one comment sets the stage for a type of response. You can see that the emotional and cognitive path followed forward between two parties is a flowing, dynamic, exchange that is mutually inspired. With practice, you get better and better at observing and analyzing how the exchange between people moves back and forth. You can pinpoint the specific comments and emotional expressions that shift the content and the tone of the interaction. Knowing something about how the parties involved "tick" can help you anticipate their behavior.

Note some of your observations in writing and re-read them over several times. Like a poem or other piece of literature, each time you revisit the writing and think about it, new insights and understanding can emerge. The more you do this, the more you can increase your sensitivity and awareness of the way each person's personality is an instrument in the symphony we call human interaction.

Needs

Closely related to "personality," the needs that are operating at a given time will motivate a person to act one way or another. Just as you gain an understanding of your own needs and how that causes you to behave to meet those needs, the same is going on for the others with whom you work. Using Maslow's hierarchy or McClelland's theory of needs, you can gain an awareness of patterns of behavior that reflect the needs of those around you.

To the extent that you can sense needs others may have, you can be a part of meeting those needs while also meeting your own needs. In the example above with Roger and Steve, needs for power in both parties were operating. Steve, being dominant, needed to maintain control. Roger, desiring to have some power in giving input to the decision making, wanted to share his idea. In scene 2 we could see both of these needs being met. It would appear that Roger also had a need for affiliation operating that was stronger than his need for power, as he addressed the issue in a different way in scene 2, one designed to avoid alienation by Steve. Roger's behavior in scene 2 paved the way for a possible win-win outcome, but in scene 1, Roger was obviously pushing for a win-lose outcome that could only further hamper their working relationship.

Social and Cultural Conventions

If we are to understand behavior exchanges we must be aware of the influences of culture, ethnicity, age, gender and other social or cultural aspects that shape our behavior and that of others. As we discussed in Chapter 11, the increasing diversity of the workplace challenges us to expand our knowledge in this area. To the extent that we can recognize the context from which a person comes, we can appreciate their differences from ourselves rather than being threatened by them.

An awareness of social conventions regarding **idioms** (expressions or sayings) in a culture is important to our understanding of others. If we take everything said in its literal meaning we may be confused and uninformed. If someone refers to a person as "a nut" someone unfamiliar with the idiom might be confused . . . wondering "a walnut, an almond? I don't get it!"

Further, the general rules of courtesy and custom, sometimes called etiquette, are important to understand lest we unknowingly offend someone by behavior that is considered by that person to be rude. Discomfort might be caused when different customs are practiced. For example, suppose someone from a culture that is more reserved regarding physical closeness is approached by someone who hugs or touches her. Both parties may feel awkward and uncomfortable. The reserved person may feel the other has violated her space; the "hugger" may see the reserved person as "cold." Ignorance of these areas can lead to embarrassment at best and disrespect at worst in our interactions with others.

Triggers for Positive and Negative Behaviors

Just as we discussed emotional intelligence as helping us recognize triggers that set off emotions and behaviors in yourself, it is helpful to be able to identify triggers that can set off other people. Returning to the Steve and Roger scenarios, perhaps Roger observed past situations where Steve came down hard in asserting his dominance over others. If he paid close attention to what happened just before Steve got "set off" he may have a clue regarding triggers for Steve. By using this information and consciously choosing how to approach Steve, Roger was able in scene 2 to avoid triggering a "shoot out" between the two of them. Watching carefully for times when Steve is especially happy and friendly, Roger may be able to figure out a pattern for initiating this positive behavior.

Being aware of what makes others "tick" can not only help you avoid "ticking them off," but can assist in contributing to their positive thoughts, feelings and behaviors. Behaviorist theories hold that all behavior is conditioned by what happens in the environment. This would suggest that we can influence those around us to behave positively. Gaining an understanding of what events initiate what responses, perhaps we can help our bosses, co-workers, and customers act positively. This, in turn, becomes a reward for us. Now is this being "people smart" or what?

Putting It All to Work

In this chapter we have examined the ideas of being people smart from the literature. We have emphasized the importance of being an astute observer and developing your people skills. We began recognizing how important it is to know yourself, your goals, personality, needs and behavioral triggers. This means having a sense of awareness about your own emotions, thoughts and behaviors. It also means using your cognitive self in concert with your emotional self to manage yourself for success.

When you turned to knowing about others, you discovered that the process is parallel to that for yourself. In fact, you could conceptualize the process as building a "People Smart Pagoda." In this model the same foundation of awareness is necessary for self and for others. You also need to know about the goals, personality, needs and triggers that guide your behavior and the behavior of others. These form the supporting columns for being people smart. Also it is necessary that you sharpen your skills in empathic listening in order to understand others. The social conventions of courtesy and etiquette and other social and cultural norms are important, too. Further you need to practice your observational skills to enhance your understanding and skill in relating to others.

In summary, if you seek to achieve career success, knowing your job and having the required work training and skills is a necessary, but not sufficient condition. To really reach excellence in your work performance, you must also be "people smart!"

SELF EXERCISES

1. Grab a piece of paper and let's do some free writing. Jot down the things that come to mind regarding your career. What do you want to accomplish in your career? How long will this take? Who are the other people who figure into the equation such as spouse, children, co-workers, clients, or boss? After you have listed about five different things you want to achieve through your career, ask yourself what these successes look like? Imagine yourself ten years from now . . . what will your life be like?

2. In your self-discovery journaling, write down three to five areas where you invest most of your time. This will reveal to you something about your motivations and the needs that are operating in your life.

3. Observe a stranger at a restaurant, in the library, or some setting for at least ten minutes focusing only on their behavior. Do not judge or evaluate or analyze the behavior. Just notice it and perhaps jot down descriptions of the behavior. This exercise is to help you sharpen your observation skills.

4. Identify someone you consider to be "people smart." Observe their behavior carefully and how their interactions are effective. Do you see any patterns?

KEY TERMS

goal	proactive	multiple intelligences
hierarchy of needs	affiliation	interpersonal
motivation	self-actualization	intrapersonal
triggers	idioms	emotional intelligence
"people smart"	personality	
peak experiences	needs	

CHAPTER 13 QUESTIONS

Short-Answer Questions

1. If I am able to understand myself and appreciate my feelings, Gardner would say this is _____ intelligence.

2. Gardner says there are how many different types of intelligence? _____

3. Goleman says being aware of feelings and changing frames positively is being _____ intelligent.

4. To determine direction and focus, it is helpful to set _____.

5. Characteristic patterns of behavior including thoughts and feelings is a definition of _____.

6. Three sources of feedback to learn about yourself are _____.

7. What three types of needs did McClelland identify?

   _____.

8. List the five levels of Maslow's hierarchy of needs.

   _____.

9. A person who realizes his or her potential and has peak experiences, is realistic, self-reliant, centered in values and ethics and identifies with all human beings. We would say that this person is _____.

10. What industry in our country works to entice us to establish certain needs for things? _____.

11. A way to understand our needs is to take an inventory of _____.

12. Environmental stimuli that causes us to have an intense emotional reaction is referred to as a _____.

13. In addition to knowing ourselves, to be "people smart" we must also know _____.

Essay Questions

1. Compare and contrast the behavior of someone you know who is "people smart" and someone who is not.

2. Discuss the advantages of setting goals.

3. Describe your own personality.

4. Describe the behavior of someone with a need for power.

5. Which of Maslow's needs is the most important? Why?

6. Discuss a "trigger" that sets you off in a positive mood.

7. Why are "people skills" so important in the workplace?

8. Discuss the difference between group goals and individual goals. Give examples.

9. Describe a personality pattern for some one whose behavior you can sometimes predict.

10. Describe a "trigger" either positive or negative you have identified for a person in your family.

14

Make Work Fun

Once upon a time there were two people sleeping in their own houses. At 6:30 a.m. alarm clocks sounded in both homes. In both bedrooms an arm stretched over to the alarm clock to find the button. And that was the end of the similarity.

GEORGE hit the snooze alarm and dozed off for a few more minutes. When the alarm sounded again, he thought, "Oh, darn, it's Monday morning already." George dragged himself out of bed and stumbled toward the kitchen to find the coffee pot. "Why does it have to be Monday?" he moaned. Eventually he grabbed a donut with his coffee, got himself dressed and dashed out thinking, "I'm going to be late again . . . oh well, who cares?"

At work, George frowned as he entered the office. "Man, it is too hot in here. Why do they keep this office so hot?" He passed a couple of co-workers who greeted him smiling. "What's with them?" he thought. "What's there to be so happy about?" He sat at his desk and stared blankly at the pile of papers on his desk. "I'll never get this all done. This is too much." For a moment he put his head down on his desk, but lifted it up and started taking the papers off the pile, to begin work.

At noontime, George decided he had to stay in and work. So he ordered a quick sandwich and brought it back to the office to eat while working over lunch. "I'm so far behind, I'll never catch up," he mumbled as the clock struck one.

In the afternoon, George kept looking at the clock. "It's moving so slowly," he muttered. "When will this day end?"

HARRY turned off the alarm and hopped out of bed to stretch. "What a sleep! Boy, I slept like a rock," he thought. He dressed eagerly and ate breakfast while reading the newspaper. Then he rose slowly and eagerly headed for the door. "What a nice day," he thought as he headed out into the morning sun. "Not a cloud in that blue sky . . . nice way to start."

At work, Harry smiled and greeted his co-workers. "How was your weekend?" he asked the fellow at the next desk, remembering that this guy was meeting his girlfriend's parents over the weekend. He settled in at his desk and reviewed his calendar. Next, he began organizing his day by making a "To Do" list. Then he launched into reviewing a report for the scheduled afternoon meeting. He mused, "This is a well-done report."

At noontime, Harry left the office to meet his friend from college for lunch. He strolled down the block to the sidewalk café they agreed on. "Couldn't have picked a better day to enjoy eating outside," he thought.

In the afternoon, Harry, report and notes in hand, entered the meeting thinking, "This'll be a challenge!"

Which of these two would you rather be? If these guys worked for Snow White, we might have Grumpy George and Happy Harry. How are their attitudes different? How are they approaching their work? Which one is making work fun?

Given how much of our lives is invested in our work, and how closely the quality of our lives is linked to our work gratification, it's something to think about. This is why in Chapter 12 we noted how important your career choice is to your happiness. The greatest occupational arrangement is when your work reflects your passion, that which you love to do. This is usually something that you do very well. It is like a positive cycle. Those things we like, we prefer to do. Since we prefer them, we do them more often. Doing them more often makes us more proficient and so we like them even more. Think of your history. What subjects did you like the best in elementary school? Did that continue into high school? Is there some connection between that subject and the career choice you've considered or decided upon? A study by British behavioral scientists found a connection between desires in youth and success in adult life. In this longitudinal study, fifty people were followed from age 7 to age 35 (a total of 28 years). The findings showed that nearly all of the subjects wound up in a professional area related to their interests during ages 7 to 14. Most strayed from these interests after childhood, but those adults who were successful returned to their childhood dreams by the age of 35. For some it was as a hobby or leisure time activity (Lonier, 1994). This suggests that we revisit our early years and look for patterns in our interests. If you have years of working experience, what have been your likes and dislikes in these experiences? Terri Levine (2002) marketing expert, author, and professional coach for people exploring work issues, suggests a "looking back exercise" where you find a quiet place to think and ask yourself questions and write down your answers. Ask questions such as "What were the activities that gave you pleasure? What jobs or volunteer activities did you really like in your teen years. How did you feel about doing the job or activity?" She relates case studies where by doing this "looking back exercise," adults seeking a career change discovered their real enthusiasm. Do you know what really engages your excitement? Are you following your passion?

Additional factors that matter for work enjoyment include autonomy, opportunities for growth and learning, and positive triggers that keep you feeling good. Also significant is the ability to cope with problems in the workplace and resolve them in a way that doesn't compromise your values and ethics. Being informed regarding potential issues can help you prevent problems or minimize their impact.

TAKING CHARGE

When you think about going to work, who are you really working for? Are you working for a company or organization? A boss? Your landlord? The auto insurance company? Or are you working for yourself? By this we don't necessarily mean that you are self-employed but that you are an employed self. Confusing? Well, look at it this way. Your whole being is involved in your career. If you change jobs, *you* are the thing that stays intact that is moving to a new position. You need to see yourself as somewhat of an entrepreneur in the workplace. More and more today, workers in all types of fields are recognizing that the stability of a life long or even several years in the same company isn't going to happen. As one study points out, before 1990 an unspoken contract existed between employer and employee. That was, "You commit to working here for the long term and we will offer you job security, good pay and promotions." However, economic recession, re-engineering and downsizing caused a breach in that contract. Now there is a new mindset among young people beginning their careers since 1990. They do not expect life-time employment with a single employer. They consider personal fulfillment in their work a birthright, and to find it they will take different options. They work as free agents or even become self-employed to find fulfillment (Hay Group, 2000). In reality, we are all self-employed. You need to sense that you are in charge of you, and that the skills and talents you possess are valuable to the organization.

As we discussed in Chapter 2, being proactive and taking responsibility for yourself is an important step to personal effectiveness. Likewise, applying this habit in your work life will contribute to your autonomy, your being in control. Remember the discussion of stress hardiness attitudes in Chapter 5. Control was the first one. If problems occur, you are the one to do something about the impact these problems have on you. If there is something you want or desire to achieve, you are the one to make that happen. Remember we referred to this as having an **internal locus of control**. If you are not in control of your life then who is? Do you want others controlling you or do you want to take charge of your life?

Being at the helm in your life leads to a sense of hope. This is an emotion that is tied to optimism. If not this, what is the alternative? Hopelessness, helplessness and despair. Who wants that in life? One German study (Goleman, 1998) examined subjects faced with a task of increasing pressure. Subjects with the highest hope of success produced brain chemicals that enabled them to keep functioning at a high level of effectiveness. Further, they did not produce levels of cortisol, a chemical which is harmful to our bodies and which a crisis mode would induce. In contrast, subjects in this study who were motivated by fear of failure had very high cortisol levels. This finding reinforces the old self-fulfilling prophecy idea that "*what I believe will happen, will happen.*" In this study those with an "*I can do this*" attitude stayed more calm, focused and productive. People who were not "taking charge" were "freaking out" from the increased pressure. This is where the ideas and strategies in Chapter 5 for mastering stress come in handy. Keep in mind the old adage: "*Can't never did anything.*"

Optimism is also related to persistence. This is an important key to career success. We hear that Michael Jordan was told by his school coach one year that he wasn't good enough to play on his high school team. Now think about it. He could have given up, given away his basketball, and quit. But he was using the other two C's of stress hardiness attitudes. He had commitment to his goal and he saw this as a challenge, not a defeat. Do you suppose Michael Jordan has made or missed most of the basketball shots he's tried? Of course, he has missed more. Look at the lesson in persistence he exemplifies.

When things don't go our way, when difficult things happen, when we make mistakes, we have the opportunity to learn. Mistakes are a blessing in disguise. Think about it. When you leave a test you have taken, which questions are you pondering in your mind? Probably not the ones you got right, but the ones you missed. This spurs you to figure things out. A workshop speaker once shared an expression that has relevance here:

Winners lose more than losers,
but they're winners because they stay in the game.

Remember this and choose to be a winner, to be the master of your life, and take charge!

INTRINSIC AND EXTRINSIC MOTIVATION

The source of your motivation can be **intrinsic** (internal) or **extrinsic** (external). We have experience with both throughout our lives in interactions with our parents, friends, teachers, and bosses.

The two types of motivation are contrasted as follows:

Intrinsic	Extrinsic
Comes from within the person	Comes from external world, from other people
Incites passion	Helps set goals
Makes you feel good	Heightens expectation
Rewards you while you work	Rewards you outside work, afterward

Examples of intrinsic motivation would include mastery, self-esteem, the joy from accomplishment, pleasure while doing the task, and intensive engagement in the work. Examples of extrinsic motivation would include money, grades, candy, and praise.

A family trying to promote learning in their child might give him money for each "A" he brings home on his report card. The child makes the connection between "A's" and money. As he gets older, he may avoid subjects in which he thinks he might not get an "A." What's happened? Getting grades has become more important than learning. Hopefully, some learning occurred in the classes in which he got the "A's", but what about the subjects he avoided in high school? When grades become the extrinsic reward we are seeking, it influences our behavior. For example, if due to procrastination, you might put off studying a subject, then stay up all night cramming for an exam to get the grade. You may pass the course but not retain much information. In contrast, what about a situation when a person wants to know? She may not even take a course. She may get a book, a video, attend a demonstration, or ask someone to learn what she wants to know. There is no grade...the knowing is the thing! And she feels the reward *while* she is doing it as she learns.

How does this show up in the workplace? Managers and supervisors try to "motivate" people to work hard and do a good job. Often they use rewards such as money, time off, or public recognition to manipulate workers into working hard. In many places we have seen an "Employee of the Month" plaque hanging on the wall with the name and picture of a worker being displayed.

Research by Teresa Amabile (1995) suggests that your job could be killing your creativity. She identifies two culprits: (1) close monitoring of your work and (2) lack of choices for getting a good evaluation or earning a reward. These factors lead to lower levels of intrinsic motivation and higher levels of extrinsic motivation that results in lower levels of creativity. She indicates that people are most creative when they are motivated by the satisfaction and challenge of the work itself rather than by external pressures. In an experiment, Amabile gathered a group of professional writers of poetry, fiction and drama. They completed a questionnaire about their attitudes toward writing. One group completed a questionnaire that dealt only with intrinsically interesting aspects of writing. Another group responded to questions only about extrinsic reasons for writing. A third group served as a control group and did not complete a questionnaire. After finishing their questionnaires, all the writers were told to write a short poem. Several poetry experts served as judges to critique the poems. The results were dramatic according to

Amabile. She found that the control group writers wrote poems judged fairly high on creativity, the intrinsic group wrote poems judged somewhat higher in creativity than the control group, and the extrinsic group wrote poems judged significantly lower in creativity than the poems of other groups. The researcher comments on the implications of these findings where she points out the *"potential effects of extrinsic constraints in everyday work environments on the creativity of people who work there."*

Flow

Mihalyi Csikzentmihalyi, former chair of the University of Chicago Department of Psychology, now at Claremont Graduate University and Director of the Quality of Life Research Center has for over 30 years been studying the lives of thousands of people seeking to find what makes people satisfied, fulfilled, and happy. He has described the concept of **flow**, a state in which people find their work exhilarating and in which they perform at their best no matter what type of work they do. Flow occurs when our skills are fully engaged and we feel ourselves stretching to meet challenges. We become lost in our work and so fully engaged that we lose all concept of time. In this state our work seems to run smoothly, effortlessly, with adaptability. The flow itself is a pleasure. In studying flow this researcher discovered that workers, on average, were in this state about half the time while on the job, and about 20 percent of time during leisure time. In contrast, workers reported the most common emotional state during leisure was apathy (Goleman, 1998). Csikzentmihalyi (pronounced chick-sent-me-high-ee) found that most people live at two extremes. They are (1) stressed by work or obligations or (2) they are bored by spending their leisure time on activities that were passive. He states that people can live enhanced, happier lives by learning new skills and increasing the challenges they face each day (Chamberlain, 1998). He has found that a typical day is full of anxiety and boredom; however "flow experiences provide the flashes of intense living against this dull background" (Csikszentmihalyi, 1990). Flow as an optimal experience is characterized by:

- a sense of playfulness
- a feeling of being in control
- concentration and highly focused attention
- mental enjoyment of activity for its own sake
- a distorted sense of time
- a match between the challenge at hand and one's skills

People experience more flow from what they do on their jobs than from leisure activities such as watching television. It seems that TV's main virtue is that is occupies the mind without demands. Flow is hard to achieve without effort. Flow is not "wasting time." Those who learn to control inner experience will be able to determine the quality of their lives, which Csikszentmihalyi says is as close as any of us can get to being happy (1993). He outlines the pathway to flow as follows:

1. **Make it a Game**—Consider tasks as games with rules, objective, challenges to be overcome and with rewards.
2. **Have a Powerful Goal**—As you play the game, think often of the overriding social, intellectual or spiritual purpose that drives your efforts.

3. **Focus**—Let all distractions, those within or without, go. Center all your attention on the game.

4. **Surrender to the Process**—Just let go. Don't try or strain to achieve your objective. Let it happen and enjoy the process of work.

5. **Experience Ecstasy**—(the feeling, not the drug!) This is the natural results of the previous four steps. It will hit you suddenly, by surprise. There is no mistaking it. This is a "natural high."

6. **Create Peak Productivity**—Your ecstatic state opens reservoirs of resourcefulness, creativity and energy. Productivity and quality of work shoot through the roof (1990).

What this researcher determined after many years of examining this concept of flow is happiness is not something that happens. It isn't from being lucky or random chance. It is not something that money can buy or power command. It doesn't depend on external events, but instead, how we interpret them. Happiness, Csikszentmihalyi writes, is a condition that must be prepared for, cultivated, and defended privately by each individual. It is in learning to control our inner selves that we create the merit of life's experience. Indeed our happiness comes not from the outer world around us, but from what we experience within. It comes from intrinsic, not extrinsic payoffs.

Although all work settings have extrinsic rewards such as performance reviews, promotions, and bonuses, Goleman (1998) also considers the most powerful motivators as those that are internal, not external. He points out that both *motivation* and *emotion* come from the same Latin root meaning "to move." The internal feelings we experience while working on a task are more intense than rewards being offered by others. He further notes a study of more than seven hundred men and women at the end of their business or professional careers who were asked what were the greatest sources of satisfaction. The first three were: (1) creative challenge of the work, (2) stimulation of the work, and (3) the chance to keep learning. The next three in order were: (1) pride in accomplishments, (2) friendships at work and (3) assisting or teaching other workers. Further down the list came status and even lower than that came the financial rewards (Goleman, 1998).

The indications from research are that what we are feeling about our work is much more significant than the external "carrots" that may be held out to us. Knowing this, it makes lots of sense to tune in once more to our self-awareness and discover our feelings. We know how high-spirited our mood is when we are doing what we love to do.

OVERCOMING PROBLEMS IN THE WORKPLACE

As we think about making work fun and functioning on an intrinsically motivated "high," it is important to come back to the reality that problems are inevitable in the workplace if we are there long enough. Being informed about some these potential problems and ways to cope with them can help us proactively prevent or lessen the intensity of these situations. Let's examine a few of the more common problems found in most work settings.

Substance Abuse

As pointed out in Chapter 4, over a billion people on this earth are dependent on alcohol and or illicit drugs. The cost of this in the workplace is seen in behaviors such as shoddy quality of work, low productivity, inconsistent performance, bizarre behaviors, absenteeism, and problems relating to others. In addition, there is often a lack of interest in work as well as a lack of concentration that adds to carelessness. This, in turn adds to health hazards in the workplace such as the 40% of on-the-job injuries and about half of all work-related deaths that occur because of alcohol or drug abuse (Dubrin, 1999, DeCenzo, 1997).

Many larger companies maintain employee assistance programs where help with substance abuse and other personal problems is provided. In the case of alcohol or drug abuse there are hospital based rehabilitation programs that help with overcoming addiction. Also there are self-help twelve step groups such as Alcoholics Anonymous and Narcotics Anonymous that are available to people who want to stop their addictions. Twelve step programs help individuals with substance abuse problems to develop a support network of people to aid in recovery and maintenance of sobriety.

Lack of Advancement

Another problem that may be experienced in the workplace is not being considered for promotions for which an employee has aspirations. As mentioned in Chapter 12, studies have shown that having a **mentor** in the work setting is significant for success. A mentor we learned is an experienced worker who takes a new worker "under his or her wing" to help one understand such realities as (1) how things work in the environment, (2) the accepted norms for behavior, (3) who key people are in the organization, and (3) how one can get ahead. One problem for female workers is that, especially in certain business and professional settings, there are few if any mentors available. In some careers, women have only recently be employed or promoted to management positions. It is important to seek out experienced workers that might serve as mentors when you begin your career. As discussed earlier, some organizations actually assign an experienced worker to function as a helper in orienting new employees.

Another strategy for moving up in the organization is to discuss your aspirations with your supervisor, especially when you meet for your annual performance appraisal. Obviously, this assumes you have rapport with your supervisor and that your evaluations of your work have been positive. Your supervisor has the information or can point you in the right direction to find it regarding position postings, availability, and educational/experience requirements for these positions. The human resource or personnel office is another source of information and guidance for exploring ways to move ahead in your organization.

Demonstrating your commitment and motivation for meeting the organization's goals is of paramount importance if you have aspirations for advancement. In your career, if you wish to make a move, you need information about the positions in which you are interested. You need to know what is required for that job and then demonstrate that you have the desired skills and knowledge. In today's terms, what we bring to an organization is referred to as our "added value." We need to know that we do, in fact, add value to a company or organization by the work we do, and be thoughtful in making this known effectively as we seek advancement. Companies are beginning to recognize that employees who truly add the most value to the organization are those who are engaged in their work and enjoying what they do. These companies are seeking to increase opportunities for intrinsic rather than extrinsic rewards (Hay Group, 2001).

You need to review your own people smarts and leadership skills since this area is especially crucial for positions that involve managing others. Inquire with the training department (if there is one in your company) for ways to secure assistance in enhancing your skills in this area if needed.

Be aware that moving up in your own department or area may be more difficult than seeking a position in a new section or division of the organization. There may be limited upward mobility in your own department. Sometimes, making a move up means making a move out . . . not only out of the department, but out of the company or organization to another employer.

Remember the power of persistence. Gather as much information and feedback as you can if you have been passed over for promotions. Try to identify your goals for preparing yourself for the position you want, and don't give up.

Burnout

Another potential problem in the workplace to be aware of is called **burnout**. This is a collection of physical, emotional and mental reactions that reflect exhaustion. Burnout is the result of constant and re-occurring emotional pressures with people in the workplace and/or at home. It can also be caused by poor management of yourself in time, feeling unable or unequal to do a job, an overwhelming workload, inability to adapt to change, lack of supervision from a manager, and an inability to meet deadlines. Burnout sufferers tend to disengage from their work and possibly the people around them. Production suffers. The person begins to have a negative self-concept and negative attitudes toward work and the workplace. The person is drained and may appear apathetic, angry, withdrawn, or lazy. Physical symptoms such as headaches, chest pains, gastrointestinal problems and back pains may occur.

Burnout can happen to anyone who is experiencing too many pressures with too little support, but it is especially found among the helping professions such as health care, social work, law enforcement, and education. Persons feeling burnout may see themselves as a failure and may be in positions where they give and give to others but lack a source of support for their own needs. Burnout can result in people behaving as if they are powerless to turn things around. They may behave like victims and begin blaming others, further comprising their relationships with co-workers.

Burnout is often found among persons who are perfectionists, idealists, or workaholics. They may start their work with great enthusiasm, very intense energy and highly positive attitudes. They are usually high achievers. Eventually they push themselves beyond their own limits and things begin to break down, leading to burnout.

Strategies for recovering from burnout include the following:

Getting appropriate and adequate support

Confronting blocking attitudes such as denial and helplessness

Releasing feelings over losses which can turn negative emotions into focused energy

Develop and use problem-solving skills

Especially if you have selected a career goal in a helping profession and/or have any of the characteristics above, monitor yourself for burnout and prevent it or get help early if symptoms occur.

Difficult People

If you work long enough undoubtedly you will find yourself faced with some people with whom you must deal with who are difficult. This is the time to get out this book and re-read the sections especially in Chapter 9 and 10 on communication. Learning to be effective in conflict resolution, in being assertive, and in listening with empathy can help you immensely in finding ways to work effectively with such difficult people.

Maintaining your own calm in these cases is half the battle and enables you to think through your plan for confronting the situation as early as possible. If you are unsuccessful in your efforts, consider seeking a third party who might act as a mediator to assist you and the person you find difficult to work with. Be alert; don't allow yourself to slip into denial. The problem doesn't go away, and could get worse.

Sexual Harassment

Sexual harassment has been around for years. Business law professors Roberts and Mann (1996) examined the extent of sexual harassment in the workplace. They report that a 1976 poll found 9 out of 10 women said they had been subjected to unwanted sexual advancement at work. A Federal Government survey found that 42 percent of women and 15 percent of men reported some sexual harassment at work. A Federal Government study for the years 1985-87 estimated government costs from the effects of sexual harassment at $267 million.

In 1992, Anita Hill (1997) accused Supreme Court nominee Clarence Thomas of sexual harassment. This case was highly publicized and the following year, the number of sexual harassment cases increased dramatically.

Sexual harassment is generally defined as any unwanted sexual activity that affects you. There are two conditions under which sexual harassment may fall. One is referred to as (1) **quid pro quo** which involves getting something for giving something, such as a person in authority demanding sexual favors to keep a job benefit. A second condition referred to as (2) **hostile environment** involves a situation where (a) a co-worker or supervisor engages in unwanted sex based behavior which renders the workplace intimidating, or hostile, or (b) the purpose is to unreasonably interfere with work performance. Hostile environment cases are more controversial since there may be so many perceptions of "intimidating" or "offensive." A company is liable if they are informed of sexual harassment and ignore it. However, a company may be held liable even if they did not know about the sexual harassment. The safest bet for a company is to have a clear policy and to be sure all employees are aware of the rules.

DeCenzo (1997) summarizes ideas for protecting yourself from sexual harassment as follows:

1. Know the organization's policy on sexual harassment.

2. Let the offending individual know you're irritated by his or her behavior.

3. Document such events.

4. If the offensive behavior is repeated, complain to someone in authority.

5. Keep records of your work.

6. Seek help from an attorney if you're not satisfied with what the organization is doing or has done.

7. Keep your spirits high.

In the interest of making work fun, it is important to be aware and alert of the rules and your rights regarding sexual harassment.

Discrimination

Since the Civil Rights movement began over thirty years ago we have become more sensitive to the need to treat all people equally. We are aware of concern for discrimination based on race or gender, but there is a broader range of areas that fall under the Equal Employment Opportunity (EEO) guidelines. The following factors are the official bases for EEO **discrimination**:

Race	Age
Color	National Origin
Religion	Sex
Disability	Reprisal

Color discrimination means situations where members of the same race are treated differently because of the color or their skin or because of the shades of brown skinned persons. National origin refers to ancestors or country of origin. **Reprisal** refers to disciplinary action for raising an allegation of discrimination.

Age discrimination involves decisions being made about employees based on their age, usually affecting older workers. Steinhauser (1998, 1999) notes that in 1994 the median age of workers was 38 years. Projections for the year 2005 are a median age of 41. In the year 2005 the number of workers fifty-five or older will rise to 2.2 million in the United States. Between 1996 and 1998 $200 million was paid out by American companies in fines for age discrimination. This amount does not include legal fees. First Union Corporation, a large bank, agreed to pay $58.5 million to 239 of its former employees who sued for age discrimination. Steinhauser says this is just the "tip of the iceberg," and notes that jury verdicts are historically higher in age discrimination than those based on race, gender or disability.

In the work situation if you are experiencing discrimination in any of the above categories, it is important to seek the guidance of the human resources representative at your place of employment charged with EEO compliance.

SUMMARY

In this chapter we have been looking at those issues related to experiencing your work as pleasurable. We have reviewed those aspects that reside primarily in your power, like taking charge and seeking intrinsic motivation. We have described exciting new findings regarding the personally rewarding feelings of "flow." We have also discussed potential problems you may encounter in the workplace including substance abuse, lack of advancement, burnout and discrimination.

In considering your work and career effectiveness, it is important that you know the workplace you are continuing in or about to enter, spend time designing or re-designing your career, and sharpen your people skills. Start with an "I can" attitude. Stay aware of what's happening to you . . . not only your work and your thoughts, but your feelings. Work with emotional intelligence. If you realize things are not right, take charge and work to change the things you can. Determine goals to revitalize your self in your current position, or determine a goal for changing positions. Consider a paradigm shift. Remember, you are in charge of your life. If you do this and remember the other points in this chapter you will be on your way to becoming like Happy Harry "flowing" through the work day and making your work fun!

SELF EXERCISES

1. Write a comparison of yourself to Grumpy George or Happy Harry.
2. Interview a friend to determine if they have more of an internal or external locus of control.
3. List three intrinsic and three extrinsic motivators operating in your life right now.
4. Think of three separate times you were in "flow" while doing a task. What were you doing in each situation?

KEY TERMS

internal locus of control	burnout
intrinsic motivation	sexual harassment
extrinsic motivation	quid pro quo
flow	hostile environment
substance abuse	discrimination
mentor	reprisal

CHAPTER 14 QUESTIONS

Short-Answer Questions

1. Who should be in charge of you in the workplace? _____
2. If you decide to change something in you that causes you problems at work, you would be exhibiting an _____ locus of control.
3. If I believe something will happen, it _____.
4. Self esteem, learning something, feeling accomplishment are found in _____ motivation.
5. If I cram all night to pass a test, I am being motivated _____trinsically.
6. In _____ motivation, the reward comes at the end of the task.
7. When people are fully engaged in their work, finding their work exhilarating and performing at their best, we would say that they are experiencing _____.
8. Watching television usually leaves people less satisfied than when they are involved in work and actively using their _____.
9. Goleman's surveys of workers at the end of their careers showed that financial rewards rank _____ in importance and source of satisfaction.

10. An experienced worker that shows "the ropes" to a newcomer is called a
    _____.

11. _____% of on-the-job injuries are related to drug or alcohol abuse.

12. Especially if you work in a helping profession, you need to be aware of the signs of _____.

13. The two types of sexual harassment are _____ and
    _____.

Essay Questions

1. Write a performance evaluation for "George" described in the opening.

2. Compare internal and external locus of control.

3. Describe extrinsic motivators you experience in your life, at home, school, or work.

4. Discuss the connection between extrinsic motivation and creativity.

5. Describe a time when you were in "flow" on a task.

6. Discuss why people in helping professions burn out easier than some other professions.

7. Discuss *quid pro quo* in sexual harassment and give examples.

8. Discuss factors that are the basis for discrimination according to the Equal Employment Opportunity Guidelines besides race, sex, religion, or age.

9. Discuss what you would do if someone made you feel sexually harassed.

10. How do the elderly fare in the workplace regarding age discrimination law suits?

References

Abascal. J. R., Brucato, L., & Brucato, D. (2001). *Stress Mastery: The Art of Coping Gracefully.* Upper Saddle River, N.J.: Prentice Hall Press.

Achtenberg, J. (1985). *Imagery in Healing.* Boston: New Science Library.

Adler, A. (1928). *Understanding Human Nature.* London: Allen & Unwin.

Adler, R. & Towne, N. (1993). *Looking Out/Looking In.* San Diego, Ca.: Harcourt Brace Jovanovich.

Alberti, R. & Emmons, M. (1974). *Your Perfect Right.* California: Impact Press.

Alexander, C., Swanson, G., Rainforth, M., Carlilse, T., Todd, C., & Oates, R. (1993). Effects of the Transcendental Meditation Program on Stress Reduction, Health, and Employee Development: A Prospective Study in two Occupational Settings. *Anxiety, Stress and Coping,* 6, 245–262.

Allred, K.D., & Smith, T.W. (1989). The Hardy Personality: Cognitive and Physiological Responses to Evaluative Threat. *Journal of Personality and Social Psychology,* 56, 257–266.

Amabile, T. (August, 1995). Do What You Enjoy: Creativity Will Follow. *American Psychological Association Monitor.*

Andreas, C., & Andreas, S. (1989). *Heart of Mind: Engaging your Inner Power to Change with Neuro-Linguistic Programming.* Moab, Utah: Real People Press.

Ardell, D. (1986). *High Level Wellness.* Berkeley: Ten Speed Press.

Atwater, E. (1986). *Human Relations.* New York: Prentice Hall.

Averill, J. R. (1983). Studies on Anger and Aggression: Implications for Theories of Emotion. *American Psychologist,* 38, 1145–1160.

Axelrod, R. (1984). *The Evolution of Cooperation.* New York: Basic Books.

Bach, G., & Wyden, P. (1968). *The Intimate Enemy.* New York: Avon.

Bandler, R. & Grinder, J. (1975). *The Structure of Magic I.* Palo Alto, California: Science and Behavior Books.

Barefoot, J. R., Dahlstrom, W. G. & Williams, R. B. (1983). Hostility, CHD Incidence and Total Mortality: A 25 Year Follow-up Study of 255 Physicians. *Psychosomatic Medicine,* 45, 559–563.

Barker, L., Edwards, R., Gaines, C., Gladney, K., & Holley, F. (1981) An Investigation of Proportional Time Spent in Various Activities by College Students. *Journal of Applied Communication Research,* 8, 101–109.

Bass, B. M. (1998). *Transformational Leadership: Industrial, Military and Educational Impact.* Mahwah, New Jersey: Lawrence Erlbaum.

Baumrind, D. (1991). Effective Parenting during the Early Adolescent Transition. Cowen, P. & Hetherington, E. (Eds.). *Advances in Family Research,* Vol. 2, Hillsdale, New Jersey: Erlbaum, 28–41.

Beck, A. (1970). Cognitive Therapy: Nature and Relation to Behavior Therapy. *Behavior Therapy,* 1, 84–200.

Beck, A. (1979). *Cognitive Therapy and Emotional Disorders.* New York: New American Library.

Benjamin, L. T., Cavell, T. A., & Shallenberger, W. R. (1987). Staying with Initial Answers on Objective Tests: Is It a Myth? In M. E. Ware & R. J. Millard (Eds.). *Handbook on Student Development: Advising, Career Development and Field Placement.* Hillsdale, N.J. : Lawrence Erlbaum Associates, 45–52.

Bennis, W.G. (1989). *On Becoming a Leader.* Reading, Pa.: Addison Wesley.

Benson, H. (1976). *The Relaxation Response.* New York: Avon Books.

Benson, H. (1979). *The Mind-Body Effect.* New York: Simon & Schuster.

Benson, H. (1985). *Beyond the Relaxation Response.* Berkeley, California: Berkeley Books.

Bernasek, A. (Feb, 2002). The Friction Economy. American Business Just Got the Bill for the Terrorist Attacks: $151 Billion a Year. *Fortune,* 145, 104.

Bourne, E. J. (1990). *The Anxiety and Phobia Workbook.* Oakland, California: New Harbinger Publications.

Bolles, R. (2002). Free On-line Tests Dealing With Careers. *http://www.JobHunters Bible.com.*

Bolles, R. (2001). *What Color Is Your Parachute?* Berkeley, California: Ten Speed Press.

Bonner, R. L., & Rich, A. R. (1991). Predicting Vulnerability to Hopelessness: A Longitudinal Analysis. *The Journal of Nervous and Mental Disease,* 179, 129–32.

Boyett, J.H. & Snyder, D.P. (1998). Twenty-First Century Workplace Trends. *On the Horizon,* 6 (2), 4–9.

Brehm, B. (1998). *Stress Management: Increasing Your Stress Resistance.* New York: Longman.

Breslow. L. (1983). The Potential of Health Promotion. In D. Mechanic (Ed.). *Handbook of Health, Health Care, and the Health Professions.* New York: Free Press.

Brockner, J., & Guare, J. (1983). Improving the Performance of Low Self-Esteem Individuals: An Attributional Approach. *Academy of Managerial Psychology,* 26, 642–656.

Brown, J. P. (1991). Staying Fit and Staying Well: Physical Fitness as a Moderator of Life Stress. *Journal of Personality and Social Psychology,* 60, 555–561

Bruner, J. & Postman, L. (1949). On the Perception of Incongruity: A Problem. *Journal of Personality,* 18, 206–233.

Buckingham, M. & Clifton, D. (2001). *Now, Discover Your Strengths.* NewYork: The Free Press.

Buscaglia, L. (1982). *Love.* New York: Ballantine Books.

Byham, W. (1999). *Landing the Job You Want.* New York: Crown Publishing Group.

Campbell, J. (1959). *Masks of God: Creative Mythology.* New York: The Viking Press.

Canfield, J., & Hansen, M. (1995). *The Aladdin Factor.* New York: The Berkeley Publishing Group.

Cannon, T., Kaprio, J., Lonnquist, J., Huttunen, M., & Koskenvuo, M. (1998). The Genetic Epidemiology of Schizophrenia in a Finnish Twin Cohort. *Archives of General Psychiatry,* 55, 67–754.

Carducci, B. (1999). *The Pocket Guide to Making Successful Small Talk.* New York: Mass Market Publishing.

Carpi, J. (Jan./Feb., 1996). Stress . . . It's Worse Than You Think. *Psychology Today,* 34–76.

Castenada, C. (1998). *The Teachings of Don Juan: A Yaqui Way of Knowledge.* California: University of California Press.

Castenada, C. (1991). *Journey to Ixtlan: The Lessons of Don Juan.* New York: Simon & Schuster.

Chamberlain, J. (July, 1998). Reaching Flow to Optimize Work and Play, *APA MonitorOnline www.apa.org/monitor.* Washington, D.C.: American Psychological Association, Vol 29, No. 7.

Chiasson, C., & Hayes, L. (1993). The Effects of Subtle Differences between Listeners and Speakers on the Referential Speech of College Freshmen. *The Psychological Record,* 43, 13–24.

Cialdini, R. B. (1988). *Influence: Science and Practice* (2nd Ed.). Glenview, Ill.: Scott, Foresman & Co.

Cohen, H. (1980). *You Can Negotiate Anything.* New York: Bantam Books

Cohen, S., & Edwards, J. (1989). Personality Characteristics as Moderators of the Relationship Between Stress and Disorder. Neufeld, R. (Ed.). *Advances in the Investigation of Psychological Stress.* New York: Wiley and Sons.

Contrada, R. (1989). Type A behaviors, Personality Hardiness and Cardiovascular Responses to Stress. *Journal of Personality and Social Psychology,* 57. 895–903.

Coopersmith, S. (1967). *Antecedents of Self-Esteem.* San Francisco: Freeman Press

Coue', E. (1922). *Self-Mastery Through Conscious Auto-Suggestion.* London: Allen & Unwin.

Covey, S. (1991). *The Seven Habits of Highly Effective People.* New York: Simon & Schuster.

Covey, S., Merrill, A., & Merrill, R. (1994). *First Things First.* New York: Simon & Schuster.

Cousins, N. (1981). *Anatomy of An Illness as Perceived by the Patient.* New York: Bantam Books.

Crane, D. R., Dollahite, D. C., Griffin, W., & Taylor, V. L. (1987). Diagnosing Relationships with Spatial Distance: An Empirical Test of a Clinical Principle. *Journal of Marital and Family Therapy,* 13, 307–318.

Csikszentmihalyi, M. (1990). *Flow: The Psychology of Optimal Experience.* New York: Harper & Row.

Csikszentmihalyi, M. (1993). *The Evolving Self: A Psychology for the Third Millennium.* New York: Harper Collins Publishers.

Dansky, K. H. (1996). The Effect of Group Mentoring on Career Outcomes. *Group and Organizational Management.* 21, 5–21.

Davis, M., Eshelman, E.R., & McKay, M. (1988). *The Relaxation and Stress Reduction Workbook.* Oakland, California: New Harbinger Publications.

DeCenzo, D. (1997). *Human Relations: Personal and Professional Development.* Upper Saddle River, N.J.: Prentice Hall.

Dekoven, B. (2001). *Discover the Fun of Work.* Washington, D.C.: Greater Washington Society of Association Executives. http//www.gwsae.org.

DePaulo, B. M. (1994). Spotting Lies: Can Humans Learn to Do Better? *Current Directions in Psychological Science,* 3, 83–86.

Deffenbacher, J. L., Oeting, E. R., & Lynch, R. S. (1994). Development of a Driving Anger Scale. *Psychological Reports,* 74, 83–91.

DiMarco, C. (1997). *Career Transitions: A Journey of Survival and Growth.* Scottsdale, Arizona: Gorsuch Scarisbrick Publishers.

Dollard, J., Miller, N. E., Doob, L. W., Mowrer, O. H., & Sears, R. R. (1939). *Frustration and Aggression.* New Haven, CT.: Yale University Press.

Donne, J. (1995). *Poems and Prose.* New York: A. A. Knopf: Distributed by Random House.

Dubrin, A. (1999). *Human Relations: Personal and Professional Development,* 5th Ed. Upper Saddle River, N.J.: Prentice Hall.

Ekman, P. (1985). *Telling Lies: Clues to Deceit in the Marketplace, Marriage and Politics.* New York: W. W. Norton.

Ekman, P., O'Sullivan, M., Friesen, W. V., & Scherer K. R. (1991). Face, Voice and Body in Detecting Deception. *Journal of Nonverbal Behavior,* 15, 125–135.

Ellis, A. (1975). *A New Guide to Rational Living.* California: Wilshire Books.

Ellis, A., & Harper, R. (1961). *A Guide to Rational Living.* California: Wilshire Books.

Ellis, A., & Knaus, W. J. (1977). *Overcoming Procrastination.* New York: Signet, New American Library.

Epstein, S. (1992). Coping Ability, Negative Self-Evaluation, and Overgeneralization: Experiment and Theory. *Journal of Personality and Social Psychology,* 62, 826–836

Fanning, P. (1988). *Visualization for Change.* Oakland, Ca.: New Harbinger Publications.

Fast, J. (1970). *Body Language.* New York: M. Evans & Co.

Felsman, J. K., & Vaillant, G. E. (1987). Resilient Children as Adults: A 40 Year Study. F. J. Anderson & Cohler, B. J. (Eds.) *The Invulnerable Child.* New York: Guilford Press.

Fensterheim, H., & Baer, J. (1975). *Don't Say Yes When You Want to Say No.* New York: David McKay.

Ferris, G. (June, 1999). *Political Skill at Work.* Champaign, Ill.: University of Illinois News Bureau.

Fleming, J., & Courtney, B. (1984). The Dimensionality of Self-Esteem: II Hierarchical Facet Model for Revised Measurement Scales. *Journal of Personality and Social Psychology,* 46, 404–421.

Flett, T. K., Blankstein, K. R., Hewitt, P. L., & Koledin, S. (1992). Components of Perfectionism and Procrastination in College Students. *Social Behavior and Personality,* 20, 85–94.

Fontana, D. (1990). *Social Skills at Work.* Leicester, England: British Psychological Society.

Frankl, V. (1959). *Man's Search for Meaning.* New York: Pocket Books.

Freedberg, S. (Nov, 17th, 1996). Mounting Cost of White Collar Stress. *Miami Herald,* 1B.

Freidman, M. & Rosenman, R. H. (1974). *Type A Behavior and Your Heart.* New York: Knopf.

Freud, S. (1924). *A General Introduction to Psychoanalysis.* London: Boni & Liveright.

Frigon, N., & Jackson, H. (1996). *The Leader: Developing the Skills and Qualities You Need to Lead Effectively.* New York: Amacom Books.

Gardner, H. (1983). *Frames of Mind: The Theory of Multiple Intelligences.* New York: Basic Books.

Gardner, H. (1993), *Multiple Intelligences: The Theory in Practice.* New York: Basic Books

Gardner, H. (1999). *Intelligence Reframed: Multiple Intelligences for the 21st Century.* New York: Basic Books.

Gardner, H., & Hatch, T. (1989). Multiple Intelligences Go to School. *Educational Researcher,* 18, 8–9.

Gardner, R. (2002). *Psychology Applied to Everyday Life.* U. S. A.: Wadsworth/ Thomson Learning, Inc.

Garfield, C. (1984). *Peak Performance.* Los Angeles, Ca.: Houghton Mifflin & Co.

Gawain, S. (1978). *Creative Visualization.* California: Whatever Publishing.

Gleick, J. (1987). *Chaos—Making a New Science.* New York: Penguin Books.

Goleman, D. (1977). *The Varieties of the Meditative Experience.* New York: E. P. Dutton

Goleman, D. (1995). *Emotional Intelligence.* New York, N.Y.: Bantam Books.

Goleman, D. (1998). *Working with Emotional Intelligence.* New York: Bantam Books.

Gomez-Mejia, L. R., Balkin, D., & Cardy, R. (1995). *Managing Human Resources.* Upper Saddle River, N.J.: Prentice Hall.

Goodman, D. (1974). *Emotional Well-Being Through Rational Behavior Training.* Springfield, Ill.: Charles C. Thomas.

Gottesmann, I. (1991). *Schizophrenia Genesis: The Origins of Madness.* New York: W. H. Freeman.

Grof, S. (1988). *The Adventure of Self Discovery.* Albany, New York: State University of New York Press.

Hamburg, D. (1994). *Today's Children: Creating a Future for a Generation in Crisis.* New York: Time Books.

Hansen, K. (2002). *Online Career Assessments: Helpful Tools of Self- Discovery.* Deland, Fl: Quintessential Careers. http//www.quintcareers.com.

Harris, T. (1967). *I'm OK, You're OK: A Practical Guide to Transactional Analysis.* New York: Avon Books.

Harvard Medical School. (April, 2002). The Mind and the Immune System—Part I. *The Harvard Mental Health Letter,* Vol. 18, No. 10, 1–3.

Harvard University. *Check Out Policy*. Harvard Botanical Library. Cambridge, Mass.: Harvard University.

Higbee, K. L. (1988). *Your Memory: How It Works and How to Improve It* (2nd Ed.). New York: Prentice Hall Press.

Hill, A. (1997). *Speaking Truth to Power*. New York: Doubleday.

Hinder, S. (1998). Time for a New Role. *Mail Tribune*. Medford, Oregon.

Holland, J. (1985). *Making Vocational Choices: A Theory of Vocational Personalities and Work Environment*, 2nd. Ed., Upper Saddle River, N.J.: Prentice-Hall.

Holmes, D. S., & Roth, D. L. (1988). Effects of Aerobic Exercise Training and Relaxation Training on Cardiovascular Activity during Psychological Stress. *Journal of Psychosomatic Research, 32*, 469–474.

Holmes, T. H., & Rahe, R. H. (1967). The Social Readjustment Rating Scale. *Journal of Psychosomatic Research, 11*, 213–218.

Holt, P., Fine, M. J., & Tollefson, N. (1987). Mediating Stress: Survival of the Hardy. *Psychology in the Schools, 24*, 51–58.

Horney, K. (1956). The Search for Glory. C. Moustakas (Ed.) *Self-Exploration and Personal Growth*. New York: Harper Colophan Books, 86–95.

Houston, J. (1987). *The Search for the Beloved*. New York: Tarcher/Putnam Books.

Hutchinson, M. (1984). *The Book of Floating*. New York: William Morris & Co.

Isen, A. (1991). The Influence of Positive Affect on Clinical Problem Solving. *Medical Decision Making*. (July–Sept.).

Jacobson, E. (1929, 1974). *Progressive Relaxation*. Chicago: The University of Chicago Press, Midway Reprint.

Kabat-Zinn, J. (1990). *Full Catastrophe Living*. New York: Dell Publishing.

Kabat-Zinn, J. (1994). *Wherever You Go There You Are*. New York: Hyperion.

Kanar, C. (1991). *The Confident Student*. Boston, Mass.: Houghton Mifflin Co.

Kemeny, M. E., Gruenewald, T. L. (2000). Affect, Cognition, the Immune System and Health. E. A. Mayer & J. Saper (Eds.). *The Biological Basis for Mind Body Interactions: Progress in Brain Research Series*. Amsterdam: Elsevier Science B.V., 291–308.

Kirkpatrick, S., & Locke, E. (1991). Leadership: Do Traits Matter? *Academy of Management Executive*. 5 (2), 48–60.

Kleinke, C. L. (1986). *Meeting and Understanding People*. New York: W. H. Freeman & Co.

Kobasa, S. C. (1979). Stressful Life Events, Personality and Health: An Inquiry into Hardiness. *Journal of Personality and Social Psychology, 37*, 1–11.

Kobasa, S. C. (1982). Commitment and Coping in Stress Resistance among Lawyers. *Journal of Personality and Social Psychology,* 42, 707–717.

Kobasa, S. C. (Sept., 1984). How Much Stress Can You Survive? *American Health,* 64–71.

Kobasa, S. C., Maddi, S. R., & Puccetti, M. C. (1982). Personality and Exercise as Buffers in the Stress-Illness Relationship. *Journal of Behavioral Medicine,* 5, 391–404.

Kopp, S. (1972). *If You Meet the Buddha on the Road, Kill Him!* Palo Alto, Ca.: Bantam Books/Science & Behavior Books.

Kuhn, T. (1962). *The Structure of Scientific Revolutions.* Chicago, Ill.: University of Chicago Press.

Lamont, K. (1975). *Escape from Stress.* New York: G. P. Putnam & Sons.

Lange, A., & Jakubowski, P. (1976). *Responsible Assertive Behavior.* U.S.A.: Research Press.

Lawler, K.A., & Smied, L.A. (1987). The Relationship of Stress, Type A Behavior and Powerlessness to Physiological Responses in Female Clerical Workers. *Journal of Psychosomatic Research,* 31, 555–563.

Lazarus, R. *Psychological Stress and the Coping Process.* New York: McGraw-Hill.

Lazarus, R., & Folkman, S. (1984). *Stress Appraisal and Coping.* New York: Springer Publishing Co.

LeDoux, J. (1993). Emotional Memory Systems in the Brain. *Behavioral Brain Research,* 58.

Lefkowitz, M. M., Eron, L. D., Walder, L. O., & Huesmann, L. R. (1977). *Growing Up to be Violent: A Longitudinal Study of the Development of Aggression.* New York: Pergamon Press.

Levine, T. (2000). *Work Yourself Happy: A Step-by-step Guide to Creating Joy in Your Life and Work.* Buckingham, PA.: Lahaska Press.

Lipman-Blumen, J. (1992). Connective Leadership: Female Leadership Styles in the 21st Century Workplace. *Sociological Perspectives.* Berkeley, California: University of California Press.

Loehr, J.E., & Migdow, J.A. (1986). *Take a Deep Breath.* New York: Villard Books.

Loftus, E., & Palmer, J. (1974). Reconstruction of Automobile Destruction: An Example of Interaction between Language and Memory. *Journal of Verbal Learning and Verbal Behavior,* 13, 585–589.

Long, B. C. (1984). Aerobic Conditioning and Stress Inoculation: A Comparison of Stress Management Interventions. *Cognitive Therapy and Research,* 8, 517–542.

Lonier, T. (1994). *Working Solo.* New York: Portico Press.

Maccoby, E. & Martin, J. (1983). Socialization in the Context of the Family. Munsen, P. (Ed.). *Handbook of Child Psychology,* 4th Ed., Vol. 4. Hillsdale, New Jersey: Erlbaum, 28–41.

Maddi, S. & Kobasa, S., (1984). *The Hardy Executive: Health Under Stress.* Homewood, Ill: Dow Jones-Irwin.

Maier, S. F., & Watkins, L. R. (1998). Cytokines for Psychologists: Implications of Bi-directional Immune-to-Brain Communication for Understanding Behavior, Mood and Cognition. *Psychological Review,* 105(1), 83–107.

Manning, M. R., Williams, R.F., & Wolfe, D.M. (1988). Hardiness and the Relationship between Stressors and Outcomes. *Work and Stress,* 2, 205–216.

Maslow, A. (1968). *Toward a Psychology of Being.* 2nd Ed. New York: Van Nostrand Reinhold.

Maslow, A. (1970). *Motivation and Personality,* 2nd. Ed., New York: Harper & Row.

McCann, I. L. & Holmes, D. S. (1984). Influence of Aerobic Exercise on Depression. *Journal of Personality and Social Psychology,* 46, 1142–1147.

McClain, L. (1987). Behavior During Examinations: A comparison of "A", "C" and "F" students. M. E. Ware & R. J. Millard (Eds.) *Handbook on Student Development: Advising, Career Development and Field Placement,* 40–42. Hillsdale, N. J.: Lawrence Erlbaum Associates

McClelland, D. (1961). *The Achieving Society.* New York: Van Nostrand.

McGilley, B. M., & Holmes, D. S. (1989). Aerobic Fitness Response to Psychological Stress. *Journal of Research on Personality,* 22, 129–139.

McGuigan, F.L. (1984). Progressive Relaxation: Origins, Principles and Clinical Applications. Woolfolk, R.L., & Lehrer, P.M. (Eds.). *Principles and Practices of Stress Management.* New York: Guilford Press.

McGregor, D. (1960). *The Human Side of Enterprise.* New York: McGraw-Hill.

McKay, M., Davis, M., & Fanning, P. (1981). *Thoughts and Feelings: The Art of Cognitive Stress Intervention.* Oakland, California: New Harbinger Publications.

McKay, M., Davis, M., & Fanning, P. (1983). *Messages: The Communication Skills Book.* Oakland, California: New Harbinger Publications.

McKay, M., & Fanning, P. (1987). *Self Esteem.* Oakland, California: New Harbinger Publications.

Mehrabian, A. (Sept., 1989). Communication Without Words. *Psychology Today,* 53–55.

Miami-Dade Community College. *Classified Staff Evaluation Form.* Miami, Fl. : Department of Human Relations.

Miami-Dade Community College. *Policy Manual.* Miami, Fl.

Miami-Dade Community College. *Procedures Manual.* Miami, Fl.

Miley, M. (1999). *The Psychology of Well Being.* Westport, CT.: Praeger.

Miller, A. (April, 1988). Stress on the Job. *Newsweek Magazine* 40–45.

Millman, D. (1991). *Sacred Journey of the Peaceful Warrior.* Tiburn, California: H. J. Kramer, Inc.

Mirsky, A., & Quinn, O. (1988). The Genain Quadruplets. *Schizophrenia Bulletin,* 14, 595–612.

Mischel, W., & Peake, P. K. (1990). Predicting Adolescent Cognitive and Self Regulatory Competencies from Preschool Delay of Gratification. *Developmental Psychology,* 26, 6, 978–986.

Mitchell, M. (1998). *The First 5 Minutes: How to Make a Great First Impression in Any Business Situation.* New York: John Wiley and Sons.

Myers, D. G., & Diener, E. (1995). Who is Happy? *Psychological Science,* 6, 10–17.

Myers-Briggs, I. (1993). *Introduction to Type: A Guide to Understanding Your Results on the Myers-Briggs Type Indicator.* Palo Alto, Ca.: Consulting Psychologists Press.

Newby, T., & Ashlyn, H. (1992). The Value of Mentoring. *Performance Improvement Quarterly.* Tallahassee, Fl.: The Learning Systems Institute, Florida State University, 54, 2–15

Nowck, K. M. (1989). Coping Style, Cognitive Hardiness and Health Status. *Journal of Behavioral Medicine,* 12, 145–158.

Nuernberger, P. (1981). *Freedom from Stress: A Holistic Approach.* Pennsylvania: Himalayan Intl. Inst. of Yoga Science and Philosophy Publishers.

Ornish, D. (1972). *Dr. Dean Ornish's Program for Reversing Coronary Heart Disease without Drugs or Surgery.* New York: Ballantine Books.

Osterkamp, L., & Press, A. (1988). *Stress? Find Your Balance.* Lawrence, Kansas: Preventive Measures, Inc.

Patel, D. (2002). *Workplace Forecast: A Strategic Outlook.* Alexandria, Va.: Society for Human Resource Management.

Pelham, B., & Swann, W. (1989). From Self-Conceptions to Self Worth: On the Sources and Structure of Global Self-Esteem. *Journal of Personality and Social Psychology,* 57, 672–680.

Pelletier, K. (1984). *Healthy People in Unhealthy Places: Stress and Fitness at Work.* New York: Delacorte Press/Seymour Lawrence.

Phelps, S., & Austin, N. (1987). *The Assertive Woman.* California: Impact Publishers.

Powell, K. E., Spain, K. G., Christenson, G. M., & Mollenkamp, M. P. (1986). The Status of the 1990 Objective for Physical Illness and Exercise. *Public Health Reports,* 101, 15–21.

Ram Dass. (1990). *Journey Of Awakening—A Meditator's Guidebook.* New York: Bantam Books

Reeves, C. (2002). *Nothing Is Impossible: Reflections on a New Life.* New York: Random House.

Reik, T. (1972). *Listening with the Third Ear.* New York: Pyramid Press.

Rhodewalt, F., & Zone, J.B. (1989). Appraisal of Life Change, Depression and Illness in Hardy and Non-Hardy Women. *Journal of Personality and Social Psychology,* 56: 81–88.

Richardson, A. (1969). *Mental Imagery.* New York: Springer-Verlag.

Roberts, B., & Mann, R. (Winter, 1996). *Sexual Harassment in the Workplace: A Primer.* Akron Law Review, 29, 269.

Robbins, A. (1986). *Unlimited Power.* New York: Ballantine Books.

Roe, A. (1972). Perspectives on Vocational Development. Whiteley, J. & Resnikoff, A. (Eds.) *Perspectives on Vocational Development.* Washington, D.C.: American Personnel and Guidance Association.

Rogers, C. (1959). A Theory of Therapy, Personality and Interpersonal Relationships as Developed in the Client-Centered Framework. Koch, S. (Ed.). *Psychology: A Study of a Science,* Vol 3. New York: McGraw Hill, 33–51.

Roper Starch Worldwide, Inc. (1999). *Baby Boomers Envision their Retirement.* Washington, D.C.: American Association of Retired Persons.

Rossi, E. (1986). *The PsychoBiology of Mind-Body Healing.* New York: W. W. Norton & Co.

Roth, D. L. , & Holmes, D. S. (1987). Influences of Aerobic Exercise Training and Relaxation Training on Physical and Psychological Health Following Stressful Life Events. *Psychosomatic Medicine, 49,* 355–365.

Roth, D., Weibe, D., Fillingian, R., & Shay, K. (1989). Life Events, Fitness, Hardiness and Health: A Simultaneous Analysis of Proposed Stress-Resistance Effects. *Journal of Personality and Social Psychology,* 57, 136–142.

Rotter, J. (1966). Generalized Expectancies for Internal vs. External Locus of Control of Reinforcement. *Psychological Monographs: General and Applied,* 80, (Whole No. 609).

Sanorajski, T., Delaney, C., Durham, L., Ordy, J. M., Johnson, J. A., & Dunlop, W. P. (1985). Effect of Exercise on Longevity, Body Weight, Locomotor Performance and Passive Aggressive Memory of Mice. *Neurobiology of Aging,* 6, 17–24.

Schacter, S., & Singer, J. (1962). Cognitive, Social and Physiological Determinants of Emotional State. *Psychological Review,* 69, 379–399.

Scheier, M. F., & Carver, C. S. (1993). On the Power of Positive Thinking: The Benefits of Being Optimistic. *Current Directions in Psychological Science,* 2, 26–30.

Schiraldi, G. (1993). *Building Self-esteem: A 125 day program.* Dubuque, Iowa: Kendall/Hunt.

Scott, D. (1980). *How to Put More Time in Your Life.* New York: Rawson, Wade Publishers.

Seaward, B. L. (1997). *Managing Stress.* Boston: Jones & Bartlett.

Seligman, M. (1991). *Learned Optimism.* New York: Knopf.

Selye, H. (1956). *The Stress of Life.* New York: McGraw Hill.

Selye, H. (1974). *Stress Without Distress.* New York: Dutton.

Selye, H. (1982). History and Present Status of the Stress Concept. Goldberg, L. & Breznitz, S. (Eds.). *Handbook of Stress; Theoretical and Clinical Aspects.* New York: Free Press.

Sheppard, J.A., & Kashani, J.H. (1991). The Relationship of Hardiness, Gender and Stress to Health Outcomes in Adolescents. *Journal of Personality,* 59, 747–768.

Siegel, B. (1986). *Love, Medicine and Miracles.* New York: Harper & Row.

Silberman, M., & Hansburg, F. (2000). *People Smart: Developing your Interpersonal Intelligence.* San Francisco, California.: Berrett-Kochler Publishers.

Simonton, O., Matthews-Simonton, S., & Creighton, J. (1978). *Getting Well Again.* New York: Bantam Books

Smith, M. (1975). *When I Say No, I Feel Guilty.* New York: The Dial Press.

Smith, T. W. (1992). Hostility and Health: Current Status of a Psychosomatic Hypothesis. *Health Psychology,* 11, 139–150.

Sonstroem, R. J. (1984). Exercise and Self-Esteem. *Exercise and Sport Sciences Review,* 12, 123–155.

State University System Board of Regents. *Policy Manual.* Atlanta: State of Georgia

Steinhauser, S. (July, 1998). Age Bias: Is Your Corporate Culture in Need of an Overhaul? *H.R. Magazine,* 87–91.

Steinhauser, S. (Sept./Oct., 1999). Beyond Age Bias: Successfully Managing an Older Workforce. *Aging Today.*

Sullivan, H.S. (1953). *The Interpersonal Theory of Psychiatry.* New York: Norton.

Talbot, M. (1991). *The Holographic Universe.* New York, New York: HarperCollins Publishers.

Tannen, D. (1990). *You Just Don't Understand: Women and Men in Conversation.* New York: Ballantine Books.

Taylor, S. E. (2000). Biobehavioral Responses to Stress in Females: Tend and Befriend, not Fight or Flight. *Psychological Review,* 107 (3), 411–429.

Tice, D., & Baumeister, R. (1993). *Handbook of Mental Control,* Vol. 5. Wegner, D., & Pennebaker, J. (Eds.). Englewood Cliffs, N.J.: Prentice Hall Press.

Toffler, A. (1971). *Future Shock*. New York, New York: Bantam Books.

Toffler, A. (1981). *The Third Wave*. New York, New York: Bantam Books.

Tulgan, B., & Martin, C. (2001). *Managing Generation Y*. Amherst, Mass.: HRD Press, Inc.

Underwood. A., & Kalb, C. (June, 1999). STRESS. *Newsweek Magazine, 56–63.*

U. S. Dept. Of Labor. (2001). *Bureau of Labor Statistics*. Washington, D.C.: U.S. Government Printing Office. Website (@www.statebls.gov.com)

U.S. Dept. Of Labor, Employment and Training Administration. (1991). *Dictionary of Occupational Titles*. Lanham, Md.: Bernan Press.

U.S. Dept. Of Labor. *Occupational Outlook Handbook*. Washington, D. C.: U.S. Government Printing Office.

U.S. Equal Employment Opportunity Commission. (April, 1997). *Technical Assistance Manual*. Washington D.C.: USEEOC Technical Assistance Program.

U. S. Surgeon General. (1979). *Healthy People: The Surgeon General's Report on Health Promotion and Disease Prevention*. U.S. Dept. Of Health, Education and Welfare (PHS) Publication No. 79-55071. Washington, D. C.: U. S. Government Printing Office.

Vaillant, G. E. (1977). *Adaptation to Life*. Boston: Little, Brown Publishers.

Wallace, R. & Benson, H. (1972). The Physiology of Meditation. *Scientific American, 226, 85–90.*

Wilber, K. (1979). *No Boundary*. Los Angeles: Center Publications.

Williams, R. (1989). *The Trusting Heart: Great News about Type A Behavior*. New York: Random House.

Wolvin, A. & Coakley, C. (1991). A Survey of the Status of Listening Training in Some Fortune 500 Corporations. *Communication Education, 40, 152–164.*

Yerkes, R. M., & Dodson, J. D. (1908). The Relation of Strength of Stimulus to Rapidity of Habit Formation. *Journal of Comparative and Neurological Psychology, 18, 459–482.*

Zillman, D. (1989). Mental Control of Angry Aggression. *Handbook of Mental Control*. Wegner, D., & Pennebaker, J. (Eds.). Englewood Cliffs, N.J.: Prentice Hall Press.

_____ *Basis of EEO Discrimination*. Washington, D. C.: Equal Employment Opportunity Commission. Website (@www.eeoc.gov.com.)

_____ Engage Employees and Boost Performance. (2001). *Working Paper*. Philadelphia, Pa.: Hay Group.

_____ (1998). Planning a Career. *Adventures in Education*, Texas Guaranteed Loan Corporation.

_____ (1998). *Self-Directed Search*. Odessa, Fl.: Psychological Assessment Resources, Inc. Website (@www.sdstest3.com).

_____ (1994). *Strong Vocational Interest Inventory*. Palo Alto, Ca.: Consulting Psychologists Press.

———— (1997). *VGM's Career Encyclopedia*. Lincolnwood, Ill. VGM Career Horizons.

Index